MAKING PROMISES

Oaths, Treaties, and Covenants in Multi-jurisdictional and Multi-religious Societies

How should we understand promises as public, private, or political commitments? What are the conditions for promise-making in religiously diverse societies with competing jurisdictions and sovereignties? *Making Promises* addresses how promises are made meaningful not only through law, but also through appeals to transcendent powers across diverse traditions.

Each contribution in this volume takes a closer look at specific kinds of promises: oaths, treaties, and covenants. The chapters reveal much about the nature of promises in multi-religious and multi-jurisdictional societies, and with contributions from scholars of religious studies, Indigenous studies, law, history, politics, and anthropology, this volume represents a comparative conversation on the making of promises. It pays close attention to Indigenous histories, visions, and conceptions of justice; comparative law within and across settler colonial states; interactions among religions and secularisms; and the ongoing importance of material culture, ritual, and emotion for these practices.

At a time of human-caused environmental devastation and political upheaval, when making promises for the future seems both urgent and futile, this volume shows that promises have long been made and unmade, kept and broken, in ways that successive generations need to acknowledge and take up anew.

BENJAMIN L. BERGER is a professor of law at Osgoode Hall Law School, York University, and the author of *Law's Religion: Religious Difference and the Claims of Constitutionalism* (University of Toronto Press, 2015).

PAMELA E. KLASSEN is a professor of the study of religion at the University of Toronto, and the author of *The Story of Radio Mind: A Missionary's Journey on Indigenous Land* (University of Chicago Press, 2018).

MONIQUE SCHEER is a professor of historical and cultural anthropology at the University of Tübingen, and the author of *Enthusiasm: Emotional Practices of Conviction in Modern Germany* (Oxford University Press, 2020).

Making Promises

Oaths, Treaties, and Covenants in Multi-jurisdictional and Multi-religious Societies

EDITED BY BENJAMIN L. BERGER, PAMELA E. KLASSEN, AND MONIQUE SCHEER

UNIVERSITY OF TORONTO PRESS
Toronto Buffalo London

© University of Toronto Press 2025
Toronto Buffalo London
utppublishing.com
Printed in Canada

ISBN 978-1-4875-4206-1 (cloth)   ISBN 978-1-4875-4209-2 (EPUB)
ISBN 978-1-4875-4207-8 (paper)   ISBN 978-1-4875-4208-5 (PDF)

Library and Archives Canada Cataloguing in Publication

Publication cataloguing information is available from Library and Archives Canada.

Cover design: Tamara Hawkins
Cover image: Christi Belcourt, *The Earth Is My Government*

We wish to acknowledge the land on which the University of Toronto Press operates. This land is the traditional territory of the Wendat, the Anishnaabeg, the Haudenosaunee, the Métis, and the Mississaugas of the Credit First Nation.

University of Toronto Press acknowledges the financial support of the Government of Canada, the Canada Council for the Arts, and the Ontario Arts Council, an agency of the Government of Ontario, for its publishing activities.

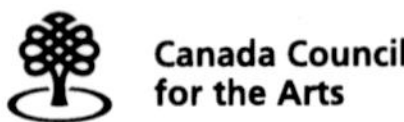

For our children

Contents

Part III

Conclusion

Promising Practices: A Preface

A promise is a promise, or so the saying goes. Honouring one's commitments or trusting in another's faithfulness, however, is not quite so easy in practice. There is a long history of religious, legal, and philosophical inquiry into what counts as a promise, and what, if anything, obliges individuals or groups of people to keep them. Historical inquiry reveals that not everyone's promises are always considered to be morally binding, and that social hierarchies often determine who can slip out of them, who is eligible for promise-making, whose "word" can be accepted as worthy. Must a promise be consensual, or can one be coerced or tricked into promissory obligations made to another? Is a promise a mere contract that can be breached at a cost, or is it a solemn pledge that, if broken, carries metaphysical consequences in this life or the next? *Making Promises* offers reflection, and perhaps even some answers, in response to these questions.

Making Promises is a journey into the plural world of promising, to borrow Jeremy Webber's phrase from his conclusion to this book. Taken as a whole, the book examines the politics and practices of promising across transnational, multi-religious, and multi-jurisdictional contexts. The chapters include attention to Indigenous histories, visions, and conceptions of justice, comparative law within and across settler colonial states, interactions among religions and secularisms, and the ongoing importance of material culture and ritual for the making of law and of promises. In particular, the chapters gathered here mark a comparative and interdisciplinary conversation about specific kinds of promises: oaths, treaties, and covenants. As speech acts or performances grounded on transcendental referents, such as God, the Creator, or a future yet to come, oaths, treaties, and covenants are particularly interesting when undertaken in societies characterized by legal and religious pluralism. In such conditions of multiplicity and competing sovereignties, how are public promises made meaningful through appeals to varied transcendent powers and diverse traditions of material culture, collective memory, embodied practices, and emotion? *Making Promises* takes these questions as its starting point, across a variety of historical contexts and practices of promising.

Swearing an oath to tell the truth in a courtroom or to declare allegiance when becoming a citizen, negotiating treaties as "sacred promises" between Indigenous and colonizing nations, and legitimizing relations of kinship through state-sanctioned ceremonies of marriage are all examples of ritualized promises in which secular politics and religious commitments conjoin. More often than not, promises also prompt sites of memory (anniversaries, documents, symbolic gifts) that further sacralize – or set apart – these commitments as specially sanctioned by law, by God, or both. In multi-jurisdictional and multi-religious societies, these public promises are far more than just examples: oaths, treaties, and covenants are generative sites of relationship out of which the very concepts and practices of religion, the sacred, law, and the secular have emerged.

Interested in the histories, ethics, and phenomenology of this range of practices of promising, we start with a few working definitions that will be explored and tested in this interdisciplinary volume. We understand oaths as promises made by an individual or group of people before witnesses, such as a judge, a religious officiant, and/or a divine being. As promises that bind a person by their own sense of a moral code that may persist after death, oaths have a sense of the sacred that extends beyond a contractual agreement. Treaties are collective promises made between parties that are meant to be carried on by future generations. In the context of treaties made between Indigenous nations and the British Crown, these promises were also sacralized with reference to the Creator, the monarch, and the natural world – the sun, the rivers, and the grasses – and through ceremonies such as sharing a pipe. Covenants, too, establish collective obligations to be honoured over time and are always sacred in some sense, though as Jeremy Webber explores in his conclusion, this need not define them as solely religious. Unlike treaties, however, covenants do not depend on equality, or even mutuality, between the parties involved. One might think here of the biblical covenant between God and the People of Israel, which was received in silence by the Israelites, or the legal device of the restrictive covenant on property, which binds though no one assented to it. It seems that we can simply find ourselves in a covenantal relationship, with all the moral and legal force that this entails.

Bringing together scholars from religious studies, Indigenous studies, law, history, politics, and anthropology, the book arises from a workshop held online in November 2020, hosted by the University of Toronto with support from the Humboldt Foundation and the University of Tübingen. What was supposed to be the final in-person workshop of the Religion and Public Memory in Multicultural Societies project, working in collaboration with the York Research Chair in Pluralism and Public Law, became an online gathering at the height of the COVID-19 pandemic. The creative, urgent, and interdisciplinary path of the workshop – and, with it, this volume – was set by a powerful public keynote by Jeffery Hewitt, entitled "Fragmented Promises, Pentimento & the Salvage Paradigm." Arguing from images as much as from texts, Hewitt took the concept and practice of pentimento – the painting and repainting of works of art that retain original visions underneath their layers of revision – as the prompt for considering the fragmented, often shattered, treaty promises of the Crown in relation to Indigenous peoples of Turtle Island.

Jeffery Hewitt's chapter became the orienting frame for *Making Promises*; a discursive and visual starting point both for the contributors as they revised their chapters and, now, for the readers of this book. After Hewitt's introductory chapter, the book is divided into three parts, each framed by a short essay by one of the co-editors setting the chapters in conversation with one another.

The first section begins with a framing essay by Pamela Klassen entitled "Promises in Place: A Great Lakes Pentimento," which maps chapters by Elizabeth Elbourne, Kate Stoehr, and Sujith Xavier as adjacent reflections on the nature of promises between Haudenosaunee, Anishinaabe, and diverse settler peoples in the southern Great Lakes. Part Two begins with "The Weight of the Promise: Material-Immaterial Practices," a reflection by Monique Scheer in which she considers how promises are acts of circulation, in which social relations are represented and embedded in materiality. With chapters by Pooyan Tamimi Arab, Jennifer Selby, Gregory Fewster, and Yaniv Feller that range from a French-Algerian wedding to the international brokering and emotional labour of museum curators, this section considers specific material representations of promises as gendered, cultural, and religious exchanges. The third section is prefaced by Benjamin Berger's discussion of "The Oath, the Law, and the 'Sense of Religion,'" in which he frames essays by Catherine Evans, Kellen Funk, and co-authors Pamela Klassen and Isabel Klassen-Marshall. Each chapter reflects on oaths as legal and state rituals that crystallize how religious and secular formations intersect in the making of promises. The volume concludes with a response from Jeremy Webber, one of Canada's leading legal and social theorists, who weaves the various contributions together, offering questions of his own about the future of oaths, treaties, and covenants in multi-jurisdictional societies.

A final prefatory word about the form of this volume: from the beginning of our conversations, a prominent feature of this project has been the integration of vivid images as not merely illustration, but also the grounds for reflection and analysis. In the pages of this book, visual and material cultures of promises and promising are just as important for prompting analysis as are words and speech-acts. Each author has included in their chapter visual sites for reflection; our invitation to readers is to also enter the conversation in this volume through these images, moving outward into the text, allowing them to inspire thought and generate insight in their own way.

One might say that we are living in a time when promises are in crisis – nations breaking treaties, politicians lying under oath, and the ever-present fear of being duped or scammed by a fraudulent actor pretending to be honourable. Who can be trusted? At a time of human-caused environmental devastation and political upheaval, when making promises for the future seems both urgent and futile, we face challenges that exceed the capacities of any single discipline to explain and address. The crisis of the promise, however, is not new. Grappling with the political and historical phenomenology of the promise at intimate and institutional levels, our collected volume shows that promises have long been made and unmade, kept and broken, in ways that successive generations need to acknowledge and take up in new ways. Promises haunt and guide, constrain and enable; we cannot live without them.

Pamela E. Klassen
Monique Scheer
Benjamin L. Berger

Acknowledgments

As we have worked together on this book, the power of promising has revealed itself to us in ways old and new, through small acts of fidelity and grander gestures of trust. For that, we have many people and organizations to thank.

We wish to thank the Alexander von Humboldt Foundation for its commitment to supporting international networks of scholarship in the humanities and interpretive social sciences. The workshop that began *Making Promises* and the resulting publication of this book were both made possible through Pamela Klassen's Anneliese Maier Research Award from the Humboldt Foundation, which she held from 2015–20. Focused on "Religion and Public Memory in Multicultural Societies," Pamela's Maier Award was hosted by Monique Scheer and the University of Tübingen and brought together international scholars and students at workshops in both Germany and Canada. We are grateful that the University of Tübingen also provided funds to support this publication. We also wish to thank York University for its generous support of Benjamin Berger's York Research Chair in Pluralism and Public Law, which provided significant funding for *Making Promises*. The Faculty of Arts and Science at the University of Toronto also provided logistical and financial support for the Religion and Public Memory Project, including for the "Making Promises" workshop. Organizationally, we are also grateful for the support and expertise of the University of Toronto Press (UTP), and its dedication to publishing rigorously reviewed, carefully copy-edited, and beautifully formatted books.

We also have many people to thank and begin with the contributors to *Making Promises*. Ranging from senior scholars to MA and JD graduates, the authors of this book have each engaged with this project with creativity and seriousness of purpose. It has been a pleasure to work, think, and write with them. We also thank Daniel Quinlan, our editor at UTP, who has been with us from the early days of the project, attending the online workshop in 2020 and helping us to realize our vision for a book about promises rich in words and images. He has our gratitude and enormous respect. Also at UTP, we are very grateful for the careful eye of our copy-editor, Emily Reiner, the organizational know-how of Natalie Garriga, our managing editor, and the savvy of Aditi Parikh, our marketing specialist. Stephen Ullstrom took on the task of indexing a book with a wide diversity of topics and authors, bringing professionalism and ingenuity to his work. We are honoured and grateful that Christi Belcourt allowed us to use her extraordinary artwork for the cover of this volume. We thank Grace Lang (JD, Osgoode Hall Law School) for so carefully reviewing the proofs. Finally, we were fortunate to have the assistance of two marvelous graduate students who helped us bring this volume into being. A sincere thank you to Paige Thombs (University of Victoria) and Charlotte Dalwood (Osgoode Hall Law School), both talented, emerging scholars of religion and public life.

Several participants in the original "Making Promises" workshop helped to shape the book and its many arguments, including Heidi Bohaker, Alan Corbiere, Tiffany Hale, Susan Hill, Dale Turner, and Elder Eileen Antone, and we are grateful to them for their early contributions. Kate Stoehr and Valeria Vergani, both MA students at U of T at the time, graciously took notes at the workshop, and we thank them for their excellent work. We also thank the anonymous peer reviewers who agreed to UTP's invitation – it is not an easy task to peer review an edited collection, and we are very appreciative of their generous and critical engagement with the book and its many authors.

Many artists kindly agreed to share images of their artwork for inclusion in *Making Promises*. Inspired by Jeffery Hewitt's keynote lecture at the workshop, we committed early on to a book that would incorporate images as both sources for and commentary on the making of promises. For their generosity, we thank Elvis Adams, Christian Chapman, Bonnie Devine, George Littlechild, Shelley Niro, Christi Belcourt, and Paul Shilling. We also thank the many archives and libraries that enabled us to include maps and images from their collections, including the Mennonite Heritage Centre, the Map and Data Library of the University of Toronto, the National Gallery of Canada, the Autry Museum of the American West, the Art Gallery of Ontario, and the College of Charleston Special Collections.

Finally, we each thank our families for their support of our work as we undertook this project. Writing this book has helped us to see anew how promises are embodied practices and powerful words that bind us into the future, demanding hope even when the times seem hopeless. For that reason, we dedicate this book to our children, who range in age from five to thirty-one. Every day, they keep us aware of how the making of promises, large and small, requires persistence, humility, integrity, and good humour; every day, they give us hope.

Pamela E. Klassen, Benjamin L. Berger, and Monique Scheer

MAKING PROMISES

INTRODUCTION

Fragmented Promises, Pentimento, and the Salvage Paradigm

JEFFERY HEWITT

I have attempted to organize this chapter in a way that is a reflective summary of the volume which follows, though I make no assertions that the structure tracks a traditional essay/story arc.[1] Still, I hope you stay with me. There is a lot for us to do together. This volume provides insights into some of the minds who are thinking about and posing complex questions that consider, in essence, how we might live well together and celebrate rather than seek to erase our differences. In particular, in our time when sometimes words and deeds may be spoken and acted on with impunity, how do we look at promises? How *should* we look at promises?

I also want to acknowledge the ongoing work of artists, a few of whom I will talk about today. Artists have much to teach us. For example, I am grateful for the image by Elvis Adams (see Figure 0.1).[2] There is a lot there to consider in Adams's work. Let me draw a few elements out. Animiike (thunderbirds), continue to fulfil their original instructions.[3] They bring thunder and rain in the spring and leave us as they gather the fog around them in the autumn as they return to the sky-world for the north wind to bring snow and usher in a time of rest and contemplation. The presence of the pipe, for me, brings in the spirit beings and the sacredness of, in this case, Treaty 3, as it is being made. The pipe inflects the presence of ancestors who guide the present and ones still to come. Imagery of land, water, animals, and grasses all participating and witnessing the ceremony are part of the solemnity and importance of treaty-making, including the wide range of life forces that are affected

Figure 0.1 Elvis Adams, *Rainy River*, 2016. Courtesy of Rainy River First Nations.

by promises made. They illustrate, as Adams has depicted, that this Treaty is eternal. On their own and together, these elements all speak to ceremony, and as Elder Fred Kelly reminds us often, our ceremonies are eternal.[4]

For the most part in Canada, we continue to follow the structures and divisions for education formed originally by the Greeks and developed in Europe with "schools" such as humanities, sciences, etc., each with their own expertise and occupations of knowledge generation.[5] It is by and large still hierarchical from professor to student and structured in a directional line from early childhood to postdoctoral.

I am not criticizing. This system works. It works particularly well for the production of and access to knowledge it was intended to produce and for whom it was intended to be produced. It provides a vital framework for classification and categorization.[6] As Leroy Little Bear, Tracey Lindberg, Doug Williams, Sylvia McAdams, Beverley Jacobs, Leanne Simpson, Sharon Venne, and a growing number of Indigenous scholars tell us, this system does not work for the production of and access to Indigenous knowledge systems.[7] It does not work because it is not Indigenous-centered, nor does it profess to be. The mainstream system of knowledge production is, like common law, formed out of a particular world view for a particular world view. That is why it works for a certain world view but not all.

I have been taught, for example, that Cree knowledge systems do not look hierarchical or siloed.[8] They do not look like an organizational flow chart with columns and rankings leading ever upward. Rather, they are interconnected and, if drawn, might look more like a spider web that has been curved into an orb as a means of demonstrating the relationality of all points of knowledge and expertise to a universe of knowledge. As knowledge expands, so too does the circle. Like the mainstream system, it too has levels of knowledge and includes expertise at a postdoctoral level but comes with an understanding that such expertise is not placed at a pinnacle. Instead, it is located in relation to other expert knowledge and so on. The system is founded in kinship. Kindship.[9] It is about how all knowledge is related not in a vague way but in a specific way, similar to how large extended families are comprised of many individuals who can be vastly different and yet remain connected through family. It is to be treated not only with respect but also to be shared and cared for.

It is a knowledge system that centres relationships and relatives. It is built on the interconnectivity of knowledge. It is a system where respect is earned, not underpinned with a hierarchical power dynamic. A means of knowing that requires actively connected relationships versus solo, subject-matter mastery. It is a system of responsibilities to be carried, not rights to be proclaimed. This is different from multidisciplinary scholarship in the mainstream system, some of which I am actively engaged in. As I understand it, the Cree system is premised on a connection to all other life forms, to energy.[10] It is also why you may sometimes hear elders state some version of "I only know a little bit," when what follows sounds like a doctoral dissertation. It is the speaker reminding the listener and themselves that what the speaker knows is interconnected to nearby knowledge, which in turn is connected to other knowledge and so on, to form a greater whole. They are part of a larger multidimensional web of knowledge that is always expanding. This last point is important to state because Indigenous knowledge is not dated, frozen, or stale. It is thriving, alive, and growing.

That said, today I start with a bit of Western science. I add the adjective "Western" because Indigenous peoples also have scientists, physicists, chemists, engineers, doctors. As journalist Robert Jago (Kwantlen First Nation) stated, it was Indigenous science that gave Europe fertilizer, subsequently bringing the continent out of the Middle Ages with a multifold increase in food production.[11] This counters a predominant narrative about the supremacy of Western science and knowledge that does not fit in well. I raise this because part of Canada's master narrative – still taught in many spaces – is that some version of Indigenous peoples handed all of the lands and resources off to the Crown and then nobly faded into the ether. Quaint, and serving the mythology of friendly settlement of Indigenous lands, but not true.

We continue to see this exoneration from a violent past, towards a more pleasant tale of Canada's founding, continue even today in the country's national reconciliation project. For example, consider how many land acknowledgments sound more like a "Canada heritage moment" without recognizing ongoing colonialism, violence against Indigenous peoples, or a stated commitment to share. There is rarely an accompanying plan of action, such as providing for land back, nor is there an open commitment to redistribute the lines of power.[12] This master narrative favours Canada the Good with a Constitution interpreted not in a modern context and alive like the living tree analogy invoked so often in constitutional law, but rather from an originalist viewpoint in relation to Indigenous peoples.[13]

We see how Canadian law and the Supreme Court of Canada generally interpret treaties, decide on which Indigenous rights exist, which were extinguished, and engage in justifying limitation, while parsing out words like *sui generis* and "moderate," while not providing a legal analysis justifying why a mythology of assumed Crown sovereignty has been so consistently adopted.[14] The Court also unilaterally sets how treaties are to be interpreted, which is to include the Indigenous perspectives but, as Val Napoleon and Hadley Friedland state, Indigenous laws are typically viewed as evidence, not law.[15] In these ways, we might see how easy it might be to believe that Indigenous peoples could not possibly have invented fertilizer because it is not in keeping with the overwhelmingly repeated use of words to form a master narrative that orders much of the modern world a different way.

Words matter. Promise. Oath. Treaty. These words continue to have meaning in both mainstream and Indigenous knowledge systems. In both Canadian and Indigenous laws.

Back to science. And art.

In mainstream science, parallax theory essentially holds that depending on one's sight line, a single object may be viewed differently.[16] For example, in an intersection there is a collision between a red car and a blue car. Witnesses standing on the north-east corner will testify that the blue car hit the red car. Witnesses on the south-west corner may testify that the red car hit the blue car and there was a squirrel that ran out causing the red car to swerve. Maybe both are correct. Where one is positioned matters. This theory also tells us that, like the human eyes, we have two different sight lines to give us a perspective of depth that is otherwise harder to perceive and navigate. And without which we may only be seeing a fragmented view. Artists know this. Some of them show us this when they draw or paint. Consider, as examples, a staircase painted on canvas as a stage backdrop with perhaps trees and plants in the foreground and distance[17] or when a small grouping of people are focused on different sights or lines, such as Leonardo da Vinci's *Virgin of the Rocks* (Figure 0.2).[18] The presence of more than one sight line offers depth.

I sometimes introduce parallax theory in my law classes in relation to the pursuit of truth and its objectivity.[19] Truth and objectivity are important, and we must be mindful when asserting either or both of them without critique because we may become vulnerable to potential soft spots. Parallax theory might help us consider objectivity here: to understand that more than one witness may be telling the honest truth, but their sight line informs what they saw. Multiple witnesses with more than one sight line should offer us a less fragmented view, a deeper perspective. Better perception of depth and thereby possibly a truth of events could, in the instance of our blue and red cars, recalibrate liability with the introduction of a squirrel, for example. When seeking to privilege some witnesses over others, maybe what we are really doing is favouring one sight line over another and deftly avoiding depth. Maybe we are opting for a single narrative that offers us a myopic view when there is more to be seen and engage with, such as Indigenous laws and understanding of words like promise, oath, and treaty. I raise parallax theory in the context of this essay because words are formed and ascribed meaning within political, social, and cultural contexts. In other words, words and their meaning are not universal.

What to do then, when more than one culture with different languages (different words), different world views, come together for a purpose, such as sharing lands and resources? Deny one and favour the other? This seems to be the prevailing practice in relation to Indigenous peoples and many promises made in and around treaties. Indigenous nations practised treaty-making through international law with other Indigenous nations long before the Crown arrived.[20] How do words like promise, oath, and treaty matter in different cultures? No doubt, linguists could tell us volumes about this.[21] I am not a linguist.

I continue to (re)learn Cree and resist trying to translate every word, because as it happens words do not always translate, which I am finding out the hard way. I am also finding a better depth of understanding of English. This may be true for other learners who study a second or third language – how it shifts and maybe deepens our understanding of our first fluent language. For me, understanding is often found

Figure 0.2 Leonardo da Vinci, *The Virgin of the Rocks*, 1491/2 and 1506–8, oil on canvas, National Gallery, London.

in world views. Cree and Anishinaabeg elders, such as Vern Harper[22] and Jim Dumont,[23] for example, have said when you want to understand why something is done, first go to the creation story. Dumont also repeatedly reminds listeners that it is a gift to hear the creation stories of others; to focus on our own; while being very clear that "all creation stories are true." He reminds listeners that no one is rightly positioned to deny the genesis of others and that we are not required to resolve any inconsistencies, rather we are to understand ourselves. Recall more than one perspective from a different sight line offers depth, not threats. Perhaps an insistence on a singular narrative is at its heart about a turn towards the simple and away from human nuance and complexities.

Short of knowing the creation stories of others, there are a myriad of ways to consider other world views that do not have to be extractive and maybe do not require words at all. Consider images located in art.

Artists play a vital role in all cultures, though that role is not necessarily the same in all cultures. That said, the work of artists is both generated and understood, like language, within a particular cultural context. I am going to draw us to a few images here; though many more should and could have easily been included, I had to edit for space.

"Pentimento" is a term in art that essentially describes when a painting reveals a different original composition or image that is not the same as the final version. In other words, there has been a painting over. Pentimento can range from reusing a canvas or board to paint something new with faint lines or subtle views of the underpainting rendered visible, to the readjustment of a hand or foot from the original composition. In her book *American Pentimento*, Patricia Seed examines the ongoing colonial project and the role of some of the Crowns of Europe.[24] She considers how cultural and legal vocabularies continue to be found in our languages, and legal systems, today in relation to Indigenous peoples. In other words, Seed examines the ongoing pentimento of language and law to paint over Indigenous peoples – language and law that paints a new composition over Indigenous peoples, building a newer narrative over an existing one. James Anaya offers us some insight into this when he writes about the legal gymnastics of the Crowns when developing and evolving the doctrine of discovery to justify the taking of Indigenous lands and resources and the use of violence against Indigenous peoples.[25]

Consider, too, the genesis of international law as we commonly know it now arrives through the Westphalian model and the treaties of the Crowns of Europe and the contributions to that peace from the then Holy Roman Empire.[26] From Westphalia in 1648, we get, among other things, the European nation states, and their successor states like Canada.

Figure 0.3 Gerard ter Borch, *The Ratification of the Treaty of Münster*, 1648, oil on copper, National Gallery, London.

Elsewhere I have written about one of the ways in which art, and in particular history painting, continues to support the premise of international law's Westphalian genesis story.[27] For example, in Gerard ter Borch's commemorative painting at the National Gallery in the United Kingdom, we see a composition of Westphalian power (Figure 0.3).[28]

Yet venturing a little further back to 1613 in what was then New Amsterdam, now Manhattan, the Haudenosaunee presented the Dutch with the Two-Row wampum belt.[29]

The Two-Row wampum is an international agreement setting out the terms by which the Haudenosaunee and Dutch would live together with peace, friendship, and respect in their own rivers. A little less than thirty-five years later, Dutch representatives would be key players in the negotiations at Westphalia. The Westphalian model offers echoes of principle elements of the Two-Row wampum. The Westphalian peace treaties sought to resolve longstanding wars for lands and resources among

European Crowns; to respect sovereignty and borders.[30] The point is, in spite of the hallmarks of the Westphalian model being similar to the Haudenosaunee's pre-existing practices of international law, there is not so much as a wampum bead on the table in Borch's painting nodding towards an Indigenous contribution.[31] Like the invention of fertilizer that continues to feed continents, there is no mention in the origin story of Westphalia of Haudenosaunne contributions to international law.

It is in these legal and public spaces where words like promise, oath, and treaty are formed and reformed, remade, and repeated in a singular sight line until it is difficult to see anything else. Where almost all of the space is consumed by one view, one narrative, that is so tremendous we can struggle to see any other. Sometimes where we think we see depth it might be merely an illusion. It is these rewrites or omissions that generate a fragmented and tilted view of superiority over Indigenous world views that I raised within the context of the workshop, "Making Promises: Oaths, Treaties and Convenants," with a hope of contributing the view from the north-east corner versus the south-west in an intersection where colonization has caused a collision. It is in considering how we understand promises where I encourage consideration of narratives, and mindfulness of pentimento. A painting over the original version. A rearranging of the original composition to suit a solo sight line, a preferred visual.

In 1492, Columbus set sail and Antonio de Nebrija – a Spanish humanist – published what is widely understood to be the first published grammar of a European language,[32] because words matter. And as de Nebrija put it, "language has always been the companion of empire."[33] But long before 1492, Indigenous peoples had already been circumnavigating the globe without colonizing.[34] Though if de Nebrija's declaration is to be considered, maybe it was either the wrong language or something lost in translation.

Though night skies may be read differently depending on world views, Columbus and other sailors and navigators, European and Indigenous, commonly understood that stars served as celestial pylons indicating where to steer their watercraft.[35] Along with that of Indigenous peoples, European thought also long saw the stars as holding stories, too, such as Orion with his dog forever chasing after him. The story of Orion, like de Nebrija himself, is a humanist one. I have also been taught that the night sky, which is part of the Cree creation story, tells us a lot about who we are. It is one of the places where knowledge is stored for the generations to come.

As Leroy Little Bear explains, Indigenous people were mainly focused on understanding knowledge for the continued existence of people and less concerned about writing down all of the rules of language in a published grammar as a means to colonizing.[36] Though, as William Buck reminds us, stars hold knowledge for all, including stories of dogs but they are not chasing after Orion. Buck tells many stories of the Cree night sky including about a constellation commonly known as the Little Dipper that in the Cree world view is the story of wolf, coyote, and fox coming together for a council. Each provides two of their pups to the people as companions and to care for communities by offering a warning of approaching dangers. It is this arrangement of stars that tells of how all of the dogs in the world came to be.

Looking through a more mainstream lens, the same stars are seen as a material object to quench physical thirst. Cree stories also offer knowledge for spiritual, emotional, mental, and physical balance. Companionship. Different viewpoints towards the same stars, which are rendered within differing contexts, inform how we see the night sky. It also informs how we see land, some of which is the subject of treaties and promises made. Cree scholar Sharon Venne writes that for Indigenous parties, treaties were made in good faith.[37] Not only treaties with the Crown, but treaties with each other, too. Promises made, which continue to be respected and honoured today. Treaties made with the sacredness exemplified in Elvis Adams's work.

You are looking at a textbook on botany, interspecies promises, and relationships to land. Métis artist Christi Belcourt layers deep knowledge into her work. In this painting (Figure 0.4), entitled *The Wisdom of the Universe*, we see relationships among the plant nation and how they are related in that orb of interrelated knowledge I mentioned earlier. We see promises made from the creation story of certain species of birds who care for and nest in plants as part of a series of interspecies treaties. We see the relationship to land as a universe of wisdom, rich in instruction, knowledge, medicine, and agreements. We see long-standing examples of oaths being kept.

In John Gast's 1872 painting *American Progress* (Figure 0.5), we see land to be expanded upon "manifest destiny."[38] Visible in the foreground is the act of erasing Indigenous peoples as blond-haired "Progress" (the centre figure), who is also referred to as Columbia, moves westward. Indigenous peoples and buffalo flee from her into the shadows as Progress brings forth a golden light. We see a visual language equating "modern" with domination and control over people, lands, and resources needing to be tamed versus Belcourt's positioning of lands that Columbia sails over as a universe of wisdom unto itself. We see rendered in oils on canvas de Nebrija's grammar that "language has always been the companion of empire." Also present are some of the hallmarks of the salvage paradigm.

Figure 0.4 Christi Belcourt, *The Wisdom of the Universe*, 2014, acrylic on canvas, unframed: 171 × 282 cm. Art Gallery of Ontario. Purchased with funds donated by Greg Latremoille, 2014. © Christi Belcourt. Photo: AGO. 2014/6.

Figure 0.5 John Gast, *American Progress*, 1872, oil on canvas, Autry Museum of the American West, Los Angeles.

Figure 0.6 Bonnie Devine, *Battle for the Woodlands: including Anishinaabitude, and Robes to Clothe the Warriors*, 2014–2015. Mixed media installation. Art Gallery of Ontario. Purchase with assistance from the Estate of P.J. Glasser, 2016. © Bonnie Devine. Photo: AGO 2016/168.

Staying for a moment with land and language, *Battle for the Woodlands* by Anishinaabe artist Bonnie Devine considers land and language through mapping some of the sites of contestation between the Anishinaabeg and the British redcoats.[39] She layers in the map of Upper Canada along with the Great Lakes, each painted as an animal being and spirit. Note how they are all connected to each other, reminding us not only of the connectedness of knowledge and water, but its sacredness as well. *Battle for the Woodlands* (Figure 0.6) shows us that the Anishinaabe world view is richly layered into the land and water. It is more than a topographical map of Upper Canada. Devine renders visually for us that land holds relational stories and if we are not careful with them, Progress may sweep them all away and leave only a pentimento of what is there. *Battle for the Woodlands* illuminates Indigenous peoples – in this instance the Anishinaabeg – as vibrant, alive, and prepared to protect knowledge, land, and peoples.

Meanwhile, American painter George Catlin,[40] arguably more directly than John Gast's *American Progress*, paints Indigenous peoples as his subject matter, including those in the American West to which Progress is bringing all of her modernity. Progress appears ironically in a Grecian robe, which had long been outdated in the nineteenth century when Gast

Figure 0.7 George Catlin, *Scalp Dance, Mouth of the Teton River*, 1835–7, oil on canvas, Smithsonian American Art Museum, Washington, DC.

painted, but which harkens back to ancient Greece and the founding of democracy.[41] The obvious counter here is that a Grecian robe is "classic," while Indigenous leggings and jerkins (also shown in shadow in the painting), are long-ago vestments for museums (Figure 0.7).

In essence, as James Clifford sets out in his essay, "Beyond the Salvage Paradigm," this anthropological term "salvage paradigm" relates to a necessity to preserve what is seen as dying or will soon be lost.[42] Artists and cultural institutions have played a key role in the salvage paradigm. As Clifford posits, it is the preservation of an "exotic culture in question, inevitably undergoing 'fatal' changes" at the actions of a dominant culture.[43] We see this in dioramas and museums when it comes to Indigenous peoples, as though Indigenous world views are not still alive in the stars, on the lands and water, but preserved forever behind glass and in the storage of public institutions. Clifford critiques the salvage paradigm for "authenticity." How can a member of one culture possibly capture the essence and realities of another when the so-called Other is only seen through a single social and cultural context, in many cases through that of the dominant culture? George Catlin (Figures 0.8 and 0.9) paints images of Indigenous peoples to "preserve" the savage nobility for the American history records. What could go wrong with titles of his works such as *Scalp Dance, Mouth of the Teton River*[44]

Figure 0.8 George Catlin, *Dance of the Chiefs, Mouth of the Teton River*, 1832–3, oil on canvas, Smithsonian American Art Museum, Washington, DC.

Figure 0.9 George Catlin, *The Last Race, Mandan O-kee-pa Ceremony*, 1832, oil on canvas, Smithsonian American Art Museum, Washington, DC.

Figure 0.10 *Mishipeshu, Lake Superior Provincial Park, Algoma.* Photo Courtesy of Wonder_Al, online: https://www.flickr.com/photos/wonderal/165250184/. Used by permission pursuant to https://creativecommons.org/licenses/by-sa/2.0/deed.en.

or *Dance of the Chiefs*?[45] If there was any lingering curiosity about Caitlin and salvage pentimento, one of his paintings is also titled, *The Last Race.*[46]

You are now looking at *Mishipeshu* (Figure 0.10).[47] This particular image is a rock painting dated pre-1492.[48] It is painted on rock on the shores of what is now called Lake Superior. In other words, not a gentle natural environment and yet after hundreds of years of exposure to the elements, it remains. Along with Jago's assertions of fertilizer as an Indigenous technological invention, so too do we see Indigenous chemistry with this rock painting. Experimenting, developing, and creating paint that would last in a harsh outdoor environment and still be visible to us centuries later offers evidence of deep Indigenous knowledge of science. For those around in the latter half of this millennia, let me know how the acrylics of today hold up. This rock painting also places humans in a canoe beside the water. It explains to travellers to the area that *Mishipeshu* lives in this lake along with serpents.[49] To those who would be travelling here, they would know, too, that a copper offering must be given in exchange for the promise of safe passage and an oath by *Mishipeshu* to ensure it. This rock painting is also about the relationship between humans, water, and the supernatural beings of the lands. It is echoed in Devine's *Battle for the Woodlands* depiction of land as relative.

Contrastingly, surveyed as an anthology, Canada's Group of Seven's[50] highly stylized landscapes[51] amplify land possessed of extraordinary beauty and wondrous light, though principally devoid of human occupation. More glaringly, Gast's *American Progress* depicts land as commodity to be claimed. While the Group of Seven's work may be both more serene and beautifully rendered with light than *American Progress*, they are landscapes influenced by a particular viewpoint.[52] We see in these creative works – *American Progress*, and the Group of Seven – hallmarks of a master narrative that Indigenous peoples are part of "once were" cultures that Catlin sought to salvage; cultures who, as Anaya points out, were not using the lands as they should be capitalized and thereby justifying the taking of lands and resources and removal of people through the doctrine of discovery.

The tensions among the rock painting and the stark, 'dominion over lands' messaging of Gast's *American Progress*, and a largely human-less compendium of Group of Seven landscapes, might also offer us some insight into the legal mythology of assumed Crown sovereignty over Indigenous peoples, lands, and resources that were not part of treaties. Whether they be the peace and friendship treaties in the east of Canada from the eighteenth century or the numbered treaties of the twentieth century or the so-called modern treaties of what is now Quebec, Ontario, and the Plains, treaties were typically underpinned by peace, friendship, and respect, as the Haudenosaunee set out with the Dutch in the seventeenth century.

Cree artist George Littlechild's *Muscle-bound Bob Talks to Birds* (Figure 0.11) is not nearly as old as the rock painting of Mizipeshu, and is rendered in a modern style that George Catlin might marvel at – considering Cree people were to disappear with the westward expansion.[53] Littlechild's piece sets out a call and response, a song between Bob and the birds. It is no accident one of the birds is a cardinal, which is representative of Cree ancestors. What we might also see depicted in Littlechild's work is an exchange between the human and the bird nation, with whom Cree people have treaties. In other words, Indigenous peoples have longer experience with interpreting treaties than Canada's courts. Venne also writes about Cree treaties with other nations, such as the Blackfoot.[54] Cree people are well-versed in treaties, which include interspecies agreements, too, as imagined in Littlechild's painting, where they are overseen by the sun and moon, and also by relatives and spiritual beings, as is seen in Elvis Adams's work.

Paul Kane, much like George Catlin, leaned towards the salvage paradigm in that he often painted Indigenous peoples in shadow, such as in *Six Black Feet Chiefs* (Figure 0.12).[55] In a similar treatment to John Gast, the light in the east moves towards the shadows over Indigenous

Figure 0.11 George Littlechild, *Muscle-bound Bob Talks to Birds*.

Figure 0.12 Paul Kane, *Six Black Feet Chiefs*, ca. 1849–55, oil on canvas, Royal Ontario Museum, Toronto. (912.1.50: ROM2010_11471_11; 300 ppi tiff, 3300 px)

Figure 0.13 Paul Kane, *Indian Encampment on Lake Huron*, 1848–50, oil on canvas, Art Gallery of Ontario, Toronto.

images in *Indian Encampment on Lake Huron* (Figure 0.13), which are either disappearing or not worth featuring in finer detail.[56] Conversely, Catlin was seeking to preserve details, which continue to be of value when looking to find insight into clothing, hairstyles, and tattooing of Indigenous peoples in prior centuries. Sometimes even in critique there is more than one sight line for us to consider and find more depth.

Across much of Kane's work that references Indigenous peoples (even in shadow), including *Chinook Indians in Front of Mount Hood* (Figure 0.14), there is an imbalance in the portrayal of Indigenous peoples. This echoes the Supreme Court of Canada's portrayal of the importance of taking into account an Indigenous perspective on treaty interpretation – as being something to consider, like including roughly painted Indigenous figures – but then treating Indigenous laws as evidence, not law, as Napoleon and Friedland remind us.[57]

Part of what I am trying to say here is that the promises made by the Crown to Indigenous peoples at the outset were in political, social, and cultural contexts that seem to make promises only to be broken. In response, some artists of the day sought to use their craft to record the existence of Indigenous peoples who would soon be extinct. Conversely, the presence of the supernatural animiike, the ancestors and

Figure 0.14 Paul Kane, *Chinook Indians in Front of Mount Hood*, 1851–6, oil on canvas, National Gallery of Canada, Ottawa. (Acc. #6918)

the pipe, in Treaty 3 in Elvis Adams's piece record something else – that treaties are a sacred promise that remain and must remain unbroken. I am also trying to say that we need to reconsider how we examine, dissect, and rule upon treaty questions that cannot be unilaterally determined by only one of the treaty parties using the laws of only one of the treaty parties. There is nothing honourable about that no matter how it is dressed up.[58]

It is vital that Canadian courts reject the unilateral assertion of Crown sovereignty, as a yet to be explained legal assumption, while offering other asymmetrically defined words to explain their work in relation to Indigenous peoples, such as *sui generis* or "moderate" or "reconcile." It does not have to be this way.[59] There are other ways of knowing. Other ways of knowing that formed the treaty relationships that are so often interpreted by one party on behalf of both parties when such an authority to do so is not within the provisions of the treaties. Indigenous knowledge systems and laws matter and must be fully applied by all parties and decision-makers – not just one. Uneven interpretations of promises made within treaties leads to distortion. It is not sustainable and should not continue to be ignored or denied. Such a singular sight line is devoid of depth and diminishes meaning for us all.

Figure 0.15 Paul Shilling (Dazaunggee – Sky Buffalo), *Time to Wake Up*.

In Anishinaabe artist Paul Shilling's *Time to Wake Up* (Figure 0.15), we are reminded that ancestors are here, too, along with our relative the sun.[60] Shilling includes fish (his dodem) coming together: one from the ancestors and the other from the mind of the human figure.[61] This echoes back to the interconnectivity of all knowledge that is not always siloed in Indigenous systems and includes inter-species knowledge.[62] Fish know, Belcourt reminds us, that knowledge is part of ceremony, and as Elder Fred Kelly says, "ceremonies are eternal." So, too, as Venne and Borrows write, are sacred promises made, such as those contained within treaties between the Crown and Indigenous peoples.

It is well past time for those professing and ruling asymmetrically for one party on the treaties. It is time to halt and search for knowledge that includes responsibility, which may be found both within and outside mainstream structures of knowledge. It is time to (re)connect to a web of relations and be good relatives, through acting respectably and honourably towards each other rather than seeking to rule over and diminish. Here, too, mainstream knowledge systems hold some key elements that are instructive. Recall that parallax theory tells us that without more than one perspective, we cannot accurately gauge depth. Our perception may be skewed one way insofar as we may only be seeing part of what we should – a fragment. But with more than one sight line (more than one perspective), we can see connectivity with, not dominance over or erasure of, what is and should be the *Wisdom of the Universe* that, at least in Belcourt's rendering, is also found in the night sky.[63]

Thank you for reading through to the end. I am grateful for your time and hope to have connected to your head minds and your heart minds because taken together they offer us enhanced sight lines with richer insights.

NOTES

1 I am grateful for being included in the original workshop, "Making Promises: Oaths, Treaties, and Covenants in Multi-jurisdictional and Multi-religious Societies," conceived of and organized by Pamela E. Klassen, Monique Scheer, and Benjamin Berger. This essay has also benefited greatly from the assistance of my research assistant, Newsha Zargaran, though any errors or omissions are mine.

2 For more on Elvis Adams's work and the Rainy River Project, see "One Diary, Many Stories: Visual Art," Art of Manidoo Ziibi, Kiinawin Kawindomowin/Story Nations, https://storynations.utoronto.ca/index.php/stories/art-of-manidoo-ziibi/.

3 There is a range of spellings for thunderbirds. The one I use here was shared with me by an Anishinaabemowin speaker from Rama First Nation.

4 Elder Fred Kelly explains "[t]hat's what our sacred law means, or, if you will, call it a constitution: it means, *kagakiwe inaakonigewin*, it means that sacred law and anything that is sacred to us is eternal," in Fred Kelly, "Let's Talk Treaty!" 25 March 2020, in Episode 12, Part 2: *The Anishinaabe in Treaty 3 with Elder Fred Kelly*, at 07:45, podcast, www.iheart.com /podcast/269-lets-talk-treaty-76110877/episode/episode-12-the -anishinaabe-in-treaty-76114961/, perma.cc/VTN9-RS9C.

5 Jacques Verger, "The Universities and Scholasticism," in *The New Cambridge Medieval History*, vol. 5, ed. David Abulafia (Cambridge: Cambridge University Press, 1999), 257.

6 Patricia J. Gumport and Stuart K. Snydman, "The Formal Organization of Knowledge: An Analysis of Academic Structure," *Journal of Higher Education* 73, no. 3 (May–June 2002): 376, 385, 402.

7 Leroy Little Bear, "Traditional Knowledge and Humanities: A Perspective by a Blackfoot," *Journal of Chinese Philosophy* 39, no. 4 (December 2012): 520; Tracey Lindberg, "Critical Indigenous Legal Theory Part 1: The Dialogue Within," *Canadian Journal of Women and the Law* 27, no. 2 (2015): 226–7; Doug Williams, *Michi Saagiig Nishnaabeg: This Is Our Territory* (Winnipeg: Arbeiter Ring Publishing, 2018); Sylvia McAdam, *Nationhood Interrupted: Revitalizing Nêhiyaw Legal Systems* (Saskatoon: Purich Publishing, 2015); Beverley Kim Jacobs, *Impacts of Industrial and Resource Development on the Wholistic Health of Akwesasronon: A Human Responsibility/Rights Solution* (PhD diss., University of Calgary, 2018); Leanne R. Simpson, "Anticolonial Strategies for the Recovery and Maintenance of Indigenous Knowledge," *American Indian Quarterly* 28, no. 3/4 (Summer–Autumn 2004): 373; Sharon H. Venne, "Treaties Made in Good Faith," *Canadian Review of Comparative Literature* 34, no. 1 (2007): 1.

8 Though I have benefited from many teachers over the years, a few who have been particularly generous with me – including on Cree structures and world view – are Vern Harper and Pauline Shirt (both now among the ancestors), and Sylvia McAdam.

9 The first person I heard speak about "kindship" was Tracey Lindberg, and I continue to be grateful as I often return to this word and unpack meaning.

10 Leroy Little Bear has written about the connection of knowledge to energy from the perspective of a Blackfoot scientist in "Traditional Knowledge," 521. My understanding of Cree knowledge systems comes from this article and discussions with Maria Campbell and Sylvia McAdam; this is my only understanding and I do not speak monolithically.

11 Robert Jago, "The Hungry People," *The Walrus*, 23 July 2020, thewalrus.ca /terra-cognita-the-hungry-people/, perma.cc/TV3J-RLE2.

12 Chelsea Vowel, "Beyond Territorial Acknowledgements," *âpihtawikosisân* (blog), 23 September 2016, apihtawikosisan.com/2016/09/beyond -territorial-acknowledgments/, perma.cc/CE7T-NV7X.

13 John Borrows, "Challenging Historical Frameworks: Aboriginal Rights, the Trickster, and Originalism," *The Canadian Historical Review* 98, no. 1 (March 2017): 122.

14 See R v. Sparrow, [1990] 1 S.C.R. 1075, 70 D.L.R. (4th) 385; R v. Van der Peet, [1996] 2 S.C.R. 507, 137 D.L.R. (4th) 289; R v. Marshall, [1999] 3 S.C.R. 456, 177 D.L.R. (4th) 513 [Marshall]; John Borrows and Michael Coyle, *The Right Relationship: Reimagining the Implementation of Historical Treaties* (Toronto: University of Toronto Press, 2017).

15 See as examples: Mikisew Cree First Nations v. Canada (Minister of Canadian Heritage), 2005 SCC 69; Marshall (see n14 above); R v. Badger, [1996] 1 S.C.R. 771, 133 D.L.R. (4th) 324; Val Napoleon and Hadley Friedland, "An Inside Job: Engaging with Indigenous Legal Traditions through Stories," *McGill Law Journal* 61, no. 4 (2016): 735, 739.

16 Ian P. Howard, *Perceiving in Depth* (Oxford: Oxford University Press, 2012), 3:84–5.

17 See https://i.pinimg.com/originals/7c/3c/03/7c3c03c6e4551671db8db1a 53c20a492.jpg, perma.cc/MYG6-YJLL.

18 Leonardo da Vinci, *The Virgin of the Rocks*, The National Gallery, London, www.nationalgallery.org.uk/paintings/leonardo-da-vinci-the-virgin-of -the-rocks, perma.cc/339A-ZE82.

19 For a technical explanation see Howard, *Perceiving in Depth*.

20 Beverley Jacobs and Jeffery Hewitt, "Indigeneity: Practices of Indigenous International Law" (forthcoming).

21 Farzad Sharifian, *Cultural Linguistics: Cultural Conceptualisations and Language* (Amsterdam: John Benjamins, 2017).

22 Vern Harper, conversation with the author, Native Canadian Centre of Toronto, Toronto, ca. 1994.

23 Jim Dumont, conversation with the author, Rama First Nation, MASK Arena, 2019.

24 Patricia Seed, *American Pentimento* (Minneapolis: University of Minnesota Press, 2001).

25 S. James Anaya, *International Law and Indigenous Peoples* (Burlington, VT: Ashgate, 2003). For more on the doctrine of discovery, see also Robert J. Miller, Jacinta Ruru, Larissa Behrendt, and Tracey Lindberg, *Discovering Indigenous Lands: The Doctrine of Discovery in the English Colonies* (Oxford: Oxford University Press, 2010).

26 For more, see James A. Caporaso, "The European Union and Forms of State: Westphalian, Regulatory or Post-Modern?" *Journal of Common Market Studies* 34, no. 1 (March 1996): 34–5; Stephen D. Krasner, "Rethinking the Sovereign State Model," *Review of International Studies* 27 (2001): 17; Stéphane Beaulac, "The Westphalian Model in Defining International Law: Challenging the Myth," *Australian Journal of Legal History* 8 (2004): 181.

27 Jeffery G. Hewitt, "Certain (mis)Conceptions," in *Routledge Handbook of International Law and the Humanities*, 1st ed., ed. Shane Chalmers and Sundhya Pahuja (London: Routledge, 2021), 159.

28 Hewitt, "Certain (mis)Conceptions," 161.

29 For more on the Two-Row wampum, see Jacobs, *Impacts of Industrial and Resource Development*, discussing "Kuswentah"; Angela M. Haas, "Wampum as Hypertext: An American Indian Intellectual Tradition of

Multimedia Theory and Practice," *Studies in American Indian Literatures* 19, no. 4 (Winter 2007): 77.

30 John J. Jackson, "Sovereignty-Modern: A New Approach to an Outdated Concept," *American Journal of International Law* 97, no. 4 (2003): 786.

31 Hewitt, "Certain (mis)Conceptions," 161.

32 Claire Gilbert, "A Grammar of Conquest: The Spanish and Arabic Reorganization of Granada After 1492," *Past & Present* 239, no. 1 (May 2018): 10–12.

33 Antonio de Nebrija, *Gramática de la Lengua Castellana* [Grammar of the Castilian Language] (Salamanca: 1492), quoted in Gilbert, "A Grammar of Conquest," 1: "siempre la lengua fue compañera del imperio."

34 Fanny Wonu Veys, *Mana Māori: The Power of New Zealand's First Inhabitants* (Leiden: Leiden University Press, 2010), 20–1.

35 Veys, *Mana Māori*, 27, 29; See, e.g., Margaret E. Schotte, *Sailing School: Navigating Science and Skill, 1550–1800* (Baltimore: Johns Hopkins University Press, 2019).

36 Leroy Little Bear, "Indigenous Knowledge and Western Science: Dr. Leroy Little Bear Talk, BanffEvents, The Banff Centre, 14 January 2015, video, 21:32, https://www.youtube.com/watch?v=gJSJ28eEUjI.

37 Venne, "Treaties Made in Good Faith."

38 *American Progress*, Library of Congress, Washington, DC,www.loc.gov /pictures/item/97507547/, perma.cc/WE4B-D9VA.

39 Bonnie Devine, *Battle for the Woodlands: Anishinaabitude*, Art Gallery of Ontario, Toronto, ago.ca/collection/object/2016/168, perma.cc /ZS5A-4LK5.

40 "George Catlin," Smithsonian American Art Museum, Washington, DC, americanart.si.edu/artist/george-catlin-782.

41 For more on styles of clothing in the founding years of the United States of America, see Sandra Tomc, *Fashion Nation: Picturing the United States in the Long Nineteenth Century* (Ann Arbor: University of Michigan Press, 2021).

42 James Clifford, "The Others: Beyond the 'Salvage' Paradigm," *Third Text* 3, no. 6 (1989): 73.

43 Clifford, "The Others," 73.

44 George Catlin, *Scalp Dance, Mouth of the Teton River*, Smithsonian American Art Museum, Washington, DC, americanart.si.edu/artwork/scalp-dance -mouth-teton-river-4347, perma.cc/Z35X-AK4C.

45 George Catlin, *Dance of the Chiefs, Mouth of the Teton River*, Smithsonian American Art Museum, Washington, DC, americanart.si.edu/artwork /dance-chiefs-mouth-teton-river-4022, perma.cc/3WRT-464E.

46 George Catlin, *The Last Race, Mandan O-kee-pa Ceremony*, Smithsonian American Art Museum, Washington, DC, americanart.si.edu/artwork /last-race-mandan-o-kee-pa-ceremony-4204.

47 Basil Johnston, *The Manitous: The Spiritual World of the Ojibway* (New York: Harper Collins, 1995). See also Agawa Rock site, Lake Superior Provincial Park, www.flickr.com/photos/wonderal/165250184/.

48 Meghan C.L. Howey, "Other-Than-Human Persons, Mishipishu, and Danger in the Late Woodland Inland Waterway Landscape of Northern Michigan," *American Antiquity* 85, no. 2 (April 2020): 350.

49 Johnston, *The Manitous*.

50 Newlands, *The Group of Seven and Tom Thomson: An Introduction* (Willowdale, Canada: Firefly Books, 1995).

51 For more, see Ian A.C. Dejardin, Sarah Milroy, ed, *A Like Vision: The Group of Seven and Tom Thomson*, (Toronto: Goose Land Editions, 2020).

52 For more on Group of Seven, see John O'Brian & Peter White, ed, *Beyond Wilderness* (Montreal: McGill-Queen's University Press, 2007).

53 For more on Mishipeshu image, which is in Lake Superior Provincial Park, Agawa Rock, see Serge Lemaître, "Agawa Pictograph Site," *The Canadian Encyclopedia*, last edited 4 March 2015, https://www .thecanadianencyclopedia.ca/en/article/agawa-pictograph -site#:~:text=It%20is%20apparently%20Shingwaukonce%20 himself,region%20after%20the%2017th%20century.

54 Venne, "Treaties Made in Good Faith," 3.

55 Paul Kane, *Six Black Feet Chiefs*, ROM Collections, Royal Ontario Museum, Toronto, collections.rom.on.ca/objects/230018/six-black-feet-chiefs -blackfoot;jsessionid=E7885C65E101974C0373AC226F405629, perma .cc/5W64-MNMN.

56 Arlene Gehmacher, "Significance & Critical Issues," Paul Kane – Life & Work, *Art Canada Institute*, www.aci-iac.ca/art-books/paul-kane /significance-and-critical-issues/, perma.cc/2GFK-SJR9, accessed 20 August 2021.

57 "Paul Kane," Culture, *Canada History*, www.canadahistory.ca/sections /culture/art/Paul%20Kane/Chinook%20Indians%20in%20Front%20 of%20Mt%20Hood.html, accessed 20 August 2021.

58 Honour of the Crown has been developed by Canadian courts and become a feature of legal analysis and decision-making since the Haida case; see Haida Nation v. British Columbia (Minister of Forests), 2004 SCC 73. For an excellent discussion on the honour of the Crown, see Robert Hamilton and Joshua Nichols, "The Tin Ear of the Court: Ktunaxa Nation and the Foundation of the Duty to Consult," *Alberta Law Review* 56, no. 3 (2019): 734–8.

59 Borrows, "Challenging Historical Frameworks."

60 Paul Shilling, *Time to Wake Up*, www.paulshilling.ca/product/time-to -wake-up/, accessed 20 August 2021.

61 For more on Anishinaabeg dodem, see Heidi Bohaker, *Doodem and Council Fire: Anishinaabe Governance Through Alliance* (Toronto: University of

Toronto Press, 2020); Leanne Simpson, "Looking after Gdoo-naaganinaa: Precolonial Nishnaabeg Diplomatic and Treaty Relationships," *Wicazo Sa Review* 23, no. 2 (Fall 2008): 33.

62 For another example, see Christi Belcourt's *Fish Fasting for Knowledge From the Stars*, https://christibelcourt.ca/products/the-fish-are-fasting -for-knowledge-from-the-stars.

63 Christi Belcourt, *The Wisdom of the Universe*, Art Gallery of Ontario, Toronto, ago.ca/collection/object/2014/6.

PART I

Promises in Place: A Great Lakes Pentimento

PAMELA E. KLASSEN

A treaty is a promise in place. In the Great Lakes region of the eighteenth and nineteenth centuries, treaties agreed to between Indigenous nations and the British Crown were made on and with land and waters. These treaties remain "sacred promises" that actively hold power and call forth responsibilities, as Jeffery Hewitt shows in his introduction to this book. When Canada refuses to remember the fullness of its promises made in place, Hewitt argues, it uses "the ongoing pentimento of language and law to paint over Indigenous peoples."[1] Pentimento, in a literary sense, means the leftover traces of changes that an author has made to the words and phrasing in a text. In the sense of painting, pentimento means "a visible trace of a mistake or an earlier composition seen through later layers of paint on a canvas."[2] In both senses, pentimento is at once a transformation and a record of that transformation capable of holding visions of the present and the past. An English word borrowed from Italian and rooted in an earlier Latin verb, pentimento also means "to repent," itself a Christian concept for acknowledging wrongdoing and working to repair it.

British imperialism envisioned Indigenous lands and waters through a continental scope: as pathways that would connect a growing global empire in a policy of expansion that tried to erase the specificity of Indigenous places and the people who belonged to them. Resisting this continental vision, Hewitt turns to the work of contemporary Anishinaabe artists such as Elvis Adams and Bonnie Devine. He draws forth a Great Lakes pentimento that illustrates the continuing power of Indigenous narratives, ceremonies, and memorialization to uphold promises in and to place, even as imperial visions sought to paint over them.

In the earliest times of treaty-making, the British understood that they were negotiating for access to specific lands and waterways of specific Indigenous nations. They sought to build alliances with those who would grant them the ability to navigate the Great Lakes as they pursued the fur trade, and who would provide them with allies in their wars with the French and later the Americans.[3] They had not yet adopted what might be called a nineteenth-century policy of pentimento, by which they claimed to have successfully blotted out Indigenous jurisdiction through treaties in which Indigenous peoples supposedly ceded and surrendered their land.

Once the British defeated the French in Quebec in 1760, and subsequently suffered defeat themselves at the hands of the Americans during the Revolutionary War, they increasingly came to see treaties not as means to move through Indigenous lands or to make Indigenous allies. Instead, they created a "legal mythology" that depicted treaties as land cessions or the extinguishment of Indigenous title. Remapping and rewriting the land as "Canada" allowed for a flood of settlers to encroach on Indigenous territory to do the work of capitalist extraction and Christian colonialism as missionaries, surveyors, farmers, loggers, miners, engineers, and builders of infrastructure.[4] As "Canada's master narrative," in Hewitt's phrase, this version of a Great Lakes pentimento was never a full erasure of Indigenous sovereignty, but a layering of memory, text, maps, images, and narrative onto Indigenous lands.[5]

The persistence and enduring significance of Indigenous governance and ceremony in the face of Canadian settler colonialism is best understood in relation to specific places and relations, as the three chapters in this section demonstrate. Elizabeth Elbourne, Kate Stoehr, and Sujith Xavier all grapple with promises made in a particular place: the land nestled into the crook of the eastern Great Lakes, where the water flows from Lake Huron along the St. Clair River to Lake Erie, and then along the Niagara River to Lake Ontario. An 1813 map (see Figure I.1) depicts this chain of lakes and rivers as "British America" and the "United States," but also recognizes the territories of the "Chippewa" (Ojibwe), Ootawas (Odawa), Miamis (Miami), and others. Based on drawings made by the British general Isaac Brock during the War of 1812, the map acknowledges Anishinaabe territories but erases Haudenosaunee presence in the region. There is no sign of the land promised to the Haudenosaunee by the British in the Haldimand Proclamation of 1784. As Elizabeth Elbourne's chapter details, Haudenosaunee who fought as allies to the British during the American Revolutionary War, and subsequently became refugees in the wake of genocidal American violence in their homelands, were given this land in recognition of their alliance. The map whites out Haudenosaunee territory, while also demonstrating that settlers knew that this

Figure I.1 Isaac Brock, et al., *A Map of the American Lakes and Adjoining Country: The Present Seat of War between Great Britain & the United States*, 1813, *Gale Nineteenth Century Collections Online*.

land was (and is) Indigenous territory. The pentimento of superimposing settler names and power on the land was, and is, never complete.

I use this 1813 map, despite its cartographic and historical errors, to situate all three of the following chapters in place, within a longer trajectory of colonial memory and forgetting. Orienting this section by way of a map helps to place these chapters in relation to a Great Lakes pentimento that allows one to notice alterations and mistakes in composition in an image, as well as the traces that retain earlier ways of seeing the world. All three chapters show that the British, and later Americans and Canadians, perceived the promises they made with Indigenous nations in treaty through visions clouded by their commitments to capitalist empire, divine providence, and white Christian superiority. They thought God intended the land to belong to them so they could enact their visions of "improvement" and "civilization," as Stoehr demonstrates. This providential view of the land runs through both US memorialization of the early "republic," as Elbourne's chapter shows, and Canadian visions of the country as a place of refuge and asylum, as Xavier argues.

Elizabeth Elbourne's chapter, "Promises Remembered and Erased: Treaties, Land, and Commemoration in the Aftermath of the American Revolution," is situated on the south and west shores of Lake Ontario, and along the Grand River (on the map this is the Y-shaped river extending north from the east side of Lake Erie). She focuses on promises that the US government and British Crown made and broke with the Haudenosaunee of Six Nations. While the 1813 map erases the Six Nations of the Grand River, Elbourne's chapter shows that the Americans and the British were both very well aware of Haudenosaunee presence. In 1879, Lyman Draper, an amateur US historian, travelled to Six Nations to collect oral history for an account he hoped to write of the American Revolution. His Six Nations conversation partners, however, agreed to speak with him motivated by their own goals. They made sure to show Draper a copy of the Haldimand Proclamation, underscoring their commitment to holding the Crown and Canada to their promises. As the "Protect the Tract" movement shows today, the Six Nations continue to articulate and live out their duties to the land as a "sacred trust."[6]

Moving northward, Kate Stoehr's paper focuses on nineteenth-century settler imaginations of Manitoulin Island, or what the Anishinaabe knew of as "Odawa Mnising" or "Mnidoo Mnising."[7] Spelled "Manatoualin Isles" on the 1813 map, with "Upper Canada" hovering over the islands in a larger upper-case font, the island is incorrectly drawn in a southerly line, but the map does acknowledge that it is within Anishinaabe territory of the "Chippewas" (Ojibwe) and the "Ootawas" (Odawa). Stoehr argues that white colonial officials in 1830s Upper Canada who debated with each other about what was "best" for the Anishinaabeg all did so to the same end: taking Anishinaabe land with justifications rooted in Christianity, capitalism, and civilization. She traces the debates between white settlers who thought of themselves as "Friends of the Indians" and Francis Bond Head, a British colonial official. Head notoriously made treaties with Anishinaabeg in the south-eastern Great Lakes area without the approval of his superiors, developing a scheme by which he would convince all of them to move to Manitoulin. Stoehr shows that despite their pitched battles, both the "Friends of the Indians" and Francis Bond Head shared the goal of Indigenous dispossession and assimilation. Convinced of their own providential claims to the land, they both agreed that the Anishinaabeg were not sufficiently "civilized" to "improve" the land without assimilating to Canadian practices. The historical record shows that Canadian claims to being civilized did not entail keeping promises; Canadians have disavowed most of their treaty promises, forgetting the ceremonies that bound them in relation to the Anishinaabeg or the Haudenosaunee. On Manitoulin and surrounding areas, this disavowal has been painstakingly detailed by the Robinson Huron Waawiindamaagewin, which successfully took Canada to court to honour its promises, and renewed its own commitments at a Treaty Gathering on Manitoulin Island in 2023.[8]

Moving back south-east from Manitoulin, and forward more than a century, Sujith Xavier's chapter, "Between Gratitude and Guilt: The Promise of a Better Life in a Settler Colony for Racialized Refugees," reflects on treaty promises from the perspective of refugees who came to Canada for asylum. Centring his reflections from his own position as a refugee from Sri Lanka who arrived in Montreal in the 1980s, Xavier shows that for refugees of colour, Indigenous law and sovereignty, and the significance of treaties, were not part of the story that Canada told them upon welcoming them to this land. Thinking of asylum as itself a kind of promise, Xavier shows how refugees in a settler colony orbit between gratitude and guilt, in their own journey of understanding what it means to build a new home in Canada on Indigenous territories. He calls for a deeper understanding of the role of racial capitalism in the building of settler colonies as ambivalent and compromised places of refuge. Demonstrating that the construction of gratitude is itself a relationship of giving and power, Xavier's chapter also connects to the theme of the gift and the question of the oath, explored more fully in Monique Scheer's comments in her introduction to Part Two and in several other chapters in this volume.

Read together, these chapters expose the cracks in a narrative of Canada as a land of promise and civilizational progress which, by the latter part of the twentieth century, also considered itself to be enthusiastically welcoming to refugees. The "Dominion of Canada" mapped and dreamed itself into a nation from sea to sea to sea by painting over Indigenous presence, law, and spirituality. Guided by a cosmology of land that prioritized extraction and accumulation, Canadian settler colonialism imagined itself on a continental scale. Working hard to forget that treaties were sacred promises which the Crown had solemnized in ceremony, federal and provincial governments (also still embodiments of the Crown in their own ways) pictured treaty lands as puzzle pieces that would fit together to give them access to resources that would build a nation.[9]

In the Great Lakes region in particular, treaties were often spurred by colonial desires for access to gold, copper, and crops in "resource-rich" places – they were promises made along the path to what Canada considered to be a god-given future of resource booms and white settlement. This version of a Great Lakes pentimento needs correction. To stick with a painting metaphor, in the world of art this correction could be called "conservation," the process by which someone with specialized knowledge and skills restores a work of art to its earlier condition. Indigenous Elders, knowledge holders, scholars, writers, and artists have been doing this work as long as Canada has been breaking its treaty promises.[10]

The constant work of correction undertaken by Indigenous people has also been an active conservation of their own traditions, as demonstrated by Jeffery Hewitt's discussion of Anishinaabe artist Bonnie Devine's installation, *Battle for the Woodlands*. Painting over a large colonial map of Upper and Lower Canada sprawling across a wall in Toronto's Art Gallery of Ontario, Devine, of the Serpent River First Nation on the north shore of Lake Huron, depicts the Great Lakes as five different spirit animals, each with their own relationship to the people of their territory (see Figures I.2 & I.3.)[11]

As Hewitt writes: "Devine renders visually for us that land holds relational stories and if we are not careful with them, Progress may sweep them all away and leave only a pentimento of what is there. *Battle for the Woodlands* illuminates Indigenous peoples – in this instance the Anishinaabeg – as vibrant, alive, and prepared to protect knowledge, land, and peoples."[12] In the public space of the art gallery, Devine engages an Anishinaabe practice of reading and visualizing through pentimento not merely as an act of historical correction, but also as an activation of a future where the people who live by the lakes could truly engage as treaty people.

As the chapters in this and other sections of the book show, the material and visual record of promises offers a chance for deeper understanding of how to live out the political and spiritual obligations of treaty: Guswenta, or the Two-Row wampum belt, as a record and reminder of the need for respectful coexistence; pipes smoked together at treaty ceremonies on Manitoulin Island; practices of memory, however partial,

Figure I.2 Bonnie Devine, *Battle for the Woodlands*, 2014–15 (detail). Acrylic paint, paper, felt, and beads, Art Gallery of Ontario, Toronto.

Figure I.3 Bonnie Devine, *Battle for the Woodlands*, including *Anishinaabitude* and *Robes to Clothe the Warriors*, 2014–15 (detail). Acrylic paint, paper, felt, and beads; maple, spruce, and willow boughs; sea grass; mixed media, felt, and beads on deer and moose hides, Art Gallery of Ontario, Toronto.

in which a US historian visited the Six Nations to better understand his own country. Painting and re-painting the land and waters, pentimento holds the possibility of both erasure and reclamation, reimagining the past and casting forward with new visions, illustrating new ways to inhabit and live out promises made and remade.

NOTES

1 See Hewitt in this volume, and Patricia Seed, *Ceremonies of Possession in Europe's Conquest of the New World, 1492–1640* (Cambridge: Cambridge University Press, 1995).
2 *Oxford English Dictionary*, s.v. "Pentimento, n.," accessed July 2023, https://doi.org/10.1093/OED/2392884272.
3 Heidi Bohaker, *Doodem and Council Fire: Anishinaabe Governance through Alliance* (Toronto: University of Toronto Press, 2021).

4 Sheldon Krasowski, *No Surrender: The Land Remains Indigenous* (Regina: University of Regina Press, 2019); Michael Coyle and John Borrows, *The Right Relationship: Reimagining the Implementation of Historical Treaties* (Toronto: University of Toronto Press, 2017).

5 See Hewitt in this volume. See also John Borrows, "Wampum at Niagara: The Royal Proclamation, Canadian Legal History, and Self-Government," in *Aboriginal and Treaty Rights in Canada: Essays on Law, Equality, and Respect for Difference*, ed. Michael Asch (Vancouver: University of British Columbia Press, 1997), 155–72; John Borrows, *Law's Indigenous Ethics* (Toronto: University of Toronto Press, 2019).

6 Council Chiefs of the Haudenosaunee, Grand River Territory, "Land Rights Statement," Protect the Tract, 4 November 2006, www.protectthetract.com/land-rights-statement.

7 Alan Ojiig Corbiere, ed., *Gechi-Piitzijig Dbaajmowag: The Stories of Our Elders*, trans. Evelyn Roy and Kate Roy (M'Chigeeng, ON: Ojibwe Cultural Foundation, 2011).

8 "About Robinson Huron Waawiindamaagewin," Treaty of 1850: Robinson Huron Waawiindamaagewin, accessed 4 June 2023, http:// waawiindamaagewin.com/.

9 Pamela E. Klassen, "God Keep Our Land: The Legal Ritual of the McKenna-McBride Royal Commission, 1913–1916," in *Religion and the Exercise of Public Authority*, ed. Benjamin L. Berger and Richard Moon (Oxford: Hart, 2016), 79–93; Pamela E. Klassen, "Spiritual Jurisdictions: Treaty People and the Queen of Canada," in *Ekklesia: Three Inquiries in Church and State*, by Paul Christopher Johnson, Pamela E. Klassen, and Winnifred Fallers Sullivan (Chicago: University of Chicago Press, 2018), 107–74.

10 Susan M. Hill, *The Clay We Are Made Of: Haudenosaunee Land Tenure on the Grand River* (Winnipeg: University of Manitoba Press, 2017); Anishinaabe Grand Council Treaty #3, "'The Creator Placed Us Here': Timeline of Significant Events of the Anishinaabeg of Treaty #3" (Kenora, ON: Anishinaabe Grand Council Treaty #3, 2013); John Borrows, *Canada's Indigenous Constitution* (Toronto: University of Toronto Press, 2010).

11 Bonnie Devine, *Battle for the Woodlands* (Detail), Resilience Project, accessed August 25, 2023, https://resilienceproject.ca/en/artists/bonnie-devine; Erica Commanda, "Bonnie Devine's *Battle for the Woodlands* Battles the Status Quo," *Muskrat Magazine*, 13 January 2016, http://muskratmagazine. com/bonnie-devines-battle-for-the-woodlands-battles-the-status-quo/.

12 See Hewitt in this volume.

Chapter One

Promises Remembered and Erased: Treaties, Land, and Commemoration in the Aftermath of the American Revolution

ELIZABETH ELBOURNE

The American Revolution was a hugely important watershed in the history of relationships between Indigenous peoples and settlers in North America. It was a way station rather than a final destination but it still marked a large-scale victory for land-hungry settlers in the context of the ongoing struggle over Indigenous lands which had shaped the Revolution itself.[1] Among other ramifications, many members of the Haudenosaunee Six Nations become refugees, fleeing core homelands in what would become New York state, in the wake of warfare and ethnic cleansing. British diplomats gave control of all Six Nations territories to the Americans at the negotiating table in 1783, despite promises to allies among the Six Nations. The Kanyen'kehá:ka (Mohawk), on whose stories this essay focuses, lost all their lands in the Mohawk Valley.

In 1784, the British governor of what was then the Province of Quebec, Frederick (or Frédéric) Haldimand, granted lands to the Haudenosaunee at Grand River and the Bay of Quinte in what is now Ontario in a scrambling partial exchange for this betrayal. The vast majority of this land in Canada had, however, passed out of Six Nations hands by the mid-nineteenth century through a variety of processes. These included the colonial state "persuading" a non-representative group to agree to allow Grand River lands to be sold by the state in the "Surrender" of 1841, with money supposedly held in trust for the Six Nations but in practice invested in a variety of ways that did not benefit the community. After a significant protest movement, rescinding of approval by some signatories, and a Commission of Inquiry, a final settlement was reached in 1847, leaving about 5 per cent of the original Grand River lands in Indigenous hands.[2] Although some of the Grand River lands were sold or gifted by Thayendenegea Joseph Brant (1743–1807),[3] including being sold to create the town of Brantford, much Six Nations land was lost to corruption and outright theft. Despite inheriting the promises of the Crown, the colonial state refused to protect Six Nations legal rights. The state consistently sided with settlers, including rewarding squatting and misappropriating Six Nations funds.[4]

It therefore may not be surprising that for many Haudenosaunee people, to remember the American Revolution in the late nineteenth century, some one hundred years later, was to remember the promises that Britain had made to its Indigenous allies. It was also to remember related promises to respect Indigenous land and self-government within the settler state of Canada. In contrast, for many settlers in the United States, the memory of the Revolution a hundred years on was tied to claims to land once occupied by Indigenous peoples. Acts of commemoration had a different weight in white towns and villages in New York. In both cases, however, telling stories about the past was a way to make claims on the present.

In this paper I look at late nineteenth-century stories about the American Revolution and its traumatic aftermath recounted by some Haudenosaunee people, particularly Kanyen'kehá:ka, as well as some contrasting ways in which members of American settler communities in New York commemorated the Revolution. The trauma of the Revolution included ethnic cleansing and the massive transfer of land from Haudenosaunee to settler hands. In new lands in what by the late nineteenth century had become the province of Ontario in the Confederation of Canada, Haudenosaunee people mobilized the memory of the past in defence of sovereignty and the right to land. Drawing on scholars such as those brought together in a major 2013 collection edited by Jill Doerfler, Niigaanwewidam James Sinclair, and Heidi Kiiwetinepinesiik Stark which argues for the importance of centring stories in Anishinaabeg studies, I suggest that stories often enshrine and reveal ideas about relationships.[5] In the context of late nineteenth-century settler Canada, reminders of past relationships and past suffering might also be also reminders of past promises about land. And if stories were about relationships, so too were treaties, as many Indigenous legal scholars and historians argue.[6] A reminder of a relationship might also be a reminder about a treaty promise. At the same time, the descendants of settlers also told stories about the American Revolution in the late nineteenth century which mostly entrenched their claims to the land. Even these stories, however, sometimes included glimmers of evidence of past relationships with Indigenous peoples, hidden under the paint like the pentimento described by Jeffery Hewitt elsewhere in this volume.

The idea for this paper was sparked by reading the research notebooks of American historian Lyman Draper, who visited Six Nations settlements at Grand River and Bay of Quinte in 1879 as part of a lifetime project of capturing memories as well as archival evidence about the American Revolution. Scattered amid much genealogical information, Draper was told a number of stories by those he met during his research. Most of those he recorded dwelt on the suffering that loyalists among the Kanyen'kehá:ka (or Mohawk) in particular had experienced in supporting the British side, including their traumatic flight from their homelands to become refugees in British territory.[7] I cannot claim to know what stories clearly "meant," not least because I am not a community member and am writing at a considerable distance. Draper himself was, as I will discuss further below, a man with his own agenda – we need to keep in mind the power relationships involved and whose pen captured stories. At a different level, however, it also matters that personal stories shape-shift and by their nature might not have a clear and direct single "meaning." Nonetheless, I would argue that Draper's notebooks did capture conversations. Storytelling is an oral performance. It is affected by context and by the relationship between teller and hearer.[8] I therefore think we might see the visiting historian of the American Revolution as also part of the picture. In that context, were people who affirmed their ancestors' loyalty making straightforward claims (even if contingently controversial in a community that was actually quite divided) or was there more at stake?

I want to suggest that stories about loyalty and suffering reminded the hearer that the Kanyen'kehá:ka had suffered in keeping their promises. In contrast, the British betrayed promises in 1783. The land at Grand River and the Bay of Quinte was the blood price of the failure of these promises. To talk about suffering and loyalty was therefore to remind the hearer, the visiting historian, of the need to keep further promises. This, at any rate, is the story that I will tell.

At the time, Draper was trying to tell his own stories. Among other projects, he wanted to write a biography of the famous and controversial Kanyen'kehá:ka leader Joseph Brant, who had fought with the British during the Revolution and later helped negotiate the creation of the Grand River settlement.[9] This biography was to go with other books that Draper also did not complete about the history of the American Revolution and the formation (as he saw it) of the early American nation. Draper was, however, an assiduous researcher who had difficulty stopping his research to write. Indeed, his legacy lies mostly in his hundreds of notebooks of research notes.[10] He never told the creation story of the American Republic but he helped create myths, some of which would live on in dangerous ways. He also caught some stories along the way.

This paper unfolds in three times. The first is the time of the American Revolution and its immediate aftermath. The second is the late nineteenth century, when stories about the past informed competing claims to land. The third is the more amorphous time of the present in which promises, broken or kept, continue to resonate.

Promises during the American Revolution

The American Revolution had a devastating impact on the Confederacy of the Six Nations, the Cayuga, Seneca, Kanyen'kehá:ka (Mohawk), Onondaga, Tuscarora, and Oneida, whose contiguous territories lay beyond the colonial province of New York and which would be taken over after the war by the new American Republic to form the much larger state of New York. During the war, the Six Nations, despite significant efforts to remain neutral in the midst of struggles over how best to protect their lands against rapacious settlers, ultimately split over what stance to adopt in a war in which neutrality proved impossible to maintain.[11] The Oneida spearheaded alliances with American rebels, while the Kanyen'kehá:ka were key players in an alliance with the British Crown. "What has happened to us all is calamitous! There is now no Long House where you and I can safely tell one another our fears, by saying to each other 'do not meddle in this affair (war) or calamity will happen to us, we will suffer this disaster, for we love our Long House,'" a speaker for a delegation from the American-allied Haudenosaunee told British-allied groups at the British fort of Niagara in 1780, where there was a large refugee community, pleading for the restoration of unity. The Kanyen'kehá:ka warrior Ka non ra ron (Aaron Hill) responded two days later, however, with reference to "faithful" promises: "[i]t is now four years, we have been going as of one mind, and our minds are now more than ever steadfast in upholding the cause of the King. We have made up our minds to be faithful […] We are not deceivers, we have all well considered our decision that no matter what will happen to us, our names will always be respected for our faithfulness."[12] This language about fidelity reflected, in my view, the importance to Haudenosaunee society of keeping promises. It would be reflected in the claims of Draper's Kanyen'kehá:ka interlocutors that despite British betrayals they had remained loyal to their agreements.

In the borderlands between Six Nations and British territories in colonial New York, settlers and Six Nations warriors fought over land. Joseph Brant helped lead raids by groups of white and Haudenosaunee "rangers" on American frontier settlements from the British base at Niagara. Joseph's sister Konwatsi'tsiaiénni (Molly Brant) had been the partner of the recently deceased Sir William Johnson ("Superintendent of Indian Affairs" for northern North America) and as a powerful woman played a leading role in counselling Kanyen'kehá:ka warriors, reflecting the importance given to women in advising on matters of war among the Haudenosaunee.[13] Almost all the borderland region was burned out, food supplies were deliberately destroyed, and many civilians on both sides were killed or taken captive. The war included the large-scale and brutal ethnic cleansing of the Sullivan-Clinton campaign during which an American army drove the western Six Nations from their territory, destroyed food supplies, and burned some forty towns. Many Haudenosaunee were driven as refugees into British-held territory.[14]

In the aftermath of conflict, in 1783 the British negotiators betrayed their allies and gave the lands of the Six Nations to the Americans. At the time, some British administrators on the ground in Canada recognized the enormity of this act. It was a violation of the 1763 Proclamation Act and the subsequent 1768 Treaty of Fort Stanwix, as well as of promises made during the war and of longer-standing alliances.[15] The soon-to-be-retired Governor of Quebec, the Swiss-born Frederick Haldimand, wrote to the Colonial Secretary in terms that recognized Haudenosaunee sovereignty:

These people, My Lord, have an enlightened Ideas of the Nature and Obligations of Treaties as the most civilized Nations have, and know that no Infringment of the Treaty in 1768 which fixed the Limits between their Country and that of the different Provinces in North America can be binding upon them without their express concurrence and Consent. Your Lordship will observe that the Object of their general Confederacy is to defend their Country against all Invaders: In case things should proceed to extremities, the Event, no doubt, will be the destruction of the Indians, but during the Contest, not only the Americans but perhaps many of His Majesty's subjects will be exposed to great distress.[16]

Seeking to prevent warfare, in 1783 Haldimand "granted" lands along the Grand River and at the Bay of Quinte to loyalist Six Nations, after British purchase from the Anishinaabeg (itself controversial). The Six Nations who moved to these new areas did not feel that they had given up their sovereignty, but they did consistently remember the British as having broken promises to protect Haudenosaunee lands. For example, in the wake of the further betrayals of Tecumseh's War and the War of 1812, Onondaga chief Echo affirmed in a council with deputy Indian Superintendent William Claus in 1819 that "The property which we owned on the other side is now possessed by the Americans. We have lost it through the means of your Wars." He went on to reference relationships with the Crown and with God: "We do not suppose, that the great King, our Father, would allow his people to suffer. He appointed Officers in this country to see that we should lose none of our property while serving under him, & you know that there is a Great Spirit above who will not allow his Children to suffer."[17] To remind the British of prior ties was to remind them of claims to the land, of treaty relationships, and of the mutual respect of sovereignty. This became all the more urgent in the late nineteenth century, after the Six Nations lands along the Grand River had been reduced to a fraction of their original size.

Stories of Exile and Belonging

In 1879, Lyman Draper, corresponding secretary of the Wisconsin Historical Society from 1854 to 1890, travelled to Six Nations communities at Grand River and the Bay of Quinte, Ontario, hoping to discuss family genealogies, particularly of the ancestors and descendants of Joseph Brant, as well as memories of the American Revolution and its aftermath. Draper's projected biography of Joseph Brant was part of the historian's lifelong project to collect information pertaining to what he saw as foundational moments in the creation of the American nation, including the American Revolution in the north-east but also the expansion of settler society westward.[18] As a would-be shaper of memory, Draper was one of a number of mid- to late nineteenth-century Euro-American historians who tried to gather oral tradition as they sought to create a new history for the young Republic.[19] This work was also informed by ideas of salvaging vanishing memory, intersecting in complex ways with the "salvage paradigm" discussed by Jeffery Hewitt in this volume.[20]

At Grand River, Draper was seemingly met, however, not only with words but also with paper. His notes begin with a copy of the 1784 Haldimand Proclamation, issued in 1784 by the Governor of Quebec, Sir Frederick Haldimand, which granted the Six Nations land "six miles deep" along the course of the Grand River.[21] Six Nations understood the Haldimand Proclamation, also remembered as the Haldimand Treaty, as a foundational grant, which needed to be protected from the purposive forgetting of malevolent colonial bureaucracies. Indeed, in 1821, Haudenosaunee envoys John Brant and William Kerr (also controversial within community memory) brought a copy of the Haldimand Treaty when visiting the Colonial Office in London in order to petition for recognition of the Six Nations' right to the land around the headwaters of the Grand River: they claimed that the Colonial Secretary might not have read it.[22] Draper the historian who was looking in the first instance for oral memory was met with the political importance of the written text of which, however, his Haudenosaunee interlocutors assumed the writer might himself need to be reminded.

Draper's conversations also included several stories from Kanyen'kehá:ka Elders, scattered among answers to questions about family genealogies, about community suffering on the trek from their lands in the Mohawk Valley to British-held territory during the Revolution. On the face of it, these might be read as stories about loyalty. Such stories about suffering and exile might equally, however, be seen as forms of commemoration that made claims, including claims to the land, and that reaffirmed webs of mutual obligation by reminding the listener of past promises. These were also stories about choices made by the Haudenosaunee, particularly the Kanyen'kehá:ka, as cohesive communities, even if these choices were painful and divisive at the time and indeed subsequently.

It is difficult to know what Draper asked to elicit the answers that he wrote in a scrawling hand in a notebook that would eventually be stored along with many hundreds of other notebooks (for Draper was a prodigious notetaker) in the library of the Wisconsin Historical Society. It is also difficult to know what respondents made of him, although they appear to have answered questions with patience and courtesy. Certainly his presence would have shaped the way in which stories were told, as theorists of oral tradition remind us. His notes were a record, however one-sided, of dialogue in context.

The aged Smoke Johnson (Sakayengwaraton), eighty-six or eighty-seven in 1879, clearly told Draper something of the origin story of the Confederacy. Johnson was a Pine Tree chief (a non-hereditary leadership position) and was known for his memory and rhetorical skills. He was also the grandfather of the poet Pauline Johnson.[23] The comment came in the midst of family histories and his own memory of travelling to Montreal with Joseph Brant and filling his pocket with pennies by dancing for the whites:

Dek-an-a-weitteh was the name of the chief of the Five Nations – a Mohawk in very early times, wise and influential, who Urged the Mohawks, Oneidas, Cayugas, Onondagas and Senecas to form a League – that they ought not to be warring against each other – but live in peace, & all the stronger to resist their enemies: made laws & good government. The Great Spirit must have given a great mind & inspired him for this great work […] This league was formed before America was settled by the whites.[24]

This was a reference to the Peacemaker, Deganawida, who persuaded the warring five nations (later joined by the Tuscarora) to form a Confederacy and who also crafted the Great Law of Peace that governed this Confederacy.

This was a different kind of story than more personal family stories. A distinction might be made between sacred narratives and other kinds of stories; Doerfler, Sinclair, and Stark underscore in parallel examples among the Anishinaabeg, for example, the distinction in Anishinaabemowin between *aadizookaanag*, "traditional" or "sacred" narratives, and *dibaajimowinan*, "histories" or "news."[25] Susan Hill underscores the centrality of foundational stories, including creation stories, to Haudenosaunee law. As Hill observes, "[s]ince the days of its formation, the Haudenosaunee have selected individuals to be students of different aspects of the Great Law, with duties ranging from the making of wampum belts to serving as a leader of a clan family. Such studies from within the Confederacy continue to this day and serve as an example of the Haudenosaunee intellectual tradition."[26] The Great Law of Peace was frequently recited, including the story of Deganawida and his collaborator Hiawatha. Johnson was thus referencing both the Haudenosaunee legal system and the stories that bound it together. Perhaps he was also subtly reminding Draper of the relative youth of the American federation compared to that of the Haudenosaunee.

Smoke Johnson also told a more recent story about fleeing from American rebels, as the Kanyen'kehá:ka left their homelands. It was about his father, Tekahionwake, or Jacob Johnson, and it was told to him by Joseph Brant:

Once when Mohawks, Brant, Jacob Johnson, warriors, women & children were retreating before the Americans – & Indians had stopped on bank of a river to prepare their dinner – with a spy behind – when latter [came] up, saying the Americans were coming, to fly instantly. They dashed into & across the river (name not remembered) on the bank of which they then were, perhaps water up to their breasts – could ford it, carrying their children, & moveables – when the whites approached, fired, & so wounded one of other warriors that he fell, & would have drowned; but Quahaock Johnson ran back, while Brant & others fired back from opposite bank […] [he] darted into the river, & dragged the wounded Indian to the friendly shore, while the water splashed up all around him, & they saved the wounded brave. Brant related this incident to Smoke Johnson & said Johnson was a braver man than himself, for he would not have done it.[27]

Near Mill Point (today Deseronto) at the Bay of Quinte, Draper met with Thomas Green, described as a "Mohawk chief," aged between seventy-seven and eighty-four.[28] After the Revolution, many of the "Lower Mohawk" community, led by Captain John Deserontyon, had chosen lands on the Bay of Quinte, an attenuated part of which is today the Kanyen'kehá:ka territory of Tyendinaga. They had lived as refugees at Lachine, outside Montreal, for much of the war, before relocating to Upper Canada. They therefore told stories of exile to Lachine.[29] Green recounted the flight to Lachine and its context:

> The Americans wanted the Mohawks to remain at their homes, & take no part in the war; but so firmly attached were they to the King, that they would not listen to their advice. They started to retire in a body to Canada; Capt. John was in the rear, to protect the women & children: They were overtaken and attacked on the way, & those in front fell back to aid the rear guard, & Capt. John was wounded.[30]

Draper clearly asked follow-up questions, seemingly trying to work out whether this was the same incident during a river crossing as described by Smoke Johnson. Green thought there might have been some "white commanders with the Indians," although it is not clear if he meant those who were attacking rather than those who were fleeing. Other testimony claims that those pursued and attacked were Haudenosaunee fighting on the American side: Elizabeth Powles, a granddaughter of Captain Isaac Hill, recounted that "[t]here were a few men to guide the women & children. American Indians followed & overtook them, & killed some."[31] Be that as it may, John Deserontyon was wounded in the thigh; whether the fight was on land or on water Green was not entirely sure but he thought on land. He was clear, however, about the suffering:

> The retreating Indians became nearly starved – children would cry of hunger – camped out; & the Indian hunters went out in every direction to hunt, killing only a few birds, & made them into gruel, so as to go as far as possible, but afforded the hungry scarcely a spoonful apiece, with small bits of the scanty meat. They were then nearly two days travel to Lachine, & without food. The journey was tardy as the children who could had to walk in their enfeebled condition – & the smaller ones had to be carried.[32]

At Grand River in September 1879, Lydia Martin, a granddaughter of Captain Isaac Hill, similarly connected loyalty with danger and exile. Her mother had been part of the trek to Lachine:

When the war broke out, the Mohawks resolved to take the king's side; & all the nation started, save a few families (Mrs. Martin thinks only three remaining) for Lachine, whence they would be safe: As Brant was most the object of Americans, he was placed in front – & all trudged along; Mrs Martin's mother was then but three years old, & of the party, & used to relate – she remembered (evidently soon after starting) they would stop at some of the homes by the way, & get buttermilk. The only food they took with them was parched corn meal – called in the Mohawk, ono-quits-ta-nah; of which each carried as much as he could. They were pursued by the Americans, & six Mohawk women, lagging behind with their heavy loads, were overtaken & made prisoners, & were put in prison & kept a long time, suffering much during their incarceration. Mrs Martin knew one of these women at Bay of Quinte. The Mohawks suffered greatly during this long journey through wilderness country to Lachine.[33]

Also at the Bay of Quinte, on 4 September, George Rokwaho Loft told the story of the journey to Lachine even more explicitly in terms of a defiant pledge of loyalty, thrown in the teeth of the Americans. Loft's grandfather was Ka-ron-ya-gi-goue, Big Clear Sky, and was the pilot sent to lead the Mohawks from the Mohawk Valley to Lachine. Loft's grandfather had fought on the British side. When the British troops left, he exchanged names with a British officer called David Loft with whom he was on "very friendly terms," and "had a great feast on the occasion – hence the origin of the Loft name among the Mohawks."[34] The exchange of names would also have created ties of mutual obligation:

On some occasion – it wd seem abt 1775 […] Washington […] spoke beautifully – saying: "Stay with me – you did not cause the war – it was the result of differences between me & the British – you stay, & share with me – if I prosper, you shall prosper – be one with us." But the Mohawks said among themselves, "we have pledged faith with our British Father, & we must keep it: We will go over the Lake to Canada – & so left the Mohawk Country […] They brought their old Church bell with them – an evidence of their devotion to their religious teachings, for it must have cost them much toil & labour; & it is now in the church near Mill Point.[35]

Whether or not the bell was carried from the Mohawk Valley at such a difficult time or retrieved later, the symbolism is significant, surely reflecting the identification of religious symbols as bearers of memory, signs of identity, and as tokens of past agreements.[36]

Stories of sacrifice and suffering recalled by particular residents of Grand River and the Bay of Quinte might on the surface express loyalty. They might, however, also be taken as a form of claims making. The Six Nations had lived up to their end of the bargains – or promises – they had made with the British. In return, they were often betrayed. In this sense, the stories told to Draper echoed the records woven into wampum belts. They also recall the weight inherent in the exchange of objects as tokens of commemoration, such as the silver vessels of the Communion silver given to a Kanyen'kehá:ka delegation to Britain by Queen Anne in 1710, buried when the Haudenosaunee fled the Mohawk Valley, recovered, and subsequently split between Grand River and the Bay of Quinte. At the Bay of Quinte, these Communion vessels were brought out at ceremonies to commemorate the arrival of the Mohawk. In 2019, Bay of Quinte chief Dan Maracle commented to a journalist reporting on this annual commemoration: "[p]romises were made that should be kept. Canada needs to dust off their history pages and reacquaint themselves with their obligation."[37]

In the years immediately after the Revolution, a military festival hosted on the first of May by Joseph Brant was another form of commemoration, at which the events of the war might be remembered, and ties reaffirmed. The event dated back to May Day celebrations hosted by William Johnson in New York, presumably with roots in both British and German traditions; in this sense Brant was claiming Johnson's role.[38] Several of Draper's informants in 1879 discussed these celebrations. Smoke Johnson recalled, for example: "The first of May, Brant used to call a meeting at Mohawk village of his old warriors – & some of the Royalists along the Niagara, John Dockstader among them – & have a great time of merriment, dancing, drinking, reminiscing […] Brant let Dockstader have a tract of land near Mount Healey don't know when he died."[39] An account from the *Upper Canada Gazette* in 1798 (also collected by Draper) reported on symbolically freighted activities. On 1 May the Six Nations volunteer militia of about four hundred people assembled at Grand River and performed military manoeuvres "in a manner which met the plaudits of the surrounding multitude, among whom were several veteran officers," firing "with such exactness as was thought not to be exceeded by the best disciplined troops." A militia of white men raised at Grand River attended and seemingly performed their own military exercises. The Mississauga, from whom the British Crown had purchased almost all their land in Upper Canada, were also in attendance, by invitation. After this, Brant gave a public dinner at his house at which many "loyal" toasts were drunk. Brant toasted "[t]he

Colonels of the different militia organizations in this Province, together with all those loyalists who were fellow sufferers with the Six Nations during the late American war." The day concluded with "several Indian dances at the council house." The following day the chiefs held a council and belts of wampum were "exchanged as a token of lasting friendship."[40] This was a public performance that reminded onlookers of the ties forged by the war and by extension of the promises made by the British during the war. The exchange of wampum was another way to entrench a relationship, with political weight.

Local historian Roger Sharpe, writing in 2015, states that the May Day celebration was a continuation of earlier May Day events encouraged by Sir William Johnson and including elements of Six Nations tradition combined with elements of the settler country fair. Under Joseph Brant, events included singing, dancing, races, wrestling, ball games, and the roasting on a fire of an entire ox, and Six Nations people came from miles around to participate. According to Sharpe, the celebration later shifted to coincide with Queen Victoria's birthday and continued to include Loyalist elements such as Union Jack flags into the 1860s.[41] My argument here is not that these celebrations necessarily imply that all members of the Grand River community were Loyalists, nor indeed that Brant united the community.[42] Instead, these performances displayed relationships that demanded reciprocal obligation and articulated parallel sovereignties: it was significant that wampum belts were exchanged and that white and Haudenosaunee militia performed exercises together but as representatives of their own communities.

Sovereignty and the Politics of History

The politics of history were evident in other ways. Cecilia Morgan has argued that from the late 1890s to 1911 the Confederacy Council of the Six Nations of Grand River maintained a particularly close relationship with the Ontario Historical Society. In 1898, Chief Dehhehnagaraneh, Speaker of the Council, welcomed members of the OHS to a special meeting at Grand River, describing delegates, in a phrase cited by Morgan, "not as strangers, but as brothers whose forefathers fought side by side with ours in the past, in defence of our country – as brothers whose fathers were devoted and loyal through many dangers and difficulties, privations and sorrows to this land and country, and to the throne of Great Britain, our great ally over the water."[43] In 1911, the Six Nations adopted David Williams, the President of the Ontario Historical Society, in a ceremony at Osheweken, echoing the long-standing Six

Nations practice of creating bonds of fictive kinship through adoption with people they wished to honour while also weaving networks of exchange and obligation. Sir William Johnson had been adopted by the Kanyen'kehá:ka before the American Revolution, for example, while the Duke of Norfolk was given a name by at least one faction in the community in 1806 in anticipation of favours, despite the fact that he lived in England.[44] In the case of David Williams, the pay-off was doubtless not what was hoped for. In that same year of 1911, Chief W.M. Elliott asked the OHS to support the Confederacy's quest for legal equality, using arguments founded in part on a shared military heritage. As Morgan shows, the OHS delegates voted against the request on the grounds that their constitution did not allow them to discuss political matters. The Six Nations allowed their OHS subscription to lapse.[45]

Even as Draper was researching the life of Joseph Brant in the 1870s, conflict was mounting between the council of hereditary chiefs at Grand River and the nascent Canadian state. Indian Agent Jasper Tough Gilkison, placed at Grand River from 1862 to 1891, tried to limit the powers of the Hereditary Council and to prevent the chiefs from leasing land to local farmers, while the 1869 Gradual Enfranchisement Act sought to dismantle customary governance and to subject certain internal decisions by the Hereditary Council of Chiefs to confirmation by the Governor-in-Council, representing the Canadian government. In 1876 the Indian Act exerted Canadian claims to control over Indigenous peoples. In 1884 the Indian Advancement Act tried to establish band councils on every reservation.[46]

The Six Nations responded in part by recalling historical promises and past relationships with other powers. As Yale Belanger argues, one important component of the Council response was to try to establish Six Nations sovereignty through researching historical treaties. In 1879, the Confederacy chiefs petitioned the British Secretary of State for the Foreign Colonies, Sir Michael Hicks Beach, requesting copies of the treaties of Utrecht, of Aix-la-Chapelle, and of Paris. In the face of intransigence, a second petition was sent in 1882 signed by Peter Powless, Henry Clench, George Buck, Jacob Silversmith, and George Key. In Yale Belanger's words, "[a]s participants in the creation and signing of the three treaties, the Iroquois considered the documents' provision to represent their inalienable rights." The Canadian government eventually conceded the role of the Six Nations in the treaties but claimed not to have copies.[47]

The historical practices of petitioning shed additional light on the seeming insistence of Grand River members on showing Draper a copy of the Haldimand Proclamation in 1879. When some thirty years later

General Levi Deskaheh attempted to take the case of the Six Nations to the League of Nations, after a failed effort to appeal to Britain over the head of the Canadian government, he called on the Queen of the Netherlands for Dutch sponsorship of the Haudenosaunee appeal to the League of Nations. This drew on seventeenth-century agreements between the Haudenosaunee and the Dutch, implicitly affirming Haudenosaunee sovereignty.[48] Despite political divides among the Six Nations exacerbated by the Indian Act, including debates over whether Grand River should be governed by a Hereditary Council of Chiefs or an elected council as the Canadian government wanted, there was wide agreement on the issue of Haudenosaunee self-determination, backed up by historical precedent. In 1923 the Royal Canadian Mounted Police (RCMP) occupied the Council House and forcibly removed the Council from power. It is telling that the RCMP also seized and removed the wampum belts from the Council House that functioned as bearers of Six Nations historical memory and as records of past agreements.[49]

Haudenosaunee people continue to actively remember this record of promises broken from the 1780s to the present, most potently through ongoing lawsuits concerning Grand River lands. To this day, the website "Mohawks of the Bay of Quinte/Kenhtè:ke Kanyen'kehá:ka" features Kanyen'kehá:ka loyalty and British betrayal under the "History of Tyendinaga" tab:

> Our ancestors were military allies of the British Crown during the American Revolution as well as many previous wars between England and France [...] Although the official position at the onset of the revolutionary war was one of neutrality, our ancestors later assisted the British as the Mohawk Valley broke out in warfare. One of the many promises made to our ancestors in order to gain their support was that their homeland villages would be restored at the end of the war. However, when the war ended with the signing of the 1783 Treaty of Paris, Britain gave up the Mohawk homelands to the American rebel forces.[50]

In the late eighteenth and early nineteenth centuries, the memory of sacrifice during the war and of the loss of lands for which the British Crown had promised restitution, and the expectation that this imposed a continuing obligation on the part of the British were also evident in political rhetoric deployed by Joseph Brant and his kin and supporters, including Joseph's son, John Brant. In negotiations over whether the community had the right to sell and lease land, the rhetoric was telling. There was significant internal conflict over whether selling land for investment income was in fact the correct strategy, as well as, at a different level of debate, whether or not Joseph Brant was personally profiting from such sales. Nonetheless, community members agreed on the importance of recognizing Six Nations independence and right to make their own choices.

In London in 1822, for example, John Brant and Robert Kerr remonstrated in a letter to the Colonial Office against the poor return that the British were giving the Six Nations for their self-sacrifice in a "foreign cause" by removing the headlands of the Grand from their territory: "The time was when you sought our aid and we gave it to you enfeebled by our connexion with you – is the return (for the blood we have shed in your cause) to be the injustice which has brought us from our distant woods to supplicate in London?"[51]

Almost two decades earlier, in 1804, John Norton, acting as an agent in Britain for the Brant faction and seeking to bypass the colonial administration, had presented a "Memorial for the Six Nations, settled on the Grand River in Upper Canada […] in their Name and by their Desire" directly to the Duke of Northumberland (with whose father Brant had longstanding connections), to pass on to the British government. The memorial requested that the Six Nations be allowed to derive economic benefit from their lands through individual ownership and the right to lease land, including hiring white sharecroppers and being given legal protection as landlords. This is hardly a straightforward document and it certainly doesn't clearly represent a majority viewpoint. Nathan Ince has recently made a convincing case that although Norton was adopted at Grand River under Brant's patronage, he was faking a part-Cherokee identity and would eventually be rejected by most community members, even before he murdered an Onondaga warrior named Big Arrow and was forced to flee Grand River in 1823.[52] Nonetheless, despite layers of complication which this paper does not have space to discuss further, it is still striking that even this memorial, which must have been approved by some at Grand River, draws on history, affirms Haudenosaunee independent choice, and underscores ongoing relationships.

The memorial begins: "By the Treaty of Peace concluded between Great Britain and the United States of America in 1783, the whole of the ancient Country of the Six Nations, the residence of their Ancestors from Times far beyond their earliest Traditions, was included within the Boundary granted to the Americans." It goes on to claim (probably incorrectly) that the Grand River tract, "although much smaller, than that they had been obliged to forsake within the United States, amply satisfied these Loyal Indians, who preferred living under the Protection of His Britannic majesty, ready to fight under His Standard again, if Occasion might require, to a more extensive Territory."[53]

Once entered into, British and Haudenosaunee relationships in both war and peace were precisely calibrated in familial terms, following Six Nations conventions. Kinship terminology, however, did not erase the reality of parallel sovereignties, as expressed in the Two-Row Wampum.[54] The Six Nations and their British or American allies were described during the war as being in relationships of brotherhood. Susan Hill observes that the Great Law of Peace on which the original Confederacy of Five Nations had been founded had "established a framework within which peoples of different blood could become family." Developing that ideology, she writes:

> familial relations were extended to Haudenosaunee allies in the same way. The idea that the British had become brethren to the Haudenosaunee was taken very seriously by the Haudenosaunee. It was seen as an extension of the Great Law, which directed that family members take care of each other and assume responsibilities for each other. The British may not have felt as strongly about the newly formed kinship bonds, but they used the terminology extensively in their relations with the Haudenosaunee and other Indigenous peoples throughout the treaty period.[55]

In sum, the stories that were told to Lyman Draper at the Bay of Quinte and at Grand River in the late 1870s were a way of remembering that had a political point: Haudenosaunee sovereignty remained alive. That point was, however, increasingly opaque to settler society.

Land, Blood, and Erasure

Draper was working during a great wave of centenary commemoration of the events of the Revolution that, as Ned Blackhawk has argued, entrenched justifications for the conquest of Indigenous lands and the supposed triumph of "civilization" and "progress."[56] If the Six Nations told stories about exile from land that was theirs, and of the subsequent claiming of new land, Draper's far more numerous stories from an American perspective not surprisingly often viewed and claimed landscapes in a different way. Draper frequently asked his US informants to reconstruct where battles took place and how they unfolded, for example. The descriptions of land and close reconstructions of battles that resulted were accounts of conquest that either left out prior Indigenous occupation altogether or acknowledged traces that were felt to make no claim on the present.

The commemoration of the pivotal battle of Oriskany provides one such example. In 1877, two years before Draper travelled to Grand River and the Bay of Quinte, the town of Utica hosted a massive centennial celebration of the brutal battle of Oriskany, New York, in which Loyalist forces including Brant and many Haudenosaunee warriors had ambushed Patriot troops trying to relieve the siege of Fort Stanwix.[57] In early 1879, in response to Draper's written queries, George Graham described the collection of memory and its attachment to place, enclosing a diagram:

> In 1844 I talked with some 7 or 8 of the patriots who were in the battle as to it – going over the ground with them and they severally very fully describing what happened in the battle. They all agreed that some 600 had passed the point marked A before any attack was made, and there were some 200 others to pass at that point – which is the ravine – That the principal fighting occurred at the place marked by me in pencil on your map AA […] Most of the hand-to-hand fighting was on what is now known as the Ringrose farm.[58]

Here, too, blood sacrifice created a personal and national claim to the land, in this case in the eyes of the Americans, calling themselves "patriots." Graham continued: "One of the patriots said that, after the fighting was over, he looked for his brother – & turning over several bodies at last turned one which was the body of his brother. Another patriot sought to find his brother in that way; but was not successful and never afterwards saw his brother."[59] Many family stories similarly recalled the violence of the frontier warfare in the borderlands between New York and Six Nations territory and the loss of kin. On the American side, however, what was remembered were atrocities committed by "Tories" and "Indians." The best-known examples were the massacres of Cherry Valley and Wyoming, which were widely publicized at the time.

Draper also, however, collected more intimate family stories. For example, Lester Klumph, whose grandparents had lived in Springfield, a small settlement in New York destroyed by raiders under Brant in 1778, told how a neighbour named Shafer fled with his wife and daughter on hearing that Brant was coming:

> His wife suddenly recollected that her bonnet had been left in the house, & desired him to return for it, while she & daughter went on. He returned & got the bonnet, & had started back, when Brant discovered him & tomahawked him on the spot, & left him where he now lies. The place is under an apple-tree on the farm formerly occupied by Mrs. Geo. Clark.[60]

A bitter and violent civil war left deep fissures and was remembered very differently on different sides. The victors, who had stayed on the land, were able, unlike the losers, to attach memory to very specific places, and in doing so lay claim to those places.

According to George Graham, writing in 1879, the recent centennial celebrations at Oriskany had been highly beneficial. The people came in many thousands, "all happy, all proud, patriotic, all better for knowing and honouring the great things done by the patriots."[61] Graham did not, however, forget the presence of the Six Nations. Its evidence was literally under his feet:

> In 1850 when the Erie Canal was enlarged Indian bones – beads, tomahawks, silver personal ornaments, broaches, coins etc, were dug out of their cemetery. My residence is at the place where this cemetery was. The Indians had a Village in the Oriskany Creek – which occupied a clearing of some 50 acres – Where the present Oriskany Village is – that is some two miles from the battle ground. The night before the battle the Americans encamped at this Indian Village.[62]

Klumph also recalled a change in tactics during the battle of Oriskany. A great storm interrupted the battle. Before the storm, Six Nations warriors were tomahawking men after they had fired their muskets; during the storm the American leader, General Herkheimer, regrouped to place two men behind each tree, "so that when one had fired his gun – and the Indian rushed forward, the other patriot 'scored one more dead Indian' – thus getting the advantage of Brandt's savages."[63] These were clearly memories of conquest and brutal, racialized warfare, although cast in terms of a larger celebration of the Revolution.

At the same time, some of the family stories collected by Draper had echoes of past relationships, particularly those collected from families that had originally settled on land with mixed European and Haudenosaunee settlement, as the British Empire spilled into Six Nations lands. A descendant of the Harper family recalled on 22 May 1879 that "Grandpa" had spoken "the language of the Six Nations" and that Joseph Brant had visited his family. Years later, when the Revolution broke out, the two men would try to kill each other one day in the snow.[64] The story continued: "Brant says 'Harper I am sorry that you were here.' He says 'why?' Brant looked him in the face as they had been school mates together 'for' he says that 'I must kill you.'" This story had many twists and turns, and included the survival of Harper. It reflected the fact, as I argue elsewhere, that families remembered people who had grown up together even as these relationships fell apart and ties of real and fictive kinship were destroyed in the violence of the war – a further layer of betrayal and trauma.[65]

In Upper Canada, commemoration around land was also oriented to claims making, but often through processes of selective forgetting.

One example will have to suffice. Most of the Grand River lands that were originally granted to the Six Nations fell into settler hands. Settlers often sought to memorialize and justify their own presence. Controversially, before his death in 1807 Joseph Brant had granted (or had persuaded the community to grant) some lands to former associates in the battles of the American Revolution, particularly men to whom the community was linked by marriage and sexual partnerships, as well as through past histories of military interaction and through the complex tentacles of the Indian Department. One such family was the Nelles family, which included men who had fought with Brant in the American Revolution and men who had Haudenosaunee partners. The Nelles family, however, took their land, put it into the Canadian land market, and brought in many additional settlers, ultimately making a lot of money, and removing the land from the force field of kinship ties to the Six Nations. By 1879, Draper's letters were revealing a Nelles family that very much wanted to keep past family ties to the Six Nations quiet – "too proud," as one Nelles family informant put it, to "own their Indian blood."[66]

Alessandro Portelli reminds us to look for the meanings of stories that might themselves not be literally true.[67] It is not certain whether the Kanyen'kehá:ka carried a church bell through the wilderness to Lachine. It is even less certain that the community as a whole decided to sacrifice out of loyalty to Britain. The accounts that are closer in time to the events of the Revolution suggest instead profound divisions, anger, and anguish. Nonetheless, what is important is the underlying sentiment that a relationship was freely forged that entailed sacrifice on the part of the Six Nations, and this is evident in a range of more formal political statements. The relationship imposed mutual obligation. In this sense, the Haudenosaunee did not forget. The same could not be said of the British or of the nascent Canadian state.

In a different register, the important Kanyen'kehá:ka artist Shelley Niro draws on memories of the American Revolution and of exile in some of her work, including in her 2007 *La Pieta*. This series of seven photographs recalls the suffering and the losses of the American Revolution, including the loss of the Kanyen'kehá:ka homeland in the Mohawk Valley (Figure 1.1). Images of water begin and end the series; in between are photographs of the Mohawk Valley, of a tree trunk, of the torso of a young man, of land at Grand River and, finally, of land from Caledonia, the subject of an ongoing land dispute between the Six Nations and the Canadian government which exploded in 2006. Each photograph is framed by wampum (Figures 1.2 and 1.3). In recorded testimony accompanying *La Pieta* in the exhibition *Shelley Niro: Five*

Figure 1.1 *La Pieta* (2007) from *Shelley Niro: Five Hundred Year Itch*, National Gallery of Canada, 2024. Photograph by Elizabeth Elbourne.

Hundred Year Itch, Niro comments that at a time of war in the Middle East in 2007, she "started thinking about the war and the American Revolution and how almost like it's a contemporary thing and it affects, still affects us." "Here we are living in the present, but these spirits are still hovering around. I wanted to acknowledge the past that's always there," she comments on an exhibition panel.[68] Niro has recounted that her father, George Oliver Doxtater, loved to tell stories about their ancestors, including about the beautiful Mohawk Valley (a place he never visited).[69] Although art, like stories, doesn't always have a set meaning and my interpretation might not be that of the artist herself, I cannot help but be struck by the language and image of the "pietà," which in classical art depicts the Virgin Mary mourning over the body of her dead son, who has died as a sacrifice. Here, Niro shows the gnarled body of a tree and body of a young man: "these are things that get lost in war," she comments. The beautiful young warrior who (it is implied) dies in the American Revolution and in wars to come, the lost land, the present land of Grand River, and the disputed land at Caledonia speak, to my mind, of sacrifice and of promises broken and to be kept.

Figure 1.2 Shelley Niro, *Hearing Trees Fall*, image from *La Pieta* (2007). My thanks to Shelley Niro for permission to reproduce this work.

Figure 1.3 Shelley Niro, *Tomorrow*, image from *La Pieta* (2007). My thanks to Shelley Niro for permission to reproduce this work.

Conclusion: Memory and the Storied Present

The wider aim of this collection is to examine the making and keeping of promises. How might telling stories about the past fit into this bigger picture? I want to close with two suggestions.

First, I have suggested in this essay that even non-sacred stories might be forms of remembering, reinforcing, and forgetting promise-making. Indeed, Heidi Kiiwetinepinesiik Stark argues that Indigenous stories constitute law (which requires promise-keeping), reflecting the fact that stories "lay out the central principles for how people order their world," just as European law in turn might be seen as a series of stories, often functioning to legitimate the settler state.[70] Whatever one makes of that larger claim, I echo Stark's argument that stories can provide insight into modes of ordering the world, summoning up ideals, even in the context of an uncertain present. I would not claim that all "stories" are alike; oral narratives are very complicated and diverse forms, particularly in an oral society. My more basic point, however, is that stories do things. In the case of stories at Grand River and the Bay of Quinte, I have argued that stories such as those of Smoke Johnson about the war and the flight to exile of the Kanyen'kehá:ka reminded the listener that they kept promises and suffered as a result of those promises. I have also suggested that many Haudenosaunee people argued in the nineteenth century that ownership of Grand River and Bay of Quinte flowed from past promises, and that this linkage continues to resonate today.

Secondly, both the settler and Haudenosaunee stories I have explored here implicitly describe past relationships. These were not neutral relationships but might be held to continue into, and to influence, the present. In this paper I have reflected on the fact that many Indigenous scholars have described treaties as being in part about cementing and continuing relationships, rather than as static documents designed to transfer land and, in that sense, cut off relationships. Treaties were bolstered by stories that were also about relationships. To take the smaller example of Draper's notebooks explored in this essay, affirmations of loyalty and statements of past suffering in the British cause might therefore arguably be seen by at least some Haudenosaunee people as ways of reminding the listener of the obligations entailed by past promises to protect land and respect sovereignty. These obligations were enshrined in treaty relationships, verbal promises by British officials during the Revolution, and the obligations imposed by military alliance.

In the United States, in contrast, memories of wartime events among settler-descended families, including frontier violence, often helped create a justificatory narrative for the formation of a new nation. Many of the settler stories and acts of commemoration recorded by Draper illustrate competing claims to the land drawing on ideas such as that of land being gained through conflict and the shedding of blood – even as stories might occasionally include echoes of alternate histories of overlapping communities and personal ties between settlers and Indigenous peoples, including family ties. Although the political implications were very different, it is worth noting that both Kanyen'kehá:ka and Euro-American stories laid claim to the land through memories of sacrifice. As Jeffery Hewitt puts it, "more than one witness may be telling the honest truth, but their sight line informs what they saw."[71] The settler stories collected by Draper (of which there were many) tended to deny Indigenous land claims by describing violent and truncated relationships and seeing ongoing Indigenous presence solely in broken relics and bones, even as glimpses of past relationships were evident in pentimento in more personal family histories. The stories told to Draper at Grand River stressed ongoing relationships with the British Crown that implicitly affirmed Six Nations sovereignty, in my view, even if on the surface they were about loyalty.

The British Crown consistently broke promises to the Haudenosaunee, most crucially the promise that Six Nations allies would not lose land through supporting the British during the American Revolution. As Kate Stoehr demonstrates in her essay in the current collection, promise-breaking continued in Upper Canada, as the nascent Canadian state failed to keep promises to the Anishinaabeg and officials were misleading over time about the benefits to be accrued through the adoption of agriculture and a sedentary lifestyle.[72] Similarly, the Canadian state would fail to protect Haudenosaunee lands on Grand River against squatters and would not support Indigenous efforts to enter the white economy on relatively equal terms. Pamela Klassen and Isabel Klassen-Marshall ask in their essay in this volume about how oaths have functioned in Canada as ceremonial promises, suggesting that the exclusion of Indigenous people from oath-taking in a variety of settler contexts was used to marginalize and exclude Indigenous interlocutors.[73] In all these cases, promises about relationships were broken. Indigenous people were never to be "modern" enough to be kept faith with. These were all tactics of exclusion. Snatches of stories relating to the American Revolution from both Indigenous and settler perspectives remind us of the tensions of the period and the claims making that subsequently flowed from its violence. In my view, it is certainly incumbent upon the inheritors of nineteenth-century settler states to remember original promises and to commit to better relationships.

NOTES

1 Ned Blackhawk, *The Rediscovery of America: Native Peoples and the Unmaking of U.S. History* (New Haven, CT: Yale University Press. 2023), 139–206; Colin G. Calloway, *The American Revolution in Indian Country: Crisis and Diversity in Native American Communities* (Cambridge: Cambridge University Press, 1995).
2 Susan M. Hill, *The Clay We Are Made Of: Haudenosaunee Land Tenure on the Grand River* (Winnipeg: University of Manitoba Press, 2017), 180–2.
3 In this essay I follow Paul Williams and Nathan Ince in placing Haudenosaunee names before names used in English at first mention for people who used different names in different contexts. Paul Williams, *Kayanerenkó:wa: The Great Law of Peace* (Winnipeg: University of Manitoba Press, 2018); Nathan Ince, "John Norton Reconsidered: Influence, Blood, and Belonging in the British Empire and Haudenosaunee Confederacy, 1786–1823," *Ethnohistory* 71, no. 2 (April 2024): 249–69.
4 Hill, *The Clay We Are Made Of*, 132–85; Sidney L. Harring, *White Man's Law: Native People in Nineteenth-Century Canadian Jurisprudence* (Toronto: University of Toronto Press, 1998), 35–61; Six Nations Lands and Resources Department, *Six Miles Deep: Land Rights of the Six Nations of the Grand River*, https://www.tidridge.com/uploads/3/8/4/1/3841927/sixmilesdeep -booklet.pdf, accessed 25 March 2025; Six Nations Lands and Resources Department, *Land Rights: A Global Solution for the Six Nations of the Grand River*, https://www.sixnations.ca/LandsResources/SNLands -GlobalSolutions-FINALyr2020.pdf, accessed 25 March 2025; Charles M. Johnson, ed., *The Valley of the Six Nations: A Collection of Documents on the Indian Lands of the Grand River* (Toronto: University of Toronto Press, 1964). Some of the land, the so-called "Brant blocks," were sold by Joseph Brant, but the Six Nations were never able to participate in colonial financial and land markets on equal terms.
5 Jill Doerfler, Niigaanwewidam James Sinclair, and Heidi Kiiwetinepinesiik Stark, eds., *Centering Anishinaabeg Studies: Understanding the World through Stories* (East Lansing: Michigan State University Press, 2013).
6 Heidi Kiiwetinepinesiik Stark and Kekek Jason Stark, "Nenabozho Goes Fishing: A Sovereignty Story," *Daedalus: The Journal of the American Academy of Arts & Sciences* 147, no. 2 (Spring 2018), 17–26; John Borrows and Michael Coyle, eds., *The Right Relationship: Reimagining the Implementation of Historical Treaties* (Toronto: University of Toronto Press, 2017).
7 Please note that I use Kanyen'kehá:ka to reflect the orthography of the western dialect of the Kanyen'kéha (Mohawk) language, rather than the eastern dialect spelling of Kanien'kehá:ka.

8 On the dynamic nature of stories, see Julie Pelletier, "And the Easter Bunny Dies: Old Traditions from New Stories," in Doerfler, Sinclair, and Stark, *Centering Anishinaabeg Studies*, 149–70. In his classic work on oral tradition in central Africa, Jan Vansina underscores forcefully the importance of performance and audience: Jan Vansina, *Oral Tradition as History*, rev. ed. (Madison: University of Wisconsin Press, 1985), 33–67.

9 Joseph Brant was controversial among some members of the Six Nations for several reasons, as well as acclaimed. Potential issues, with different weight for different people, might include his strategy of alliance with the British during the American Revolution; related conflict between different nations of the Confederacy during the Revolution, notably the Kanyen'kehá:ka (Mohawk) and the Oneida, and the related extinction of the council fire of the Confederacy; his later policy of selling and gifting land at Grand River in hoped-for exchange for investment income and influence; his claim to overall leadership of the Grand River community; his role in the negotiation of the 1768 Treaty of Fort Stanwix; and his personal benefit from land sales. Brant was also at the heart of debates over strategy in the wake of American settler conquest during the Revolution, including the drive to unify disparate Indigenous groups. Some of this controversy reflected profound ontological debates among the Six Nations and more broadly among north-eastern Indigenous communities about the best way to navigate the dramatic expansion of settler colonial states. As Rick Monture points out, Brant could not have acted alone given the nature of Haudenosaunee governance, and historical memory may be too focused on Brant. Rick Monture, *We Share Our Matters: Teionkwakhashion Tsi niionkwariho:ten: Two Centuries of Writing and Resistance at Six Nations of the Grand River* (Winnipeg: University of Manitoba Press, 2014), 29–61; Lisa Tanya Brooks, *The Common Pot: The Recovery of Native Space in the Northeast* (Minneapolis: University of Minnesota Press, 2008), 106–62; Hill, *Clay We Are Made Of*, 155–62; Isabel Thompson Kelsay, *Joseph Brant, 1743–1807: Man of Two Worlds* (Syracuse, NY: Syracuse University Press, 1984). It seems appropriate that Susan Hill terms him "the complicated Joseph Brant" (Hill, *Clay We Are Made Of*, 155). My thanks to Karl Hele, Angus Hemlock, and Rick Hill for very helpful discussion.

10 The originals are held in the archives of the Wisconsin Historical Society. They are also available on microfilm, which is how I have accessed the papers. They are difficult to read as they are not fully catalogued and Draper's notes and collected papers can seem somewhat incoherent. Some of the stories have escaped Draper's notebooks to become canonical; others need to be recaptured. Draper was also picking over the oral traditions of settler society which were explored by other historians with

similar aims, notably William Stone. I discuss the collection further in Elizabeth Elbourne, "Orality and Literacy on the New York Frontier: Evidence from the Draper Papers," in *Critical Perspectives on Colonialism: Writing the Empire from Below*. ed. Kirsty Reid and Fiona Paisley (New York: Routledge, 2014), 58–82. The volume of papers on which I draw in the current essay is volume 13 of series F, on Joseph Brant. I thank Priya Grant and Matthew Wyman-McCarthy for stellar assistance in transcribing this volume.

11 Caitlin A. Fitz, "'Suspected on Both Sides': Little Abraham, Iroquois Neutrality, and the American Revolution," *Journal of the Early Republic* 28, no. 3 (Fall 2008): 299–335; Karim M. Tiro, "A 'Civil' War? Rethinking Iroquois Participation in the American Revolution," *Explorations in Early American Culture* 4 (2000), 148–65; Alan Taylor, *The Divided Ground: Indians, Settlers and the Northern Borderlands of the American Revolution* (New York: Knopf, 2006); Calloway, *The American Revolution in Indian Country*; Barbara Graymont, *The Iroquois in the American Revolution* (Syracuse, NY: Syracuse University Press, 1972).

12 Library and Archives Canada [LAC], Claus family fonds, vol. 24, 2–6: "Translation of a Document, in Mohawk, on page 165, vol. 2, Claus Papers." It begins "Niagara, February 17th, 1780 was the first meeting." See also Elizabeth Elbourne, *Empire, Kinship and Violence: Family Histories, Indigenous Rights and the Making of Settler Colonialism, 1770–1842* (Cambridge: Cambridge University Press, 2022), 70–113, especially 110–12.

13 Brooks, *The Common Pot*, 118–21.

14 Rhiannon Koehler, "Hostile Nations: Quantifying the Destruction of the Sullivan-Clinton Genocide of 1779," *The American Indian Quarterly* 42, no. 4 (Fall 2018): 427–53; Chad Anderson, "The Built Landscape and the Conquest of Iroquoia, 1750–1820," in *Investing in the Early Modern Built Environment: Europeans, Asians, Settlers and Indigenous Societies*, ed. Carole Shammas (Leiden: Brill, 2012), 265–94; Max M. Mintz, *Seeds of Empire: The American Revolutionary Conquest of the Iroquois* (New York: New York University Press, 2002).

15 John Borrows, "Wampum at Niagara: The Royal Proclamation, Canadian Legal History and Self-Government," in *Aboriginal and Treaty Rights in Canada: Essays on Law, Equality, and Respect for Difference*, ed. Michael Asch (Vancouver: University of British Columbia Press, 1997), 155–72; Hill, *The Clay We Are Made Of*, 130–1, 135–7.

16 The National Archives [TNA], London, UK, CO 42/45: General Haldimand to Lord North, Quebec, 27 November 1783. The National Archives henceforth annotated as TNA.

17 LAC RG-10, vol. 716. Mfm C-13411. Six Nations council, Ancaster, 1819. Speech of Echo.

18 Joseph Schafer, *The Draper Collection of Manuscripts* (Madison: State Historical Society of Wisconsin, 1922); Josephine L. Harper, *Guide to the Draper Manuscripts* (Madison: Wisconsin Historical Society, 1983). Draper did not, however, publish very much, being "less ready in composition than expert in accumulating notes, documents and memoirs" (Schafer 4).

19 Compare William L. Stone, *Life of Joseph Brant – Thayendanegea: including the border wars of the American Revolution, and sketches of the Indian campaigns of Generals Harmar, St. Clair and Wayne.* 2 vols (New York: Alexander V. Blake, 1838); Jeptha R. Simms, *History of Schoharie County and Border Wars of New York* (Albany, NY: Munsell & Tanner, 1845); William W. Campbell, *Annals of Tryon County; or, The Border Warfare of New York, during the Revolution* (New York: J. & J. Harper, 1831).

20 Jeffery Hewitt, "Fragmented Promises," this volume.

21 Wisconsin Historical Society, Draper papers, Series F, vol. 13, pp. 18–19. Henceforth annotated as Draper papers.

22 TNA, CO 42/369: Robert Kerr and John Brant to R. Wilmot, 31 January 1822, for example.

23 Monture, *We Share our Matters*, 66–8; Douglas Leighton, "Johnson, John," *Dictionary of Canadian Biography*, University of Toronto/Université Laval, 1982–2025, accessed December 28, 2022, https://www.biographi .ca/en/bio/johnson_john_11E.html.

24 Draper papers, Series F, vol. 13, pp. 26–7.

25 Doerfler, Sinclair, and Stark, "Bagijige: Making an Offering," in *Centering Anishinaabeg Studies*, xvii-xviii.

26 Williams, *Kayanerenkó:wa*; Monture, *We Share Our Matters*, xiii, 6–10; Hill, *The Clay We Are Made Of*, 27–46.

27 Draper papers, Series F, vol. 13, 26 September 1879, p. 28.

28 "Born, his older sister says, near close of 1802 – he claims to be 84 – his wife says 81." From "Ths. [Thomas] Green – Mohawk chief," Draper papers, Series F, vol. 13, p. 67.

29 On Niagara, see Calloway, *American Revolution in Indian Country*, 129–57.

30 Draper papers, Series F, vol. 13, 6 October 1879, p. 67.

31 Draper papers, Series F, vol. 13, 6 October 1879, p. 75.

32 Draper papers, Series F, vol. 13, 6 October 1879, p. 68.

33 Draper papers, Series F, vol. 13, 28 September 1879, p. 34.

34 Draper papers, Series F, vol. 13, 4 September 1879, 48. Loft's son, Fred Loft, was an important Kanyen'kehá:ka activist.

35 Draper papers, Series F, vol. 13, 30 September 1879, p. 48–9.

36 On another bell that was important to a community, see stories about the Kanyen'kehá:ka raiding Deerfield in 1704 to win back their captured church bell: E.A. Smith, "The Story of the Bell, 1882" and Taiaiake Alfred, "A Different View: A Descendant Recounts the 1704, 1995," in *Captive*

Histories: English, French, and Native Narratives of the 1704 Deerfield Raid, ed. Evan Haefali and Kevin Sweeney (Boston: University of Massachusetts Press, 2006), 213–20, 244–52. See also Elizabeth Elbourne, "Managing Alliance, Negotiating Christianity: Haudenosaunee Uses of Anglicanism in Northeastern North America, 1760s–1830s," in *Mixed Blessings: Indigenous Encounters with Christianity in Canada*, ed. Tolly Bradford and Chelsea Horton (Vancouver: University of British Columbia Press, 2016), 38–60.

37 Haley Lewis, "'Our People Should Always Be Honoured: Re-enacting the Landing of the Mohawks of the Bay of Quinte," 12 June 2019, TVO.org. www.tvo.org/article/our-people-should-always-be-honoured-re-enacting -the-landing-of-the-mohawks-of-the-bay-of-quinte. Compare to Nathan Ince, "'As Long as That Fire Burned': Indigenous Warriors and Political Order in Upper Canada, 1837–42," *Canadian Historical Review* 103, no. 3 (September 2022): 384–407.

38 As I comment in n9 above, however, it must be noted that there were tensions around Brant's leadership in ways that this paper does not have room fully to explore.

39 Draper papers, Series F, vol. 13, p. 5. Draper took notes on his interview with "John Smoke Johnson" on 26 September 1879.

40 *Upper Canada Gazette*, West Niagara, 12 May 1798.

41 Roger Sharpe, "The Indian Department and Six Nations Martial Tradition," County of Brant Public Library Digital Collections, http://images.ourontario.ca/brant/2710274/data, 2012.

42 The idea of leadership by a single person was not in line with traditional Haudenosaunee governance practice. Furthermore, a dissident council headed by Seneca and based in Buffalo, NY, tried to oust Brant in 1804, despite resistance from Grand River chiefs. Although he was not deposed, Brant withdrew from Grand River after these events and retired to his home at Brantford. Monture, *We Share Our Matters*, 29–62; Kelsay, *Joseph Brant*; LAC, MG 19, F10, Edward Walsh Papers, Folder 1, items 6 and 7: "Captain Brant's answer," Grand River (1 May 1805) and Council minutes (no heading; no date).

43 Cecilia Morgan, *Creating Colonial Pasts: History, Memory, and Commemoration in Southern Ontario, 1860–1980* (Toronto: University of Toronto Press, 2015), 59.

44 Alnwick Castle, Percy Family Papers: MS DNP 63. Joseph Brant to Duke of Northumberland, Grand River (24 January 1806): f. 5–6. I consulted the microfilm copy in the British Library. On diverse and changing forms of adoption, including the adoption of academics, see Kevin J. White, "Adoption, Incorporation, and a Sense of Citizenship and Belonging in Indigenous Nations and Culture: A Haudenosaunee Perspective," *AlterNative: An International Journal of Indigenous Peoples* 14, no. 4 (December 2018), 333–42.

45 Morgan, *Creating Colonial Pasts*, 60–2.

46 Monture, *We Share Our Matters*, 68–9.

47 Yale D. Belanger, "The Six Nations of Grand River Territory's Attempts at Renewing International Political Relationships, 1921–1924," *Canadian Foreign Policy* 13, no. 3 (2007): 34.

48 Belanger, "Six Nations," 37; Grace Woo, "Canada's Forgotten Founders: The Modern Significance of the Haudenosaunee (Iroquois) Application for Membership in the League of Nations," *Law, Social Justice, and Global Development* 1 (2003), University of Warwick, https://warwick.ac.uk/fac/soc/law/elj/lgd/2003_1/woo/#a9.

49 Hill, *Clay We Are Made Of*: 212–236; Belanger, "Six Nations," 39–40. For Six Nations sovereignty and identity claims, see also Alan Downey, *The Creator's Game: Lacrosse, Identity, and Indigenous Nationhood* (Vancouver: University of British Columbia Press, 2018).

50 "History," Mohawks of the Bay of Quinte/Kenhtè:ke Kanyen'kehá:ka, https://mbq-tmt.org/history/, accessed 26 March 2025.

51 TNA, CO 42/369: Robert Kerr and John Brant to R. Wilmot, 31 January 1822.

52 Gaining freehold title would potentially enable individuals to sell land; this was a subject of controversy. Joseph Brant wanted to facilitate land sales, while others opposed them. Norton was born in Scotland to a Scottish mother but claimed that his father was a Cherokee war captive raised in Britain. At the same time, he was adopted by the Mohawk in accordance with Haudenosaunee custom, arguably making biological ancestry less relevant; Ince argues, however, that this would not necessarily have given him an equivalent status to all community members. Norton fled Grand River after the killing of Big Arrow (despite being exonerated by a colonial court), becoming lost to the archival record after his departure. For fuller discussion, including a re-evaluation of evidence concerning Norton's identity, see Nathan Ince, "John Norton Reconsidered: Influence, Blood, and Belonging in the British Empire and Haudenosaunee Confederacy, 1786–1823," *Ethnohistory* 71, no. 2 (April 2024): 249–69.

53 Alnwick Castle, Percy Papers, MS 62, ff. 22–24: "Memorial for the Six Nations […]."

54 Jon Parmenter, "The Meaning of *Kaswentha* and the Two Row Wampum Belt in Haudenosaunee (Iroquois) History: Can Indigenous Oral Tradition Be Reconciled with the Documentary Record?" *Journal of Early American History* 3, no. 1 (2013): 82–109.

55 Hill, *The Clay We Are Made Of*, 97. See also David L. Preston, *The Texture of Contact: European and Indian Settler Communities on the Frontiers of Iroquoia, 1667–1783* (Lincoln: University of Nebraska Press, 2009), 282.

56 Blackhawk, *The Rediscovery of America*, 365–8.

57 "Preparations for the centennial celebration of the battle of Oriskany on Monday are complete, and the indications are that it will be the grandest demonstration which has ever occurred in Central New-York," enthused the *New York Times*. "All of the interior towns are aroused, and will send thousands of representatives and numberless organizations." *New York Times*, 5 August 1877.

58 Draper papers, Series F, vol. 4, item 60: George Graham to Lyman Draper, Oriskany, NY, 20 February 1879.

59 Draper papers, Series F, vol. 4, item 60: George Graham to Lyman Draper, Oriskany, NY, 20 February 1879.

60 Draper papers, Series F, vol. 4, item 57: Lester Klumph to Lyman Draper, Conneautville, PA, 30 March 1879.

61 Draper papers, Series F, vol. 4, item 60: George Graham to Lyman Draper, Oriskany, NY, 20 February 1879.

62 Draper Papers, Series F, vol. 4, item 64: George Graham to Lyman Draper, Oriskany, 27 March 1879.

63 Draper Papers, Series F, vol. 4, item 64: George Graham to Lyman Draper, Oriskany, 27 March 1879.

64 Draper Papers, Series F, vol. 5, 12–12^6 : [E.C. Stuart?] to Lyman Draper, Swallowhill, NY, 22 May 1879. Note: name of author is hard to decipher.

65 Draper Papers, Series F, vol. 5, 12–12^6 : [E.C. Stuart?] to Lyman Draper, Swallowhill, NY, 22 May 1879; Elbourne, *Empire, Kinship and Violence*.

66 Draper Papers, Series F: Julia Nelles to Lyman Draper, Grimsby, 2 April 1879.

67 Alessandro Portelli, *The Death of Luigi Trastulli and Other Stories: Form and Meaning in Oral History* (Albany: State University of New York Press, 1991).

68 Shelley Niro, *La Pieta*, 2007, exhibition panel, *Shelley Niro: 500 Year Itch*, National Gallery of Canada, Ottawa.

69 Melissa Bennett, "It Starts with a Whisper," in *Shelly Niro: 500 Year Itch*, ed. Melissa Bennett (Hamilton, ON: Art Gallery of Hamilton and the Smithsonian Museum of the American Indian, 2023), 32.

70 Heidi Kiiwetinepinesiik Stark, "Stories as Law: A New Method to Live By," *Sources and Methods in Indigenous Studies*, ed. Chris Andersen and Jean O'Brien (New York: Routledge, 2017), 250.

71 Jeffery Hewitt, "Fragmented Promises, Pentimento, and the Salvage Paradigm," this volume, 9.

72 Kate Stoehr, "'The Culture of the Soil': Agriculture, Improvement, and Settler Colonial Landscapes of Nineteenth Century Manitoulin Island," this volume.

73 Pamela Klassen and Isabel Klassen-Marshall, "Ceremonial Promises: Oath, Treaties, and the Transformation of Christian Privilege in Canada," this volume.

Chapter Two

"The Culture of the Soil": Agriculture, Improvement, and Settler Colonial Landscapes of Nineteenth Century Manitoulin Island

KATE STOEHR

In this chapter, I analyse competing Christian, settler-colonial justifications for the dispossession of Indigenous land in nineteenth-century Upper Canada. My analysis is rooted in an exploration of constructions of Manitoulin Island in colonial texts. More specifically, I look at the ways in which the colonial government interpreted and manipulated the 1836 Treaty with the Anishinaabeg of Manitoulin, negotiated by Lieutenant Governor Sir Francis Bond Head on behalf of the Crown.

The interpretations of the 1836 Manitoulin Treaty included in the texts I examine do not reflect Anishinaabe understandings of the Treaty and its terms. According to Head's written account, the Treaty relinquished "Ottawa and Chippewa" claims to Manitoulin and its surrounding islands and made them the property of all Indigenous people, under their "Great Father's control."[1] However, the Treaty was not and is not understood by the Anishinaabeg as a land cession. Anishinaabe legal scholar John Borrows points out that the decision of the Anishinaabeg to take part in the Treaty was rooted in a drive to maintain traditional decision-making practices, ratify Indigenous title to the Island, and "irrevocably affirm that Manitoulin Island would be under exclusive Indian jurisdiction."[2]

In his work on Anishinaabe treaty-making in the eighteenth- and nineteenth-century northern Great Lakes, Alan Corbiere notes that Head engaged in a number of Anishinaabe treaty practices and ceremonies in the process of negotiating with the Anishinaabeg. Practices such as the smoking of a peace pipe and the exchange of a wampum string referenced and, from the point of view of the Anishinaabeg, renewed the existing relationship between the Western Nations and the Crown. The relationship in question was established by the Covenant Chain wampum and the 1764 Treaty of Niagara and was based in alliance, peace, and respect. Through his actions and references, Head made promises to the Anishinaabeg based on longer-standing promises he clearly did not fully understand. Corbiere points out that Head did not see the promises made by the Crown through the Covenant Chain as binding.[3] In reference to the Convent Chain in an 1836 letter to his superior, Head stated that "on our part, little or nothing documentary exists – the promises which were made, whatever they might have been, were almost invariably verbal; those who expressed them are now mouldering in their graves."[4] Corbiere notes that describing the Treaty in this way "served to diminish its legitimacy in the eyes of subsequent colonial officials who privileged the written record."[5]

Head's depiction of the Covenant Chain is predictive of the ways in which written versions of treaties, including the 1836 Manitoulin Treaty, would be centred by the colonial state in order to absolve itself of responsibility, nullify promises, and apprehend Indigenous land. In this chapter, I examine the ways in which Euro-Christian ideas about land and the improvement of land work in Head's Treaty text and in colonial constructions of Manitoulin to justify settler emplacement throughout Upper Canada. In examining the story of Manitoulin as it is depicted through colonial documents, I argue that the Canadian government employed the concept of improvement in its civilizing policies and treaty interpretations as a way to religiously authorize the colonial appropriation of Indigenous land.

Between 1835 and 1839, Manitoulin Island and its agricultural potential, or supposed lack thereof, became the centre of a conflict between colonizing agents about the government's policy of civilization and the future of Indigenous peoples in Upper Canada. The conflict stemmed from Lieutenant Governor Sir Francis Bond Head's proposal to remove all Indigenous people to Manitoulin to keep them away from white settlers in what was becoming southern Ontario. Head intended to put an end to the colony's agriculturally based Indigenous civilizing programs which he believed were ineffective. Supporters of the existing policy argued against Head's proposal on the grounds that some Indigenous people had proved themselves civilized by converting to Christianity and farming their land. According to policy supporters, these select groups of Indigenous people were already landholders by virtue of improving their land through agriculture. In their arguments, both Head and his opponents made claims about what kinds of landscapes could be made into property as well as what kinds of human relationships to land signified civility, validated ownership, and justified settler appropriation. Active in both the Treaty and the arguments that followed it was the Euro-Christian concept of "improvement."

I take improvement to mean the transformation of land, and by extension, people through agricultural cultivation according to colonial standards of civility. For the British Colonial Office in the nineteenth century, the improvement of land through cultivation served as the foundation of property ownership, which was a prerequisite for a civilized society. To improve land was, in effect, to make it into property under the legal framework of colonial jurisdiction and real estate law.[6] In this sense, uncultivated land – including Indigenous territory – was unnamed, purposeless, and ownerless. Thus, the British colonial civilizing programs of the 1830s outlined civilization as both a spiritual and a material process. Conversion to and participation in a Christian religion alone did not denote civility, rather it was embodied through the physical act of continuously cultivating, and thereby improving, land.

The accounts of Manitoulin that I explore in this chapter are not representative of the Island's physical landscape in the nineteenth century, nor do they convey Indigenous perspectives on the land. As I will show, each text depicted Manitoulin in ways that supported arguments for policies that aimed to control and contain Indigenous people and to justify the colonial apprehension of their land. These accounts certainly did not depict Manitoulin as it was understood and seen by the Anishinaabeg who lived and continue to live there.[7] Anishinaabe scholar Alan Corbiere describes Manitoulin Island as a place that was and continues to be sacred:

> The creator had made this place last, this Manitoulin Island. He made the world, created everything, worked hard and he wanted to have a place for himself. So what he did was he took all the best, cleanest water, best air, all the plants that would be needed, all the medicines and food, and he put it here on this island so that he could have a place for himself. It is a sacred place and it continues to be a sacred place and it was treated as a sacred place in the past.[8]

In their depictions of Manitoulin, I argue that the authors of the colonial texts I examine imbued the Island's landscape with religio-racial meaning. Judith Weisenfeld defines religio-racial identity as the ways in which members of a group "understand individual and collective identity in the conjunction of religion and race."[9] Weisenfeld notes that group members' "attitudes about the social and political worlds around them generated material approaches to organising space and the built environment to support their communities and invested city spaces with religio-racial meaning."[10] In the texts I analyse, I see these authors as constructing the "national character" of Indigenous people as a collective religio-racial identity. They imposed this identity upon the Island itself, constructing a textual landscape that supported their colonial understanding of Indigeneity. On the surface, the depictions of Manitoulin I examine appear at odds with each other. However, I show that they were all deeply enmeshed within the same Euro-Christian cosmology of land that prescribed improvement through cultivation as a mode through which settlers and Indigenous people could attain civility and claim land.[11] The authors of these sources differed in their understandings of who could become civilized and own property; nonetheless, their arguments all worked towards similar goals of dispossession or displacement of Indigenous people and their land, albeit to different degrees and with different motivations.

The Construction of Canada's Agricultural "Civilizing" Policy

Scholars of British colonial policy note that the colony's desire to acquire land for the expansion of white settlement and to cut spending in the Indian Affairs Department led Canada's colonial government to establish programs of "civilization" in place of past alliance-based relationships with Indigenous nations.[12] The colonial government claimed that their decision to deliver treaty annuities in the form of farming implements and to eventually cease paying annuities altogether supported their "duty" to induce Indigenous people to live as self-sustaining, civilized agriculturalists.[13] According to the government, this so-called duty superseded past promises of autonomy and reciprocity. Scholars Lisa Ford and Paul McHugh note that by the 1830s, "the idea that Indians were sovereign nations with their own territory, hunting economy and law had all but collapsed"; this idea was replaced, they write, "by a vision of Upper Canada as a land in which a minority of 'civilized' farming Indians would survive in the midst of a flourishing settler colonial economy."[14]

The British civilizing policies of the 1830s developed alongside a rise in Protestant humanitarianism in the Colonial Office and were rooted within Christian notions of the salvation of the soul and improvement of the land.[15] For Christian missionaries, cultivation was a duty required by God, one they assigned to their converts before it became a component of the colonial civilizing policy. Scholars have shown how Euro-Christian missionaries from Jesuits to Methodists viewed wild or "idle" land in the New World as something akin to the biblical wilderness in which Jesus was tempted by Satan, as both the location and condition of sin.[16] For such missionaries, agricultural practices, or a lack thereof, served as a moral barometer for measuring spiritual progress. Undergirding ideas surrounding improvement through cultivation was the concept of Christian monogenism, an idea of racial hierarchy that held sway from the sixteenth century into the mid-nineteenth.[17] Monogenism assumed a teleological end in which all humans, specifically non-white races, would rise out of their ostensibly denigrated states and advance towards a new Eden. From the viewpoint of monogenists, agricultural civilization was a natural, predetermined next step in the transformation of the Indigenous inhabitants of the New World.[18]

In the early nineteenth century, Britain saw a rise in lobby groups that aimed to ensure the "humane" treatment of colonized peoples.[19] Groups like the Aborigines Protection Society (APS) were adamant supporters of Canada's agricultural civilizing policy. Historian Cole Harris notes that the APS "emerged directly out of the struggle for the abolition of slavery, and counted among its leaders prominent members of the Church Missionary Society and of the Liberal (free trade) party."[20] The British civilizing programs the APS supported sought to convert Indigenous people into productive Christian agriculturalists in three steps: first, by gathering them into permanent villages, then by administering instruction in the Christian faith, and finally by inducing them to take up European practices of farming over hunting, fishing, and harvesting.[21]

Within the British civilizing policies of the nineteenth century, agriculture, improvement, and property were tied to each other by a deeply rooted Christian cosmology of land. Scholar Pamela Klassen defines cosmologies of land as "religiously authorised visions of what land is for, who owns it, how it is mapped, and where sites of spiritual power are located."[22] Within a Christian cosmology of land, land exists to provide subsistence for humans through cultivation. The "obligation to cultivate the earth" was located at the centre of the European system of domestication, though its origins did not stem solely from economic arguments about the apprehension of land. They were equally rooted within a Euro-Christian understanding of what constituted biblical relationships to land. Agriculture, performed within the context of civilizing programs, was intended to alter not only the landscapes on which it was enacted, but the relationships between Indigenous people and the land they tilled. The colonial government, along with its agents and missionaries, sought to shift Indigenous people from "a wandering to a settled life" and "attach them to the soil" on the basis of ownership, making them into individual, private landowners.[23]

Canada's intention of making Indigenous people into individual landowners served a much larger settler-colonial goal. By discouraging Indigenous people from "wandering," the colonial government sought to limit Indigenous claims to large areas of land. Additionally, the colonial state hoped that the focus of single-family farming within civilizing programs would replace and eliminate communal ownership. Notably, the notion of ownership within Indigenous world views differs in significant ways from Euro-colonial conceptions. When Anishinaabe scholar Leanne Simpson speaks of her nation's relationships with land, she notes a "connectivity based on the sanctity of land," which encompasses the love her people have for their families, language, and way of life.[24] Anishinaabe nationhood, she notes, "is based on the idea that the earth is our first mother, that 'natural resources' are not 'natural resources' at all, but gifts from our mother."[25]

The colonial government constructed Canada's civilizing policy to serve the growth of the colony and the prosperity of its settler population. The aim of inducing Indigenous people to "undertake the culture of the soil" was not to ensure a secure future for Indigenous people as successful farmers.[26] Scholars of Canada's policies regarding agriculture on reserves have shown that throughout the nineteenth century, the colonial government made a concentrated effort to "undermine and atrophy agricultural development" in Indigenous communities.[27] In 1881, the government revised the Indian Act to place prohibitions on the sale of Indigenous produce in the prairies and north-western Ontario. Alongside the implementation of a "peasant agriculture" policy on reserves in 1889, these policies reveal that the colonial government did not intend Indigenous communities to progress beyond self-sufficiency, or even achieve it.[28]

The Legal and Religious Foundations of "Improvement"

The origins of agriculture as a means and a signifier of civilization stemmed from Enlightenment ideals of natural rights. Natural rights served to justify the appropriation of Indigenous lands via the supposition that, in nature, uncultivated lands could be lawfully apprehended by those who could make the land productive, namely white settlers.[29] Much of the foundation of nineteenth-century ideas about land and its proper uses in England and the colonies derived from thinkers such as John Locke and Emmerich de Vattel.[30] For Locke, the highest form of labour was agriculture, the value of which was evidenced by the paradigmatic Devonshire farmer, whose ten acres of farmland was superior to a thousand acres of land in "the wild woods and uncultivated waste of America."[31] Similarly, Vattel maintained that every nation on earth was required to cultivate the land on which they lived.

Like Locke, Vattel labelled uncultivated land as unclaimed and therefore free for the taking, though in Vattel's case such lands could only be appropriated if the conquering nation did not have enough land to support its existing population, as in the case of the nations of Europe. Canada's 1845 *Report on the Affairs of the Indians in Canada* referenced Vattel as a source of wisdom for the government's previous dealings with Indigenous people and their land. The report's authors claimed that the government's choice to offer Indigenous people compensation to "remove quietly to more distant hunting grounds or confine themselves within more limited reserves" was the most humane course of action given that the path of white settlement would eventually lead to a "protracted struggle for ownership" that Indigenous people would necessarily lose.[32] To support its supposition, the report cited a large passage from Vattel's 1758 treatise *The Law of Nations: or, Principles of the Law of Nature Applied to the Conduct and Affairs of Nations and Sovereigns*:

> We have already observed in establishing the obligation to cultivate the earth, that these nations cannot exclusively appropriate to themselves more land than they have occasion for, or more than they are able to settle or cultivate. Their unsettled habitation in those immense regions, cannot be accounted a true and legal possession, and the people of Europe, too closely pent up at home, finding land of which the savage had no particular need, and of which they made no actual constant use, were lawfully entitled to take possession of it and to settle it with colonies. The Earth, as we have already observed, belongs to mankind in general, and was designed to furnish them with subsistence. If each nation had from beginning resolved to appropriate to itself a vast country, that the people might live only by hunting, fishing and wild fruits, our globe would not be sufficient to maintain a tenth part of its present inhabitants. We do not, therefore, deviate from the views of nature, in confining the Indians within narrower limits.[33]

Following Vattel's passage, the report stated that the present economic value of the acquired lands only recently came into being and was "created solely by the presence and industry of the white settlers."[34] At the time of the acquisitions, the report argued, the only value of such lands to the "denizen of the forest" was "as a hunting ground, as the source of his supply of game and furs." The land as stewarded by Indigenous people was previously worthless expressly because Indigenous people allegedly "knew nothing" of the cultivation of the soil.[35] Indigenous ways of interacting with and using land, including traditional cultivation methods such as clearing land through the use of fire and changing growing location from season to season, did not qualify as valuable or as evidence of ownership in the European sense.[36] Instead, Indigenous mobility served as testimony to what Locke and Vattel, and later Canada's colonial government, perceived as impermanence on the land and a lack of territorial claim.[37]

Locke's and Vattel's political theories of property were connected to Christian cosmologies of land. Monogenism and the biblical rhetoric of cultivation were tightly entwined within the nineteenth-century Christian cosmology of land, and they worked together discursively within the concept of improvement. Through the binding together of church and state within Canada's civilizing programs of the 1830s, agricultural improvement was reified as a spiritual process that brought both land and people into Christian civilization. Within this context, agricultural improvement acted like cartography, as a "key tool in the story and infrastructure of colonial dispossession."[38] The process of improving land was a medium through which territory was physically and ideologically made and unmade.

Manitoulin Island as a Transitional Space: Anderson's Initial Evaluations

In 1835, Manitoulin Island came into the view of Canada's colonial government by way of a suggestion from Captain Thomas G. Anderson. Anderson, a supporter of the government's civilizing policy, was the Indian Agent and superintendent from 1830 to 1836 at the Coldwater-Narrows Reserve, located about five hundred kilometres south-east of Manitoulin Island. Anderson wrote a number of letters to his superiors making a case for both the necessity of Canada's agricultural civilizing program, as evidenced by the progress at Coldwater, and the viability of Manitoulin as an ideal location for the program to continue. In his letters, Anderson depicted civility as a state of being that could be embodied through habits, behaviours, and tasks centred around a Euro-agrarian way of life. Further, he associated civility as well as Indigeneity with particular kinds of landscapes.

The Coldwater-Narrows Reserve was a community of Methodist Chippewa (Ojibwe), Odaawaa, and Potawatomi farmers led by Chiefs John Aisance, William Snake, and William Yellowhead.[39] The aim of the Coldwater "experiment," as Anderson referred to it, fell in line with the colonial understanding of Christianization and agricultural instruction as pathways to civility.[40] In 1836, Francis Bond Head ordered the dissolution of the Coldwater-Narrows Reserve for sale to white settlers when he took over as lieutenant governor from John Colborne.[41] Anderson, however, viewed Coldwater as evidence of success for the department's civilizing policy. In a letter to Lieutenant Governor Colborne, Anderson emphasized what he viewed as the progress of his charges at Coldwater. He claimed that prior to the government's intervention, the Anishinaabeg in the area were "much demoralised," bordering on starvation, in the "habit of drunkenness," and without knowledge of religion.[42] Anderson juxtaposed the practice of single-family farming at Coldwater in 1836 with what he claimed was the state of the community at the time of his arrival:

> Miserable as was their state, it will hardly be credited that their minds were so debased, their listlessness and lethargy so great, that it required considerable persuasion to prevail on them to accept the bounty of government. By studious attention to their habits and prejudices, they were at length gradually brought to assist, and the general result has been that each Indian with a family, has now a little farm under cultivation, on which he raises not only potatoes and Indian corn, but also wheat, oats, and peas.[43]

The practice of Christianity alongside the institution of European agricultural methods, Anderson argued, helped wean the residents of Coldwater from the "toils of the chase," transforming them into "good members of the Church of Christ and dutiful loyal subjects."[44]

Coldwater's only obstacle, Anderson argued, was its growing proximity to white settlers. Manitoulin Island, however, was far from the compromising settlers and traders of the mainland and had the capacity to accommodate the Indigenous people of Georgian Bay and its surrounding regions. In July of 1834, Chief Aisance approached Anderson in the Council House at Penetanguishene and told him that his people were "desirous of being civilised; but they wished to settle on Manitoulin Island, and not at Coldwater."[45] The following summer Anderson and Reverend Adam Elliot, a traveling Anglican missionary, set out for Manitoulin to speak with the Indigenous people living on the north shore of Lake Huron about settling at a potential mission on Manitoulin in the hopes of promoting their conversion to Christianity. On Manitoulin, Anderson and Elliot found established "Indian plantations" and an abundance of soil "suitable for an Indian farm."[46] Taking into account Manitoulin's favourable landscape and his experience at Coldwater, Anderson wrote to Colborne emphasizing the necessity of founding a "complete settlement" on Manitoulin as soon as possible, "for the civilization of the Indians as well as to prevent the total extinction of their race."

Notably, Anderson understood civilization to be a gradual and effortful process. For an Indigenous person to become civilized he had to "bestow great labour in cultivating the ground and sowing his seed." In order to do this, he had to leave behind those habits that were indicative of Indigenous ways of life which, for Anderson, included "the arts of canoe and wigwam building," fishing, and hunting.[47] Manitoulin in its present state offered the conditions necessary for the temporary continuation of "Indian habits of life," but its soil held a future in which Christian Indigenous farmers would conform with colonial expectations:

> Its immediate vicinity to the present lands of the Indians will induce them to make the change without difficulty. The land is good, it is well watered by rivers and interior lakes, and its numerous bays abound in fish. All these are important considerations, for the Indian cannot be expected all at once to change his habits of life.[48]

Anderson conceived of "natural Indian" and "civilised Indian" as two distinct identities centred around ways of interacting with land and water. Each identity was tied to a corresponding landscape: an Indigenous landscape enabled hunting and gathering while a civilized landscape encouraged static cultivation. As Indigenous people changed their habits, so too would they change their landscape. In Anderson's view, Manitoulin was primed for such a transformation.

Manitoulin as a Refuge for the "Noble Savage": Head's Removal Plan

In 1836 Francis Bond Head succeeded Colborne as Lieutenant Governor of Upper Canada. Before leaving office, Colborne appealed to the British Secretary of State, Lord Glenelg, to sanction the founding of the civilizing settlement headed by Anderson on Manitoulin Island. Head, by contrast, had different plans for Manitoulin Island. Head's political views were driven by his belief in the concept of the "noble savage" who was, in his view, incapable of adjusting to or taking on European religion or lifestyles. He favoured a policy of complete removal, in which the government would withdraw Indigenous peoples from areas inhabited by white settlers and relocate them to remote regions of the colony.

At the time of Head's appointment, British officials were evaluating the supposed benefits and successes of the Indian Department's civilizing program compared to its costs.[49] Glenelg tasked Head with crafting a report to support the alleged efficacy of the department's policy. In August of 1836 Head travelled to Manitoulin to gather information about the Indigenous nations present at the government's annual distribution of treaty annuities.[50] The gathering took place at Manitowaning, a village on the north-east shore of the Island and the intended location of Anderson's civilizing mission. In attendance were the Indigenous nations of the Upper Great Lakes with treaty relationships to the Crown. Some Manitoulin Chiefs were signatories and descendants of signatories to previous treaties with the colonial government, such as the 1764 Treaty of Niagara, however Manitoulin Island itself was not covered by a treaty at the time of Head's arrival.[51]

At the treaty gathering, Head approached the Anishinaabe nations he believed to have ancestral claims to Manitoulin. In his address, Head alleged that white farmers were seeking their land and that the colonial government was without the power to protect it:

> In all parts of the world, farmers seek for uncultivated lands as eagerly as you, my red children, hunt in your great forests for game. If you would cultivate your land, it would then be considered your own property; in the same way as your dogs are considered among yourselves to belong to those who have reared them; but uncultivated land is like wild animals, and your Great Father who has hitherto protected you, has now great difficulty in securing it for you from the whites who are hunting to cultivate it.[52]

Head's speech did not introduce or allude to his removal policy, rather he sought to heighten for the Anishinaabeg the necessity of a treaty with the Crown on the grounds that their lands were under immediate threat. Following Head's reasoning, the Anishinaabeg had not laboured on the land in a way that rendered it into property. According to Head's analogy, in order to lay claim to land one must rear it as one rears feral dogs, that is, through domestication. In keeping with a Euro-Christian cosmology of improvement, the domestication of land could only be achieved by cultivating it according to colonial standards. Thus, without evidence of domestication through cultivation Manitoulin was a place legally unclaimed. As a result, the government allegedly could not defend the Island against settlers who wished to improve the land. If the Anishinaabeg entered into Head's Treaty, however, King William IV, or "The Great Father," would withdraw his claim to Manitoulin and its surrounding islands.[53]

The treaty Head proposed was unique in that, purportedly, it did not seek to open Indigenous land for white settlement. Rather, in exchange for each nation's individual claim to the land, the government (according to Head) would protect the Island from white encroachment so long as it remained open to all Indigenous people who wished to live there and be, as Head phrased it in his treaty speech, "civilised as well as totally separated from Whites."[54] John Borrows notes the Treaty gave the Anishinaabeg the unique power under colonial law to exclude white settlers from Manitoulin. From Head's point of view, however, the Treaty laid the groundwork for his removal policy, and it did so without explicitly revealing his further political goals. Head's references to civilization and cultivation in the treaty speeches may have concealed the potential implications of the treaties from their witnesses and signatories, including Anderson and Reverend Elliot. In this way, the Treaty functioned as a tool of removal under the guise of a promise of protection. At the same gathering at Manitowaning, Head proposed a treaty with similarly veiled intentions to the Saugeen Ojibway, whose territory stretches along the Saugeen Peninsula, currently known as the Bruce Peninsula. Head proposed that the Saugeen should surrender their land in exchange for houses further north, assistance cultivating their land, and protection from white encroachment.[55]

Head's correspondence following the treaty signings discloses his plan to remove the people he viewed as barriers to progress. In a letter following the signings, Head wrote to Glenelg about his belief in Manitoulin's capacity to serve the colonial nation:

> It was evident to me that we would reap a very great benefit if we could persuade these Indians, who are now impeding the progress of civilization in Upper Canada, to resort to a place possessing the double advantage of being admirably adapted to them (inasmuch as it affords fishing, hunting, bird shooting and fruit), and yet in no way adapted to the White population.[56]

This passage also provides a window into Head's complicated understanding of the relationships between Indigenous peoples and land, as well as his conception of Manitoulin. The fish, fruit, forests, and animals of the Island would enable Indigenous people to live in nature as Head believed they were intended to do. Crucially, Head did not categorize cultivation as a natural occupation of Indigenous peoples. Manitoulin's apparent lack of agrarian potential, with its rocky and wooded landscape, characterized it as a distinctly Indigenous space, in other words, superfluous land unfit for European settlers.

Despite his belief in the archetype of the noble savage, Head's personal philosophy and his colonial policy were still informed by the property-making power of improvement. The connections between improvement, cultivation, and property served as another source of justification for the 1836 Treaty, in his view. In his letter to Glenelg, Head echoes Vattel's argument for the appropriation of Indigenous land in the *Law of Nations*:

> It must always be kept in mind, that, however useful rich land may be to us, yet its only value to an Indian consists in the game it contains: he is in fact lord of the manor, but it is against his nature to cultivate the soil – he has neither right nor power to sell it. As soon therefore as his game is frightened away, or its influx of immigration cut off by the surrounding settlements of the Whites, his land, however rich it may be, becomes a "rudis indigestaque moles," of little value or importance, and in this state much of the Indian property in Upper Canada at present exists.[57]

For Head, uncultivated land was a waste, and as follows could not be truly and legally possessed. Thus, the supposed natural aversion of Indigenous people to agriculture prohibited civility indefinitely.

Based on Glenelg and Head's 1836 and 1837 correspondence, it seems Head's impassioned arguments and not insignificantly, his acquisition by way of the Treaty of tens of thousands of acres of Indigenous land for the nascent colony, made Glenelg into a supporter of Head's new policy of removal. In a letter responding to Head's plans for Manitoulin, Glenelg wrote that he "feared it impossible" to question the accuracy of Head's conviction that attempts to convert Indigenous people into Christian farmers were futile and ultimately destructive:

> I should most reluctantly yield to the conviction that in the prosecution of this object we must abandon the hope of imparting to the Indians the blessings of Christianity, on the ground that those blessings were necessarily more than counterbalanced by the evils, with which they have hitherto been unhappily associated.[58]

Deferring to Head's supposed expertise, Glenelg ratified both treaties Head negotiated at the 1836 gathering. The ratification of the 1836 treaties, however, was seen as highly controversial by those who viewed themselves as acting "in the real interests of the Indians," namely missionaries and white members of Christian humanitarian organizations like the Aborigines Protection Society.[59]

A Pan-Indigenous Space: The Aborigines Protection Society's Views of Manitoulin

For members of the Aborigines Protection Society, the prospect of the Colonial Office's adoption of Head's policy of removal was both unjust and immoral. A group of missionaries, philanthropists, and self-appointed "friends of the Indians," the APS considered Head's Treaties to put the survival as well as the spiritual and social salvation of Indigenous people in Upper Canada at risk. At the centre of the ensuing debates were firmly held beliefs about what constituted natural relationships between Indigenous people and land, as well as colonial perceptions of the landscape of Manitoulin. Head's removal policy was unjust, the APS argued, on the grounds that it would appropriate land from Indigenous communities the APS believed had earned title through cultivation. It was immoral in that removal to the relatively remote and allegedly infertile Manitoulin Island would cause Indigenous converts on the path to civilization to abandon both agriculture and Christianity and return to their earlier habits and dispositions as hunters, fishers, and gatherers. Though they were seeking different ends, both Head and the Aborigines Protection Society hinged their arguments upon physical relationships to land. Their notions of colonial property, how it was constructed and claimed, depended on the same cosmology of improvement, at the centre of which was the act of cultivation. Both parties drew from this cosmology of improvement to make cases for varying degrees of exclusion.

The 1839 *Report on the Indians of Upper Canada by a Sub-committee of the Aborigines Protection Society* made several criticisms of the 1836 Treaties, Head's policy, and the claims he made in his appeals to Glenelg and the Colonial Office. An 1837 memorial within the report claimed in its title to be written on behalf of the Saugeen Indians in Upper Canada.[60] The authors argued that Head's removal plan had three major errors:

1. That the Indians removed voluntarily, and that therefore no injury was done them.
2. That the Manitoulin Islands are really *fit* for them, supposing them to become civilised cultivators of the ground.
3. That the Indians are so certainly contaminated by contact with the white people, that nothing but removal out of their reach can prevent it.[61]

The first point of contention dealt with the issue of consent. Following the Treaties, Head planned that over time *all* Indigenous people in Upper Canada would relocate to Manitoulin to fortify themselves against the whites.[62] Those implicated in this removal clause, the memorialists pointed out, did not volunteer to relocate to Manitoulin. The APS, however, did not seek to defend all non-consenting Indigenous nations who would be affected by Head's stipulation of removal.

Rather, they sought only to exempt the Indigenous communities "in which, with much labour, and after repeated disappointments, the germs of Christianity and civilisation have at length taken root with fair promise of fruitfulness."[63] The society aimed to protect Indigenous communities made up of Christian farmers such as the Anishinaabeg of the Saugeen Peninsula, who had entered into a separate treaty with Head at the 1836 gathering at Manitowaning. The memorialists differentiated the Saugeen from those "wandering and uncivilised Indians" who also inhabited the newly ceded territories.[64] Such examples served as success stories for the missionaries the society supported and proved that its beliefs in colonial civilizing programs were well founded. It was communities like these, composed of civilized converts, whose consent and claims to land mattered to the APS.

The APS constructed a quasi-legal, theological argument based on the notion that communities like that of the Saugeen had made themselves into property holders by virtue of their religiously sanctioned agricultural relationship to land. In an 1837 memorial, the APS claimed that the actions the Saugeen undertook in farming the land elevated the validity of their attachment:

> It appeals to your memorialists that those Indians who have cleared the land, ploughed and sowed fields, erected houses, homes, and places of worship upon it, have rendered themselves possessors of the soil by a stronger title than that by which their wandering brethren have held other portions of districts as common hunting grounds.[65]

For the APS, the Saugeen transformed unused space into a claimable place by cultivating their land. They possessed land that was not in a state of "little value or importance," as Head had claimed.[66] Their land was outside of the common, as it were, and therefore spared from the processes of appropriation that applied to land that existed in the so-called state of nature. Indigenous people were capable of improvement and, as follows, holding property, only if they embodied the teachings of civility through their interactions with land. Much like Head, the APS wielded the power of improvement as a tool of colonial apprehension and Indigenous dispossession.[67]

The authors of the 1837 memorial also refuted the notion that Manitoulin was a suitable living place. The island, they alleged, was not "fit" for Indigenous people who intended to become "civilised cultivators of the ground."[68] Its rocky, barren landscape made it a place hostile to colonial organization. Much of the APS's 1839 report concentrated on discrediting Head's claims by proving the necessity and historical effectiveness of Canada's civilizing programs. Along with petitions from British philanthropists the report contained testimonies from missionaries in Canada stationed within Indigenous communities. The missionaries quoted in the report measured advancement by what they saw as the proliferation of industrious habits among Indigenous people. Notably, many of these habits were centred around improving land, primarily through agriculture. Following such a metric, the progress of a community depended on the arability of its land. Not only did the act of cultivation make land into property, it also served as a signifier for civility and successful conversion. Further, in designating Manitoulin as unfit for cultivation, the report marked the island as a symbolic and physical threat to the colony's growth and values.

One unidentified missionary whose letter to Glenelg was quoted in the 1839 report challenged Head's assessment that "great mortality" followed efforts to convert and civilize Indigenous people:

> It is admitted that Christianity does not impart to the Indian a *new body*, although it implants within him *a new heart*; and therefore constitutions impaired by intemperance, vice, and exposure, may become a prey to consumption and other diseases, after the Christian conversion and reformation of the Indians as well as before. But is this mortality *increased or lessened* by the "Christianizing and civilizing process"?[69]

As the missionary made clear, he did not believe Christianization altered the body of a convert in a physical way. It did, however, prime new disciples to embrace a particular set of bodily habits that allegedly lessened mortality. In his letter, the missionary provided an example in the River-Credit Mission, which he claimed thrived after the community's conversion, as evidenced by a decrease in deaths. The missionary claimed that the River-Credit Council had ascertained that ten years immediately prior to the community's conversion, there had been three hundred deaths whereas in the whole of the ten years following there had been from fifty to sixty.[70] According to the letter, an old chief who spoke as a representative for the council "feelingly ascribed" the difference in numbers "to their becoming Christians."[71] In place of the heathen lifestyle that had led to deaths by starving, fighting, burning in a fire, or exposure, residents of the River-Credit Mission now led civilized lives, which they demonstrated by diligently sowing crops and ordering the landscape.[72] The missionary quantified their moral improvement in bushels and acres:

> Previous to the conversion of this tribe, they did not cultivate an acre of land; since the conversion of this tribe, they have cleared from the forest,

brought under cultivation and enclosed 820 acres of land; have grown the last year nearly 900 bushels of wheat and corn, nearly 1100 bushels of potatoes, 84 tons of hay, besides garden vegetables and various descriptions.[73]

Notably, the Mississauga Ojibway of the River-Credit Mission practised agriculture long before the missionary's introduction to the community in 1827.[74] The River-Credit Mission was directed by the Reverend Peter Jones who was a member of the Mississauga nation. The brief history of the River-Credit Mission outlined in the letter makes no mention of Jones or the nation's other chiefs who played central roles in helping the community to prosper and who spoke out against Head's policy of removal.

The accuracy of the missionary's River-Credit anecdote and whether or not it proved Head's arguments false is not as significant as the conversion narrative it presents. In the letter, the missionary stages a story of the transformation of souls, bodies, and land. Conversion begins with the metaphorical implanting of a new heart. It then takes root in the body and manifests in physical habits of industry which involve the completion of tasks fixated on improving land: clearing forests, milling wheat, and raising cattle. In her work on the religious landscapes of nineteenth-century America's Western Reserve, known today as Ohio, Amy DeRogatis notes that in the view of frontier missionaries, "bodily signs of piety demonstrated the relationship between physical and moral order."[75] For the missionaries featured in the APS's report, the communities they worked within displayed their newly acquired morals through the physical alteration of their landscapes, primarily through cultivation. Another anonymous missionary quoted by the report noted that in only one year the community he ministered to had turned 140 acres of heavily wooded territory into valuable space by clearing and enclosing it.[76] According to the APS's missionary testimonies, moral communities enclosed gardens and constructed orderly houses by virtue of individual obedience to moral habits of temperance, prudence, and industriousness. Moral bodies, in this view, created and maintained moral spaces.

The descriptions of Manitoulin in the APS's report function in two significant ways. First, they outline a static form of Indigeneity which its authors equated with the Island's supposedly primitive, barren landscape. In their letters, the missionaries depicted this version of Indigeneity as a condition that converts could surmount or shed through devotion to moral habits and civilized tasks. Second, they imply that Manitoulin possessed a kind of power of reversal over the Indigenous people who lived there. Not only would it prevent the seeds of conversion and civilization from germinating, it would cause those who had previously made progress to devolve into their former state. The image of Manitoulin constructed by the report racialized the land itself, marking it as a pan-Indigenous space, similar in some ways to Head's characterization of the Island. For the APS, however, it was an inherently dangerous space, one that fostered the types of habits that missionaries categorized as intrinsically immoral.

A second 1838 memorial included in the report, addressed to Lord Durham, the Governor General and High Commissioner of British North America, characterized Manitoulin as a hinterland hospitable only to the nature of the "Indian heart."[77] The memorial asserted that removal to Manitoulin would cause Indigenous people to abandon their pursuit of Christianity and civilization. Worse yet, the threat of removal to Manitoulin came at a time when conditions in the settled regions of Upper Canada would ensure that civilizing programs were the only viable option to prevent the "annihilation" of Indigenous people:

> At the very time at which the affairs of the Aborigines within the province seemed to have reached the point of their lowest decline, when the contracting of their borders and the extinction of their game appear to have brought the absolute necessity of a new mode of subsistence, to second the gentle persuasions of the Missionaries, alluring them to the industrious and peaceful habits of civilized life, they are called to abandon the advantages which they are just beginning to enjoy, and are to be banished to the 23,000 rocks of granite, dignified by the name of Manitoulin Islands.[78]

The authors of the memorial depicted Manitoulin as if it was unchanged by the effects of settler colonialism in the Great Lakes. Unlike mainland Upper Canada, the Island was still an untamed space. Thus, it provided an environment that was naturally suited to what the memorialists called "the life of the savage."[79] If square lots and croplands were markers of the civilized Indigenous Christian farmer then fish-filled waters and rocky terrain were synonymous with the "national character" of Indigenous people:

> On these islands, from ancient motives of veneration, calculated to render permanent their native superstitions, but perfectly useless as Sir Francis admits, for every purpose of civilized life, the Indians flattered with the prospect of retaining their national character, and of finding enjoyments which their forefathers possessed, when they had the range of the whole country, are doomed to live on berries yielded by the few shrubs which can take root between the crevices of the rocks, and on the fish which frequent the shallow waters.[80]

The memorialists' notion that the Island was unfit for every purpose of civilized life yet well suited to the "national character" of Indigenous people implied that Manitoulin's landscape matched a former, instinctual version of Indigenousness.[81] These "native superstitions" embodied the inverse of civility and belonged to the predecessors of the Indigenous converts whom the Society extolled.

The memorialists' assertion that Manitoulin was "calculated to render permanent" so-called "native superstitions" implied that its effects went beyond encouraging uncivilized habits and beliefs: it had the power, it seems, to undo civility. The idea that converts could unwittingly backslide to their former "simple-minded state," as one missionary put it, reveals that the APS saw and depicted supposedly civilized Indigenous converts as "mimic people" rather than equals.[82] Drawing from critical theorist Homi Bhabha's concept of colonial mimicry, historian Cecelia Morgan writes that in missionary writing, Indigenous adults appear as "'mimic' people": as embodied examples "of a reformed, recognisable Other."[83] Bhabha notes that "the discourse of mimicry is constructed around an ambivalence; in order to be effective, mimicry must continually produce its slippage, its excess, its difference."[84] Manitoulin's apparent ability to induce Indigenous people to retain their supposedly native dispositions unveils the inherent slippage within the colonial concept of Indigenous civilization and the idea of cultivation as a means to that end. Following the APS's logic, Indigenous people were always vulnerable to their instinct. Thus, civilization was a process with no finish line. The memorial's final appeal to Lord Durham makes clear that civility, even in its most convincing performance, was and would always be an ongoing act of mimicry:

> Whatever fame may accrue to Lord Durham for extinguishing the prejudices of party, calming the turbulence of passion and softening the asperities of opposing factions at Canada, he will receive the rich reward of internal satisfaction no less solid and lasting from having rescued from annihilation protected and elevated the North American Aborigines and thereby set a new and noble example for the *imitation* of the civilized world.[85]

The Promise to Cultivate: Manitoulin as Fertile in 1861

Notably, the colonial government did not use Head's Treaties to remove Indigenous people from their land in the years immediately following the Treaties' ratification. Nor, however, did they live up to its promises to protect Manitoulin Island from white incursion. When the colony recognized Manitoulin as a potential resource roughly three decades later, Canada's colonial agents utilized the 1836 Manitoulin Treaty as a tool of apprehension aided by an argument once again based in a Christian cosmology of improvement.[86]

When Glenelg recommended Head's Treaties for approval, he claimed that the colonial government's motive for doing so was rooted in a belief that Manitoulin's location would protect Indigenous people from negative influences. In an 1837 letter addressed to Head, Glenelg maintained that the Island's distance from white settlements would at least allow for the inculcation of "the doctrines and precepts of Christianity, without interference with the ordinary habits of life hitherto pursued by the Indians, and apart from the deteriorating influence of a general intercourse with another race of men."[87] Thus, Glenelg's reconfiguration of Head's policy allowed the colonial government to encourage removal under the guise that it was a smoother pathway to civilization. Further, in 1838 Glenelg reinstated Colborne's initial plans to establish an agricultural settlement on Manitoulin, which was led by Thomas G. Anderson with the help of Reverend C.C. Brough of the Anglican Church of Canada. Notably, depictions of Manitoulin's landscape, specifically its arability, looked radically different in reports from Anderson, Brough, and other Anglican missionaries on the ground compared to the descriptions of Head and the Aborigines Protection Society. In one of Brough's reports for the Department of Indian Affairs, he noted that Manitoulin appeared to be "a well-chosen location for the Indians," specifying that he had never seen "finer spring crops than those raised by the Indians there."[88]

The colonial government administered the civilizing program at Manitowaning or "the Establishment," as Anderson referred to it, until they dissolved it in 1856, echoing the earlier seizure of Georgian Bay agricultural "experiments" on Beausoleil Island and Coldwater. A description of the village from the "Report of the Special Commissioners Appointed on the 8th of September, 1856, to Investigate Indian Affairs in Canada" depicted Manitowaning as a failure due to disregard on the part of its inhabitants:

> The village of Manitowaning no longer presents the appearance which it did twelve years ago. Many of the inhabitants have emigrated, some to join the Newash Band, others to settle themselves at Garden River, and a few have founded the new village of Wiabejiwong … The condition of the farms near the settlement was in keeping with that of the village itself: fields without fences, and gardens lying uncultivated, presented a picture of complete neglect and indifference.[89]

The Anishinaabeg never agreed to move to Manitowaning and live according to the guidelines set out by the resident missionary and Indian Agent. Attributing the settlement's failure to inconsistent, incorrect methods of cultivation allowed the government to place the blame upon Indigenous people. The 1856 assessment of Manitowaning laid the necessary groundwork for the government to later frame the theft of Anishinaabe land for white settlement as the natural consequence of the inability of Indigenous people to use land properly.

Rather than fulfilling their treaty obligations, in 1861 the colonial government began formal efforts to coerce the Anishinaabeg to cede Manitoulin. In October of the same year, treaty commissioners Lindsay and Bartlett arrived on Manitoulin. They began their case by stating that the Anishinaabeg had not fulfilled their end of the 1836 agreement. In reference to the phrase in the 1836 Treaty "the property (under your Great Father's control) of all Indians whom he shall allow to reside here," the commissioners argued that in order for the 1836 Treaty to remain valid, thousands of Indigenous people should have migrated to Manitoulin to become "cultivators of the soil":[90]

> At that time there were 9,300 Indians, under the protection of your Great Father, who assembled at an appointed place every year in Upper Canada. It was then thought that this large number would make this Island the place of future settlement. If they had done so, and followed your examples in becoming cultivators of the soil, the intention of the Government in settling this Island with Indians would have been carried out. Unfortunately, however, your people have not availed themselves of the opportunity of collecting, as settlers, upon this Island in a body by whom a large portion of its best soil might be cultivated … We are instructed to tell you that 25 acres will be secured by a Crown Deed to every head of a family upon this Island … In default of the Indians neglecting to come here and settle this Island, your Great Father deems it equitable to grant the remainder of the land to his white children, of whom, as well as yourselves, it is his duty to take care.[91]

The very fact that the colonial government attempted to make a second treaty on Manitoulin for the purposes of attaining Anishinaabe surrender hints that to some degree, they knew that the 1836 Treaty was not a land cession but instead had an affirmation of Indigenous sovereignty over Manitoulin Island. The commissioners' manipulation and misinterpretation of the 1836 Treaty terms, however, reveal that the colonial government was never truly concerned about the survival of Indigenous people. By 1861, it seems that the 1836 Treaty no longer aided in the flourishing of Canada's settler society. The colonial government once again utilized the power of improvement to attempt to dispossess the Anishinaabeg of their land. Ultimately, in the nineteenth century, the colonial government's goals were to obtain land for expansion and to cut financial ties with all Indigenous nations – ending any relationships of responsibility and reciprocity. Indigenous agricultural success and land ownership were never in the government's interest.

NOTES

1 Odaawaa and Ojibwe, *Canada Sessional Papers*, no. 63, 1863, *Proposals Made by Sir Francis Bond Head, August 1836*, in Eleanor Charlton, "Manitoulin Island, 1862: Anishinaabe Strategies of Resistance and Survival" (master's thesis, Trent University, 2005), 23.

2 John Borrows, "Negotiating Treaties and Land Claims: The Impact of Diversity Within First Nations Property Interests," *The Windsor Yearbook of Access to Justice* 12 (1992): 191.

3 Alan Ojiig Corbiere, "Anishinaabe Treaty-Making in the 18th- and 19th-Century Northern Great Lakes: From Shared Meanings to Epistemological Chasms" (PhD diss., York University, 2019), 243.

4 Corbiere, "Anishinaabe Treaty-Making," 243.

5 Corbiere, "Anishinaabe Treaty-Making," 243.

6 Lisa Ford, *Settler Sovereignty: Jurisdiction and Indigenous People in America and Australia, 1788–1836* (Cambridge, MA: Harvard University Press, 2010), 9.

7 The Anishinaabeg include the Ojibwe, Odaawaa, Potawatomi, Mississauga, Algonquin, and Saulteux people. In this paper, I use Anishinaabe and Anishinaabeg (plural) to refer specifically to the Odaawaa, Ojibwe, and Potawatomi people who lived and continue to live on Manitoulin Island. Corbiere, "Anishinaabe Treaty-Making," 1.

8 Alan Corbiere in "Island of the Great Spirit: The Legacy of Manitoulin," directed by Zach Melnick (2008, Ontario Visual Heritage Project), https://www.youtube.com/watch?v=Q2kL3An1MxE.

9 Judith Weisenfeld, *New World a-Coming: Black Religion and Racial Identity During the Great Migration* (New York: New York University Press, 2016), 5.

10 Weisenfeld, *New World a-Coming*, 5.

11 Pamela E. Klassen, *The Story of Radio Mind: A Missionary's Journey on Indigenous Land* (Chicago: University of Chicago Press, 2018).

12 Paul McHugh and Lisa Ford, "Settler Sovereignty and the Shapeshifting Crown," in *Between Indigenous and Settler Governance*, ed. Lisa Ford, Tim Rowse, and Anna Yeatman (Oxford: Routledge, 2012), 23–34; Cole Harris, *The Reluctant Land: Society, Space, and Environment in Canada before Federation* (Vancouver: University of British Columbia Press, 2008); Sarah

Carter, "Aboriginal People of Canada and the British Empire," in *Canada and the British Empire*, ed. Phillip A. Buckner (Oxford: Oxford University Press, 2008), 200–19.

13 Sir James Kempt to Secretary of State Sir G. Murray, 1829, in *Report on the Indians of Upper Canada, 1839*, Aborigines Protection Society (London: William Ball, Arnold, and Co, 1839), 8.

14 McHugh and Ford, "Settler Sovereignty," 25.

15 McHugh and Ford, "Settler Sovereignty," 26.

16 Carole Blackburn, *Harvest of Souls: The Jesuit Missions and Colonialism in North America, 1632–1650* (Montreal: McGill-Queen's University Press, 2000); Cecilia Morgan, "Turning Strangers into Sisters: Missionaries and Colonization in Upper Canada," in *Sisters or Strangers?: Immigrant, Ethnic and Racialized Women in Canadian History*, ed. Marlene Epp and Franca Iacovetta (Toronto: University of Toronto Press, 2016), 89–107; J. Edward Chamberlin, *The Harrowing of Eden: White Attitudes Toward Native Americans* (Toronto: Fitzhenry and Whiteside, 1977); William Cronon, *Changes in the Land: Indians, Colonists, and the Ecology of New England* (New York: Hill & Wang, 1983).

17 Weisenfeld, *A New World a-Coming*, 2016.

18 Yael Ben-zvi, "Where Did the Red Go?: Lewis Henry Morgan's Evolutionary Inheritance and U.S. Racial Imagination," *The New Centennial Review* 7, no. 2 (Fall 2007): 201–29.

19 Cole Harris, *Making Native Space: Colonialism, Resistance, and Reserves in British Columbia* (Vancouver: University of British Columbia Press, 2002), 9.

20 Harris, *Making Native Space*, 9.

21 This summarizes the recommendations made by Sir James Kempt for "settling the Indians" in an 1829 report commissioned by Secretary of State Sir G. Murray. The report served as a foundational document for the civilizing policy of the 1830s. Sir James Kempt to Secretary of State Sir G. Murray, 22 April 1829, in *Report on the Indians of Upper Canada*, 9.

22 Klassen, *The Story of Radio Mind*, 95.

23 "Copies or Extracts of Correspondence since 1st April, 1835, between the Secretary of State for the Colonies and the Governors of the British North American Provinces Respecting the Indians in Those Provinces," *House of Commons Sessional Papers*, 1839, XXXIV.

24 Leanne Betasamosake Simpson, "Coming into Wisdom: Community, Family, Land, and Love," *Northern Public Affairs* 6, special issue no. 1 (July 2018): 12–17 .

25 Simpson, "Coming into Wisdom," 16.

26 Sir James Kempt Report to Sir George Murray, Castle of St. Lewis, Quebec, 20 May 1830, in *Report on the Indians of Upper Canada*, 12.

27 Sarah Carter, *Lost Harvests: Prairie Indian Reserve Farmers and Government Policy* (Montreal: McGill-Queen's University Press, 1993), 234.

28 Leo G. Waisberg and Tim E. Holzkamm, "'A Tendency to Discourage Them from Cultivating': Ojibwa Agriculture and Indian Affairs Administration in Northwestern Ontario," *Ethnohistory* 40, no. 2 (Spring 1993): 191.

29 Shaunnagh Dorsett, "Civilisation and Cultivation: Colonial Policy and Indigenous Peoples in Canada and Australia," *Griffith Law Review* 4, no. 2 (1995): 215.

30 Allan Greer, *Property and Dispossession: Natives, Empires and Land in Early Modern North America* (Cambridge: Cambridge University Press, 2018), 425.

31 Greer, *Property and Dispossession*, 244.

32 William Rawson, John Davidson, and William Hepburn, "History of the Relations between the Government and the Indians," in *Report on the Affairs of the Indians in Canada* laid *before the Legislative Assembly, 20th March, 1845* (Ottawa: Claims and Historical Research Centre, 1845), Appendix E.E.E, Section I.

33 Rawson, Davidson, and Hepburn, "History of the Relations."

34 Rawson, Davidson, and Hepburn, "History of the Relations."

35 Rawson, Davidson, and Hepburn, "History of the Relations."

36 "Anderson's reports on Manitowaning." Appendix to the sixth volume of the journals of the Legislative Assembly of the Province of Canada, from the 2nd day of June to the 28th day of July, 1847, both days inclusive, and in the tenth and eleventh years of the reign of Our Sovereign Lady Queen Victoria, being the third session of the second provincial Parliament of Canada, session 1847.

37 Susan E. Gray, "The Border Difference: The Anishinaabeg, Benevolence, and State Indigenous Policy in the Nineteenth-Century Great Lakes Basin," *American Studies in Scandinavia* 50, no. 1 (2018): 111.

38 Klassen, *Radio Mind*, 95.

39 Heather N. Smith, "'We Are One Nation': The Legacy of the Coldwater-Narrows Reserve (1830–1836)," *The Great Lakes Journal of Undergraduate History* 6, no. 1 (2018): 61.

40 Smith, "We are One Nation," 62.

41 Smith, "We are One Nation," 70.

42 "Extracts from a letter to Colborne from Anderson, communicated by his excellency to the Bishop of Quebec, and by the Bishop to 'The Society at Toronto for Converting and Civilizing the Indians and Propagating the Gospel among Destitute Settlers in Upper Canada' dated September 24th, 1835," in *The Stewart Missions*, ed. W.J.D Waddilove (London: J. Hatchard, 1838), 90.

43 "Extracts from a letter to Colborne from Anderson," 90.

44 "Extracts from a letter to Colborne from Anderson," 90.

45 *The Stewart Missions*, ed. Waddilove, 81.

46 *The Stewart Missions*, ed. Waddilove, 116.

47 *The Stewart Missions*, ed. Waddilove, 116.

48 "Report from Superintendent Anderson to Lieutenant Governor Colborne, Sept 24, 1835," in Robert J. Surtees, *The Manitoulin Treaties* (Ottawa: Treaties and Historical Research Centre, 1986), 20.

49 Surtees, *The Manitoulin Treaties*, 20.

50 Prior to Head's appointment, Colborne had shifted the location of annuity distribution from Penetanguishene to Manitoulin Island. Head was also tasked with putting a stop to treaty annuities as a means of cutting costs. He did not inform those present at the gathering of the government's intention of stopping presents.

51 Corbiere, "Anishinaabe Treaty-Making," 129.

52 Corbiere, "Anishinaabe Treaty-Making."

53 "Proposals Made by Sir Francis Bond Head, August 1836," *Canada Sessional Papers*, No. 63, 1863, in Charlton, "Manitoulin Island, 1862," 23.

54 "Proposals Made by Sir Francis Bond Head," 23.

55 "Proposals Made by Sir Francis Bond Head," 23.

56 Library and Archives Canada (LAC) RG 10, Vol. 391, Head to Glenelg, 20 August 1836.

57 LAC RG 10, Vol. 391, Head to Glenelg, 20 August 1836.

58 Lord Glenelg to Sir F.B. Head, 20 January 1837, in *Report on the Indians of Upper Canada*, 21.

59 "Memorial from the spring of 1838, to the Earl of Durham, High Commissioners of her Majesty's Provinces in North America, London, 3 April 1838. Signed on behalf of the Committee J.J. Freeman and J.H. Tredgold," in *Report on the Indians of Upper Canada*, 24.

60 In this context, the memorial is functioning in the same way as a petition.

61 "Memorial to Lord Glenelg in February 1837 by upwards of eighty gentlemen in London, on behalf of the Saugeen Indians in Upper Canada," in *Report on the Indians of Upper Canada*, 22.

62 Sir Francis Bond Head to Lord Glenelg, 20 November 1836, in Borrows, "Negotiating Treaties and Land Claims," 199.

63 "Memorial from the spring of 1838," 26.

64 "Memorial to Lord Glenelg in February 1837," 21.

65 "Memorial to Lord Glenelg in February 1837," 22.

66 LAC RG 10, Vol. 391, Head to Glenelg, 20 August 1836.

67 Audra Simpson, *Mohawk Interruptus: Political Life Across the Borders of Settler States* (Durham, NC: Duke University Press, 2014), 39.

68 "Memorial to Lord Glenelg in February 1837," 22.

69 "Extract of a Letter to Lord Glenelg, relative to Sir Francis Head's despatches on the affairs of the Indians," in *Report on the Indians of Upper Canada*, 31.

70 "Extract of a Letter to Lord Glenelg," 33.
71 "Extract of a Letter to Lord Glenelg," 33.
72 "Extract of a Letter to Lord Glenelg," 33.
73 "Extract of a Letter to Lord Glenelg," 33.
74 Praxis Research Associates, *The History of the Mississaugas of the New Credit First Nation* (Hagersville, ON: Mississauga of the New Credit First Nation, 2006).
75 Amy DeRogatis, *Moral Geography: Maps, Missionaries, and the American Frontier* (New York: Columbia University Press, 2003), 95.
76 "Extract of a Letter to Lord Glenelg," 35.
77 "Extract of a Letter to Lord Glenelg," 31.
78 "Extract of a Letter to Lord Glenelg," 31.
79 "Extract of a Letter to Lord Glenelg," 24.
80 "Memorial from the spring of 1838," 26.
81 "Memorial from the spring of 1838," 26.
82 Morgan, "The Making of White Settler Societies," 41
83 Morgan, "The Making of White Settler Societies."
84 Homi Bhabha, "Of Mimicry and Man: The Ambivalence of Colonial Discourse," in *Tensions of Empire: Colonial Cultures in a Bourgeois World*, 8th ed., ed. Frederick Cooper and Ann Laura Stoler (Berkeley: University of California Press, 2009), 126.
85 "Memorial from the spring of 1838," 27. (Emphasis added.)
86 Simpson, *Mohawk Interruptus*, 39.
87 Lord Glenelg to Bond Head, 20 January 1837, in *Report on the Indians of Upper Canada*, 21.
88 *Appendix to the sixth volume of the journals of the Legislative Assembly of the Province of Canada, from the 2nd day of June to the 28th day of July, 1847, both days inclusive, and in the tenth and eleventh years of the reign of Our Sovereign Lady Queen Victoria, being the third session of the second provincial Parliament of Canada*, session 1847, 174.
89 Canada, "Report of the Special Commissioners Appointed on the 8th of September, 1856, to Investigate Indian Affairs in Canada," *Canada Sessional Papers*, no. 16, Appendix 21, 1858, in Allyshia West, "Indigenous and Settler Understandings of the Manitoulin Island Treaties of 1836 (Treaty 45) and 1862" (master's thesis, University of Victoria, 2008), 33.
90 Canada, "1863 Report of Indian Affairs," *Canada Sessional Papers* 26, no. 63, in West, "Indigenous and Settler Understandings," 38.
91 Canada, "1863 Report of Indian Affairs."

Chapter Three

Between Gratitude and Guilt: The Promise of a Better Life in a Settler Colony for Racialized Refugees

SUJITH XAVIER

In this chapter, I explore the notion of promise encompassed within the Canadian refugee regime, that domesticated the 1951 Convention Relating to the Status of the Refugees (Refugee Convention).[1] Relying on my own lived experience as a survivor of war fleeing to what is now Canada, I contrast the promises embedded within the refugee system alongside the erasure of the original peoples of Turtle Island.[2] My aim is to situate the grateful racialized refugee within this settler colony.[3] I argue that the symbolic aspirations of the international refugee convention, coupled with the promises built into its implementing legal framework in Canada, trap refugees between gratitude and guilt.[4]

The promise built into this system is however contingent on how refugees integrate into our adopted home. Integration is predicated on values determined by the Canadian racial state,[5] including the settler colonial impetus for the erasure of Indigenous peoples on these stolen lands.[6] The Canadian integration model moreover is based on how refugees abide by "Canadian" norms by learning whiteness, performing whiteness, and more importantly "acting white."[7] The performance of whiteness insidiously works to eliminate Indigenous peoples through a "methodological nationalism"[8] that necessitates fidelity to the racial settler state.[9] This erasure is made possible for example by obscuring the history of the ongoing genocide of Indigenous peoples.[10]

Viewed from another perspective, this promise has affective elements that structure the experience of a racialized refugee settler, above and beyond the intimate and the emotional.[11] In this analysis, I focus on my own sense of gratitude and guilt, noting that there is a larger body of critical scholarship that explores the relationship between affect and racialization within a racial capitalist structure.[12] For example, the promise of safety and home is contingent on the expectations intimately connected to whiteness. Devon Carbado and Mitu Gulati have theorized this type of performance as "acting white."[13] In a similar, albeit different, manner, Cheryl Harris has reflected on her grandmother's painful experience of "passing as white to work in Chicago's central business district" in the segregated 1930s United States.[14] Others have chronicled the effects of the white supremacist expectations to "cover" one's own sexual orientation to blend in.[15]

Returning to my own experience, the type of performance that I explore in this short chapter requires an allegiance to the Canadian sovereign and a deep sense of gratitude. This gratitude moreover requires a specific set of performances, that ultimately lead to the erasure of Indigenous peoples, precipitating a form of emotional guilt. My analysis will unfold in three sections. First, I will examine the promises contained within the refugee regime to afford protection to those fleeing "by reason of a well-founded fear of persecution for reasons of race, religion, nationality, membership in a particular social group or political opinion."[16] I will chronicle my own experiences of fleeing war-torn Sri Lanka and arriving in Canada to seek asylum. I will examine how refugees are selected and are expected to conform to the white ideal, precipitated by the exclusion clauses of the Refugee Convention and the inadmissibility requirements of the Canadian Immigration and Refugee Protection Act. In the final section, I will turn to my own journey of uncovering the place and space of Indigenous peoples of the territories that I now call home. It is an account of how I became aware of my own complicity in the ongoing genocide of Indigenous peoples of Turtle Island and how I have started to reconcile and contend with my own gratitude and guilt on these stolen lands.

For international lawyers, complicity has several significant connotations. Within international criminal law, there is a focus on individual criminal responsibility, where complicity is ascribed to prohibited conduct, criminalized through four international crimes.[17] With the ratification and domestic implementation of the Rome Statute of the International Criminal Court,[18] the Canadian government entrenched these prohibitions within the national criminal code and in other statutory frameworks.[19] Importantly within the refugee context, the exclusion clauses of the Refugee Convention operate to limit admissibility of those complicit in international crimes.[20] I, however, deploy complicity not in the vernacular of individual criminal responsibility.

Critical race theorists have long chronicled the impact of white supremacy[21] and they have illustrated how the white supremacist system functions to privilege whiteness, for example over Blackness.[22] In fact, some scholars have pointed to the race-to-innocence as a means of maintaining the existing power structures, and ultimately promoting white supremacy.[23] Building on the work of Canadian critical race scholars and Indigenous scholars like Enakshi Dua and Bonita Lawrence, it is important to openly explore the complicity of racialized refugees within the Canadian national narrative.[24] In a similar fashion, I locate my own complicity within this settler colonial space, where refugees perform a truncated version of the race-to-innocence and ignore the ongoing genocide of Indigenous peoples.

I draw inspiration from several methodological positions, ranging from autoethnography,[25] to reflexive inquiry,[26] to storytelling.[27] Relying on my own lived experience, I tease out pivotal moments in my own life as a set of "counterstories" to illustrate the way both gratitude and guilt structure my experiences in Canada.[28] Of course, relying on memory may be challenging, especially given what we know about victims of trauma and their ability to remember.[29] To overcome some of these challenges, I rely on stories that have played a prominent role in my daily conversations with my family.

Asylum as a Promise: The International and Domestic Refugee System

The desire to protect civilians fleeing violence began in the early 1900s. To some, the origin of refugee law starts with Fridtjof Nansen and his appointment as the High Commissioner for Russian Refugees of the League of Nations.[30] The Western drive to ensure protection of those fleeing violence became even more acute as a result of the Second World War, and the ensuing mass exodus caused by the extreme violence of the Nazis.[31] Based on the experiences of Europe at this time, the United Nations commenced the task of drafting an international convention that would enshrine the protection of refugees. In 1947, the Commission of Human Rights, tasked with drafting the Universal Declaration of Human Rights (UDHR), "adopted a Resolution by which it expressed the wish that 'early consideration be given by the United Nations to the legal status of persons who do not enjoy the protection of any government.'"[32] Such initiatives would lead to the Refugee Convention in 1951, followed by the 1967 Protocol Relating to the Status of Refugees.[33]

The Refugee Convention is perceived as a highly successful international treaty with 146 member states.[34] It was grounded in the language of Article 14 of the UDHR, recognizing the right to claim asylum.[35] The universalism of the convention ensured that those fleeing violence would have a refuge in another nation.[36] The convention created legal obligations on signatories to protect vulnerable peoples fleeing their countries of origin. It ensured that refugees had legal rights wherever they claimed asylum. These legal rights, subject to domestic implementation, are promises of asylum, implicitly providing for health and safety. The universalism of the convention nonetheless enabled the "myth of difference" between European and racialized Third World refugees.[37] The myth of difference coupled with various historical and contextual factors have led to restrictive asylum policies promoted by developed nation states.[38]

The convention defined a refugee as someone fleeing their country of origin with a well-founded fear of persecution based on the enumerated grounds identified earlier. Three foundational principles of non-discrimination, non-penalization, and non-refoulement are central to the convention.[39] Non-discrimination is built into the legal definition of a refugee. The other two principles operate to ensure that those fleeing are not penalized for illegally crossing international borders and they are not sent back to their country of origin to face violence or worse, death.

The convention is a commitment by the international community to protect refugees and provide asylum to those who have a well-founded fear of persecution. The legal protection and rights that ensue are a promise by the international community to a convention refugee. Broadly, it is a promise by the international community to protect those who are fleeing violence from their "home" jurisdictions. This promise, however, cannot be fulfilled if a refugee claimant acted in contravention to the purposes of the convention.[40] The exclusion clause of the convention deems a refugee to be inadmissible in three distinct instances. A refugee may be inadmissible if they are suspected of committing international crimes, if they allegedly committed non-political crimes, or the more nebulous element of conduct contrary to the principles and purposes of the United Nations.[41] The signatory nations to the convention domesticated their international legal obligations[42] and in turn, the Canadian federal government promulgated the Immigration Act in 1976.

Canada played a significant role in drafting the 1951 Convention. A Canadian representative – Leslie Chance – chaired the drafting committee. Yet Canada did not ratify the convention and accompanying protocol until 1969.[43] The convention moreover was not fully implemented domestically until 1976, even though refugees claimed asylum in Canada before this period.[44] Since then, Canadian courts have engaged in a robust interpretation of the convention and the domestic legislation.[45]

While Canada may have played a significant role in the construction of an international promise for refugees, it did not distinguish between immigrants and refugees within its national borders.[46] Historically, Canada's immigration policies, particularly its policies tied to those fleeing their home, can be traced back to Confederation. Jamie Chai Yun Liew and Donald Galloway suggest that after Confederation, European settlers were encouraged to settle while racialized people were excluded.[47] Canada's "open" immigration regime with broad exceptions significantly changed in the early 1900s.[48] During this period, the immigration regime was radically altered from one that was permissive to one that was exclusionary. Only certain classes of people were allowed into the country. Canadian immigration policies centred on economic needs of the fledgling confederacy. From this early articulation, Canada's legislative and regulatory approach to immigration remained static until the 1976 Immigration Act.

The Canadian racial settler state set up a large infrastructure to regulate and process asylum seekers. Following the landmark 1985 *Singh* decision, the Canadian government created the Immigration and Refugee Board (IRB) to process refugee claimants.[49] The IRB is now Canada's largest administrative agency. In 2020, for example, the agency made 25,866 decisions.[50] During the same year, it received over 70,000 refugee claims.[51] It is clear that the IRB plays a strategic role in determining the composition of Canada's population.

Canada is viewed as a welcoming nation. In fact, Canada was awarded the Fridtjof Nansen Medal in 1986 for helping refugees.[52] Canadian critical race theory scholars have illustrated the contrary. From a historical perspective, Black-identified enslaved peoples who came to Canada as refugees were not entitled to the same kind of rights as their European counterparts.[53] More recently, Laura Madokoro has made powerful linkages between Canada's hesitation to adopt the refugee convention to its desire to maintain white supremacy within its settled territories.[54] Historically, there has been remarkable hesitation to change the racial make-up of the Canadian population. In fact, these hesitations are visible in the very nature of the IRB and how it operates. In the next section, I chronicle my own experience of claiming asylum as means to illustrate these hesitations and how they form the "background norms" in creating the grateful refugee.[55]

Claiming Asylum: Becoming Grateful

I was born in a small village forty-five minutes outside of Jaffna town in the Northern Province of Sri Lanka (formerly known as Ceylon). I was nine when my mother and I fled our village of Vilan because of the civil war. The protracted conflict between "Eelam Tamils" in the Northern and Eastern Provinces, and the majority-supported Sinhala Buddhist government based in the southern part of the country would continue years after we had left.[56] The root cause of the conflict is intimately connected to Western colonialism.[57] Once independence was achieved from the British, the Eelam Tamils of Sri Lanka faced harassment, discrimination, and death by those left in charge.[58]

This struggle for power resulted in the daily military shelling of the North and East by the Sri Lankan state. I cannot forget the first bunker that my mother built in front of our house under the mango trees. My mother's father planted the mango trees with care many years before I was born. My memory of free-flowing bullets from the black, grey, and sometimes green helicopters and the loud thud of the shells landing somewhere near our village often returns when I think about our home. The bunker would serve as our refuge from the military combat between the Eelam Tamil insurgents and the Sri Lankan military. The mango trees would provide cover as we ran into the bunker. When the fighting intensified, my mother and I first fled to Colombo, the country's capital. As the repression of political dissent intensified, our family could no longer stay there. We left, travelling through various safe third countries. We landed in Montreal, Quebec, in November 1988. We claimed asylum and settled as convention refugees in Canada, first in Montreal and then later in Toronto, Ontario. I would eventually make my way to the traditional territories of the Three Fires Confederacy in south-western Ontario.[59]

In claiming asylum in Montreal, we followed the processes described earlier. Sometime during the cold winter of 1989, my mother and I travelled by Metro to the newly established IRB. She completed a Personal Information Form (now known as the Basis of Claim Form) using her then-limited English language skills.[60] Within a few weeks, we received acknowledgment of our application and information about the next steps, including details about where to access French class, so we could begin our integration in Quebec. We then waited for our hearing before the board. The hearing took place sometime during the summer months of 1989. Once the board member was satisfied with the credibility of my mother's well-founded fear of persecution based on ethnic and national identity, we were accepted as convention refugees on the same day.[61]

In making the determination of whether we qualified as refugees, the board member relied on the domesticated version of the refugee definition. The member ascertained whether we had a well-founded fear of persecution based on the enumerated grounds. They made a determination about the fear, trauma, and violence that we experienced through a set of objective criteria. The narrative that my mother presented through her Personal Information Form to the IRB member with the help of our lawyer was deemed credible, based on the legislative scheme and the jurisprudential elements.[62] Once the hearing was over, the board member returned with their decision. The member greeted us with a hug and a "welcome to Canada."

Of course, our experience is an anomaly as the refugee determination system is notoriously slow, particularly in more recent times. We were eternally grateful for our newfound home and thrilled at the prospect of starting our lives in Montreal. This is the narrative that I grew up with. This is how I continue to narrate how we arrived and settled within this settler colonial place.

The scholarship on gratitude is complex and rich, paying close attention to both psychological and social aspects of this emotion.[63] While recent interventions have explored the meaning and scope of gratitude in the migration context,[64] there is some focus on cultural and social aspects as well. As chronicled by Arjun Appadurai, appreciation in South Indian Tamil culture is deeply structured by social class, caste, and religion.[65] Appadurai makes the following astute reflection: if "giving is axiomatically (even if temporarily) the sign of superiority and receiving the sign of inferiority, then it is easy to see that the symbolism of gratitude and the language of hierarchy are closely connected [...]."[66] Gratitude is structured around duties and obligations, and is ultimately based on power. Eelam Tamils share some cultural similarities with South Indian Tamils, especially in how gratitude is constructed.

Reading Appadurai's insights into my own lived experience, the board member's simple gesture of warmth and welcoming words were often deployed in our household to signal our gratitude to the Canadian racial settler state. Of course, we were grateful to the powerful Canadian state for allowing us access to a privileged white space. Power is manifested through the racial settler state's violence against Indigenous peoples, Black people, and other racialized people. It was broadcast daily into our living room through the national media. Importantly, the power of the racial state also manifested in our interactions with our white French neighbours and the broader public infrastructure in the eastern (and conservative) suburbs of Montreal. By giving us this gift of safety, we were locked into a hierarchical relationship with the racial settler state. While culturally, we were predisposed to this type of hierarchical relationship, there are important affective elements that were at play as well.

Our performances of gratitude manifested through our daily efforts to become francophone while we were in Montreal. We showed our gratitude by learning to recite by heart the allegiance to the Queen when we received our citizenship a few years later, even though there was no mention of the original peoples of the land that we lived on. Our gratitude played out as we learned the national anthem in both official languages and became well-meaning "Canadians" who abided by the laws of the sovereign, as we strove to speak English without an accent when we moved to Ontario.[67] We struggled to get an education and gainfully work without staying on social assistance for too long. We understood that we were lucky that we were able to flee to Canada given our middle-class privilege in Sri Lanka. We wanted to become contributing members of Canadian society. In this effort, we made sure that we became friends with white people to illustrate our commitment to integrate. Fleeing from a state with an active terrorist group also necessitated that we create relationships in which white folks can vouch for us. We engaged in the manifold "performances of subordination" that the racial settler state required.[68]

Our gratitude and our efforts, however, did not trigger the "hidden switch" to assimilation.[69] As Dina Nayeri suggests:

> But there were unspoken conditions to our acceptance, and that was the secret we were meant to glean on our own: we had to be grateful. The hate wasn't about being darker, or from elsewhere. It was about being those things and daring to be unaware of it. As refugees, we owed them our previous identity. We had to lay it at their door like an offering, and gleefully deny it to earn our place in this new country. There would be no straddling. No third culture here.[70]

Scholars across disciplines have explored the role of gratitude in the everyday experiences of ordinary people.[71] While gratitude itself is positive, some scholars have nonetheless troubled the deceptively simple nature of the emotion in contested spaces.[72] As I reflect upon the board member's warm words of "welcome to Canada" and the kind gesture of a hug, I cannot ignore the background norms and the affective expectations of the performances of subordination that are built into policies of integration and fidelity to the racial settler state.[73] My own experience of learning French first and then learning all the other subjects in French in primary school through the lens of whiteness is just the starting point.[74] The educational processes in Canada are built on a "master script […]" of whiteness, maleness, and straightness, coupled with the daily microaggressions, overt forms of racism, and homophobia, for example.[75] In this context, I was assiduously socialized in particular ways given my intersecting social markers to perform whiteness.[76] Beneath this expectation of gratitude, other socializing norms work to police and regulate those who are new to Canada. For example, Frantz Fanon and Audre Lorde's exposure to violent racialization on their respective trains signals to the affective elements that structure our daily experiences in white supremacist spaces.[77] Our experiences are not only culturally coded (as I have set out), they can also be located within the broader social context that triggers violent emotional responses and causes racial trauma.

Carbado and Gulati have theorized the various means by which racial identities are policed to ensure that whiteness is sustained within both public and private spheres.[78] In thinking through the various means by which racialized people, in particular African Americans, must navigate their daily existence, Carbado and Gulati suggest that they must adopt various forms of "working identity."[79] Adopting a working identity, similar to Harris's "passing," is a conscious decision that racialized people must make in their daily lives and how they navigate their social relations in the wake of the violence they encounter.[80] Within a professional environment, for example, "acting white" may allow Black employees to navigate their workplace in a seamless manner without challenging the existing racial hierarchy.[81] Taking this American critical race theory insight to the experiences of racialized asylum seekers in Canada opens up another window into our understanding of gratitude. By adopting the successful techniques of assimilation, dropping the accent, and the affinity for spicy (and smelly) food, and by not eating with my hand in my case, the refugee can seamlessly integrate within our respective spaces.[82] We become the grateful refugee, invested in performing whiteness all the while knowing our place within the white supremacist hierarchical structure that sustains the settler colony. Our investment in whiteness is predicated on the desire not to be expelled, a possibility clearly demarcated within the refugee legal framework.

The Refugee Convention includes text that can be deployed to render a refugee claimant inadmissible if their conduct does not fall within the expected boundaries. The convention has carved out instances in which an asylum seeker may be made inadmissible through the application of Article 1F (exclusion clause) of the Refugee Convention. Canadian domestic law has adopted these provisions and the more recent version of the Immigration and Refugee Protection Act includes further grounds on which a refugee claimant may be made inadmissible. These grounds range from security reasons, commission of international crimes or international human rights violations, serious criminality, organized crime, and health reasons, among others.[83] In 2012, for example, former Prime Minister Stephen Harper sought to promulgate legislation that would make it easier to deport permanent residents (e.g., successful refugee claimants) for serious and minor criminal conduct.[84]

There exist central forms of regulation as a result of the convention and its domestic adaptation to make undesirable refugees inadmissible. The undesirability is built around the racial settler state's problematic notions of criminality and health, for example. This legislative framework then works to persistently reinforce existing racial scripts predicated on binaries that refugees must abide by, with accompanying threats of deportation for any violation.[85] Importantly this fear of exclusion is built into the legal system that sets out the promise to provide refugees asylum, based on the expected performance of the "good" refugee. There are various types of examples available within the jurisprudence that illustrate the real-life possibilities of what may happen if a refugee decides to forego the expected gratitude towards the settler colony.[86]

These state-sponsored threats are part of broader legal and non-legal frameworks and structures that are committed to the racial settler colonial project and the ensuing attempts to eliminate and dispossess Indigenous peoples.[87] These legal and non-legal frameworks and structures create the affective elements needed to maintain racial hierarchies necessary for the system to function. In performing the grateful refugee and acting white within the settler colonial space, asylum seekers become implicated and imbricated in the attempted erasure and dispossession of Indigenous peoples. Not only are they implicated through their performance of whiteness in terms of conduct, but refugees also participate in purchasing land, stolen from Indigenous peoples. In the following section, I explore this element further.

Refugee Settler Complicity on Stolen Land: Sitting with Guilt[88]

There are varying descriptions of the different treaties to regulate the relationship between Indigenous peoples and the initial wave of European settlers. These treaties are of course unfulfilled promises. The Truth and Reconciliation Commission of Canada's 2015 report chronicles this violent and exploitative encounter and the ensuing unequal relationship built by public law.[89] The 94 Calls to Action specifically address the role of education in righting the relationship through accurate portrayals of what happened.[90] This is relevant for racialized refugees, especially for our socialization and integration in Canada. Only in June 2021 did the Federal Government amend the Canadian oath of citizenship to recognize "First Nations, Inuit and Métis, and the obligation that all citizens have to uphold the treaties" between Canada and the various Indigenous nations.[91]

Indigenous peoples and European settlers entered into promises that set in motion two legal orders: one for the European settlers and the other for Indigenous peoples.[92] Mohawk scholar Dr. Beverley Jacobs describes it through the metaphor of two distinct ships that travelled parallel to each other in the river of life with their own laws.[93] But these orders did not stay distinct. The European order began to encroach on Indigenous peoples and ultimately exercise sovereign rights over Indigenous lands.[94] This process of expansion started to take a drastic turn where lands and waters were appropriated violently and Indigenous peoples were displaced and forced to assimilate.[95] In concert with these policies of assimilation, the fledgling racial settler state of Canada sought to remove the various Indigenous nations' capacity to deploy international law by working to limit their claims to statehood.[96] These policies further solidified Canada's ability to regulate Indigenous peoples within the national borders.

In an analogous manner, the Refugee Convention and the domestic incorporation of the refugee frameworks operate to erase Indigenous peoples from this process of resettlement that racialized refugees embark on. For example, I was not aware of the multi-jurisdictional legal orders that operate in Canada. I only learned of the multiple legal orders of the diverse Indigenous communities much later in life. Importantly, refugees that do not have my level of privilege are not afforded these types of opportunities and they are susceptible to the racial settler state's myths about the founding of Canada. While the promise of asylum and the processes of assimilation work to solidify the refugees' gratitude, technologies of erasure are simultaneously at work to cover over the presence of Indigenous peoples and the policies of genocide. In what follows I draw from my own lived experiences as means to explore this process of settlement for refugees. I situate my refugee experience in this context, where I confront settler colonialism all the while riddled with guilt.

As settler colonialism continues, we are witnessing its power in the western part of the country with the construction of pipelines. In the eastern region, the Mi'kmaq are facing discriminatory treatment as they continue to harvest lobsters. We know that, throughout Canada, Indigenous children continue to be stolen and placed in the child welfare system. More importantly, we are also witnessing the results of the forced assimilations that took place within the residential schools set up to "kill the Indian in the child."[97] These forced assimilation practices included the murder of Indigenous children, and some of their remains were recently uncovered in and around residential schools across the country.[98]

This process of settlement, conversion, and adaptation of the lands and waters by white settlers at the outset, to the detriment of Indigenous peoples, has enabled the creation of the racial settler state of Canada.[99] This process of creating the Canadian racial state through displacement and settlement was further reinforced by the burgeoning immigration policy of white-only Canada during the early stages of nation building.[100] This policy worked to ensure that racialized cheap labour was available to facilitate the construction of railways and other necessary infrastructure.[101] This reliance on cheap migrant labour continues to this day as more racialized migrant workers arrive to work on the traditional territories of Indigenous peoples in, for example, southwestern Ontario.[102]

As Canadian higher educational institutions move forward in implementing the Calls to Action of the Truth and Reconciliation Commission, I am engaged in challenging conversations as a law professor teaching on the traditional territories of the Three Fires Confederacy. These conversations are spurred on by the "anti-violence work of decolonizing our disciplines, our institutions, our private spaces, and our lives."[103] Arab, Black, East Asian, Latinx, and South Asian communities are confronting the Truth and Reconciliation Commission's Calls to Action in their own ways. As I have suggested elsewhere, there are multiple approaches to dealing with these calls.[104]

One approach focuses on the common experiences of racism that Indigenous peoples and racialized peoples on Turtle Island have encountered, in various iterations. Under this rubric, by centring the experiences of Indigenous peoples and the descendants of enslaved peoples,[105] we can understand the racial Canadian state's violence. This particular framing, though, does not take account what Bonita Lawrence and Enakshi Dua call the uncomfortable truth of the erasure of Indigenous peoples from antiracism practices, theories, and analysis.[106] They powerfully suggest that the impact of colonization on Indigenous peoples is not centred in our antiracism discourse, and in fact this has resulted in a bifurcated set of anti-racist practices.[107] Taking these insights into the space of new arrivants, integration policies similarly point to a decentring of Indigenous peoples.[108] Racialized people, and refugees specifically, continue to benefit from the ongoing settler colonial dispossession of Indigenous peoples and the theft of their lands. Importantly, refugees may be willing participants in this process of genocide. This is a particularly salient, albeit difficult point to grapple with: while the racial settler state may keep its promise of granting safety and asylum (resulting in gratitude), it is at the expense of Indigenous peoples. Racialized refugees in conforming to the demands of the racial settler state are implicated in the ongoing genocide of Indigenous people as they perform whiteness and integrate within Canada.

Another approach may be more complex. Questions about settler complicity are often met with opposition. The argument is that racialized people do not have the same type of complicity in the ongoing genocide of Indigenous peoples. In particular, the homogenizing effects of lumping all racialized peoples into the category of settlers erases the very real lived experiences of the descendants of enslaved peoples who may not bear the same kind of complicity as, for example, "new arrivants."[109] They do not benefit in the same ways, either.[110]

In the context of Indigenous peoples' dispossession, we must bring back the refugees who fled to Canada to claim asylum, relying on the international community's promise of safety. It is often said that refugees fleeing their respective spaces of violence arrive in Canada for a better life, fleeing, for example, immediate "hot violence."[111] This better life is made possible by satisfying the legal requirements of the definition of a refugee. But what is hidden from these conversations and processes is the material reality of the lands that refugees must now settle. The erasure of the Indigenous peoples from this hopeful promissory narrative of flight and refuge then is part of the larger racist myth-making of Canada and the allure of the international promise of safety. Shaista Patel captured these tensions in the following manner: "While we may share some histories, it is critical for us Muslims and other non-Indigenous peoples here to not fall into the trap of equating the struggles of Muslims with that of Indigenous peoples in white settler colonies, where Indigenous peoples who have been living here since time immemorial have now been outnumbered by whites through illegal land grab, dispossession, and outright genocide."[112]

Turning to my own experience and reflecting on Patel's astute claim, I fled war-torn Sri Lanka with my mother in the late 1980s. Given my context, "Does my flight not immunise me from this type of accountability"?[113] This is a complex question and I do not have a fulsome answer. Rather, as I continue to learn about the Anishinaabe and the Three Fires Confederacy in whose territory I am now a guest, it is impossible to ignore the location of our homes that we may have purchased in the region. The University of Windsor, more importantly, is also situated on

Anishinaabe land. In this vein, I cannot ignore the fact that I live, love, and work on lands that were taken from Indigenous peoples. I continue to benefit from this dispossession. This is an unsettling fact that is tremendously difficult to contend with as a racialized refugee settler.

This type of recognition, then, produces a particular form of guilt. For those working on criminal law, the determination of guilt is an essential ingredient in the adjudicatory criminal process. Similarly, within the refugee determination scheme, credibility is an essential component. Yet the guilt that I reference is beyond these conceptualizations. Rather, this type of guilt is tied to the complicity of refugees in the ongoing genocide of Indigenous peoples and our role in its facilitation by becoming well-meaning, white-acting members of the racial state of Canada. Sitting with the guilt of complicity, then, is difficult but necessary.

As a survivor of war, it is challenging for me to contend with the idea that I am now an active participant in Canada's genocidal settlements. Yet I believe that I am in fact complicit. Sitting with this guilt is part of the journey of building a better future that fundamentally acknowledges the histories that connect my experience of escaping conflict to settling on Indigenous territories. Of course, it is undeniable that there are important historical connections between why I was forced to leave my home and settle on the traditional territories of the Indigenous peoples.[114]

The British Empire created the conditions that lead to the Sri Lankan civil war.[115] The very same empire also took control of the territories of Indigenous peoples on Turtle Island. Acknowledging the temporal and jurisdictional histories as forming the background norms helps us understand the various rationales as to why people like me are forced to flee and how we become implicated in the genocidal processes of racial settler states like Canada.[116] In this vein, Third World Approaches to International Law scholars and Indigenous scholars are exploring some of these interrelated historical questions and they are building bridges between their respective communities as a means to overcome the insularity of their fields. In fact, there is a recent concerted effort to build "better relations within our communities, with each other and with the lands, waters and nature that are part of our daily lives."[117] From this perspective, there is a need to question and challenge the expected fidelity and gratitude required of refugees to the racial settler state for the promise and gift of asylum while simultaneously locating and situating the guilt of complicity accompanied with settling on stolen lands. Engaging in this reflexive discourse[118] is part of the necessary unlearning. It paves the way forward for the potential of decolonizing migration.[119]

Conclusion

In this chapter, I have sought to situate the grateful refugee in Canada within a racial settler colonial place. I suggested that grateful refugees are caught between gratitude and guilt as they become accustomed to life in their new homes. I deployed insights from critical race theory to illustrate the demands of gratitude by the settler colonial racial state while simultaneously pointing to the guilt stemming from complicity in the ongoing genocide of Indigenous peoples on Turtle Island. Ultimately, I illustrated the dynamics of gratitude and guilt built into the promise of refuge for which Canada has gained global recognition.

Yet, as I conclude this chapter, there are lingering questions. What are the historical and contemporary jurisdictional connections between refugees fleeing their respective homes and settling on Indigenous lands? Can the disparate experiences of refugees and Indigenous peoples be connected through histories of empire and capital exploitation?[120] Are histories of racial capitalism relevant in describing the experience of refugees in racial settler colonial spaces? Are there possibilities for refugees to build community with, and alongside, Indigenous peoples? Are there decolonial practices that refugees can adopt as they arrive in Canada seeking asylum?[121] These questions must be answered as we move forward in solidarity with marginalized communities. While remaining tethered to my gratitude and guilt in this racial settler colonial place, I look forward to co-conspiring with allies as we engage in fostering new paths built on dignity, respect, trust, and common desires for a better future.

NOTES

1 My understanding of a promise is predicated on my own Judaeo-Christian values. My nuclear family is part of the small Catholic minority community of Eelam Tamils and some members of my family continue to practice a conservative form of Catholicism. I no longer practise this faith. Immigration and Refugee Protection Act, S.C. 2001, c. 27, s. 96; Convention Relating to the Status of Refugees, 28 July 1951, 189 U.N.T.S. 150.

2 For a meaningful description of Turtle Island, see Leanne Betasamosake Simpson, *Dancing on our Turtle's Back: Stories of Nishnaabeg Re-creation, Resurgence and a New Emergence* (Winnipeg: Arbeiter Ring Publishing, 2015), 65–70.

3 Haunani-Kay Trask, "Settlers of Color and 'Immigrant' Hegemony: 'Locals' in Hawai'i," in *Asian Settler Colonialism: From Local Governance to the Habits of Everyday Life in Hawai'i*, ed. Candace Fujikane and Jonathan Y.

Okamura (Honolulu: University of Hawai'i Press, 2008), 45–65, https://doi.org/10.21313/hawaii/9780824830151.003.0001; Patrick Wolfe, *Settler Colonialism and the Transformation of Anthropology: The Politics and Poetics of an Ethnographic Event* (London: Cassell, 1999), 1–6.

4 Nishhza Thiruselvam, "Care Ethics and Narratives of the 'Grateful Refugee' and 'Model Minority': A Postcolonial Feminist Observation of New Zealand in the Wake of the Christchurch Terror Attacks," *Women's Studies Journal* 33, no. 1/2 (2019): 9; Christine Schwöbel-Patel and Deger Ozkaramanli, "The Construction of the 'Grateful' Refugee in Law and Design," *Queen Mary Human Rights Review* 4, no. 1 (2017), 10.

5 Victoria M. Esses, Leah K. Hamilton, Caroline Bennett-AbuAyyash, and Meyer Burstein, "Characteristics of a Welcoming Community," Pathways to Prosperity: Canada (Ottawa: Integration Branch of Citizenship and Immigration Canada, 2010), http://p2pcanada.ca/library/characteristics-of-a-welcoming-community-report/.

6 This type of erasure is not limited to Indigenous peoples. Through various "integration" programs, the Canadian settler state promotes a certain type of citizen. See for example Glynis George, Erwin D. Selimos, and Jane Ku, "Welcoming Initiatives and Immigrant Attachment: The Case of Windsor," *Journal of International Migration and Integration* 18 (2017): 29–45, https://doi.org/10.1007/s12134-015-0463-8; Aryan Karimi, Sandra M. Bucerius, and Sara Thompson, "Gender Identity and Integration: Second-Generation Somali Immigrants Navigating Gender in Canada," *Ethnic and Racial Studies* 42, no. 9 (2019): 1534–53, https://doi.org/10.1080/01419870.2018.1494847.

7 Devon W. Carbado and Mitu Gulati, *Acting White? Rethinking Race in "Post-Racial" America* (New York: Oxford University Press, 2013). For an earlier articulation of this process of "passing," see Cheryl I. Harris, "Whiteness as Property," *Harvard Law Review* 106, no. 8 (June 1993), 1713.

8 Amar Bhatia, "Reflections on Teaching Critical Migration Law in a Settler-Colonial Context (Dispatch)," *Studies in Social Justice* 14, no. 2 (2020): 510.

9 I borrow the idea of the racial state from Barrington Walker and will explore it further in the sections below. See generally, Barrington Walker, "Immigration Policy, Colonization and the Development of White Canada," in *Canada and The Third World: Overlapping Histories*, ed. Karen Dubinsky, Scott Rutherford, and Sean Mills (Toronto: University of Toronto Press, 2016), 38–9.

10 The Canadian Federal Government recently changed the oath of citizenship but the old guide to citizenship continues to be used. See Rhiannon Johnson, "Citizenship Oath Sworn by New Canadians Now Recognizes Indigenous Rights," *CBC*, 29 June 2021, www.cbc.ca/news/indigenous/new-citizenship-oath-ndigenous-rights-1.6080274.

11 For a sophisticated account of affect and racialization, see Frantz Fanon, *Black Skin, White Masks* (New York: Grove Press, 2008). See also Sara

Ahmed, "Collective Feelings: Or, the Impressions Left by Others," *Theory, Culture & Society* 21, no. 2, (2004): 25–42; Eric Shouse, "Feeling, Emotion, Affect," *M/C Journal* 8, no. 6 (2005), https://doi.org/10.5204/mcj.2443.

12 Fanon, *Black Skin, White Masks*; Ghassan Hage, "The Affective Politics of Racial Mis-interpellation," *Theory, Culture & Society* 27, no.7–8 (2010): 112–29.

13 Carbado and Gulati, *Acting White?*, 21–45.

14 Harris, "Whiteness as Property," 1710.

15 Kenji Yoshino, *Covering: The Hidden Assault on Our Civil Rights* (New York: Random House, 2007).

16 Immigration and Refugee Protection Act, S.C. 2001, c. 27, s. 96.

17 Rome Statute of the International Criminal Court, 17 July 1998, 2187 U.N.T.S. 90 arts. 6–8*bis* (entered into force 1 July 2002, in accordance with Article 126, ratification by Canada 7 July 2000).

18 Crimes Against Humanity and War Crimes Act, S.C. 2000, c. 24.

19 S.318, Criminal Code, R.S.C. 1985, c. C-46; Crimes Against Humanity and War Crimes Act, S.C. 2000, c. 24; Fannie Lafontaine, "Canada's Crimes against Humanity and War Crimes Act on Trial: An Analysis of the *Munyaneza* Case," *Journal of International Criminal Justice* 8, no. 1 (March 2010): 269–88, https://doi.org/10.1093/jicj/mqq002.

20 Convention Relating to the Status of Refugees, 28 July 1951, 189 U.N.T.S. 150, art. 1F; Jennifer Bond, Nathan Benson, and Jared Porter, "Guilt by Association: Ezokola's Unfinished Business in Canadian Refugee Law," *Refugee Survey Quarterly* 39, no. 1 (March 2020): 1–25, https://doi .org/10.1093/rsq/hdz019.

21 Various social scientists from varying disciplinary bounds understand white supremacy in a similar manner. For example, critical race feminist scholar, Sunera Thobani, has characterized white supremacy as a master narrative "which takes as its point of departure the essentially law-abiding character of its enterprising nationals, who are presented […] as responsible citizens […]. Having overcome great adversity in founding the nation, these subjects face numerous challenges from outsiders – 'Indians,' immigrants, and refugees – who threaten their collective welfare and prosperity." Sunera Thobani, *Exalted Subjects: Studies in the Making of Race and Nation in Canada* (Toronto: University of Toronto Press, 2007), 4. Philosopher Charles W. Mills has characterized white supremacy as "the most important political system of recent global history – the system of domination by which white people have historically ruled over and, in certain important ways, continue to rule over nonwhite people […]." Charles W. Mills, *The Racial Contract* (Ithaca, NY: Cornell University Press, 1997), 1.

22 Derrick Bell, "The Power of Narrative," *Legal Studies Forum* 23, no. 3 (1999): 315–48.

23 Richard Delgado, Jean Stefancic, and Angela P. Harris, *Critical Race Theory: An Introduction*, 3rd ed. (New York: New York University Press, 2017), 85–6.

24 Bonita Lawrence and Enakshi Dua, "Decolonizing Antiracism," *Social Justice* 32, no. 4 (2005): 120.

25 Sarah Wall, "Easier Said than Done: Writing an Autoethnography," *International Journal of Qualitative Methods* 7, no. 1 (March 2008): 38–53, https://doi.org/10.1177/160940690800700103; Sarah Stahlke Wall, "Toward a Moderate Autoethnography," *International Journal of Qualitative Methods* 15, no. 1 (2016), https://doi.org/10.1177/1609406916674966; Pamela Moss and Kathryn Besio, "Auto-methods in Feminist Geography," *GeoHumanities* 5, no. 2 (2019): 313–25, https://doi.org/10.1080/23735 66X.2019.1654904; Paul Richard Blum, "American Slave Narratives as Autoethnographic Paradigm," *Human Affairs* 31, no. 2 (2021): 236–45, https://doi.org/10.1515/humaff-2021-0019.

26 Ellyn Lyle, *Of Books, Barns, and Boardrooms: Exploring Praxis through Reflexive Inquiry* (Boston: Sense Publishers, 2017); Sujith Xavier and Jeffery G. Hewitt, "Introduction: Decolonizing Law in the Global North and South: Expanding the Circle," in *Decolonizing Law: Indigenous, Third World and Settler Perspectives*, ed. Sujith Xavier, Beverley Jacobs, Valarie Waboose, Jeffery G. Hewitt, and Amar Bhatia (Milton, UK: Taylor & Francis, 2021), 1–14.

27 Bell, "The Power of Narrative"; Delgado, Stefancic, and Harris, *Critical Race Theory*, 44–57; Patricia J. Williams, *The Alchemy of Race and Rights* (Cambridge, MA: Harvard University Press, 1991); Robert A. Williams, "Vampires Anonymous and Critical Race Practice," *Michigan Law Review* 95, no. 4 (1997): 741.

28 Delgado, Stefancic, and Harris, *Critical Race Theory*, 49–50.

29 Nancy A. Combs, *Fact-finding without Facts: The Uncertain Evidentiary Foundations of International Criminal Convictions* (Cambridge: Cambridge University Press, 2010), https://doi.org/10.1017/CBO9780511760259; Alexander Zahar, "The Problem of False Testimony at the International Criminal Tribunal for Rwanda," in *Annotated Leading Cases of International Criminal Tribunals, vol. 25: International Criminal Tribunal for Rwanda, 2006–2007*, ed. André Clip and Göran Sluiter (Cambridge: Intersentia, 2010), 509–22, https://papers.ssrn.com/abstract=1443124.

30 Paul Weis, "The Development of Refugee Law," *Michigan Journal of International Law* 3, no. 1 (1982): 28.

31 Lucy Mayblin, *Asylum after Empire: Colonial Legacies in the Politics of Asylum Seeking* (London: Rowman & Littlefield, 2017); Laura Barnett, "Global Governance and the Evolution of the International Refugee Regime," *International Journal of Refugee Law* 14, nos. 2 and 3 (2002): 243, https://doi.org/10.1093/ijrl/14.2_and_3.238.

32 Paul Weis, ed., *The Refugee Convention,1951: The Travaux préparatoires Analysed, with a Commentary* (New York: Cambridge University Press, 1995), 1.

33 Weis, "The Development of Refugee Law," 28–32; James C. Hathaway, "The Evolution of Refugee Status in International Law: 1920–1950," *International and Comparative Law Quarterly* 33, no. 2 (April 1984): 348–80.

34 The initial 1951 Convention included a geographic and temporal limit that restricted the application of the convention to events that occurred before 1951 in Europe. The 1967 protocol eliminated these restrictions. For more details, see Office of the United Nations High Commissioner for Refugees (UNHCR), "Introductory Note," *Convention and Protocol Relating to the Status of Refugees* (Geneva: UNHCR, 2010), 4, www.unhcr.org/3b66c2aa10.

35 Universal Declaration of Human Rights, G.A. res. 217A (III), UNGAOR, 3rd Sess., Supp. No. 13, U.N. Doc A/810 at 71 art. 14 (1948).

36 Sujith Xavier, "False Western Universalism of Global Governance Theories: Global Constitutionalism, Global Administrative Law, International Criminal Institutions and the Global South" (PhD diss., York University Osgoode Hall Law School, 2015).

37 B.S. Chimni, "The Geopolitics of Refugee Studies: A View from the South", *Journal of Refugee Studies* 11, no. 4 (1998): 350.

38 Mayblin, *Asylum after Empire*, 5.

39 UNHCR, "Introductory Note," 5

40 Suresh v. Canada (Minister of Citizenship and Immigration), 2002 SCC 1, [2002] 1 S.C.R. 3; Pushpanathan v. Canada (Minister of Citizenship and Immigration), [1998] 1 S.C.R. 982.

41 A good example of this element is Pushpanathan v. Canada (Minister of Citizenship and Immigration), [1998] 1 S.C.R. 982.

42 Canada is a dualist nation. International treaties must be domesticated via the consent of the Canadian federal parliament. See Philip Saunders et al., *Kindred's International Law, Chiefly as Interpreted and Applied in Canada*, 8th ed. (Toronto: Emond Montgomery, 2019), 149–98; for an in-depth discussion of Canada's approach to implementing international obligations, see Nevsun Resources Ltd. v. Araya, 2020 SCC 5, [2020] 1 S.C.R. 166.

43 "As Hathaway documents, this was because 'the Department of Citizenship and Immigration was of the view that the Convention was inconsistent with Canadian interests both because its definition [of refugee] was conceptually open-ended and because the duty to avoid the return of refugees might inhibit Canada's ability to turn away undesirable immigrants.'" Jamie Chai Yun Liew and Donald Galloway, *Immigration Law*, 2nd ed. (Toronto: Irwin Law, 2015), 23.

44 Laura Madokoro, "A Decade of Change: Refugee Movements from the Global South and the Transformation of Canada's Immigration

Framework," in *Canada and the Third World: Overlapping Histories*, ed. Karen Dubinsky, Sean Mills, and Scott Rutherford (Toronto: University of Toronto Press, 2016), 222–7.

45 Singh v. Minister of Employment and Immigration, [1985] 1 S.C.R. 177.

46 Liew and Galloway, *Immigration Law*, 22.

47 Liew and Galloway, *Immigration Law*, 15.

48 Liew and Galloway, *Immigration Law*, 16.

49 Singh v. Minister of Employment and Immigration, [1985] 1 SCR 177.

50 "Refugee Protection Claims (New System) by Country of Alleged Persecution – 2020," Immigration and Refugee Board of Canada, last modified 1 September 2023, https://irb.gc.ca/en/statistics/protection /Pages/RPDStat2020.aspx.

51 "Refugee Protection Claims."

52 Reuters, "U.N. Awards Medal to Canada for Its Contributions to Cause of Refugees," *Los Angeles Times*, 7 October 1986, www.latimes.com/archives /la-xpm-1986-10-07-mn-5066-story.html.

53 Barrington Walker, *Race on Trial: Black Defendants in Ontario's Criminal Courts, 1858–1958* (Toronto: University of Toronto Press, 2010); Marlene Epp, *Refugees in Canada: A Brief History* (Ottawa: Canadian Historical Association, 2017), 5. Canada continues to be celebrated for adopting a welcoming position, notwithstanding the ongoing delays in processing refugee claims, illegal prolonged detentions, and deportations. For a recent assessment, see Patti Tamara Lenard, "How Exceptional? Welcoming Refugees the Canadian Way," *American Review of Canadian Studies* 51, no. 1 (2021): 78–94, https://doi.org/10.1080/02722011.2021.1874230.

54 Madokoro, "A Decade of Change," 222.

55 David Kennedy, "Challenging Expert Rule: The Politics of Global Governance," *Sydney Law Review* 27, no. 1 (2005): 6–8.

56 I use Eelam Tamils as a means to distinguish between South Indian Tamils. The use of the signifier "Eelam" is contested and challenged by the racist Sri Lankan Buddhist nationalist state.

57 Sujith Xavier, Adrian A. Smith, and Amar Bhatia, "Indebted Impunity and Violence in a Lesser State: Ethno-racial Capitalism in Sri Lanka," *Journal of International Economic Law* 25, no. 2 (June 2022): 277–93.

58 Nira Wickramasinghe, *Sri Lanka in the Modern Age: A History* (New York: Oxford University Press, 2015).

59 Sujith Xavier, "Loving, Working, and Living on Stolen Land: People of Colour, Settler Colonialism & White Supremacy," *reconciliationsyllabus* (blog), 8 December 2018, https://scholar.uwindsor.ca/lawpub/95.

60 Bill C-55 came into force in January 1989. "The Immigration and Refugee Board of Canada Celebrates 30 Years," *Immigration and Refugee Board of Canada*, modified 22 May 2019, https://irb-cisr.gc.ca/en/stay-connected

/Pages/30-years-irb.aspx; Immigration Act, 1988 Amendment, R.S.C. 1985, c. I-2, ss 59–76.

61 This account is based on years of conversation with my mother about our experiences of claiming asylum. I was twelve years old when we were accepted as refugees.

62 This assessment would later be set out in 1993 in Canada (Attorney General) v. Ward, [1993] 2 S.C.R. 689.

63 Adam B. Cohen, "On Gratitude," *Social Justice Research* 19, no. 2 (June 2006): 254–76, https://doi.org/10.1007/s11211-006-0005-9.

64 Pauline Gardiner Barber, "'Grateful' Subjects: Class and Capital at the Border in Philippine–Canada Migration," *Dialectical Anthropology* 37, no. 3–4 (December 2013): 383–400, https://doi.org/10.1007/s10624-013-9321 -2; Shiva Nourpanah, "The Construction of Gratitude in the Workplace: Temporary Foreign Workers Employed in Health Care," *International Migration* 59, no. 2 (April 2021): 57–71, https://doi.org/10.1111 /imig.12769.

65 Arjun Appadurai, "Gratitude as a Social Mode in South India," *Ethos* 13, no. 3 (Fall 1985): 237, https://doi.org/10.1525/eth.1985.13.3.02a00020.

66 Appadurai, "Gratitude as a Social Mode," 237.

67 There is wealth of social science scholarship that has examined acculturation of refugees in Canada. See, for example, Katharine M. Donato and Elizabeth Ferris's reflections: "In an updated assessment of refugee integration, Wilkinson and Garcea (2017) analysed data from two large Canadian surveys and found that refugees and Canadian-born natives differed in economic outcomes, although after 10 years, these differences disappeared. Before then, however, refugees experienced higher unemployment and underemployment, they received lower income, and they were more likely to receive social benefits. The two key obstacles affecting how quickly refugees achieved economic parity with Canadian natives were language competency and whether education was completed in Canada. After 10 years, however, most refugees' earnings had improved and supported a middle-class lifestyle." Katharine M. Donato and Elizabeth Ferris, "Refugee Integration in Canada, Europe, and the United States: Perspectives from Research," *The Annals of the American Academy of Political and Social Science* 690, no. 1 (July 2020): 17, https://doi .org/10.1177/0002716220943169.

68 Barber, "'Grateful' Subjects," 391.

69 Dina Nayeri, "The Ungrateful Refugee: 'We Have No Debt to Repay,'" *The Guardian*, 4 April 2017, www.theguardian.com/world/2017/apr/04 /dina-nayeri-ungrateful-refugee.

70 Nayeri, "The Ungrateful Refugee."

71 Cohen, "On Gratitude"; Appadurai, "Gratitude as a Social Mode."

72 Barber, "'Grateful' Subjects"; Nourpanah, "The Construction of Gratitude."

73 George, Selimos, and Ku, "Welcoming Initiatives and Immigrant Attachment"; Matthew Wright and Irene Bloemraad, "Is There a Trade-Off between Multiculturalism and Socio-political Integration? Policy Regimes and Immigrant Incorporation in Comparative Perspective," *Perspectives on Politics* 10, no. 1 (March 2012): 77–95, https://doi.org/10.1017/S1537592711004919.

74 Robin Diangelo and Özlem Sensoy, "Leaning in: A Student's Guide to Engaging Constructively with Social Justice Content," *Radical Pedagogy* 11 (January 2014).

75 Gloria Ladson-Billings, "Just What Is Critical Race Theory and What's It Doing in a Nice Field like Education?," in *Foundations of Critical Race Theory in Education*, 2nd. ed., ed. Edward Taylor, David Gillborn, and Gloria Ladson-Billings (New York ; Routledge, 2016), 24–5; Patt Dodds, "Are Hunters of the Function Curriculum Seeking Quarks or Snarks?," *Journal of Teaching in Physical Education* 4, no. 2 (January 1985): 91–9.

76 Patricia Hill Collins, "Reflections on the Outsider Within," *Journal of Career Development* 26, no. 1 (Fall 1999): 85–8, https://doi.org/10.1177/089484539902600107; Kimberle Crenshaw, "Mapping the Margins: Intersectionality, Identity Politics, and Violence against Women of Color," *Stanford Law Review* 43, no. 6 (July 1991): 1241–1300.

77 Shiloh Whitney, "The Affective Forces of Racialization: Affects and Body Schemas in Fanon and Lorde," *Knowledge Cultures* 3, no. 1 (January 2015): 45; Hage, "The Affective Politics of Racial Mis-interpellation," 112.

78 Carbado and Gulati, *Acting White?*, 21–45

79 Carbado and Gulati, *Acting White?*, 10–19, 21–6.

80 Harris, "Whiteness as Property."

81 Carbado and Gulati, *Acting White?*, 35–45.

82 See for example Audmax Inc. v. Ontario Human Rights Tribunal, 2011 ONSC 315, 328 D.L.R. (4th) 506; Margaret Wente, "The Case of the Smelly Lunch," *The Globe and Mail*, 3 February 3 2011, www.theglobeandmail.com/opinion/the-case-of-the-smelly-lunch/article622015/.

83 Immigration and Refugee Protection Act, ss. 35–42.

84 "Conservatives' Bill to Deport 'Foreign' Criminals Goes Too Far," *Toronto Star*, 17 November 2012, www.thestar.com/opinion/editorials/2012/11/17/conservatives_bill_to_deport_foreign_criminals_goes_too_far.html.

85 Lucie E. White, "Subordination, Rhetorical Survival Skills, and Sunday Shoes: Notes on the Hearing of Mrs. G.," in *Feminist Legal Theory*, ed. Katharine T. Bartlett and Roseanne Terese Kennedy (Boulder, CO: Westview Press, 1991), 158–69.

86 For a striking example, see Es-Sayyid v. Canada (Minister of Public Safety & Emergency Preparedness), 2012 FCA 59; Suresh v. Canada (Minister of Citizenship and Immigration), 2002 SCC 1, [2002] 1 S.C.R. 3.

87 John Borrows, "Unextinguished: Rights and the Indian Act," *University of New Brunswick Law Journal* 67 (January 2016): 3–35.

88 Portions of this section are adapted from Sujith Xavier, "Loving, Working, and Living on Stolen Land."

89 Sujith Xavier, "False Western Universalism in Constitutionalism? The 1867 Canadian Constitution and the Legacy of the Residential Schools," in *The Canadian Constitution in Transition*, ed. Paul Daly, Richard Albert, and Vanessa MacDonnell (Toronto: University of Toronto Press, 2019), 270–87.

90 The Truth and Reconciliation Commission of Canada, *Honouring the Truth, Reconciling for the Future: Summary of the Final Report of the Truth and Reconciliation Commission of Canada*, (The Truth and Reconciliation Commission of Canada, 2015), Calls to Action 62–5, 93–4, 289–96, 362, https://publications.gc.ca/collections/collection_2015/trc/IR4-7-2015-eng.pdf.

91 Immigration, Refugees and Citizenship Canada, "Canada's Oath of Citizenship Now Recognizes First Nations, Inuit and Métis Rights," News Release, 21 June 2021, www.canada.ca/en/immigration-refugees-citizenship/news/2021/06/canadas-oath-of-citizenship-now-recognizes-first-nations-inuit-and-metis-rights.html.

92 John Borrows, "Wampum at Niagara: The Royal Proclamation, Canadian Legal History, and Self-Government," in *Aboriginal and Treaty Rights in Canada: Essays on Law, Equity, and Respect for Difference*, ed. Michael Asch (Vancouver: UBC Press, 1999), 155–60.

93 Beverly K. Jacobs, "International Law/the Great Law of Peace," (master of laws thesis, University of Saskatchewan, 2000), 144, https://harvest.usask.ca/handle/10388/etd-07042007-083651; Amar Bhatia, Beverley Jacobs, Jonathan Rudin, Douglas Sanderson, and Mark Waters, "Reconciliation and the Constitution: A Transcript of the Roundtable," *The Supreme Court Law Review: Osgoode's Annual Constitutional Cases Conference* 81 (2017): 277.

94 Irene Watson, *Aboriginal Peoples, Colonialism and International Law: Raw Law* (Milton Park, UK: Routledge, 2015); Wolfe, *Settler Colonialism*.

95 The Truth and Reconciliation Commission of Canada, *Honouring the Truth*, 37–70.

96 Amar Bhatia, "Statehood, Canadian Sovereignty, and the Attempted Domestication of Indigenous Legal Relations," in Xavier, Jacobs, Waboose, Hewitt, and Bhatia, *Decolonizing Law*, 34–59.

97 The Truth and Reconciliation Commission of Canada, *Honouring the Truth*, 129

98 Valarie Waboose, "The Children Have Awakened Canada," *Third World Approaches to International Law Review: Reflections*, 12 August 2021, https://twailr.com/the-children-have-awakened-canada/.

99   Patricia A. Monture, *Thunder in My Soul: A Mohawk Woman Speaks* (Halifax: Fernwood, 1995); Sylvia McAdam and Sujith Xavier, "Truth, Freedom and Solidarity: A Reflection on Solidarity between Indigenous Peoples and Settler Refugees of Colour," *28 Magazine* (forthcoming).

100   Bhatia et al., "Reconciliation and the Constitution," 277; Walker, "Immigration Policy," 285–7.

101   Walker, "Immigration Policy."

102   Adrian A. Smith, "Racialized In Justice: The Legal and Extra-legal Struggles of Migrant Agricultural Workers in Canada," *Windsor Yearbook of Access to Justice* 31, no. 2 (2013): 15–38, https://doi.org/10.22329/wyaj.v31i2.4410; Adrian A. Smith, "The Bunk House Rules: A Materialist Approach to Legal Consciousness in the Context of Migrant Workers' Housing in Ontario," *Osgoode Hall Law Journal* 52, no. 3 (2016): 863–904.

103   Xavier, "Loving, Working, and Living on Stolen Land."

104   Xavier, "Loving, Working, and Living on Stolen Land."

105   Eve Tuck and K. Wayne Yang, "Decolonization Is Not a Metaphor," *Decolonization: Indigeneity, Education & Society* 1, no. 1 (2012): 1–40, https://jps.library.utoronto.ca/index.php/des/article/view/18630.

106   Lawrence and Dua, "Decolonizing Antiracism," 123–4.

107   Lawrence and Dua "Decolonizing Antiracism," 123–4; Amar Bhatia, "We Are All Here to Stay? Indigeneity, Migration, and 'Decolonizing' the Treaty Right to Be Here," *Windsor Yearbook of Access to Justice* 31, no. 2 (2013): 42–7, https://doi.org/10.22329/wyaj.v31i2.4411.

108   Kamau Brathwaite, *The Arrivants: A New World Trilogy* (Oxford: Oxford University Press, 1973).

109   Brathwaite, *The Arrivants.*

110   Allison Guess, Eve Tuck, and Hannah Sultan, "Not Nowhere: Collaborating on Selfsame Land," *Decolonization: Indigeneity, Education & Society* (June 2014), https://decolonization.files.wordpress.com/2014/06/notnowhere-pdf.pdf; Tapji Garba and Sara-Maria Sorentino, "Slavery Is a Metaphor: A Critical Commentary on Eve Tuck and K. Wayne Yang's 'Decolonization Is Not a Metaphor,'" *Antipode* 52, no. 3 (May 2020): 764–82, https://doi.org/10.1111/anti.12615.

111   For reflection on Teju Cole's "hot" and "cold violence," see Noura Erakat and John Reynolds, "We Charge Apartheid? Palestine and the International Criminal Court," *Third World Approaches to International Law Review: Reflections*, 20 April 2021, https://twailr.com/we-charge-apartheid-palestine-and-the-international-criminal-court/.

112   Shaista Patel, "Defining Muslim Feminist Politics through Indigenous Solidarity Activism," *The Feminist Wire*, 1 August 2012, https://thefeministwire.com/2012/08/defining-muslim-feminist-politics-through-indigenous-solidarity-activism/.

113 Xavier, "Loving, Working, and Living on Stolen Land."

114 Xavier, Smith, and Bhatia, "Indebted Impunity and Violence," 277–93.

115 Sujith Xavier, *Reconciliation as Violence: Truth and Justice in Canada and Sri Lanka* (on file with author, in progress).

116 Kennedy, "Challenging Expert Rule"; Sujith Xavier, "Theorising Global Governance Inside Out: A Response to Professor Ladeur," *Transnational Legal Theory* 3, no. 3 (2012): 268–84.

117 Xavier and Hewitt, "Introduction: Decolonizing Law," 3.

118 Xavier and Hewitt, "Introduction: Decolonizing Law," 4–5.

119 E. Tendayi Achiume, "Migration as Decolonization," *Stanford Law Review* 71, no. 6 (June 2019): 1509–74.

120 I am currently pursuing these questions as part of a larger project on reconciliation: Sujith Xavier, "They're talkin' 'bout a reconciliation: Listening to the Whispers in the Chelvanayakam Archives" (on file with author, in progress), https://tamil.digital.utsc.utoronto.ca/node/10674.

121 Shiri Pasternak and Hayden King, *Executive Summary. Land Back: A Yellowhead Institute Red Paper* (Toronto: Yellowhead Institute, 2019) , 68.

PART II

The Weight of a Promise: Material/Immaterial Practices

MONIQUE SCHEER

Social life is built on the circulation of things. Sharing food, giving gifts, trading wares – all these activities involve material objects changing hands between people in relationships. And in these acts, it has been argued, the material objects acquire an additional, immaterial dimension. Relying heavily on Indigenous theory and practice, as mediated through anthropologists, Marcel Mauss called it *hau*, adopting a Maōri term to describe the spirit which imbues the gift, a power obliging its receiver to reciprocate.[1] According to this idea, the immaterial dimension of an object is more than mere symbolic meaning (though it is also that); that is, the transaction does more than stand for the social relationship, it creates and maintains the obligation, commitment, or bond through what Mauss called "spiritual mechanisms."[2] The key model on which he builds his theory is, moreover, the "potlatch," characterized by rivalry, which also fills the exchange that forms the basis of the contract with the energy of competition. Drawing from Chinook, Tlingit, Haida, Kwakwakawakw, and other Indigenous examples, he argued that European society also knew this kind of agonistic gift-giving: "In the same way we vie with one another in our presents of thanks, banquets, and weddings, and in simple invitations. We still feel the need to *revanchieren*, as the Germans say."[3] Following this reasoning, the ties that hold us together as families, communities, and societies have a strong immaterial dimension, but they regularly require materialization – the material practices which forge them – to keep them alive.

It follows, then, that the practices of contractual agreements, of oath-taking and promise-making, which are themselves acts of forging bonds between people (individuals as well as collectivities), would rely on material objects exchanged and/or displayed. There is hardly an example of a promise that is not mediated and buttressed by some form of materiality. Jeffery Hewitt's introductory essay in this volume points to the role that the pipe and wampum played in sealing a sacred promise between Indigenous people and the Crown. In Europe, it is a piece of paper, ritually signed and sealed: the drops of liquid ink on parchment, melted wax, and cord or ribbon form a constellation of materiality in which the solemnity of the promise is made real and irrevocable. The vow to submit to the rules of the religious order and devote one's life to its holy discipline manifests in the shaving off of hair and the donning of special robes, each and every day renewing and maintaining that vow. Marriage is sealed with the trading of rings, outwardly legible as the commitment to each other. And when a promise is revoked, its material marker is also usually removed or destroyed, signifying a release from the bonds of obligation. Even un-promising has a material dimension.

Such practices can also feel threatening, as anyone knows who has received a gift "with strings attached." The Kantian-inspired (certainly now in many quarters everyday) theory of subject-object relations has revolved around disempowering the object, disentangling subjectivity from materiality, and discrediting certain material practices as "fetishization," that is, the improper attribution of power to things. But such obsessive ring-fencing would seem to confirm that very notion: matter itself has a binding, constraining, sometimes overpowering quality, and this it shares with oaths and promises, making them colluders in bondage. The "not-me" objectivity of the material must be reckoned with, and cannot be ignored or elided without considerable effort.

As the chapter by Pooyan Tamimi Arab in the following section shows, this effort lurks behind Spinoza's formulation of an ethics of freedom. Spinoza recounts the story of the promise made to a Japanese shogun by Dutch traders, stipulating that the latter refrain from outward displays of religion on the island. The philosopher approves of the agreement since it dovetails with the interiority and immateriality of Dutch Reformed piety, which he views as desirable in any case. And just as one should not be bound by bodily exercised and outwardly visible religious practices, neither should one be bound by a promise to a foreign potentate, he claims. In one stroke, the philosopher has identified the link between materiality and the promise, while denying them both their moral power over the autonomous subject. Maintaining interiority in religious observance appears to be a practice ground for cultivating distance from a sense of obligation towards certain people. This sort of emotional work is part of the "political, social, and cultural contexts that seem to make promises only to be broken" by the Crown to the Indigenous peoples.[4] Overcoming the binding power of promises requires considerable cultural preconditions and cognitive preparation, such as the formulation and inculcation of an ideology which denies the recipient of the promise equal standing.

The effort required to overcome the moral power of the promise corresponds to its weight. As the chapter by Jennifer Selby on a French-Algerian wedding vividly demonstrates, obligations which ensue from promises can be very burdensome. Marriage ceremonies are in many ways archetypal for the imbrications of materiality and promise-making: they are rich in symbolism and the ritual practice that instantiates the change in social status and publicly forges the bond between the couple. No wonder the wedding vow has served as a prime example for John Austin's definition of the performative utterance, one that does not merely describe the world, but is itself an act which affects the world.[5]

Selby's chapter shows how material culture is also harnessed into navigating the cultural differences between the key players of the ritual. The French-Algerian woman at the centre of the chapter longs to wear a Parisian-style white wedding dress, but commits to wearing a traditional Algerian dress, whose heavy material and cumbersome headdress are redolent of the weight of the multiple obligations she is carrying on her wedding day, with nauseating consequences. This story of the power of the marriage ritual over the supposedly autonomous actors who choose to celebrate it together illustrates the deep entanglement of materiality and subjectivity. Speaking the vow before the community is as much an intentional act of the will as it is a material, bodily practice, mobilizing the muscles of the heart, the flow of blood through the veins, the work of neurons and skin to exert a moral force over the oath-takers. Even if a bride eschews the weight of heavy silk and long, trailing veils, her very speaking the words of commitment activates her body, generating feelings which validate the promise.

It is the same for the audience viewing the couple and the officiant, hearing them speak, rehearsing their words in their own minds, reminding them, perhaps, of their own commitments and feeling them renewed as well. The wedding vow is an example of what William Reddy has called an "emotive," adapting Austin's concept to emotional utterances. Reddy argues that statements about our own feelings are both constative and performative, as they organize thoughts and physical arousals into a meaningful pattern, creating something that was not there before.[6] Arguably, hearing another person's utterance organizes an observer's own thoughts and feelings as well, meaning that emotives act as a bridge between bodies.[7] Ritual is implemented to get all this individual and collective material activity going, and its experience creates the satisfying sense that a commitment has been fully and properly made.

Rather than adopting the view that the binding quality of materiality is a threat to individual autonomy, we can think of it as an enabling factor. Things, spaces, and material practices are part of the infrastructure of the promise, without which it would not be as secure. From this perspective, the power of materiality becomes an asset, can make a promise entangled with objects more potent than one that is not. This conclusion is suggested by Gregory Fewster's chapter in this section, which describes the competition between two forms of contract – a gentleman's word of honour vs. concrete quid pro quo arrangements. In the story of a Canadian museum curator's failed attempt to leverage the (merely) verbal promise of a deceased business partner in a world in which transactions were carefully documented in an elaborate distributional bureaucracy, the materiality of account records and inventories, papers, and signatures, proved more powerful. Is this typical for the modern world, one wonders, or is the power of bureaucratic materializations augmented in the museum context, where so much value is derived from physical objects?

If we think of such objects that are wrangled into the work of sealing promises as agents, as actor-network-theory has encouraged us to do, we might ask whether they can refuse to be effective.[8] Or more precisely, we might be more mindful of the fact that their efficacy is not automatic but dependent on affordances they offer, and bodies habituated to recognizing and using them. An unfamiliar object may not have any power at all. Yaniv Feller explores this possibility in his chapter, which looks at the museum, whose special task it is to present objects to audiences that may be familiar or completely unfamiliar with them. Here the question becomes whether the affective and epistemological effect of these objects on unprepared bodies can be aided by skilful curatorial practices. Focusing on displays of the Torah as the material manifestation of God's covenant with his people, Feller compares two museums and how they each, in different ways, silence aspects of this promise. The museums fail to mediate its full meaning, and Feller concedes that this is true of all curatorial practices. The chapter therefore highlights two aspects of materiality and promise-making in pluralistic settings: it is as much about the promise that the museum makes to visitors (which it can never really fulfil) as it is about the ways that the Torah materializes God's covenant (of which only a part is made legible in the museum). The failure of the museum is indicative of the inability of materiality to fully represent the promise, even as it enables it.

Taken together, the chapters in this section highlight the multifaceted interplay of materiality and immateriality in promise-making. Words, gifts, documents, and feelings are more than mere vehicles of the solemn oath that forges ties, they embody the spirit of the promise in the sense of giving it weight and a binding power. These are essential factors in the struggle for the recognition of promises made and the obligations they imply.

NOTES

1 Marcel Mauss, *The Gift: The Form and Reason for Exchange in Archaic Societies*, trans. W.D. Halls (London: Routledge, 2002), 14–15.
2 Mauss, *The Gift*, 9.
3 Mauss, *The Gift*, 8.
4 See Hewitt, page 22, in this volume.
5 J.L. Austin, *How To Do Things With Words* (Oxford: Oxford University Press, 1962), 6.
6 William M. Reddy, *The Navigation of Feeling: A Framework for the History of Emotions* (Cambridge: Cambridge University Press, 2001), 105.
7 Deborah B. Gould, *Moving Politics: Emotion and ACT UP's Fight Against AIDS* (Chicago: University of Chicago Press, 2009), 38n49.
8 Bruno Latour, *Reassembling the Social: An Introduction to Actor-Network-Theory* (Oxford: Oxford University Press, 2005), 62.

Chapter Four

Making Promises to the Shogun: Spinoza on the Dutch East India Company in Japan

POOYAN TAMIMI ARAB

In his *Theological-Political Treatise*, published in 1670 in Amsterdam, the Early Modern philosopher Benedictus de Spinoza (1632–77) presents the case of Dutch Protestant inward-directed religiosity in Japan as both theologically sound and politically justified. The Tokugawa shogunate's *Sakoku* edicts imposed strict restrictions on entry and exit from Japan and prohibited all forms of Christian worship as a condition for conducting trade on the small island of Dejima, near Nagasaki. Spinoza argues that the Dutch Protestants who lived and worked there exemplify how piety can be maintained without ceremonies or public worship. For him, there is no contradiction between adhering to the shogunate's edicts, engaging in commerce, and living a pious Christian life:

> Indeed, someone who lives in a state where the Christian religion is forbidden is bound to abstain from these ceremonies. But he can still live blessedly. We have an example of this in Japan, where the Christian religion is forbidden, and the Dutch who live there are bound by a command of the East India Company to abstain from all external worship.[1]

Spinoza's reasoning assumes that his target audience is familiar with relations between sovereign nations. This audience included philosophers, theologians from universities and the Dutch Reformed Church, and elite members of the regent class, whose families profited from international commerce.

By invoking the example of Japan, Spinoza seeks to convince them that "all external [forms of] worship" (*omni cultu externo*) are inessential to Christianity. Rituals, which he describes in the *Theological-Political Treatise* as "ceremonies" (*ceremoniae*), are, in his view, instituted for social and political purposes rather than out of pure religious necessity. Although Spinoza often describes Christians critically in other writings – portraying them as ignorant and superstitious[2] or in a state of delirium, that is, emotional and mental confusion[3] – he nevertheless distills from the Bible fundamental religious values that he regards as essential, meaningful, and universally valid. The most important of these is obedience to God, which, according to Spinoza, simply means practicing justice and loving one's neighbor.[4] His plea comes down to saying that all the agitations and conflicts over externalities, squabbles over miracles and particular rituals, have obscured religion's moral core, which is simple and easy to understand for all, and does not require philosophical or scientific knowledge.

This reading of Spinoza's passage in the *Theological-Political Treatise* only scratches the surface of what is at stake when promises are made and agreements are signed. It remains within the framework of his theological-political perspective, which in his time meant deriving political arguments from scripture. But how should Spinoza's reference to the trade relationship with Japan be understood within the broader framework of his philosophy, beyond religious considerations? How does his historically situated perspective on Dutch-Japanese relations follow from his view of human beings as subject to shifting power dynamics and emotions? And what insights about promises, oaths, and international treaties emerge from this conception of human nature? To answer these questions, I situate Spinoza's reference to Dutch presence in Japan within his metaphysics of power and his interest-based understanding of promises, oaths, and international treaties as conditional and non-binding. I also consider the historical context of Dutch commitments to the shogun, exploring how the Dutch approached material and religious boundaries in their dealings with the Tokugawa shogunate – some objects threatening the agreement, others securing it. A material approach, attending to the role of these objects, can offer a critical perspective and help illustrate how Spinoza interpreted Dutch-Japanese relations within his broader philosophical framework.

Although the *Theological-Political Treatise* mentions Japan only twice and seemingly in passing, such references – both in Spinoza's work and in the writings of other Early Modern and Enlightenment philosophers – highlight how the contact zones of international relations, where imperial networks exposed thinkers to both intra- and inter-religious diversity, functioned as "laboratories" for reimagining European political thought.[5] The reference to Japan is politically significant because it aligns with the Dutch ambition to establish what historian Arthur Weststeijn describes as a vast "empire by treaty" in Asia.[6]

By the time Spinoza was writing, Catholic nations such as Portugal had already been expelled from Japan, a process completed in 1641. The Dutch Protestants, having declared their independence from Spanish Catholic rule, were granted permission to trade only after being subordinated to the authority of what the United East India Company (VOC: *Verenigde Oostindische Compagnie*) commander François Caron described as the "powerful kingdom of Japan" (*het machtigh coninckrijke Japan*), which had committed "abominable cruelty against the Roman Christians" (*grouwelijcke wreedtheydt teghen de Roomsche Christenen*).[7] Since the Tokugawa shogunate was too powerful to be subdued militarily, the Dutch had no choice but to accept its terms for commercial exchange. In this context, the Protestant emphasis on inward faith and sober material culture and religion proved advantageous. It provided a justification – despite objections from some Protestant authorities in the Netherlands – for adopting a pragmatic approach to balancing piety with economic gain. The East India Company, evidently embracing this pragmatism, secured exclusive maritime access to Japan, a privilege that provoked derision from other European nations.[8] Well into the nineteenth century, only the Dutch, having agreed to purge Christian symbols, texts, and even gestures from their daily lives in Japan, were permitted to trade in Dejima.[9]

Spinoza's view on making promises to the shogun was rooted in social contract theory, drawing inspiration from Thomas Hobbes's *Leviathan* (first published in 1651). Both philosophers were frequently denounced by church authorities, and Spinoza's *Theological-Political Treatise* was officially banned in the Dutch Republic just four years after its publication. His purely immanent conception of sovereignty shocked contemporaries, including Hobbes himself, who, upon reading the *Theological-Political Treatise*, is said to have exclaimed that he "durst not write so boldly."[10] Like Hobbes, Spinoza envisioned a state whose governance of external religious matters extended across all jurisdictions where its power was exercised. This radical philosophy, in which power and right are one and the same, shaped Spinoza's understanding of agreements – such as those between the Tokugawa shogunate and the East India Company, the de facto main branch of the emerging Dutch state as a "Company-Republic"[11] – as expressions of this unity.

In what follows, I begin by examining the status of promises in Spinoza's metaphysics and politics. I then return to the *Theological-Political*

Treatise's proposal for a universal religion and consider how Spinoza distinguishes this moral core of religion from public worship, which he argues should be regulated by the state. Next, I explore the similarities and differences between Spinoza's religious and political ideals and the development of a distinctively sober Protestant aesthetic in the Dutch Republic during the sixteenth and seventeenth centuries. This so-called Protestant style, with a "semiotic ideology" that privileged interiority – to use anthropologist Webb Keane's concept[12] – shaped what was possible for Dutch merchants as they approached the material boundaries of cultural and religious presence set by Japan.

Promises in Spinoza's Metaphysics and Politics

Spinoza's conceptualization of promises, oaths, and contracts in the *Theological-Political Treatise* extends to international relations in the *Political Treatise*. The arguments in these two works of political philosophy are grounded in Spinoza's metaphysics of immanence, as outlined in the *Ethics* – published posthumously alongside the unfinished *Political Treatise* in 1677. His analysis of the political significance of promises is theoretically consistent with both his naturalist world view and his social contract theory.[13] To fully grasp the reference to Japan in the *Theological-Political Treatise*, it is therefore useful to keep the *Ethics* in mind.

The *Ethics* starts by identifying God with Nature. Spinoza conceives of Nature as infinite, without beginning or end, whereas humanity, by contrast, is finite – a manifestation of that same Nature. From this philosophical foundation, the book leads us through an exploration of human emotions and the question of what is required for people to live freely and in accordance with the dictates of reason. It is within this context that Spinoza discusses promises and deception. In Part IV of the *Ethics*, we read that "A free man always acts honestly, not deceptively."[14] But who is truly free? Although Spinoza explicitly speaks of the "free man" (*homo liber*, which can be interpreted also to mean "free person," but we should consider seventeenth-century gender bias in our interpretation), there is no free will in a determined world. People become freer as their power increases – that is, as they live more in accordance with the dictates of reason. The more this is the case, the less room there is for deception (*dolus malus*).

Being affected by forces in myriad ways, Spinoza sees actual humankind as enslaved by their emotions, with largely inadequate understandings of their surrounding environments. Even in the most ideal circumstances, he suggests, we may succeed in using the power of reason to better regulate our emotions, but never to break free from their influence entirely. And even if we were wise philosophers, all human beings remain at the mercy of others. Under such conditions, deception may at times be justified (we need look no further than the first edition of Spinoza's *Theological-Political Treatise*, which was published anonymously and falsely claimed to have been printed in Hamburg). Concerned with political stability, Spinoza must explain how a promise – potentially formalized into a mutually beneficial contract – is possible at all. How can people, given that they "are necessarily subject to affects, inconstant and changeable," trust one another? The answer follows from Spinoza's conception of the human subject as a product of natural forces:

> No affect can be restrained except by an affect stronger than and contrary to the affect to be restrained, and everyone refrains from doing harm out of timidity regarding a greater harm.[15]

In the *Theological-Political Treatise*, Spinoza similarly describes this emotional process, which both forms and dissolves promises, as a "universal law of human nature": "Between two goods, each person chooses the one he judges to be greater; between two evils, the one which seems to him lesser."[16] Moreover, individuals act within the limits of their power, selecting what is possible in situations that are in constant flux. There is no intrinsic reason to avoid deception or to uphold a promise – only contingent affect-power relations determine whether one does so. As Spinoza puts it: "absolutely no one will stand by his promises [*neminem absque dolo promissurum*] unless he fears a greater evil or hopes for a greater good."[17]

At first glance, it might seem that promises hold no validity for Spinoza. Philosopher Michael Rosenthal formulates this more cautiously, noting that Spinoza "attaches no special status to promises,"[18] despite being influenced by Hobbes's social contract theory, which suggests that humankind can overcome the chaos of the state of nature through cooperation. The Dutch translator of the *Political Treatise*, Karel D'huyvetters, similarly argues that promises do play a role in Spinoza's ethics and political philosophy but that their status is conditional – not absolute.[19] In the *Theological-Political Treatise*, Spinoza argues that people have no reason to abide by promises if circumstances change. He illustrates this point with the example of a robber: according to natural right – that is, by virtue of one's power in a given situation – one may deceive a robber with a false promise. Another example concerns a promise to abstain from eating for twenty days: if fulfilling such a promise proves irrational and contrary to self-preservation, and if breaking it can be done without fear, then one has the right to do so. Like Hobbes, Spinoza suggests that it is virtually impossible – or at least unrealistic – to assume that the fundamental right to self-preservation, which he defines as nothing more than the striving to persevere in one's essence,[20] can be annulled by a social contract.[21]

From these reflections, Spinoza makes a far more consequential political claim – one with direct implications for his treatment of international relations – namely, that "a contract [*pactum*] can have no force except by reason of utility [*ratione utilitatis*]."[22] In other words, political and social bonds do not rest on superior moral imperatives but on mutual interests and changing circumstances. Spinoza emphasizes that people are barely receptive to reason and struggle to pursue long-term goals, which undermines the reliability of their promises. Promises are only effective when reinforced by something that directs behavior in the desired direction. He writes:

> Everyone is drawn by his own pleasure. Most of the time the mind is so filled with greed, love of esteem, envy, anger, etc., that there's no room for reason. That's why, though men may promise with definite signs of an ingenuous intention, and contract to maintain trust, still, no one can be certain of another's good faith unless something else is added to the promise.[23]

This passage does not suggest that trust is impossible. On the contrary, Spinoza argues that trust arises from a complex balance of forces. However, this trust is not absolute: if the balance of forces shifts, it directly affects mutual trust.

Given these fundamental aspects of the human condition – that our actions are determined by how we are affected – Spinoza makes fear of the state, whether the one to which we belong as citizens or a foreign power, central to his account of how promises are upheld. Fear of the sovereign state's ability to punish discourages people from breaking their promises. Ideally, this supreme authority (*summa potestas*) also acquires the right to regulate all external religious matters (*jus circa sacra*)[24] and fosters a democratic religious sensibility among citizens, ensuring social and political stability. This must, however, be achieved without excessive authoritarianism or absolutism, which Spinoza – following Seneca's advice – believed would inevitably lead to a nation's destabilization and possible destruction: "no one has sustained a violent rule for long; moderate ones last."[25] In this way, Spinoza seeks to buttress the possibility of freedom through the necessary authority of the state.

A treaty or promise between nations, therefore, holds only when sovereignty is actively exercised and the safety of those who break the agreement is at risk. In the seventeenth-century Asian context, the young Dutch Republic's East India Company had to contend with powerful entities such as the Mughal Empire and the Tokugawa shogunate. It is against the absence of a sovereign power capable of establishing a Reformed public church that Spinoza's stance on the possibility of an entirely inward Christian piety must be understood – an idea distinct from the *pietas* of Roman antiquity, which also influenced his political thought and encompassed outward forms of worship and material culture (Spinoza regarded such external practices as essential to maintaining a well-ordered democratic society). In contrast to Dutch subservience in Japan, the conquest of Batavia – now Jakarta, the capital of Indonesia – led to efforts at conversion, suppression, and eventual toleration of non-Christians. In his account of religious experiments made possible by Dutch overseas expansion in the second half of the seventeenth century, Weststeijn argues that "occupation and ownership (in other words, legitimate sovereignty) were the essential conditions for establishing a Reformed church order and spreading the Gospel in the colonial world."[26] Spinoza's reflections on Japan align with, or at the very least do not contradict, this general rule, demonstrating that even under conditions of subordination, commercial activity does not preclude inner piety.

For Spinoza, a promise between two individuals could be structurally compared to one between sovereign states. He collapses the distinctions between oaths, covenants, vows, and treaties, analyzing promises and potential deception as products of social and natural mechanisms rather than expressions of free will.[27] The legal philosopher Tilman Altwicker persuasively argues that this does not mean Spinoza completely denies the possibility of international law: states, like individuals, will be "compelled to cooperate with one another" by the same sociological and psychological mechanisms.[28] Even under this more optimistic reading, however, Spinoza's account of promises between nations remains grim. He follows the maxim that there is no distinction between the laws of nations and the laws of nature[29] and goes further than Hobbes by asserting that humankind can never leave the state of Nature – with a capital N, as this conception of nature is identified with God – nor can a civil order deny natural rights, which are inseparable from power.

As in the *Theological-Political Treatise*, Spinoza's argument about international relations in the *Political Treatise* follows from his metaphysical account of the affects as argued for in the *Ethics*. Promises, oaths, and covenants will persist only as long as the balance of fear and hope continues to favor honesty:

> This alliance remains firmly established so long as the reason for making the alliance – the fear of loss or hope of profit – continues to motivate both parties. But if either Commonwealth loses its hope or fear, it is once again its own master, and the chain by which the Commonwealths were bound to one another is broken of its own accord. So each Commonwealth has a complete right to dissolve the alliance whenever it wants to. It can't be said that it acts deceitfully or treacherously because it rescinds its assurance as soon as the cause of fear or hope is taken away. This condition was the same for each of the contracting parties: whichever one could first be free of fear would be its own master, and would use its freedom as it thought best.
>
> Moreover, no one contracts for the future unless he assumes that certain circumstances will prevail. If these circumstances change, then the nature of the whole situation also changes. That's why each of the allied Commonwealths retains the right to look out for itself, and why each of them strives, as far as it can, to get beyond fear, and hence, to be its own master. That's also why each of them strives to prevent the other from becoming more powerful.
>
> So, if any Commonwealth complains that it has been deceived, it can't condemn the good faith of the allied Commonwealth, but only its own foolishness, because it entrusted its own well-being to another Commonwealth, which was its own master and for which the well-being of its own state is the supreme law.[30]

According to Spinoza, a combination of fear of loss and hope for profit explains the East India Company's willingness to comply with the Tokugawa shogunate's demands. Likewise, the Japanese would not have permitted the Dutch to enter the island of Dejima without expecting some form of benefit or tribute in return. In Spinoza's view, such trading relations are both lucrative and pragmatic – yet ultimately founded on conditional agreements. Each party is likely to renege on its promise should the balance of power shift in its favor or alter in a way that diminishes the agreement's utility. A contract holds validity only insofar as it serves an interest.

Universal Religion and Protestant Style

From the above, it should now be clear that Spinoza's view of promises, grounded in Hobbesian power relations, bears little resemblance to the Protestant conceptions of sincerity that emerged in the sixteenth century.[31] While a free person, in his philosophy, would act sincerely – that is, honestly – this would be solely because they have the power to do so without jeopardizing their own safety. Spinoza's broader views on religion do share certain similarities with the Dutch and Protestant context in which he lived. On closer examination, however, they turn out to be sharply critical of Christian concepts such as sin and moral emotions like indignation and remorse. In contrast to the abundance of seventeenth-century Dutch still life paintings, intended as visual reminders of mortality, Spinoza's ideal is freedom. As he writes, "a free man thinks of nothing less than of death, and his wisdom is a meditation on life, not on death."[32] Moving from Spinoza's philosophy to the Christian historical context to which it responds is, therefore, tricky. One might too easily conflate the two. Yet, if we acknowledge the distinctiveness of Spinoza's thought, we must also consider that the *Theological-Political Treatise* was a political pamphlet, crafted to appeal to learned audiences who were, in all likelihood, more sympathetic to Protestantism than to Catholicism, Judaism, or other religious traditions.

The first time Spinoza refers to the Dutch in Japan, his concern is not to theorize promises or international relations. Rather, he presents an example that reinforces his critique of religious aesthetics and material religion in chapter five, titled *The Reason why ceremonies were instituted, and on faith in historical narratives, for what reason and for whom it is necessary*. The following section will elaborate on this argument and clarify why his views on promises are relevant in this context. Before addressing this connection, however, it is crucial to understand that Spinoza advocates a radical separation between theological content and aesthetic ritual or ceremonial form. His aim is to emancipate individual believers from their social surroundings and to disentangle the very idea of religion from external forms:

> As for the Christian ceremonies, viz., Baptism, the lord's Supper, the festivals, public statements, and whatever others there may be which are and always have been common to all Christianity, if Christ or the Apostles ever instituted these (which so far I do not find to be sufficiently established), they were instituted only as external signs of the universal Church, not as things which contribute to blessedness or have any holiness in them.[33]

In downgrading the religious significance of rituals and ceremonies, Spinoza locates the essence of Christianity in the inner space of private conviction. In this regard, he goes further than his Dutch and Protestant contemporaries, who rejected the perceived magic of Catholicism yet continued to uphold the intrinsic value of public worship (*de eredienst*).

Spinoza does recognize – just as Luther and Calvin did – that the language and aesthetic forms of rituals shape conceptions of piety and influence how one understands and practices a devout life.[34] By disentangling a universal religious core from particular rituals, Spinoza argues that the latter can and should serve a social function – one that philosophers understand as purely political. Specific rituals, in his view, provide the aesthetic framework that shapes a distinct and cohesive society, characteristics that are essential for good governance. More sharply put, this means that in matters of public worship, politics takes precedence over religion. In Spinoza's framework, public worship does not contribute to citizens' "blessedness" (*beatitudo*). Public worship does, however, serve the worldly and politicals goal of ensuring "the temporal happiness of the body and the peace of the state."[35] Moreover, Spinoza does not advocate a separation of church and state,[36] reinforcing his view that religious practices should be subordinated to political authority.[37] Religion, in other words, is institutionalized for social and political purposes, not because it is inherently necessary in a religious sense.

According to the *Theological-Political Treatise*, religious minorities who do not belong to the majority are comparable to strangers living in solitude – a notion that recalls Spinoza himself, an excommunicated Jew of Portuguese descent. They may or may not participate in the majority's ceremonies, but either way, this does not prevent them from leading ethical and religious lives. Extending this idea from individuals to minority groups, Spinoza invokes the example of the Dutch living in Japan. Their solitude and private religiosity – practiced without the church architecture and public services they had in Holland – did nothing to diminish their capacity to live blessed lives.

In the Dutch context, Spinoza's argument amounted to advocating a balance between Amsterdam's cosmopolitan atmosphere, which accommodated freethinkers, migrants, and refugees of diverse religious backgrounds, and a model of governance that fostered a sense of belonging to the nascent Dutch Republic. He held that collective emotions should be shaped by an official religion (*religio patriae*, literally "the religion of the fatherland"), administered by civil rather than ecclesiastical authorities. Special architecture, commemorative rituals, and public feasts played a crucial role in his analysis, as nothing, in Spinoza's view, could more effectively reach people's hearts and cultivate a shared understanding and sense of purpose.[38] The Dutch Republic in which Spinoza lived and wrote had, in fact, become closely tied to a distinct Protestant aesthetic. Despite his criticism of Christianity and the demagogic use of "superstitions" by religious authorities, these Protestant aesthetics likely aligned more closely

Figure 4.1 Gerrit Berckheyde, *The Interior of the Grote Kerk in Haarlem*, 1673, National Gallery, London, NG1451.

with Spinoza's democratic ideal than what he described as vain and pompous ceremonies, of Muslims and presumably also of the Catholic Church.[39] In any case, this preference would have certainly resonated with many of his readers.

The Protestant aesthetics I refer to are exemplified in Gerrit Berckheyde's painting of the interior of St. Bavo Church in Haarlem, completed three years after the publication of the *Theological-Political Treatise* (Figure 4.1). Although the various elements in the painting may appear profane, they are imbued with religious significance. The white walls and absence of statues, the preacher's austere clothing as he commands the congregation's attention from the pulpit, and even the chandelier (Figure 4.2) serve as recognizable symbols that both reflected and reinforced an ideal Dutch Protestant identity. To this day, such chandeliers are primarily found in Protestant churches.[40] It so happens that such chandeliers were also gifted by the East India Company to Japan as part of their efforts to secure the continuity of their trade agreement. What does this tell us? I would argue that these

Figure 4.2 Gerrit Berckheyde, *Hanging Chandelier*, detail of *The Interior of the Grote Kerk in Haarlem*, 1673, National Gallery, London, NG1451.

objects reveal something about the symbolic possibilities that Protestant styles of material culture and religion enabled. In this sense, they can help illuminate the historical context of Spinoza's argument for a universal religion – one that did not inherently require public worship.

A sceptic might argue that these chandeliers are nothing more than lamps – objects of Dutch material culture without inherent Protestant or religious significance. However, art historian Mia Mochizuki challenges this view, noting that lamps in this style were produced after the Reformation and donated by guilds to Reformed churches following the Iconoclastic Fury (*de Beeldenstorm*).[41] Stripped of medieval iconographic references to Mary, these stylized lamps, with their octopus-shaped arms and spherical ornaments, marked a subtle theological transition: from a Catholic church centred on the altar to an enlightened, Protestant space designed for reading the Word.[42] At the same time, in Amsterdam, similar chandeliers also adorned the seventeenth-century Portuguese Synagogue, which adapted to the prevailing Dutch aesthetic. The fact that the synagogue could incorporate the same object without difficulty suggests that, like white walls or black garments, the lamp was not necessarily an exclusively Protestant symbol. As we will see in the next section, this flexibility proved beneficial in maintaining Dutch-Japanese relations.

Contingent Boundaries of Material Culture and Religion

The second time Spinoza refers to the Dutch in Japan in the *Theological-Political Treatise* is at the end of chapter sixteen, titled *On the Foundations of the Republic; on the natural and civil right of each person; and on the Right of the Supreme Powers*. It is fascinating to see how Spinoza analyses international politics, without hesitation, from a completely areligious and, in that sense, secular perspective. He presents his reasoning as nothing more than an observation of worldly facts. At the same time, he seems intent on convincing readers that relations between states *should not* be determined by religious interests:

> For those who rule as Christian sovereigns do not hesitate, for the sake of their greater security, to conclude treaties with the Turks and Pagans, and to command their subjects, who go to live among them, not to assume a greater freedom in their practices, whether secular or religious, than they have explicitly agreed to or than that state has granted. This is evident from the agreement of the Dutch with the Japanese, which we have previously spoken about.[43]

Although Spinoza believes that the sovereign has the right to regulate, restrict, or even prohibit religious expressions, this does not mean that these passages can be read as an endorsement of the Tokugawa shogunate's policies. After all, the *Theological-Political Treatise* warns that authoritarian and absolutist forms of government are unwise, and seventeenth-century Edo – now Tokyo – bore little resemblance to the cosmopolitan Amsterdam that Spinoza praised. In Altwicker's interpretation of the *Political Treatise*, Spinoza's description of relations between states, shaped by affects and power, can be understood as an Early Modern theory of the psychological and sociological mechanisms that enable the effective force of laws.[44] From this perspective, in which states, like individuals, are driven by passions – "the fear of loss or hope of profit"[45] – it becomes clear why Christian rulers enter into treaties with "Turks" (that is, Muslims) and "Pagans" (that is, the Japanese, whose Tokugawa shogunate had made Buddhism a state religion; only in the nineteenth century would this status be granted to Shinto). It is natural, Spinoza reasons, that the citizens or subjects of Christian states obey the laws of non-Christian rulers when the circumstances require it.

We can better appreciate the extent to which the Dutch were willing to go to secure friendly relations with Japan – and, in turn, better understand the world Spinoza refers to in just a few sentences – by considering the role of material culture and religion. Objects, from buildings and books to artworks and everyday devices, not only reveal the practicalities involved in making promises but also delineate the contingent boundaries of inclusion and exclusion between the parties involved.

Dutch adaptation to Japanese demands began even before their arrival in Dejima. A warning was placed on the masts of Dutch ships, strictly forbidding the transport of Bibles or participation in any external forms of worship – no matter how mundane, such as praying before and after a meal – deeming them dangerous in Japan. The East India Company advised its personnel to endure these restrictions and to serve God only in their "sacred inner thoughts" (*ondertusschen betrachte een ijder met heijlige innerlijcke gedachten sijnen Godt te dienen*).[46] The Dutch position as "Others" in seventeenth-century Japan was precarious. Those who survived the treacherous journey at sea still had to navigate the delicate politics of avoiding offense to Japanese authorities. As Mochizuki describes, their operations proceeded with extreme caution:

> The Dutch went to great pains to obliterate or hide any signs of their religion that could even vaguely be interpreted as openly serving a Christian god. When a warehouse was built in Hirado with the inscription "Anno Domini 1640" above the doorway, its reference to Christ seemed provocative to the Japanese, so Caron, the current Dutch governor of the trading post on Deshima,[47] agreed to raze the whole offending building, thereby securing continued trade access.[48]

A notorious practice of this period was image-stepping (*beeldtrappen*), a ceremony in which Japanese suspected of conversion could demonstrate their rejection of Christianity by stepping on images of Jesus or Mary. The Wereldmuseum Leiden (formerly Museum Volkenkunde) holds one such ghostly stepping plate (Figure 4.3). Dutch-speaking Protestants and others – including the diverse groups employed by the East India Company – would have occasionally participated in these ceremonies, during which the emotions of those tested were closely monitored. Observers believed that a person's "true" feelings could be revealed by subtle physical reactions: discomfort, sweating, or a reddening face. Any sign of hesitation or failure to trample the image properly could lead to accusations of disloyalty. For Japanese subjects, failing to pass the Tokugawa regime's inquisition-like tests of orthodoxy carried the ultimate penalty – death.[49] This practice aligns with what Catherine Evans, in her chapter in this volume, describes as "truth technologies."

Figure 4.3 Fumi-e, Japan, 1661–73, Wereldmuseum Leiden, The Netherlands, RV-2984-5. Photograph by the author.

Mochizuki suggests that, for the Dutch, the practice of stepping on images (*fumi-e* for the object and *e-fumi* for the practice) not only reflected ideals of inner religious experience – consistent with Protestant disregard for external rituals – but also served as a rejection of

Catholicism: an iconoclasm in absentia that reinforced Dutch Reformed identity. However, she provides no direct historical evidence for this interpretation and may be overestimating the significance of the practice. The ritual was designed to provoke "authentic" emotional responses from believers, and in a potentially life-threatening situation, deception may have been a necessary means of self-preservation.[50] Whatever the case, Mochizuki's broader argument finds support in historian Benjamin Schmidt's characterization of the Dutch overseas enterprise as shaped by an "anti-Habsburg model of empire," which aimed to weaken Spanish and Portuguese influence while, where possible, establishing "pious Protestant governance."[51] Mochizuki similarly contends that the economic activities of the East India Company cannot be separated from Protestant ideals and their material expressions, which Weststeijn summarizes as the belief that the pursuit of wealth could be compatible with godliness.[52] When the Dutch razed a building bearing the suspicious inscription "Anno Domini 1640," iconoclasm – symbolic of Dutch independence from Catholic rule – also secured their trading relationship with Japan.

Beyond avoiding overt displays of Christianity, the Dutch success in Japan relied on carefully chosen gifts that piqued the curiosity and admiration of their hosts. The selection of these gifts was itself a complex matter, requiring written and oral communication with both authorities in Japan and Company officials back home. Art historian Theodoor Lunsingh Scheurleer describes this diplomatic challenge as follows:

> For [the East India Company in] Japan, the choice of gifts was a recurring problem. Each year, the chief in command of the Company's business in that empire undertook a court trip to Edo, where he met with the shogun and presented diplomatic gifts [*een "schenkagie"*]. If these were accepted and reciprocated with gifts in return, the Dutch were free to return to the settlement [in Dejima] and had a reasonable chance that business could continue for another year.[53]

Lunsingh Scheurleer meticulously catalogued the extravagant gifts sent to Japan, including a hanging chandelier in the characteristic Dutch style, presented in 1636 (Figure 4.4); a large standing chandelier, gifted in 1640 (Figure 4.5); and a massive bronze lantern, sent in 1643 – all crafted by Joost Gerritszoon (and possibly designed by Johannes Lutma). Other gifts included three large paintings, which appeared to make little impression, and a pair of binoculars that delighted the shogun when he was informed of the gift in advance. As Lunsingh Scheurleer notes, this strategy of diplomatic gifting was common across Asia.[54] Similar chandeliers were gifted in the early seventeenth century to the Ottoman

Figure 4.4 Joost Gerritszoon, Hanging chandelier in copper lantern, ca. 1636, Tōshōgū Mausoleum, Nikkō. Photograph by Theodoor Lunsingh Scheurleer.[56]

sultan and, around the same time as in Japan, to the Mughal emperor during a court trip to Lahore in 1642. In Mughal India, Dutch metalwork was mocked for being made of copper rather than silver or gold, whereas in Japan, the curious elites expressed admiration for the craftsmanship. The hanging chandelier was presented before an audience of

Figure 4.5 Joost Gerritszoon, Standing chandelier, ca. 1640, Tōshōgū Mausoleum, Nikkō. Photograph by Theodoor Lunsingh Scheurleer.[57]

several hundred and meticulously prepared, with instructions in Japanese script ensuring it was suitably arranged for the shogun.

These chandeliers were not perceived by the Dutch as potentially Christian or Protestant objects; had they been, the fear of jeopardizing their trade relations would have deterred them from offering such gifts. Nor did the Japanese interpret them as expressions of Dutch post-Reformation aesthetics. The limited mutual knowledge between the two cultures allowed the chandelier to be regarded primarily as a technical device – a lamp – its stylized form devoid of explicit religious references.[55] Moreover, for the Japanese, Christianity was strongly associated with Catholicism. Even if the chandelier's implicit connection to a Protestant culture had been recognized, it may not have carried the same symbolic threat. Once placed within a sacred Tokugawa space – where they remain to this day – the chandeliers became integrated into a new environment shaped by Japanese political spirituality.

Conclusion

Why would Spinoza – celebrated for his defence of democracy, freedom of inquiry, and expression, and known for his critique of authoritarian regimes as threats to peace and stability – invoke an example from the intolerant Tokugawa shogunate? Even considering Spinoza's metaphysics of power and his realist politics, his use of the Dutch experience in Japan in the *Theological-Political Treatise* remains strikingly uncritical, especially when compared to his portrayal of the Ottomans in the same text as authoritarian and theocratic. In this chapter, I have proposed that Spinoza's reference to Japan functions as a rhetorical device aimed at reassuring Dutch readers that the text's defense of freedom of inquiry (*libertas philosophandi*) did not threaten religious sincerity, commercial interests, or the stability of the state. His argument could even be read as providing justification for the East India Company's approach, framing its compliance with Japanese restrictions as a means of preventing conflict and securing free trade. The promise to the shogun was, in essence, to refrain from introducing alien transcendent powers through material Christianity – ensuring that Christian views, emotions, and practices were not promoted among the Japanese, who regarded these as disloyal and subversive and sought to eradicate such influences through the *e-fumi* ceremony, which tested one's willingness to step on a symbol of the proscribed religion.

Moreover, actual Protestant authorities were, unsurprisingly, less enthusiastic about the Dutch acquiescence to Japanese demands. Between 1653 and 1660, the provincial synod of Utrecht protested against the edict that strictly banned or regulated Christian rituals, denouncing it as a "horrible decree" imposed by "pagan" Japan.[58] The gifts the Dutch presented to non-Christian authorities also drew criticism. Catholic poet Jan Vos, for instance, wrote a scathing poem condemning the production of chandeliers and lanterns for the sho-gun, likening it to selling one's soul to the devil.[59] By the time Spinoza's *Theological-Political Treatise* was published in 1670, Dutch debates on the issue appear to have subsided. However, the treatise's reduction of cer-emonies and public worship to mere political instruments diverged too sharply from authorized religiosity and was swiftly condemned as a book "forged in hell" (*gesmeed in de hel*).[60] Protestant critics warned that a true confessional state could not tolerate the religious errors that Spi-noza sought to include under the banner of freedom of inquiry. Catho-lic critics agreed, and in 1679, the Vatican promptly placed Spinoza's works on its *Index of Forbidden Books*.

That Spinoza's reference should be understood within an interna-tional context – one in which others also mobilized the case for politi-cal arguments applicable to Europe – is evident from John Locke's *An Essay Concerning Toleration*, composed in 1667, three years before the publication of Spinoza's *Theological-Political Treatise* (Japan is not men-tioned in Locke's later *Letter Concerning Toleration*, written after Louis XIV's revocation of the Edict of Nantes in 1685). In contrast to Spinoza, Locke invokes the Tokugawa example to highlight the dangers of entangling religion and politics, warning of the "danger of establishing uniformity." He cites the early seventeenth-century massacres and tor-ture carried out in the name of purging Japan of Christianity, arguing that the political enforcement of religious uniformity would lead to its ultimate conclusion: "the total destruction and extirpation of all dis-senters at once."[61] Locke was equally critical of the conditions securing Dutch presence in Dejima, warning that the suppression of religious expression in Japan was not a model that should ever be imposed in England:

> Nor are the Christians that trade there to this day suffered to discourse, fold their hands, or use any gesture that may show the difference of their religion. If anyone think uniformity in our church ought to be restored though by such a method as this, he will do well to consider how many subjects the king will have left by that time it is done.[62]

In light of such explicit criticisms of Tokugawa policies, Spinoza's engagement with the same example appears strikingly different. Unlike Locke, Spinoza does not condemn Japanese policies. Nor does he seek to justify them within an anti-colonial framework, as Pierre Bayle would a generation later.[63] And unlike the Swiss minister Jean Baptiste Stoupe, who accused the Dutch of prioritizing commerce over faith in *La Religion des Hollandais*, Spinoza does not frame Dutch actions as a mere subordination of religion to political expediency. According to

Stoupe, Spinoza's argument in the *Theological-Political Treatise* aligned with the policies of the Company-Republic, reducing religion to nothing more than a political instrument.[64]

Yet, I believe Spinoza's concern was more profound than his critics acknowledged. He was not simply offering a pragmatic defense of Dutch policies. Instead, he genuinely sought to reconcile the idea of a universal religion with a political philosophy in which right and power were one and the same. There is no reason to doubt that Spinoza, who risked his life by writing his treatise, sincerely held that universal religion consisted of obedience to God in practising justice and love for one's neighbour. However – and this remains a deeply unsettling perspective even today – sovereign power, regardless of this love, can do whatever it is capable of doing. At the very least, this naturalist view serves as a warning about political realities. The Dutch were wise not to provoke what the East India Company's governor, Caron, described as the "powerful kingdom of Japan," for in Spinoza's view, the laws of nature ultimately determine political outcomes: "It is by the supreme right of nature that fish are masters of the water, and that the large ones eat the smaller."[65]

Acknowledgments

I am grateful for the conversations and support of Jo Spaans, Ernst van den Hemel, Mia Mochizuki, Benjamin Schmidt, Daan Kok, Henri Krop, and Piet Steenbakkers, as well as to the Association of the Spinoza House for inviting me to their 2022 annual conference and for publishing a shorter version of this essay in Dutch. I also thank copyeditor Emily Reiner and the editors of this volume for their patience and insightful comments.

NOTES

1 *Theological-Political Treatise (TTP)* V.33–4 in Benedictus de Spinoza, *The Collected Works of Spinoza*, trans. Edwin M. Curley (Princeton, NJ: Princeton University Press, 2016), 2:147.

2 Letter 73, *The* Collected *Works of Spinoza*, 2:467–8.

3 *TTP*, Preface, *The Collected Works of* Spinoza, vol. 2.

4 *TTP* XIII.20–9, *The Collected Works of Spinoza*, 2:261–3.

5 Arthur Weststeijn, "Colonies of Concord: Religious Escapism and Experimentation in Dutch Overseas Expansion, circa 1650–1700," in *Enlightened Religion: From Confessional Churches to Polite Piety in the Dutch Republic*, ed. Joke Spaans and Jetze Touber (Leiden: Brill, 2019), 106.

6 Weststeijn, "Colonies of Concord," 112.

7 François Caron, *Beschrijvinghe van het machtigh coninckrijcke Japan, vervattende den aerdt en eygenschappen van 't landt, manieren der volckeren, als mede hare grouwelijcke wreedtheydt teghen de Roomsche Christenen* (Amsterdam: Joost Hartgens, 1652).

8 Jonathan Israel, *Democratic Enlightenment: Philosophy, Revolution, and Human Rights 1750–1790* (Oxford: Oxford University Press, 2011), 547.

9 See, for example, Adam Clulow, The *Company and the Shogun: The Dutch Encounter with Tokugawa Japan* (New York: Columbia University Press, 2013).

10 Edwin Curley, "'I Durst Not Write So Boldly,' or How to Read Hobbes' Theological-Political Treatise," in *Hobbes e Spinoza, scienza e politica: atti del Convegno Internazionale, Urbino, 14–17 ottobre, 1988*, ed. Daniela Bostrenghi and Emilia Giancotti Boscherini (Naples: Bibliopolis, 1992), 497–593.

11 Arthur Weststeijn, "Empire of Riches: Visions of Dutch Commercial Imperialism, c. 1600–1750," in *The Dutch Empire between Ideas and Practice, 1600–2000*, ed. René Koekkoek, Anne-Isabelle Richard, and Arthur Weststeijn (Cham: Palgrave Macmillan, 2019), 37–66.

12 Webb Keane, *Christian Moderns: Freedom and Fetish in the Mission Encounter* (Berkeley: University of California Press, 2007).

13 Compare with Michael A. Rosenthal, "Two Collective Action Problems in Spinoza's Social Contract Theory," *History of Philosophy Quarterly* 15, no. 4 (October 1998): 389–409.

14 Ethics 4, Proposition 72; for an analysis, see Don Garrett, *Nature and Necessity in Spinoza's Philosophy* (New York: Oxford University Press, 2018), ch. 16.

15 E4P37S2 in Benedictus de Spinoza, *The Collected Works of Spinoza*, trans. Edwin M. Curley (Princeton, NJ: Princeton University Press, 1986), 1:567.

16 *TTP* XVI.15, *The Collected Works of Spinoza*, 2:285.

17 TTP XVI.16, *The Collected Works of Spinoza*, 2:285.

18 Rosenthal, "Two Collective Action Problems," 406n8.

19 Benedictus de Spinoza, *Staatkundige Verhandeling*, trans. Karel D'huyvetters (Amsterdam: Wereldbibliotheek, 2015), 78n57.

20 E3P7.

21 *TTP* XVII.1–3, *The Collected Works of Spinoza*, 2:296.

22 *TTP* XVI.18–20, *The Collected Works of Spinoza*, 2:285–6.

23 *TTP* XVI.22–23, *The Collected Works of Spinoza*, 2:286.

24 *TTP* XIX, *The Collected Works of Spinoza*, 2:332; for an analysis, see Atsuko Fukuoka, *The Sovereign and the Prophets: Spinoza on Grotian and Hobbesian Biblical Argumentation* (Leiden: Brill, 2018), ch. 4.

25 *TTP* V.22, *The Collected Works of Spinoza*, 2:144.

26 Weststeijn, "Colonies of Concord," 110.

27 Also see Jeremy Webber's analysis of these distinctions in this volume.

28 Tilmann Altwicker, "The International Legal Argument in Spinoza," in *System, Order, and International Law: The Early History of International Legal Thought from Machiavelli to Hegel*, ed. Stefan Kadelbach, Thomas Kleinlein, and David Roth-Isigkeit (Oxford: Oxford University Press, 2017), 183–98 (quote is from the abstract).

29 Letter 50, *The Collected Works of Spinoza*, 2:406–7.

30 *TP* III.14, *The Collected Works of Spinoza*, 2:523.

31 Compare with Monique Scheer, *Enthusiasm: Emotional Practices of Conviction in Modern Germany* (Oxford: Oxford University Press, 2020); and with Keane, *Christian Moderns*.

32 E4P67.

33 *TTP* V.32, *The Collected Works of Spinoza*, 2:146–7.

34 Among Protestant theologians in the seventeenth century there existed diverse interpretations of the relation between internal and external faith. For a new study of Early Modern Protestant aesthetics in art and theology, see William A. Dyrness, *The Origins of Protestant Aesthetics in Early Modern Europe: Calvin's Reformation Poetics* (Cambridge: Cambridge University Press, 2019). For a study of the multiple perspectives on the relation between internal faith and scripture, which can only be understood through signs, see Brian Cummings, *The Literary Culture of the Reformation: Grammar and Grace* (Oxford: Oxford University Press, 2002).

35 *TTP* V.2, *The Collected Works of Spinoza*, 2:138.

36 *TTP* XIX, *The Collected Works of Spinoza*, vol. 2.

37 Spinoza's theory of the political function of the human imagination set material boundaries of inclusion to his ideal state. For a discussion of the role of material religion in his philosophy and politics, see Pooyan Tamimi Arab, *Why Do Religious Forms Matter? Reflections on Materialism, Toleration, and Public Reason* (London: Palgrave MacMillan, 2022).

38 For a charitable reading of Spinoza's national religion, see Mogens Lærke, "Spinoza on National Religion," in *Spinoza's Political Treatise: A Critical Guide*, ed. Yitzhak Y. Melamed and Hasana Sharp (Cambridge: Cambridge University Press, 2018), 111–27. Some Spinoza scholars write that in hindsight, Spinoza's political philosophy does not sufficiently protect against authoritarian or even totalitarian solutions, comparable with criticisms voiced against Rousseau's *The Social Contract*, but we could also understand Spinoza's plea as comparable to an early instance of a civil religion which in the liberal and republican tradition should inculcate a "sense of justice," to use Rawls's phrase, in people who are no longer mere subjects of the sovereign but citizens who need to agree on the basic structure of their political institutions.

39 *TTP*, Preface.9, *The Collected Works of Spinoza*, 2:68.

40 Catholic churches' chandeliers looked different, in the form of a wheel with candles on the circumference, or with three chains in the case of the sanctuary lamp. Christian exceptions are from later periods, for example when a Protestant church came into Catholic hands after the French Revolution.

41 Mia M. Mochizuki, "Deciphering the Dutch in Deshima," in *Boundaries and Their Meanings in the History of the Netherlands*, ed. Benjamin J. Kaplan, Marybeth Carlson, and Laura Cruz (Leiden: Brill, 2009), 63–94.

42 On street lighting in Spinoza's time, see Craig Koslofsky, *Evening's Empire: A History of the Night in Early Modern Europe* (Cambridge: Cambridge University Press, 2013); on the symbolic status of lit candles during the Reformation, see Joke Spaans, "Faces of the Reformation," *Church History and Religious Culture* 97, no. 3/4 (2017): 408–51.

43 *TTP* XVI.67, *The Collected Works of Spinoza*, 2:295–6.

44 Tilmann Altwicker, "Spinoza's Theory of International Relations," in *Naturalism and Democracy: A Commentary on Spinoza's "Political Treatise" in the Context of His System*, ed. Wolfgang Bartuschat, Stephan Kirste, and Manfred Walther, trans. James Fontini (Leiden and Boston: Brill, 2019), 57–67; Altwicker, "The International Legal Argument in Spinoza," 183–98.

45 *TP* III.14, *The Collected Works of Spinoza*, 2:523.

46 Quoted in Caspar A.L. van Troostenburg de Bruijn, *De Hervormde Kerk in Nederlandsch Oost-Indië onder de Oost-Indische Compagnie (1602–1795)* (Arnhem: Tjeenk, 1884), 579–80.

47 "Deshima" is a Dutch-influenced transcription of "Dejima," which follows modern Hepburn romanization.

48 Mia M. Mochizuki, *The Netherlandish Image after Iconoclasm, 1566–1672: Material Religion in the Dutch Golden Age* (New York: Ashgate, 2008), 319; see also Mochizuki, "Deciphering the Dutch in Deshima."

49 Xavier Guillaume, "Misdirected Understandings: Narrative Matrices in Japanese Politics of Alterity toward the West," *Japanstudien: Jahrbuch des Deutschen Instituts für Japanstudien* 15, no. 1 (2004): 96–7.

50 The *e-fumi* ritual's presuppositions about how religious emotions work can be fruitfully compared to Protestant ideals of sincerity. See Scheer, *Enthusiasm*, Ch. 4.

51 Benjamin Schmidt, "Hyper-Imperialism: The Dutch Vision of Empire and the Expansion of the European World," in Koekkoek, Richard, and Weststeijn, *The Dutch Empire*, 73–4.

52 Weststeijn, "Empire of Riches."

53 My translation. From Theodoor H. Lunsingh Scheurleer, "Koperen kronen en waskaarsen voor Japan," *Oud Holland* 93, no. 2 (1979): 69.

54 For a broader account of Dutch art and the gift in the seventeenth century, see Michael Zell, *Rembrandt, Vermeer, and the Gift in Seventeenth-Century Dutch Art* (Amsterdam: Amsterdam University Press, 2021).

55 Compare with Mochizuki, "Deciphering the Dutch in Deshima."

56 Lunsingh Scheurleer, "Koperen kronen en waskaarsen voor Japan," 71.

57 Lunsingh Scheurleer, "Koperen kronen en waskaarsen voor Japan," 72.

58 Jan A.B. Jongeneel, *Utrecht University: 375 Years Mission Studies, Mission Activities, and Overseas Ministries* (Frankfurt: Peter Lang, 2012), 21. Also see Acta classis Utrecht 9–10 August 1653, Utrechts Archief, T 24-1, inv. nr. 3, 312–14.

59 Lunsingh Scheurleer, "Koperen kronen en waskaarsen voor Japan," 93.

60 Steven M. Nadler, *A Book Forged in Hell: Spinoza's Scandalous Treatise and the Birth of the Secular Age* (Princeton, NJ: Princeton University Press, 2011).

61 John Locke, *A Letter Concerning Toleration and Other Writings*, ed. and introd. Mark Goldie (Indianapolis: Liberty Fund, 2010), 130.

62 Locke, *A Letter Concerning Toleration*, 130.

63 Jonathan Israel, *Enlightenment Contested: Philosophy, Modernity, and the Emancipation of Man, 1670–1752* (Oxford: Oxford University Press, 2006), 595–6.

64 Henri Krop and Pooyan Tamimi Arab, eds., *Spinoza's Theological-Political Treatise (1670–2020). Commemorating A Long-Forgotten Masterpiece* (Basel: MDPI, 2021), 2.

65 *TTP* XVI.2, *The Collected Works of Spinoza*, 2:282.

Chapter Five

Longing and Belonging in France and Algeria: The Promise of Amel's *Chedda*

JENNIFER A. SELBY

This chapter considers how colonial legacies are brokered through relationships and through ritual, with attention to promises made at the time of marriage.[1] It draws from a larger research project that examined the marriage partner preferences and wedding rituals of individuals of Algerian origin who live in a suburb of Paris and in Montreal, Quebec. Here I focus on one interlocutor, Amel, twenty-five, born in northern France.[2] In her telling, following *mektoub* (or that which is willed by God), she marries an Algerian groom, Yacine, twenty-six, in Ghazaouet, Algeria. In five ethnographic vignettes – at her wedding procession in Ghazaouet; at a wedding show; at a meeting with some of her friends outside of Paris; in preparations before the wedding; and in the dress's removal – we will see how longing (or desire), belonging (kinship), intergenerational promises, and coloniality thread through Amel's *chedda* dress.[3]

The forest-green three-piece gold-threaded velvet caftan-style top and golden skirt are traditionally accompanied by a heavy headpiece, gold bracelets on both arms, a half dozen gold rings, and strings of pearls that cover the chest. It is traditionally worn in the province of Tlemcen at the time of marriage. Its materiality, especially its weight, carries gender-specific burdens.[4] In what follows, I suggest that its rituality ignites transnational and intergenerational tensions that reflect complex promises in Amel's "colonial" life. Debates surrounding her wearing of the *chedda* reflect three competing sites: first, with the French state. Amel's desire for an Algerian groom, for whom French

Figure 5.1 Amel's *chedda*, July 2016. Photograph by J.A. Selby.

citizenship is at play, triggers scrutiny of the legitimacy of their union. Second, her self-identity as a racialized, Muslim, and Algerian-origin young woman born in France. And third, as they debate the garment's meaning, the "colonial" situatedness of Amel's family in France and in Algeria tells us about transnational kinship ties. Amel's ritual wishes on her wedding day may bridge two worlds, but they also confirm her sophisticated "coloniality,"[5] a concept that helps to conceptualize Amel's brokering of kinship ties through marriage, and to think about transnational promise-making.

The *chedda* embodies numerous obligations, burdens, and bonds, as Jeremy Webber so elegantly theorizes in his contribution to this volume. While the garment is physically challenging, this chapter aims to quantify the *chedda*'s symbolic weight. Its presence in Amel's wedding festivities in Algeria triggered often disparate familial and personal values about the ritualization of sexuality and "tradition." Despite the risks its symbolism could pose vis-à-vis the French state's scrutiny of Yacine and their transnational union, and despite her wish to feature the stylish white dress first, we will see how Amel ultimately does not disrupt the intergenerational meanings the *chedda* holds.

Downtown Ghazaouet, Algeria, July 2016

It's 10:00 p.m., and the sun has set on a scorching, humid July evening in the coastal Algerian city of Ghazaouet. I'm in the backseat of Amel's older brother Rayan's small rental car. He's leaning out of his open window, his new haircut firmly gelled in place, happily shouting and honking as he drives along dimly lit downtown streets. We are sandwiched amid another dozen cars in Amel's wedding procession. Amel is in the car ahead of us. As the car winds down a hill towards the city centre, Rayan shouts, "Oh! Look!" and the five of us laugh with excitement as another wedding procession zooms towards us. Despite the speeds at which both parties travel, and despite being in the backseat, I can make out the other bride's torso and head, visible through the oncoming car's sunroof. Our headlight beams illuminate her white princess gown and blowing veil, contrasting against the night sky. This bride's posture appears carefree, surely enabled by the white lightweight partial veil. Despite the gaiety of the moment, I think with regret about Amel on her way to celebrate her wedding to Algerian-born Yacine. The sight of this other bride will upset her. How did this oncoming bride negotiate the white princess dress for her procession?

Amel and I have known each other for only seven months, but our friendship had deepened in the past weeks and with the intensity of the past five days at her grandmother's house. We met because of my ethnographic research on the transnational marriage preferences and migratory lives of French and Quebecois Algerians. With her sister and mother busily preparing themselves and Amel's elderly grandmother and aunt for the wedding events and her female cousins largely occupied with their young children, I quickly and appreciatively fell into a maid-of-honour role, helping tie hundreds of wedding favours, washing dishes, organizing jewellery, opining on shoes, and attending to Amel.

The other bride no longer visible, the car turns towards a large two-story rental hall. Amel's extended family and her husband-to-be's female family members continue hooting and honking as they park, stopping when they exit their vehicles and enter the hall. I, too, get out of the backseat and walk towards the bride's car, just ahead of us. I can see that Amel is flustered as she manoeuvres the *chedda*'s weight. For months, her mother, Wafa, had unwaveringly insisted that Amel wear the heavy traditional *chedda* ensemble as the first of her wedding gowns. Amel's wedding preparations uncovered many familial debates and discussions about kinship, proper tradition, decorum, and ritual. One of the most heated of these centred on the *chedda*.

I see Amel carefully shuffle out of the backseat of her cousin's compact car. She closes her eyes as she balances the weight of the *chedda* and its accessories. We make eye contact and in a low sharp voice, Amel asks me, "Did you *see* the other bride? WhatEVER! [*N'importe quoi!*] My mom has no idea. *Seriously.*" She adeptly moves only her eyes and mouth in anger so as not to disturb the weighty cone-shaped layers of her stacked, gold-plated, bejewelled headdress and to keep her heavy neck-covering earrings from swinging. I nod and focus my attention on vigorously fanning her face and neck with the small folded fan I have tucked in my purse. Amel breathes deeply and is careful not to touch the beads of sweat on her face. She sways a bit on the shiny two-inch pearl-coloured heels she wears for the first time. I quietly assure her that her make-up has remained unsmeared.

In the meantime, Amel's younger sister, Hafsa, and Djouer, the hired make-up artist/hairstylist/dress coordinator who had been in the backseat with Amel, go ahead inside the hall to ensure everything is ready for her entrance. Just up from the cars, guests spill out from the main hall, the honking having alerted them to the procession's arrival. An easy chatter fills the night air.

Like generations of women from western Algeria before her, Amel wears a traditional *chedda*. Unlike generations of women in her family before her, she was born in France. A religiously practising X-ray technician who works at a clinic in the La Défense business district just outside Paris, Amel had debated the festivities' dress order with her sister, mother, aunts and grandmother for months before the wedding: first in France as she purchased and was fitted for her white princess gown and six others, and later in her grandmother's house in Algeria in the days before the wedding.[6] Given their cost, Amel rented her *chedda* gown and accessories from Djouer. While she would wear eight gowns in succession that evening, for her, the first gown was the most important: it would be the most photographed, would be in the procession from her grandmother's home, through the city and to the hall, and would be the gown in which the groom, Yacine, and his extended family would first see her. She told me that what started with joking remarks about respecting the *Bled* (Arabic for "home country") by her mother and aunts became caustic as the wedding celebration approached and she had not assured them she would wear it first.[7] Amel had threatened to thwart family pressure and wear her white princess gown no matter their opinion, but her resolve waned in the days before the wedding party.[8]

Why did her maternal family insist on her wearing the *chedda* first? On the surface, Amel's mother is less "traditional" than her daughter, who wears hijab, is careful with her prayers, and, for these reasons and because of her darker complexion, is racialized as Muslim in France more than her mother. With the exception of her more intermittent prayers when she dons a hijab, Wafa wears a long and stylish light brown wig, which, at times, she swings dramatically, and with which she often pairs with loose-fitting, bright pantsuits. Wafa is known for being brash and outspoken, as she alternates between French and Arabic. She loves to debate issues of propriety with her sons and Algerian-born nephews. Divorced, her five children's acceptability and acceptance in her Algerian hometown matters to her. Wafa aims to avoid reinforcing stereotypes of migrants to France, namely of those who return to the *Bled* with suitcases (and sometimes cars and trailers) filled with sought-after household goods and gifts, and also with airs of pretension, judging the practices and habits of those left behind. Her mother Wafa wore a *chedda* first at her own arranged transnational wedding to her father, who is French-born and of Algerian origin, as did her mother and grandmothers before her.

Anticipating the heat of July and seeking markers of sophistication, Amel preferred to wear the white princess dress first, pairing it with a silver-bejewelled crown and an attached white hijab. But she enters the debate in a weak position: *mektoub* (destiny) led her to a practising Muslim, Ghazaouet-born spouse.[9] Like her older brother Rayan, Amel waited until she finished her studies and secured employment and an apartment before considering marriage possibilities. Unlike Rayan, because she holds modest markers of privilege – a French degree, employment, and a rented apartment – traditionally held by men, her willingness to cede to ritual gender expressions was perhaps scrutinized to a greater extent. In agreeing to celebrate the wedding in Ghazaouet, she had thus already implicitly accepted an unstated family contract: the "traditional trappings" of a family-focused Algerian (Sunni) wedding.

Longing and belonging for Amel are blurred. For as long as she can remember, she has spent summer holidays at her maternal grandmother's home in this small seaside city. Coinciding with her non-practising father's departure in her early teens – leaving her mother alone to raise five children – Algerian familial ties and her religious practice took on greater meaning for her. Unlike her three younger siblings, she speaks Arabic fluently with her maternal family. Given Wafa's limited earnings as an office cleaner, Amel saved her teenage retail earnings for plane tickets.

Transnational life has meant that in real ways, Amel lives two lives: summer days in her grandmother's breezy, three-story multi-generational concrete home in western Algeria, and her significantly different life as a single working woman living alone in a small student studio residence outside of Paris. Family life in Ghazaouet revolves around playing with and caring for her younger cousins (whose single mother, Amel's aunt, has a degenerative disease and is bedridden), keeping house, schlepping and hanging clothes to dry on the flat roof's clothesline, and preparing and washing up after loud shared meals. It is lively and family focused. In the five days before her wedding, in addition to the four adults and two children who typically live in her grandmother's house, more than twenty additional family members sleep on floor mats and eat together at makeshift white plastic tables set up in the house's cooler lower-level garage. Amel's life outside Paris is also busy, but there her days are filled by two paid jobs, shopping, and attending movies with her friends, traveling by subway, and eating ready-made meals in the evenings alone in her studio apartment.

Admittedly, as we stand about to enter the wedding hall, I, too, am nervous. While I feel like I know him a little bit from a few stories Amel has shared and while we corresponded electronically when he helped me secure my visitor's visa to Algeria, tonight I will actually interact with Yacine and see with whom Amel will begin married life. Amel met Yacine during an annual summer visit two years ago, after her maternal grandmother had moved the three-generational household next door to his parents' home. By all accounts, he's a very suitable marriage candidate. Amel appreciates that he is at ease in familial environs like her grandmother's home. Importantly, he is open to migrating to her Parisian suburb, a move understood in the match. He has completed some university education in the nearby city of Tlemcen and speaks some French. Yacine's family is well-to-do by Ghazaouet standards, but it's clear that his potential euro earnings and the remittances he will send home mean class mobility for him and his family.

The fan now back in my purse, I catch Amel's eye and see that she's already ably concealed her anger and exhaustion. She starts walking towards the entrance. Her pace quickens as she walks up the steps. Amid the *youyous* (a celebratory staccato-like shouting of "you") of female guests and clapping of men and children who stand on each side as though to make an entrance aisle, she makes her way to a double throne at the back of the hall. Djouer follows a few steps behind, catching up to support her as she sits, checking the headdress before more photographs are taken.

Twenty minutes pass. Amel greets guests who approach her at the throne, posing in her *chedda*. Suddenly gunshots and music announcing Yacine's arrival by single horse are heard in the distance. Amel carefully rises back onto her heels to meet him at the doorway. The party is about to begin. For the first time that day, Amel's face relaxes. She smiles.[10]

The *Salon du mariage orientale,* outside Paris, April 2016

It's a cool and sunny Sunday morning. Buds are blooming and summer weddings are being planned. Excitement fills the air as several dozen women and young children, some pulling their mothers' arms expectantly, others strapped into strollers, stand in line at a convention centre just outside Paris. With the three-euro entry fee in hand, two young women in stylishly twisted hijabs wearing polished make-up smile from behind a registration table. One stamps attendees' hands, so they can come and go through to the eight-hour event; the other gestures towards heavy black curtains to indicate the entrance to the city of Nanterre's 2016 *Salon du mariage orientale.*[11] The women and children spill into the 1,400-square-metre space, eager to explore the stands organized in a series of U-shaped rows in the back half of the convention centre.

Vendors smile invitingly, many offering sweets and small gifts to draw attention to their wares. A raised catwalk across from the stands is flanked by dark velvet drapes to create a backstage. The far side of the space features two rooms: one designated for prayer [*espace salât*] and the other for free child-minding [*espace enfants*]. Catered halal food options mean many will spend the day at the salon. Loud *rai*-style dance music blasts through two raised speakers at either end of the cat-walk, successfully muffling the low drone of children's cries. Women mingle, and most booths are busy, renting and selling *orientale*-style gowns, Maghrebian-influenced catering options, elaborate gold- and silver-coloured jewellery, make-up products, deals on beauty sessions (for epilation, make-up, henna application), and *neggafa* bridal-assistance services (like what Djouer offers in Ghazaouet). Also popular are wedding party décor and kits for making *dragées* [wedding favours]. I saw advertisements at local interurban train interchanges for weeks announcing the salon and hoped to meet local brides-to-be, including Amel and her work friend, Sara.

The 3:00 p.m. fashion show is the salon's main attraction. Women claim their seats around the stage by draping their jackets hours beforehand. When the early afternoon *dhuhr* prayer finishes, the lights dim and loud dance music begins. Met with a standing ovation and shouts of approval from the crowd, the first models laugh and wave. Most of the audience is standing; many of the women watch the show through their smart phones. Phone cameras flash and videos are shot to share on social media and for future style reference. Scanning the crowd, it appears unlikely that all the women present are brides-to-be. Some attend to spend an afternoon with female family or friends – the child-minding space makes it easy to bring young kids along. Others attend for fun and for inspiration; and still others are brides, who, like Amel, are looking for specific ritual items, whether dresses, jewellery, candles, or favours.

Amel and I find each other after a flurry of text messages. We had met a few months earlier through a mutual friend and had met in person twice beforehand. She arrives after the fashion show begins with Sara, who is also engaged to be married that summer, the daughter of a Tunisian-born mother and French-born father of Tunisian origin. Sara will marry a second-generation young man of Moroccan origin she met at university; they will celebrate their marriage in Nanterre. Both women take many photos. Amel's also looking for two tiaras and backup headscarves to match the dresses she's had made in the north of France, where she grew up. The tailor she's hired is of Algerian origin and familiar with the preferred styles and materials. Amel adds that because he's located outside Île-de-France, he is less expensive, too.

The fashion show features garments tailored to its *"orientale"* theme: bejewelled Moroccan caftans, Kabyle-style colourful gowns, Tunisian *keswas*, other more provocative "orientalized" styles, and *one* Algerian *chedda*. A procession of at least a dozen white wedding gowns receives the most wows and mobile phone attention. For the first time, I hear Amel mention she wants to wear her white princess gown at her wedding first. Sara nods silently while intently photographing one. Before they leave, we stop for some mint tea and sweets. Amel purchases a faux-diamond tiara, which she will wear with her white princess gown in three months. But this is her only purchase. A skilled shopper, Amel notes the better prices at the *marché* in St-Denis, north of Paris.

La Défense Shopping Centre, outside Paris, Late June 2016

I meet Amel after 8:00 p.m. at a café outside a large department store after her evening shift, where she works part-time. It's Ramadan, and her day has been marathon-like: she has fasted since daybreak, through her day job at the radiology clinic, and then at her second job as a cashier. I wait for her at a table inside the La Défense shopping complex west of Paris. Amel waves and smiles broadly as she walks towards me, adjusting the hijab she has just reapplied after her shift.[12] We greet with *la bise* and sit. Amel opens her large purse and finds some Algerian dates – making sure to note that they are from Algeria and *not* Morocco – and sips on a small bottle of milk to break her fast. She then joins me for an iced tea and a boxed chicken sandwich, a meal very different from those we would share with her extended family in the basement of her grandmother's house in Ghazaouet the next month.

Amel began this part-time job when she first moved to Nanterre for studies in radiology.[13] Her original plan had been to quit at the store when she began her full-time position, but with the wedding planned for right after Ramadan, she needed the extra income. Plane tickets, new luggage, make-up, lingerie, dresses, and shoes are expensive. And, she wants to "do it right." Because her family in France lives several hours away by train, most of Amel's social life involves friends made at the store.

She has a lot going on. In addition to these long workdays in the summer heat during Ramadan, Amel tells me she has just started packing up her student housing studio apartment. She applied for and was allocated a one-bedroom social housing apartment in Puteaux, a suburb adjacent to La Défense, where she'll move with the help of work friends in a few days. Having completed her studies, she is no longer eligible for student housing. She and Yacine will live there together when he migrates from Ghazaouet after their wedding. Amel knows that the size of their apartment will impact his post-wedding eligibility for residency.

Amel stops chatting to wave to two department store colleagues, who wave back and walk over to say hello. One wears hijab, but neither has fasted that day. She encourages the women to join us for tea. She introduces me, making sure to point out I had just received a travel visa to attend her wedding. I knew she hoped they would attend, too. With the complication of attaining a visa for non-nationals and the expense of the flights, none of her French friends will travel to Ghazaouet.

Our conversation shifts to Yacine. One of the young women, with long braids and bright black eyes, teases Amel about Yacine's intentions. She laughs, taps Amel's shoulder to emphasize her point, and makes a joke about *blédards* [young men from the *Bled*], implicitly invoking contemporary politics in France that, since the 2000s, have scrutinized non-European Union transnational unions. Amel mostly ignores her friend's judgment, responding lightly that she prefers not to think about the administrative hurdles ahead to secure legal residency in France for Yacine. Indeed, four months before the wedding, in one of our formal interviews, Amel told me, "I don't even want to think about it [the paperwork] for the moment." Because Amel is usually gregarious and expressive, her friends read her tone and don't press further.

Amel pulls out her phone and shifts the conversation by sharing photos of her dresses. The three of us lean in to look at the small screen and oohh and ahhh. They are beautiful, elaborate, long sequined gowns in grey, pink, red, blue, and light blue. The last one is a princess-style white gown with intricate silver beading on the front and a cinching belt.

Amel's colleagues' concerns with Yacine's intentions mirror those of the French state. In both cases, the concerns are highly gendered: women, and not men, are the likely victims of *escroquerie sentimentale à but migratoire* [love fraud, with a migratory aim]. They may be falsely lured into marriage to facilitate papers. At that point, Amel had undertaken almost all ritual negotiation and preparation for his arrival in France; Yacine was physically absent from celebration preparations in France, but also from those in Algeria, even when he was just next door. Moreover, in our brief interactions after the wedding, my impression was that he was unconcerned by how his agency was perceived. Except for his dramatic and physically demanding evening entrance into their marriage celebration – on a bucking white horse wearing a cape surrounded by guests' celebratory *youyous*, fire torches, and gunshots – in both appearance and in conversation, Yacine appeared to be comfortable with the performative nature of their nuptials. On numerous occasions, Amel, however, expressed fatigue with the pressure she felt to be both "traditional" and "French." She and her sister Hafsa's outfits and comportment are closely scrutinized by their mother and aunts. In contrast, her younger brother Victor's "Euro-urban" wedding attire of a black tuxedo with white Converse high-tops was ignored by his mother and aunts.

Amel's "individualism" as a French woman and the "traditionalism" of the match are surveilled by her family, by herself, and by the state.[14] Despite having spent considerable time and money in the last few months purchasing the right products in France, once in Ghazaouet Amel downplays the suitcase of cosmetics, creams, perfume, and jewellery she has brought with her. She wants to be accepted by her female relatives, but I know from having gone shopping with her outside of Paris, she also wants to assert her individuality and present herself as chic.

For now, Amel's young friends seem happy to chat about Amel's wedding dresses as they pass her phone between them. We finish our sandwiches, chat for a few more minutes and then walk down several escalator flights to the interurban trains. Amel must get home to eat again and finish her prayers before waking up and doing it all again tomorrow.

Wedding Day, July 2016

The morning before the *Jour J* ["big day"], Amel's sister Hafsa, Wafa, and I visit Djouer's hair salon to confirm hair, make-up, and accessory choices for the next day. Djouer is a *neggafa*, or bridal assistant.[15] The next day, she will play a significant role in counselling Amel in her beauty choices, ensuring her hair, make-up, and accessories match and that the ensembles translate well for local family and guests. Amel has gone alone to the hammam.

Djouer's presence on the day of the wedding shifts the balance of the *chedda* debate definitively. As a wedding ritual expert, Djouer takes a gentler approach than Wafa, the three aunts, and the grandmother. She quickly grasps that Amel doesn't want to wear the dress and heavy accessories. She coaxes her with compliments and delicately questions the suitability of the princess dress. In Amel's place, I would be convinced by Djouer. Her soothing voice, however, betrays the rigidity with which she polices this tradition. As she dresses Amel and secures the layers of the crown with dozens of bobby pins, Djouer memorably tells her, "*Elle est lourde avec la tradition.*" [It's heavy with tradition.] In the years since, this observation has stayed with me. Djouer stresses that to wear the *chedda* ensemble is to knowingly and publicly bear its weight and to make it look effortless. Amel must keep this intergenerational promise. As a French-born woman with deep emotional and kinship ties to the *Bled*, Amel feels this pressure in a particularly visceral way. Its promises of inclusion are not straightforward for her.

The morning of the wedding party, Amel relaxes on a floor mat in an upstairs bedroom, knowing the long night that awaits. Her mood is melancholic. Without a working mobile phone, I lie down on an adjacent mat and stare up at a light bulb dangling from the ceiling. It is already above 30°C. Several times Amel notes her disappointment with her Algerian family. She says that if she were not from France, her aunts would have prepared her a special lunch, as they had done the previous year for her cousin. In addition, when she realizes she's missing a backup pair of nylons, no one offers to go downtown to get them for her. To add insult to injury, she complains that the downtown hammam she visited the day before was not luxurious. Using tweezers to remove remaining hair from her waxed shins, she notes, "Had I been in Paris, I would have spent the whole day at a beauty institute where everything would have been perfect."

When Djouer arrives in the early afternoon, however, Amel's mood shifts. She showers, eats some fried chicken and potatoes, and feels calmer. I help Djouer bring up several suitcases and make-up boxes from the van her husband drives. Djouer closes the door to the bedroom, removes her headscarf, and sits cross-legged on one of the sleeping mats. Amel opens her own suitcases and shows Djouer her make-up and *combinaisons* [outfits]. Djouer runs her hands over the dresses approvingly. Djouer begins by drawing intricate henna designs on Amel's ankles and wrists. As the design dries, Djouer dries Amel's hair with a *brushing*, pulling the hair straight. With adjacent squealing and slammed doors, she locks the bedroom door to ward off Amel's young nephews, curious about the preparations and looking for leftover sweets from the wedding favour production line a few nights before. We ignore their pleas from the other side of the door. Thankfully, their curiosity wanes. Djouer insists on styling my shorter hair too. We sip water from large, recycled water bottles, but the stillness of the afternoon heat is oppressive under the hot hair dryer.

Djouer does not rest. She opens her large make-up bag, and searches for a specific eyeshadow. Even if gentle in her approach, Djouer engages in little consultation. She doesn't ask about the dress order. She simply dresses Amel with the *chedda*'s layers. The long skirt's elastic waist is easy. Djouer then turns her attention to the matching make-up, then the layered jewellery, and last, the crown. It all goes smoothly until Djouer applies a dark green eyeshadow that matches the *chedda*'s deep green velvet. Amel has a less flashy palette in mind, but Djouer continues applying her choice.

Djouer's role in assuring the *chedda* cannot be discounted. Amel's responses to her mother, aunts, and grandmother calls for tradition are reactive; she sees them as lodged in the past, as backward. As a third party and a professional aware of local trends and fashions, Djouer is a more effective marital ritual expert. As she adds an additional layer of "touching up" foundation, Djouer coaches Amel: "We all found the *chedda*'s weight difficult. You must be focused. You must be strong." These words will be repeated by Djouer that evening and, strikingly, she says them in French, perhaps to translate the point and to rally my support.

Amel expects Yacine's family to arrive to bring her to the hall shortly after 7:00 p.m., and so we finish preparing. Hearing me unlock the door, the young cousins rush over to the see the results. They jump with excitement. Amel enlists the oldest to help her down the wide concrete staircase to the front hall. Her mother and aunts rise from their chairs in the kitchen; their *youyous* and excitement reveal their approval.

But Yacine's family is late. As Amel waits in the 34°C heat, perched on a flat Moroccan-style couch in the living room, nearly *two hours* pass. Her head and neck waiver. Yacine is not responding to her text messages. She is understandably agitated. Amel's brother Victor aims to lighten the mood, cracking jokes about the backward mentality of the *Bled*, urging Amel not to be uptight like French women. Amel looks at him wearily. She does not laugh.

Suddenly, under the weight of the *chedda*, the rising strain of Yacine's text silence and the uninterrupted heat, Amel retches. She manages to miss her new heels, but the pool of vomit threatens to meet the bottom of the dress. As she shudders, everyone else springs into action, anxious to remove all traces before the guests arrived. One aunt kicks off her heels and runs for a mop and bucket while another races to the kitchen, opening lower cabinets to find a can of air freshener, which she begins spraying as she swings her arms so to guide its vanilla odour in all directions. A cousin lifts the bottom of the gown to ensure it remains clean. Like a NASCAR support team, they clean up in moments. All evidence is erased. Fortunately, despite her unexpected heave forward, Amel resisted jerking her head, so her heavy earrings and jewels remain in place. Djouer checks the pins holding the crown and opens up her make-up case to find some pressed powder to blot the sweat on Amel's face. Amel suppresses tears as she sips a fresh glass of water brought by her sister. I pick up a handheld folding fan and focus my energy on vigorously fanning her face and neck.

After the vomit crisis, the mood in the living room is decidedly more subdued. The night sky grows darker and cooler. It seems like only minutes later we hear *youyous*, this time outside the front door. Yacine's aunts and mother have arrived to invite Amel to the ceremony. Amel stands and accepts her brothers' aid in walking outside towards the car. She embraces Yacine's female family members in the entryway. Children squish into vehicles. The procession begins.

Removing the *Chedda*, Ghazaouet Wedding Hall, July 2016

Yacine wears one outfit for their wedding celebration – a slim-fitted black suit with a black tie and pointed black patent shoes. His sole accessory is a broad white cape he wears for his brief theatrical horseback arrival. His black hair is cut short, his beard closely shaven. After receiving a ceremonial glass of milk and being fed some dates by his teary-eyed mother, who knows that their marriage also means the departure of her eldest son, Yacine joins Amel at the throne. They embrace and sit as they are photographed. The evening will be followed by dance performances, a gender-segregated sit-down meal in the hall's lower level, guest dancing, racing children, invited musicians, cake, the distribution of the wedding favours, and more dancing.

Soon after the initial couple photos, and a brief tour to greet guests, Djouer gestures discreetly to Amel to return to the dressing room for the first dress change. Yacine leaves the stage to greet family members. Amel catches my eye, so I walk out from behind the crowd to follow her. The hall's private dressing room has its own air-conditioning gauge, and Djouer has turned it up. The cool air feels divine. Careful to lock the door from the inside, she ushers Amel to sit in front of a wall of mirrors and begins carefully removing the pins holding up the crown. Djouer crouches on the floor to pull off Amel's tight ivory heels, and she and I organize the jewellery into separate bags. The outfit's physical, familial, and symbolic weight is more easily quantified in its many pieces. Once the sections of the crown are removed, Amel sighs. She allows her head to slump forward.

When one of the aunts knocks on the door, asking questions about her evening meal, Amel yells, "Come back in ten minutes!" She laughs a little. Once the remaining garments are removed, without a word, Amel lies down on the cool marble floor, as though to ground herself and cool her whole body. Past and future challenges are momentarily forgotten: Wafa's insistence on the *chedda* worn first, Djouer's complicity, Yacine's upcoming paperwork to secure permanent residency in France, his as-of-yet unknown hurdles in finding paid work, the challenges their marriage will face in France. She closes her eyes for a moment and seems to relax. She's upheld her part in a silent contract. Now, she can share her chosen dresses.

The evening ends as the sun begins to rise and with Amel and Yacine leaving for their two-day honeymoon. As I squish into the backseat of Rayan's car with two aunts and Wafa in the front seat, I find myself wondering whether the other bride we saw on our way to the hall that night wore a *chedda* at all. Perhaps yes. But, perhaps not. While they attend and are aware of other weddings in Ghazaouet, Wafa and Amel's debate about tradition and what it means to be a transnational French bride likely do not reflect the changing range of dresses, styles, rituals, meals, and customs of the region.

Discussion: Ritual and "Coloniality"

I became aware of the marriage partner preferences for "traditional" partners of Algerian origin, like Amel's desire to marry Yacine, when I began conducting doctoral fieldwork in a Parisian suburb in 2004. These preferences are tangled with cosmopolitanism, kinship ties and colonial politics. In light of the problematized public spaces of the *cités* (or housing projects) that house many Muslim French in the suburbs, a prevalent scholarly argument characterizes a taking up of "tradition" at the time of marriage as a religious response to an exclusionary, secular France that, increasingly, demands the relegation of visible religiosity out of the public sphere.[16] This explanation would likely frame Amel's decision to marry a practising so-called traditional Algerian Muslim as a strategy to ensure her acceptability as a Muslim who wears hijab.

But Amel herself does not centralize her hijab in her accounts of marriage. She and many of the other Muslim French youths of Algerian origin I have interviewed both seek *and* constitute traditionalism and the *Bled* at the time of marriage, in which Islam is sometimes referenced and sometimes ignored.[17] By focusing on the *chedda*, I have aimed to develop a different angle. Given how the control of intimacy and sexuality are central to colonial politics, including in French Algeria, I frame her desire for this marriage partner as also evoking and repossessing her kinship ties with the *Bled*. Tradition is not "orthodoxy," but a dynamic group of practices and ideas that provide and secure social bonds.[18] France is home for Amel. But the *Bled* acts as a touchstone that includes, but not always, religion. For many of my interlocutors, the social bond or cohesiveness of tradition is expressed through kinship ties. These desires occur in tandem with and contrary to legislation by the French state since 2006 that aims to control and impede transnational unions.[19]

How should the imagined tension of these desires and relations be framed? Based on France's 132-year occupation (1830–1962), "postcolonial" may seem most apt. The prefix can mark an ongoing aftermath, as Alana Lentin uses it to describe "being worked over by colonialism."[20] Other scholars have argued that the term may falsely relay the notion of a conclusion.[21] Most scholars acknowledge that either/or demarcations (post- or not) are not helpful. Nacira Guénif-Souilamas, for one, insightfully argues that colonial power dynamics in France are "still colonial and already postcolonial."[22] In relation to the vignettes presented here, I would not situate Amel's marriage partner preference and marriage rituals as "anti-colonial" responses that reject French colonial histories of biopower and sexual imperialism.[23] Nor are they "post." The "anti" perspective does not capture the life-affirming element to these transnational commitments to Algeria and the sophisticated awareness of systems of power that make renewed kinship with the *Bled* at the time of marriage sought after. If anything, they centre pleasure and connection. In delineating what he calls "the coloniality of power," Aníbal Quijano notes the power of European colonialisms to shape knowledges and realities long past the end of the colonial era. If the French colonial project in Algeria clearly delineated proper sexuality as part of its civilizing mission, in this context, young people of Algerian origin in France like Amel may partially reclaim that critique through kinship ties at the time of marriage.[24]

Unsurprisingly, Amel never uses iterations of the term "colonial" to describe the longing and belonging invoked by her marriage partner preference for Yacine, their transnational wedding, and its rituals. Yet, as a young cosmopolitan French woman, she sought out a marriage partner who ensured the continuance of her central beliefs. Thus, in aiming to think through how colonial histories and relationships emerge in my interlocutors' description of the *Bled* in their marital lives, and the way these linkages (or promises) materialize on the body and through ritual, coloniality is therefore useful in considering the expressions of desire and relationships of power at stake for many in relation to enduring structures of colonial oppression. Centring relations in this desire helps underscore the *Bled*'s continued presence for young people like Amel, not solely as a desired expression of authentic Islam, but also of kinship and transnationalism.

Conclusions: On a Wedding Dress's Promises

Amel's preference for a white princess gown reflects both practical and idealized goals: she seeks some control of the day's rituals; she seeks to distinguish her taste and sophistication, with the white gown's matching France-purchased jewellery and make-up; and she seeks to perform romance in ways that follow well-circulated tropes of modern love and signs of consent, and signal her adeptness with consumer culture. Despite these competing hopes, that Amel wears the *chedda* first is unsurprising. The couple's limited budget and large extended families near Ghazaouet make hosting the wedding there a necessary choice; it is unlikely that their families would receive visitor visas for France. When I asked her mother Wafa about her investment in this ritual on a few occasions, she offered brief explanations, including, "It's tradition. And that's it." Perhaps, given Amel's Frenchness, Wafa sensed potential critique of Amel's customs and decorum. Perhaps she knew that Amel's future kinship ties in Ghazaouet would be strengthened through this performance. Perhaps Wafa felt insecure about her own belonging in Ghazaouet, having now lived almost thirty years in France.

The presence of Djouer as ritual expert cannot be discounted. Djouer's literal and metaphorical warning of the *chedda* headdress's weight as she secured it offered a challenge Amel wanted to meet. Lastly, and the primary point in my exploration of this garment, is that no matter her stylistic preferences, Amel's choice to marry Yacine – with his upbringing, geographical ties, values, and *Algerianité* – forge her wearing of the *chedda* as part of her access to kinship in the *Bled*. Silently bearing the *chedda* in the public wedding ritual became a marker of Amel's promise to maintain Algerian traditions. It came to symbolize her kinship. Amid these seemingly competing pulls – of *longing for* an Algerian connection and *belonging to* the French state through access to (and surveillance of) citizenship – the ritual choices surrounding the *chedda* illuminate how individuals like Amel forge their own relationships of kinship and desire through promise-making amid ongoing colonial and immigration politics. Still, the other unknown Ghazaouet bride's seemingly carefree ability to wear the princess gown in her procession shows that perhaps the *chedda*'s promise of intergenerational cultural tradition is not as rigid as it has been imagined by Amel's transnational family.

NOTES

1 I am indebted to Amel and Yacine and their families for generously including me in their wedding preparations and wedding day. I sincerely thank them. The photograph is used with Amel's permission. I also gratefully acknowledge funding from the Social Sciences and Humanities Research Council of Canada, and to Benjamin Berger, Pamela Klassen, and Monique Scheer for holding such a generative online workshop amid the COVID-19 pandemic in November 2020. Some parts of Amel's story

are featured in *Secular Sensibilities: Romance, Marriage and Contemporary Algerian Immigration to France and Québec* (Chapel Hill, NC: University of North Carolina Press, 2025). All names have been anonymized. Translations from French are my own.

2 This transnational ethnographic project includes fieldwork and 187 interviews conducted in Petit-Nanterre, France, in four Algerian locations, and in Montreal, Quebec from 2011–19. As elaborated in the second vignette, I met Amel in early 2016 in a Parisian suburb approximately fifteen kilometres north-west of the Arc de Triomphe. Owing to a history of family regroupment immigration and other migratory patterns, this French suburb remains primarily of Algerian origin, which is not the case for most Parisian suburbs. No official data exist, but there are an estimated seven million inhabitants in France of Algerian origin. I do not assume that the suburb's Algerians and inhabitants of Algerian origin are Muslim. But, in the more than 150 interviews I have conducted in the neighbourhood since 2004, I have met one Algerian Christian who was a recent convert and half a dozen atheists. Compared with non-Algerians, Algerian French marry more often, seek out heteronormative unions, and do not cohabitate before marriage (at least officially). See Christelle Hamel, Bertrand L'Hommeau, Ariane Pailhé, and Emmanuelle Santelli, "La formation du couple entre ici et là-bas," in *Trajectoires et origines: Enquête sur la diversité des populations en France*, ed. Cris Beauchemin, Christelle Hamel, and Patrick Simon (Paris: Ined Éditions, 2010), 85–7.

3 Known as the *Chedda of Tlemcen*, this garment and its accessories are notable in this region of Algeria. Ghazaouet, the city of Amel and Yacine's wedding celebration, is seventy kilometres north-west of the province's capital city of Tlemcen. Traditionally, women of socially upwardly mobile families in this province begin putting together their wedding trousseau in girlhood. Given the cost of the pieces and accessories (rarely reworn, unlike most of the other gowns Amel wore), it is common today to rent the *chedda* and its trimmings, as Amel did from Djouer.

4 See Jane Bennett, *Vibrant Matter: A Political Ecology of Things* (Durham, NC: Duke University Press, 2010).

5 Walter D. Mignolo and Catherine E. Walsh, *On Decoloniality: Concepts, Analytics, Praxis* (Durham, NC: Duke University Press, 2018).

6 Amel's father's whereabouts are unknown. Her mother and siblings live three hours north of Paris. Amel moved to Nanterre for her studies, and because of her full-time job and the allure of the nearby capital city, she plans to stay and live nearby with Yacine.

7 With the notion of the *bled*, Algeria is imagined as a repository of a range of sociocultural (via holidays, foodways, dress, etc.), political, familial, sexual, and religiously infused values. See Jennifer A. Selby, "*C'est plus*

traditionnel ici qu'au bled! Analyse socio-spatiale du traditionalisme religieux dans une banlieue parisienne," *Ethnologie française* 44, no. 3 (2014): 515–26.

8 Amel's maternal entourage did concede to break two traditions related to virginity: first, that an older female family member did *not* draw red circles and apply red lipstick accentuated with white dots on her face, an outward marker of her purity. Second, there was no mention of checking for blood-stained sheets post-consummation. These rituals were seen by women in her family as in poor taste.

9 Many of my interlocutors who migrate to France from Algeria to marry are women, but approximately one in five are men like Yacine. Unlike their father's arrangement with their mother in the early 1980s, Amel's and Rayan's transnational unions followed new French laws passed in 2006 and 2011 that seek to impede transnational marriages owing to fears that facilitating entry into France through family regroupment encourages immigration fraud. See Jennifer A. Selby, "Le *bled* en banlieue: Le mariage musulman face à l'État français," *Ethnologie française* 47, no. 4 (2017): 703–715.

10 Since accepting his proposal – made in the company of his parents, her mother, and grandmother at the kitchen table of her grandmother's home – Amel has been careful to keep their interactions "appropriate," and so, until the wedding night, the couple communicated almost exclusively through online text messaging. Their first moments physically alone together were dining together in her dressing room midway through the wedding party. Djouer and I ate our three-course, family-style dinner together in a sex-segregated dining room in the lower level of the hall.

11 *Orientale* in this wedding show in Nanterre, France, is meant as a reference not to East Asia, but to Maghrebian or North African wedding styles, vendors, and colours. The mobilization of the Orient/Orientalism and its relation to coloniality is not lost on me.

12 As part of the "hijab generation," Amel attended public school after the 2004 law prohibiting visible religious signs in public schools. She is therefore accustomed to a "pivoting" hijab. She is less careful at the department store, but noted proudly that her colleagues at the X-ray clinic have never seen her pray or wear hijab and did not know she was fasting.

13 Because her mother works as an office cleaner and her father did not participate financially (or physically) in the wedding, Amel's part-time department-store job and full-time work covered most expenses. Her mother and four siblings contributed, Yacine's parents paid for half the party expenses, and Yacine paid for expenses related to his move to France.

14 While governmentality around their mixed union hovered in the backdrop of the wedding preparations, official state scrutiny began two days after

the wedding when the couple visited the French consulate in Oran to have their wedding act "translated." Amel and Yacine, both nervous, were questioned separately by French officials but without incident. The next afternoon, they boarded a flight from Oran to the Orly airport, and Yacine migrated to Nanterre, initially with a tourist visa. Again, even if some, like her co-workers, worried his intentions were dubious, her family's, friends', and the state's concerns about their marriage, regarding consent, individualism, and sexual freedom, were directed towards Amel.

15 The notion of a *neggafate* (dresser and organizer) is a Moroccan-related reference to decorum and the defenders of tradition, but it captures Djouer's tasks of dressing and preparing Amel throughout the evening and of keeping her calm. Had she lived in Ghazaouet, Djouer would have accompanied Amel in the months beforehand and have had a hand in all her sartorial decisions.

16 For earlier studies of Muslim practice in France, see Nacira Guénif-Souilamas, *Des "beurettes" aux descendantes d'immigrants nord-africains* (Paris: Bernard Grasset, 2000); Nathalie Kakpo, *L'islam, un recours pour les jeunes* (Paris: Presses de la fondation nationale des sciences politiques, 2007); John R. Bowen, *Why the French Don't Like Headscarves: Islam, the State, and Public Space* (Princeton, NJ: Princeton University Press, 2007); and Leyla Arslan, *Enfants d'islam et de Marianne: Des banlieues à l'université* (Paris: Presses universitaires de France, 2010).

17 The larger project includes interviews with eighty-nine individuals of Algerian origin in Montreal; cisgender women's relationship to the *Bled* and marriage rituals differs there significantly, see Selby, *Secular Sensibilities*.

18 Armando Salvatore, "Tradition and Modernity within Islamic Civilisation and the West," in *Islam and Modernity: Key Issues and Debates*, ed. Muhammad Khalid Masud, Armando Salvatore, and Martin van Bruinessen (Edinburgh: Edinburgh University Press, 2009), 5.

19 Most notable are restrictions and surveillance imposed on non-EU transnational marriage, beginning in 2006 that become increasingly strict in 2011 and 2021. See Manuela Salcedo Robledo, "Bleu, blanc, gris … la couleur des mariages," *L'Espace politique* 13 (May 2011), doi.10.4000/espacepolitique.1869; Selby, "Le *bled* en banlieue."

20 Alana Lentin, "Decolonising Epistemologies," *alanalentin.net* (blog), 10 February 2017, https://www.alanalentin.net/2017/02/10/decolonising-epistemologies/.

21 Teresa Macías, "Postcolonialism and Decoloniality," in *Critical Social Work Praxis*, ed. Sobia Shaheen Shaikh, Brenda Anne-Marie LeFrançois, and Teresa Macías (Halifax: Fernwood Publishing, 2022), 331–45.

22 Nacira Guénif-Souilamas, "The Other French Exception: Virtuous Racism and the War of the Sexes in Postcolonial France," *French Politics, Culture*

and Society 24, no. 3, (Winter 2006): 24. Several terms have been coined based on these concepts. For instance, historian Todd Shepard introduces a "post-decolonisation" formulation to capture the ongoing Algeria-France relationship. The "post-de" prefix, he says, makes evident that French colonialization did not abruptly end in 1962 and the "de" allows clearer attention to Algerian perspectives. See Todd Shepard, "The Global Erotics of the French Sexual Revolution: Politics and 'Arab Men' in Post-decolonization France, 1962–1974," in *The Global 1960s: Convention, Contest, and Counterculture,* ed. Jadwiga E. Mooney and Tamara Chaplin (Abingdon, UK: Routledge, 2018), 115–39. Still other scholars have argued for an expressly "anti-colonial" (or "uncolonial") position, effectively centring anti-imperialist politics. See Frantz Fanon, *The Wretched of the Earth,* trans. Richard Philcox (New York: Grove, 2004).

23 See Ann Laura Stoler, *Carnal Knowledge and Imperial Power: Race and the Intimate in Colonial Rule* (Berkeley: University of California Press, 2002).

24 Aníbal Quijano, "Coloniality of Power, Eurocentrism, and Latin America," in *Coloniality at Large: Latin America and the Postcolonial Debate,* ed. Mabel Moraña, Enrique D. Dussel, and Carlos A. Jáuregui (Durham, NC: Duke University Press, 2008), 181–224. On the French "civilizing" mission in Algeria, see Judith Surkis, *Sex, Law, and Sovereignty in French Algeria, 1830–1930* (Cornell, NY: Cornell University Press, 2019); and Todd Shepard, "'Something Notably Erotic': Politics, 'Arab Men,' and Sexual Revolution in Post-decolonization France, 1962–1974," *Journal of Modern History* 84, no. 1 (March 2012): 80–115.

Chapter Six

Quid pro quo? Egyptian Papyri Distributions and the Bureaucracy of a Promise

GREGORY FEWSTER

The Thomas Fisher Rare Book Library at the University of Toronto and the nearby Royal Ontario Museum (ROM) have in their possession somewhere in the ballpark of four hundred papyrus manuscripts that were excavated in Egypt around the turn of the twentieth century.[1] On the face of it, this is not a remarkable fact. Museums and libraries especially in Europe and North America have collections of ancient artefacts that originated elsewhere. They are used to teach students and the wider public about world cultures and by researchers in historical and anthropological study. There is a growing effort, however, among archaeologists, museum professionals, and others to think more deeply about these collections and to examine the conditions that enabled the extraction, appropriation, and dispersal of cultural heritage objects. One crucial component of this work is critical provenance research: the attempt to document as clearly as possible the chain of ownership back to the original context of an artefact's excavation while interrogating the structures that legitimized the movement of artefacts.[2] This essay contributes to that effort by documenting and explaining the energies of Charles Trick Currelly, the first official collector and then Director of the ROM, to compile a diverse and representative collection of Egyptian papyrus manuscripts in Toronto.

Provenance research relies first and foremost on archives that preserve records of artefact acquisition and excavation. But for artefacts that were acquired by colonial powers in the nineteenth and early twentieth centuries, such records can be minimal or absent altogether.

This is the case for many of the papyri in Toronto, particularly a small unpublished collection currently at the ROM, reducing the possibility of a thorough and critical treatment of their provenance. In order to address this relative absence, this essay examines archival records of a different sort, what I am calling the "Currelly correspondence": a series of letters initiated by Currelly in an attempt to acquire from the Egypt Exploration Society (EES) "quite a large number of bits of paper, and I think, papyrus, with inscriptions in Arabic on them" and add them to the existing ROM collections.[3]

At the centre of the Currelly correspondence is a promise. Currelly felt entitled to the papyri because – as he repeatedly insisted – they had been promised to him. As his story went: a male colleague in the EES had offered the papyri to Currelly because he secured a rather sizable donation to support the colleague's excavations. It is a fascinating claim. As this essay argues, Currelly was rooting this gentleman's agreement squarely within a formalized framework of artefact distributions, whereby museums were encouraged to sponsor EES excavations in return for a portion of the finds. In the effort to acquire more papyri for his museum, Currelly was testing the limits of official EES policy in practice, and he did so by holding out for consideration the power of a promise. He thus invited the EES to imagine their distributions as a flexible system held together by masculine, homosocial relationships of exchange and favour. For that was what the "promise" encapsulated.

Building on recent studies of EES distribution practices, this essay considers the logic behind Currelly's own interpretation of the distributions framework, by investigating how his request for papyri was received by EES officials.[4] There are multiple ways to view an object, Jeffery Hewitt reminds us in this volume, a function of parallax vision. And the reception of Currelly's request was accordingly multiple, exemplifying a diversity of ways that EES officials were able to conceive of distributions as quid pro quo or as a promise, that is, as a strictly formalized transaction or as a flexible and informal relationship of exchange. Against a singular understanding of EES distributions, the Currelly correspondence reveals how competing views existed within the EES itself. And it reflects the very mechanisms, namely, bureaucracy, that would regulate that diversity of views into practice, the actual movement of artefacts.

Although Currelly's leveraging of promise would fail in that instance – no more papyri would come to the ROM – the correspondence nevertheless sheds light on Currelly's methods of antiquities acquisition, hinting at his strategies of assembling another papyri collection for the ROM, whose documentation is otherwise absent. On a broader level, the correspondence places Currelly's collecting activity for a museum in Toronto on the stage of British colonial appropriation and dissemination of Egyptian antiquities in the early twentieth century. Analysis of the correspondence thus contributes to critical provenance research for a specific museum collection as well as to our understanding of the complexity of bureaucratic and relational aspects of the colonial antiquities trade and the operations of the Egypt Exploration Society, in particular.

The Currelly Correspondence in the EES Archives as Evidence for Provenance

On 14 September 1926, C.T. Currelly sent a letter to Mary Jonas, the General Secretary of the Egypt Exploration Society. Both parties were actually fairly regular correspondents. Jonas would write to inform Currelly that a box of artefacts was on its way from London to Toronto. Currelly would respond, informing her of the artefacts' safe arrival, often thanking her for their secure packing. Although the letter of 14 September included such pleasantries, it was also notably different from their standard exchange. The famous papyrologist Bernard P. Grenfell had recently died, and Currelly seized the moment to dredge up a promise that Grenfell had made in the field some twenty years prior, though not without expressing sympathy for his passing. According to Currelly, Grenfell had made a promise that the Toronto museum should receive a small collection of Arabic papyri as a token of thanks after Currelly had secured the substantial sum of £1,200 to support EES excavations, which Grenfell had been supervising.[5] Currelly thought that it was high time for the EES to fulfil Grenfell's promise.

Although some have admired Currelly for his "energy and foresight" in compiling the ROM's archaeological and historical collections, others are more critical of his activities, raising questions about his professionalism, credentials, and methods.[6] Currelly's request for Arabic papyri could be interpreted quite naturally in that critical light. For it was only upon Grenfell's death that Currelly seems to have recalled a decades-old promise that would benefit the ROM. No doubt, the ROM's Director can be read as tactlessly opportunistic, and his belated request suspicious, consistent with what many would see as his overall approach to antiquities collection. Reducing Currelly's request for Arabic papyri to this caricature, however, is to miss an opportunity to peer into the contexts of the antiquities trade that made this request legible.

To take a more historically situated approach to the request for papyri requires placing the Currelly correspondence in its archival context – the Lucy Gura Archive in London – which documents the activities of the EES from its founding as a subscription fund for Egyptian excavation to the present.[7] Housed in the archives are excavation records, site photographs, accounts of archaeological finds, and letters between EES secretaries and museums officials. These documents can be incredibly banal – rows of concise artefact descriptions, lamentations about dwindling finances, and brief yet polite exchanges concerning the acquisition and delivery of artefacts. Bureaucracy, however banal it may be, was nevertheless an important dimension of the British imperial apparatus, including the antiquities trade in the nineteenth and twentieth centuries. Its interpretation is now an essential component of postcolonial scholarship on the twin spheres of archaeology and museum collections.[8] The Lucy Gura Archive thus places Currelly's specific request for Arabic papyri within the much broader dynamics of the British colonial excavation and trade in Egyptian antiquities.

EES Excavations and the Distribution of Egyptian Antiquities

The rationale for the Egypt Exploration Society followed a familiar colonial logic that capitalized on the mystique of ancient Egypt in the eyes of British society: unable to fully grasp the significance of the artefacts of the once-great civilization, the inferior local population was mismanaging and even destroying their cultural heritage. Tourists and the French administration were no better, the Society's founder Amelia Edwards observed. Only scientific excavation and study, she claimed, would preserve these artefacts of antiquity against sure obliteration.[9] The Egypt Exploration Society (then: Fund) was thus founded in 1882 to sponsor British-led excavations "especially on sites of Biblical and classical interest."[10]

Although Egyptology conjures up images of the Great Pyramids of Giza, the Sphinx, and monumental temples of Dynastic-period Egypt, the EES established its Graeco-Roman Branch in 1896 to dig at sites likely to have been populated during the periods of Ptolemaic/Macedonian (305–30 BCE) and Roman (30 BCE–646 CE) rule.[11] For at these sites, the archaeologists knew, they could recover the most common ephemeral medium for writing in the ancient Mediterranean: papyri.[12] Bernard Grenfell and Arthur Hunt assembled teams of local Egyptians to do the heavy lifting at such sites as Oxyrhynchus and towns scattered throughout the Fayyūm Oasis, and together they unearthed Greek fragments of classical and biblical works along with records of the day-to-day life of residents of those towns.[13]

By the late nineteenth century, British archaeologists had a practised tradition of financing their digs by subscription, in contrast to the state-support models of France or Germany.[14] The Egypt Exploration Fund joined numerous other archaeological societies (e.g., the Palestinian Exploration Fund) in soliciting donations from members of British society and abroad, promising some sort of token in return. Egyptian law prohibited the export of antiquities, initially constituting a legal barrier to the use of excavated artefacts as tokens in exchange for subscriptions. But this was soon overcome through an agreement negotiated by the leading British archaeologist, Flinders Petrie, with Gaston Maspero, the Director of the French-run antiquities service.[15] The system they initiated is known as *partage*, which allows for a division of antiquities between those who administered the country of origin and the excavating body; in this case, antiquities were divided between the Bulaq Museum in Cairo and the Egypt Exploration Society.

As a result of Petrie's negotiations, Egyptian antiquities – including papyri – began to flood back to the EES headquarters in London. According to Tim Barringer, "the procession of objects from peripheries to centre symbolically enacted the idea of London as the heart of empire," while the display of artefacts in that heart construed their meaning as evidence of British cultural supremacy.[16] Indeed, imperial ambitions had energized EES activities from the start – the founding of the EES occurred conspicuously close to the British seizure of Alexandria. As an expression of British civilizing power, the EES was now successfully "saving" Egyptian and Graeco-Roman antiquities from potential destruction with their excavations. And in London, those antiquities were now available to be ordered and displayed in the British Museum according to scientific principles.[17]

The movement of antiquities under EES control, however, was not unidirectional, thus complicating Barringer's schematic. Under Petrie's *partage* agreement, artefacts were moving to London in order to be distributed almost immediately as tangible gratuities for the growing number of subscribers to the EES. Subscribers could now physically possess artefacts to which they had entitled themselves (at least in their view) when they supported colonial excavations with their financial donations. Distribution was, admittedly, not so straightforward. Artefacts were never meant to be distributed to individual subscribers, but rather to public institutions (libraries and museums) that could effectively partner in the mission of the EES.[18] Wealthy donors, like J.P. Morgan, could forward money to the Fund, but they would have to select a public institution, like New York City's Metropolitan Museum of Art, to actually take possession of the artefacts.

The EES thus established relationships with a range of public institutions and their financiers, mainly in England, the Commonwealth, and the United States, but also in Europe, South Africa, and even Japan. It was an elegant system. The EES needed funds for their excavations while public institutions required artefacts to fill their museums; the subscription-distribution model would satisfy both agendas. And the relationships between the EES and museums quickly evolved into what Alice Stevenson has called a "symbiotic dependency," generating a steady and reciprocal flow of financial support and artefacts.[19] Distributing these artefacts was a complicated affair indeed, but also essential to the continued existence of the EES. Thus, their ledgers demonstrate concerted efforts to maintain its symbiotic relationships, as clerks checked and double-checked that each subscribing institution was given their due.[20]

From the legal prohibition of the removal of antiquities from Egypt to the EEF's maintenance of a symbiotic dependency with public museums and libraries, artefact distribution was an emergent property that governed how antiquities moved from Egypt itself to museums scattered across the globe. On a broad level, this movement from colonized periphery to imperial core to its colonizing appendages reflected the confluence of British imperial knowledge and power. But at their most basic, distributions appear to have operated according to a very simple principle, one that EES officials would repeat over and over in their correspondence and publications: donation to the Fund for the sake of preserving the archaeological record of ancient Egypt would be returned with its equivalence in antiquities. Very simply, the EES declared that they distributed artefacts according to a principle of quid pro quo.

C.T. Currelly and the Archaeological Collections of the Royal Ontario Museum

The quid pro quo arrangement between the EES and numerous public institutions was predicated upon broadly shared convictions about the value of extracting antiquities from Egypt. Underneath this general agreement, institutions followed differing taxonomic ideologies, rationales of display, and motives for collecting, influenced especially by their respective social, economic, cultural, and geopolitical situations.[21] The story of quid pro quo is not just about the EES and its need for regular financing. It is about the specific institutions that used the EES as a means of expanding their collections.

The particular situation of the ROM, in the context of colonial collecting, has been well documented.[22] In the early twentieth century, the city of Toronto was trying to establish itself as an international city. It needed to distinguish itself against such nearby large American cities as New York and Chicago, while shaking off its identity as merely a British colonial outpost. Establishing a world-class "encyclopaedic" museum in Toronto, by assembling artefacts that offered a representative cross section of the world's cultures and their development for display, research, and teaching, was an integral part of its emergence on the international stage.[23] But to establish an individual, international reputation, the ROM had to compete using its limited resources against the voracious and well-funded collecting habits of American institutions.[24]

C.T. Currelly would prove to be an integral asset in the pursuit of these goals. When it officially opened its doors on 19 March 1914, the ROM revealed to the public collections associated with five distinct "Museums" within it: Geology; Mineralogy; Palaeontology; Zoology; and Archaeology. The Archaeological collection was by far the most substantial and would continue to grow under Currelly's directorship, the core of the Egyptological and Graeco-Roman collections being constituted by EES distributions in direct proportion to Toronto subscriptions. This symbiotic relationship established between the EES and the ROM was a product of Currelly's unique relation to both institutions, one that had actually been initiated over a decade before the Museum ever opened.

Currelly's involvement in both EES archaeology and a Toronto museum commenced during a trip to London in 1902. His work with the EES was the consequence of a somewhat serendipitous meeting with Flinders Petrie, which would ensure Currelly's employment for several years. He began by conducting more mundane work for the Society, which included collecting subscriptions and packing artefacts for distribution, before eventually contributing to excavations at the ancient Egyptian sites of Abydos and Deir el-Bahari. Currelly's work as a museum professional resulted from a similarly unexpected encounter, this time with an old schoolmate, Ned Burwash. At the annual exhibition of the EES, Currelly met Ned and his father, Nathanael, now Chancellor of Victoria College, recently federated with the University of Toronto.[25] The exhibit displayed finds acquired in the most recent excavation season prior to their distribution, and they provoked Chancellor Burwash to express his interest in starting a museum in Toronto. Burwash saw the EES as a means to that end, apparently believing the Egyptian artefacts on display were for sale. This was a mistake that Currelly quickly corrected, by explaining the quid pro quo dynamics of EES distributions.[26]

Having recently come under the mentorship of the very architect of the EES distribution system (i.e., Petrie), Currelly was uniquely positioned to leverage that experience to the benefit of a Toronto museum in its incipient stages, with himself at its centre. He was able to explain to the Burwashes that distributions were how one acquired artefacts, rather than direct purchase. Upon his return to Toronto, Ned thus embarked upon a campaign to secure subscriptions to the EES and "did what [he] could to further Mr. Currelly's ambition to start a good museum in Toronto."[27] Currelly, meanwhile, worked out that ambition while still employed by the EES. For example, while packing artefacts for distribution, he supplemented the Toronto allotment with "prehistoric objects" from a storeroom he was permitted by the current president to "ransack."[28] With first-hand experience of the actual procedures by which artefacts were assembled and sent to their destination, Currelly quickly learned that personal connections moved artefacts around, adding more complex and unofficial dimensions to the basic policy of institutional quid pro quo.

Currelly's role as a collector for the ROM quickly eclipsed his activities with the EES. From 1902 onwards, he built up wide-ranging collections for the Archaeology Museum, which would place the ROM among leading museums internationally.[29] Within the more expansive purview of the Archaeology Museum, however, Egyptological artefacts remained an important part of its collection – its growth an expression of the ROM's symbiotic dependency with the EES, first initiated by Chancellor Burwash at the recommendation of Currelly. Over 1,500 Egyptian antiquities, including one hundred or so Greek papyri, would be shipped at regular intervals first to Toronto's Victoria College and later directly to the ROM, in proportion to the subscriptions collected in Toronto.[30] If Currelly's insider status at the EES was a crucial element to the initial distribution of artefacts to Toronto, it remained an ever-present feature of their symbiosis, ready to be leveraged in the perennial pursuit of a broader and more representative trove of archaeological artefacts of any kind, which would include, of course, papyri.

The Bureaucracy of a Promise and the Politics of Distribution

When Currelly wrote to Mary Jonas on 14 September 1926, he did so both as the Director of the Royal Ontario Museum of Archaeology and as someone who was invested in the interests of the EES and well connected to its inner circle. He portrayed his relationship with the late B.P. Grenfell as one of friendly rapport, established through their shared experiences in EES excavations and reinforced when Currelly secured funds to finance Grenfell's work. And he used that rapport as a foundation for his request to receive an assemblage of Arabic papyri.[31] But Currelly's leveraging of his relationship with Grenfell – encapsulated in the "promise" – gestured beyond itself to the larger framework of EES artefact distributions. For Grenfell had allegedly offered the papyri on account of Currelly's role in securing a financial donation to Society activities. It was within that framework of artefact distributions that Currelly's claim to Arabic papyri would be interpreted.

According to the logic of Currelly's request, then, the very procedures governing how the EES distributed its artefacts were at stake. Did Grenfell's promise fall under the purview of distributions, or not? And at the centre of this question sat Mary Jonas. For as Stevenson has noted, during her tenure as EES Secretary, Jonas was "the diplomatic pivot around which competing views on the significance and nature of archaeological finds for museum acquisitions were balanced."[32] The Currelly correspondence is thus a testament to Jonas's bureaucratic management of the peculiar request, mediating between Currelly on one side and various members of EES committees (and their potentially differing views) on the other.

From Currelly's perspective, the matter was worth the effort of some brief back-and-forth exchange, to see what he could get out of the Society by appealing to his relationship with Grenfell, after the distinguished archaeologist's passing. But in some sense, Jonas beat Currelly at his own game. As she explained in her reply, Jonas had mobilized a relationship closer to Grenfell. After consulting Grenfell's long-time colleague Arthur S. Hunt, she could report that "there are no Arabic papyri available at the present moment" but Hunt would "bear in mind the needs of the Toronto Museum at the next distribution of papyri."[33] To this Currelly protested that "the papyri and paper were promised," sending a third letter to Hunt himself.[34] But that is as far as it went for Currelly: Hunt's position in the Society and relationship to Grenfell were superior to Currelly's own. By the following year, the papyri were forgotten and he would return to his usual expressions of gratitude for the delivery of well-packed boxes of Egyptian artefacts.[35] Even without a new batch of papyri, the symbiosis between the ROM and the EES remained intact.

What Currelly did not know is that even after Jonas replied so conclusively, his letter had initiated considerable deliberation among influential members of the EES. It demanded the attention of the Executive Sub-Committee, who instructed Jonas to solicit corroboration from D.G. Hogarth, another of Grenfell's former colleagues, while she continued her exchange with Hunt.[36] The resulting correspondence, with Jonas at its centre, reflects striking disagreement among the EES officials over the factuality of Grenfell's promise and its legitimacy as a model of artefact distribution.

The facts of Grenfell's promise to Currelly are decidedly opaque, as much now as they were in 1926, which no doubt contributed to the disagreement. Arthur Hunt stated that he had no recollection of any promise that Grenfell may have made to Currelly.[37] D.G. Hogarth likewise claimed neither knowledge of finances for the relevant excavation season nor anything about the papyri.[38] Mary Jonas, however, was more than a mediator of Hunt's and Hogarth's recollections to the EES board. She acted as institutional memory with ready access to EES records, advocating for that recorded past. When she consulted a *Report* detailing donations, subscriptions, and expenditures, she found that "a large sum of money was received by the Society about the date that Mr. C. mentions."[39] In fact, her reading of the *Report* was generous to Currelly's recollection. The *Report* did devote considerable attention to the donation of £1,000 (not £1,200), offered in early in 1906 by William M. Laffan, an associate of J.P. Morgan and member of the Metropolitan Museum of Art's Executive Committee. But this date places the donation during the first of Currelly's excavation seasons, not the second.[40] Most significantly, the so-called "Laffan Fund" came with specific conditions, which the EES had accepted: the Fund must support the ongoing excavation at Deir el-Bahari under Prof. E. Naville (with any leftover funds used to support other excavations), while antiquities from Deir el-Bahari should be distributed pro rata to the Met.[41] No mention of Grenfell and Oxyrhynchus, let alone Currelly and the ROM. According to these records, the EES and the Met participated in a straightforward case of distribution quid pro quo, and one that necessarily excluded the ROM as a beneficiary of the donation. Twenty years after the fact, Currelly's letter had to persuade against the grain of official EES records and the strict stipulations afforded by the Laffan Fund.

The decision whether Grenfell's promise in 1906 should influence the distribution of papyri in 1926 turned, at least from Jonas's perspective, on two factors: the factuality of the donation and the legitimacy of the promise. In spite of the fact that the Laffan Fund restricted artefact distribution to the Met, Jonas allowed that Currelly's own involvement in securing that donation may have been muted in the *Report*. But she shared with Hunt the sentiment that, fundamentally, the papyri were the property of the EES and therefore not Grenfell's to promise to anyone, adding elsewhere, "I think that a vague informal promise made in the field is not a very binding one."[42] Even if Currelly had been instrumental in securing the £1,000, Grenfell's promise, in the view of Jonas and Hunt, did not satisfy a strict formulation of distribution procedures as quid pro quo.

The EES Sub-Committee, however, did not share this view. Without the benefit of other evidence, we know only their conclusion as described by Jonas in a letter to D.G. Hogarth:

> At the meeting I was asked to write to you asking that you would perhaps stir up Professor Hunt about further distributions. […] The feeling of the Committee is that there is a very large amount of papyri still untouched, and that an occasional letter to speed up its publication and distribution may do good.[43]

Whatever concerns Jonas or Hunt may have raised concerning the factuality or legitimacy of Grenfell's promise made no difference to the Executive Sub-Committee. Their instructions to Jonas reveal, rather, a more flexible view towards the flow of artefacts and money. Just as Grenfell's promise fell outside the purview of the Laffan Fund, so too would the suggestion of future papyri for the ROM fall outside Currelly's particular request for *Arabic* papyri. In fact, it was precisely this more generic flow that mattered. Papyri should not remain tucked away in lead boxes in Queen's College, Oxford, when they could be moving and thus ensuring future donations to the Society. However fanciful Currelly's letter may have been, it spoke to a long and enduring relationship between himself and Grenfell, and the EES as a whole. Grenfell's promise, in that sense, was more than just a transaction, it reflected a much broader dimension of EES distributions: the enduring relationship of exchange, regardless of how seamlessly it did (or did not) comport to official, stated policy or stipulation. For that reason, the Executive Sub-Committee resolved to do their best to ensure the delivery of papyri to the ROM, at least at some point in the future.

Conclusion

No Arabic papyri would ever make it to Toronto. It turns out that the year 1924 saw the final formal distribution of papyri to subscribing institutions; they never got around to the Arabic papyri, which remain unpublished.[44] In the years since Grenfell allegedly made his promise to Currelly, the EES had even ceased digging for papyri altogether, occupied now by the demands of institutions for "museum-quality" objects from excavations at Amarna and other such sites that energized the current wave of Egyptomania.[45] This endless flow of excavation and distribution of antiquities, however, gets to the heart of the bureaucratic negotiations of the Currelly correspondence. Both sides were invested in maintaining their symbiotic dependence, which transcended individual allotments of artefacts. For Currelly to press any further for the Arabic papyri was to risk damaging his rapport with the EES – more than twenty years in the making – and thus halt the flow of new artefacts to Toronto. And some members of the EES administration knew that the ROM and its financiers were a reliable source of funding, evidenced in a letter from Jonas composed only a month before Currelly's own.[46] To brush off his request could equally jeopardize further subscriptions and donations from Toronto.

The Currelly correspondence reveals the tenuous nature of the system of artefact distributions and its limits. In his failed attempt to acquire an assemblage of Arabic papyri from the EES, C.T. Currelly put their procedures of distribution to the test. The varied reactions to his request demonstrate considerable disagreement among concurrent ranking members of the EES in their respective vision for distributions. But it is disagreement that, on some level, was resolved by the bureaucratic activity of Mary Jonas. For the answer she gave Currelly – both the refusal to send Arabic papyri and the suggestion of future distributions – aligns precisely with neither of the views expressed by Jonas and Hunt nor by the Executive Sub-Committee. Rather, it reflects a curious compromise that both acknowledged Currelly's relationship with the EES while refusing to grant his specific request. Both dimensions of distributions – quid pro quo and promise – were maintained in the final outcome and its consequences. This is a testament to the regulating power of bureaucratic activity in the face of parallax vision, concerning the movement of Egyptian antiquities on the colonial stage.

This episode in the history of the Egyptian Exploration Society and the Royal Ontario Museum, finally, holds lessons for analysing the modern antiquities trade and the histories of (un)provenanced artefacts. Both interpretive models of EES distributions – the rigid quid pro quo or the flexible, relational promise – can dominate the scholarly imagination. But as the Currelly correspondence illustrates, neither options can fully do justice to the on-the-ground practices of colonial extraction and artefact relocation that lasted for half a century or more. Artefacts were not moved precisely according to policies published by excavating bodies such as the EES, and neither were they moved entirely through unregulated relational systems of exchange. Rather, these were idealized options regulated in the context of their distinct circumstances by the mechanisms of bureaucracy and the tenacity of such figures as Mary Jonas. In the case of undocumented Egyptian papyri currently held in the storerooms of the Royal Ontario Museum, the Currelly correspondence thus shows us that, whereas Currelly may have wished to acquire them on the strength of the promise, the bureaucratic mechanisms of the EES must have demanded at least a little bit more quid pro quo.

Appendix: Currelly's two letters to Mary Jonas (images and transcription)

THE ROYAL ONTARIO MUSEUM OF ARCHAEOLOGY

TORONTO 5, CANADA

CABLE ADDRESS:
ROMA, TORONTO

AGENTS IN ENGLAND:
THOMAS MEADOWS & CO., LTD.,
35, MILK STREET,
LONDON, E.C. 2.

OFFICE OF THE DIRECTOR

September 14th, 1926.

Miss Mary C. Jonas, Secretary,
Egypt Exploration Society,
13, Tavistock Square,
London, W.C.I.

Dear Miss Jonas,

The few Egyptian things arrived quite safely, for which many thanks for the good packing.

I was extremely sorry to learn just recently that poor Grenfell was dead. Now, may I go into some back history? I think it was the second year that I was at Deir el Bahri that the Fund ran very short of money, and it was possible to finance the work only because I begged something over £1000 from an American. There was also some other money I begged that was never collected, through some mistake in the office. This threw me in touch with Mr. Pierpont Morgan, and he gave a subscription for the Graeco-Roman branch that enabled Hunt and Grenfell to go on with their work, which was threatened with being held up.

Grenfell at that time suggested that as they had found a good many Arabic documents, scraps of paper, and so forth, these could be turned over to us together with some papyri, as an acknowledgment of my services in enabling them to go on that year with their work. He said there was quite a large number of bits of paper and, I think, papyrus, with inscriptions in Arabic on them, and he was quite anxious that we should have them.

I should be very grateful if you would bring this matter before the Council and have what are sorted out by Hunt sent on to us, and also a few of the regular wills and stock papyri.

Yours very sincerely,

C. T. Currelly

Director.

DIST 23.34 [Sept 14th, 1926 – typescript on ROMA letterhead]
September 14, 1926
Miss Mary C. Jonas, Secretary
Egypt Exploration Society,
13, Tavistock Square,
London, W.C.I.

Dear Miss Jonas,
The few Egyptian things arrived quite safely, for which many thanks for the good packing.

I was extremely sorry to learn just recently that poor Grenfell was dead. Now, may I go into some back history? I think it was the second year that I was at Deir el Bahri that the Fund ran very short of money, and it was possible to finance the work only because I begged something over £1200 from an American. There was also some other money I begged that was never collected, through some mistake in the office. This threw me in touch with Mr. Pierpont Morgan, and he gave a subscription for the Graeco-Roman Branch that enabled Hunt and Grenfell to go on with their work, which was threatened with being held up.

Grenfell at that time suggested that as they had found a good many Arabic documents, scraps of paper, and so forth, these could be turned over to us together with some papyri, as an acknowledgment of my services in enabling them to go on that year with their work. He said there was quite a large number of bits of paper and, I think, papyrus, with inscriptions in Arabic on them, and he was quite anxious that we should have them.

I should be very grateful if you would bring this matter before the Council and have what are sorted out by Hunt sent on to us, and also a few of the regular wills and stock papyri.

Yours very sincerely,
C.T. Currelly [signed]
Director.

Disr. 23, 38

12069

THE ROYAL ONTARIO MUSEUM OF ARCHAEOLOGY

TORONTO 5, CANADA

October 26th, 1926.

CABLE ADDRESS:
ROMA, TORONTO
AGENTS IN ENGLAND:
THOMAS MEADOWS & CO., LTD.,
55, MILK STREET,
LONDON, E.C. 2.
OFFICE OF THE DIRECTOR

Miss Mary C. Jonas,

    Secretary, Egypt Exploration Society,

      13, Tavistock Square,

        London, W.C.I.

Dear Miss Jonas,

    Your letter of October 13th has just arrived.   You leave out one thing: the papyri and paper were promised.

    Now, I wonder if you could find out just what has happened to the Arabic papyri and paper, because Grenfell promised them as definitely as could be just at the time when I obtained the American money that to such a large extent enabled him to finish up the work that had been going on for such a long time at Oxyrrhynchos.   I know there were roughly six tons of material in the cellars and elsewhere, that were being worked over, and I am certainly very anxious that we should get a decent bunch. I have known manuscript to be deliberately wasted in England that would have been of enormous interest in many other places. So please do your best for us.

        Yours sincerely,

        Director.

190   Gregory Fewster

DIST 23.38 (Oct 26, 1926 – typescript, on ROMA letterhead)
Miss Mary C. Jonas,
Secretary, Egypt Exploration Society,
13 Tavistock Square,
London, W.C.I.

Dear Miss Jonas,
Your letter of October 13th has just arrived. You leave out one thing: the
papyri and paper were promised.

   Now, I wonder if you could find out just what happened to the Arabic
papyri and paper, because Grenfell promised them as definitely as could be
just at the time when I obtained the American money that to such a large
extent enabled him to finish up the work that had been going on for such
a long time at Oxyrhynchos. I know there were roughly six tons of material in the cellars and elsewhere, that were being worked over, and I am
certainly very anxious that we should get a decent bunch. I have known
manuscript to be deliberately wasted in England that would have been of
enormous interest in many other places. So please do your best for us.

Yours sincerely,
C.T. Currelly [signed]
Director.

NOTES

1 Research for this chapter was supported by the Social Sciences and
   Humanities Research Council of Canada.
2 For papyrologists, Roberta Mazza's recent article is paradigmatic:
   "Papyrology and Ethics," in *Proceedings of the 28th Congress of Papyrology,
   Barcelona 1–6 August 2016*, ed. Alberto Nodar and Sofía Torallas Tovar
   (Barcelona: Publicacions de l'Abadia de Monserrat, 2019), 15–27.
3 Quotations from C.T. Currelly to Mary C. Jonas, 14 September 1926
   (Egypt Exploration Society, Lucy Gura Archive, DIST.23.34). Institutional
   designations on all sides have changed over the years and it is important
   to keep track of these changes in order to make sense of the primary
   documentation. The Egypt Exploration Society (EES) received its name
   in 1912, having been established in 1882 as the Egypt Exploration Fund
   (EEF). Likewise, the Royal Ontario Museum (ROM) was first established
   as five museums, including the Royal Ontario Museum of Archaeology
   (ROMA). In this paper, I will use the current designations, but readers may
   have to infer institutional continuity with reference to primary sources.
4 On papyri distributions, see William A. Johnson, "The Oxyrhynchus
   Distributions in America: Papyri and Ethics," *Bulletin of the American Society*

of Papyrologists 49 (2012): 209–22; building on R.J. Schork, "The Singular Circumstances of an Errant Papyrus," *Arion* 16, no. 2 (Fall 2008): 25–47; Kilian Fleischer, "Die Teilung von P.Oxy.III 448," *Zeitschrift für Papyrologie und Epigraphik* 172 (2010): 201–2; now also Roberta Mazza, "Papyri, Ethics, and Economics: A Biography of P.Oxy.15.1780 (P39)," *Bulletin of the American Society of Papyrologists* 52 (2015): 113–42. On Egyptian artefact distributions more broadly, see Alice Stevenson, *Scattered Finds: Archaeology, Egyptology and Museums* (London: University College London Press, 2019).

5 According to the Bank of England's inflation calculator, this donation would be worth almost £150,000 (or $260,000 CAD) today.

6 Quotation from Northrop Fry's forward to Currelly's *I Brought the Ages Home* (Toronto: Ryerson Press, 1956), viii. Generally positive portrayals of Currelly include Lovat Dickson, *The Museum Makers: The Story of the Royal Ontario Museum* (Toronto: University of Toronto Press, 1986), 53; Julia Matthews, "The Right Man in the Right Place at the Right Time: A Look at the Visionary Who Was Instrumental in Founding the ROM," *Rotunda* 38, no. 3 (2006): 15–18. Compare the more critical assessments in John M. MacKenzie, *Museums and Empire: Natural History, Human Cultures and Colonial Identities*, Studies in Imperialism (Manchester: University of Manchester Press, 2009), 45; and Stevenson, *Scattered Finds*, 123–4.

7 Thanks are due to Stephanie Boonstra at the Egypt Exploration Society for helping me to access and navigate their digitized archive. Some of the records held in the Lucy Gura Archives are actually copies of letters sent abroad. But there are, unfortunately, no originals or additional pieces of this correspondence preserved in the ROM archives.

8 See especially Thomas Richards, *The Imperial Archive: Knowledge and the Fantasy of Empire* (London: Verso, 1993); Ann Laura Stoler, *Along the Archival Grain: Epistemic Anxieties and Colonial Common Sense* (Princeton, NJ: Princeton University Press, 2009).

9 Concerns over the destruction of Egyptian artefacts by local Egyptians and tourists is a perennial sentiment expressed in the *Annual Reports* of the EEF/EES as well as, famously, in one of Amelia Edwards's early works. Of course, some of this sentiment was meant to legitimize the excavations and drum up support. See Amelia Ann Blanford Edwards, *A Thousand Miles Up the Nile* (B. Tauchnitz, 1878), 136.

10 These words, quoted from the first circulated leaflet of the Fund, are drawn from Margaret S. Drower, "The Early Years," in *Excavating Egypt: The Egypt Exploration Society, 1882–1982*, ed. T.G.H. James (Chicago: University of Chicago Press, 1982), 15.

11 See discussion in Eric G. Turner, "The Graeco-Roman Branch," in James, *Excavating Egypt*, 161–78.

12 Papyrus had been manufactured and used in Egypt for numerous purposes, including as a writing surface, for millennia. Paper was introduced to Egypt in the ninth century and began to be manufactured there in the tenth, where it was used alongside papyrus as a writing surface. See Jonathan M. Bloom, *Paper before Print: The History and Impact of Paper in the Islamic World* (New Haven, CT: Yale University Press, 2001), 74–85, on the manufacture and use of paper in Egypt.

13 Some work has been done on the contributions of local Egyptians in Stephen Quirke, *Hidden Hands: Egyptian Workforces in Petrie Excavation Archives, 1880–1924* (London: Bloomsbury Academic, 2010). Roberta Mazza has shown that the brother of Shaykh Amed Sayad of the village of Sandafa, nearby ancient Oxyrhynchus, provided essential local knowledge for the first discovery of papyri there, rather than the insights of Grenfell and Hunt, as is usually claimed. See Roberta Mazza, "Narratives of Discovery: Petrie, Grenfell and Hunt, and the First Finding of the Oxyrhynchus Papyri," *Bulletin of the American Society of Papyrologists* 59 (2022): 221–58.

14 See discussion in Amara Thornton, "' … a Certain Faculty for Extricating Cash': Collective Sponsorship in Late 19th and Early 20th Century British Archaeology," *Present Pasts* 5, no. 1 (2013): 4–5. In fact, these archaeological societies had missionary societies as their precursors, which also relied on subscriptions to fund their efforts to convert the world to Christianity. The most notable example is probably the London Missionary Society (LMS). See Richard Lovett, *The History of the London Missionary Society, 1795–1895, in Two Volumes* (London: H. Frowde, 1899), among others. The LMS had soon developed its own museum, featuring artefacts (e.g., "idols") variously acquired in missionary efforts that evidenced both the need for and success of its activity. It was recognized that the museum and its artefact displays justified the Society's work and even prompted further subscriptions, while serving as a primary means of mediating world cultures to the British public long before the development of "scientific" museums. See discussion in Chris Wingfield, "'Scarcely More than a Christian Trophy Case'? The Global Collections of the London Missionary Society Museum (1814–1910)," *Journal of the History of Collections* 29, no. 1 (2017): 109–28; cf. Richard Daniel Altick, *The Shows of London* (Cambridge, MA: Belknap Press, 1978), 298–9.

15 The first public announcement of the EEF's formation made this legal prohibition clear: "It must be distinctly understood that by the law of Egypt no antiquities can be removed from the country." "Egyptian Antiquities," *The Times* (London), 30 March 1882. Such laws date back to 1835, and have undergone modification with new administrative regimes and geopolitical situations. See the comprehensive discussion

in Antoine Khater, *Le régime juridique des fouilles et des antiquités en Égypt* (Cairo: Imprimerie de l'Institut français d'archéologie orientale, 1960); with briefer accounts in Dalia N. Osman, "Occupier's Title to Cultural Property: Nineteenth-Century Removal of Egyptian Artifacts," *Columbia Journal of Transnational Law* 37, no. 3 (1999): 969–1002; and Salima Ikram, "Collecting and Repatriating Egypt's Past: Toward a New Nationalism," in *Contested Cultural Heritage: Religion, Nationalism, Erasure, and Exclusion in a Global World*, ed. Helaine Silverman (New York: Springer, 2011), 142–5.

16 Tim Barringer, "The South Kensington Museum and the Colonial Project," in *Colonialism and the Object: Empire, Material Culture, and the Museum*, ed. Tim Barringer and Tom Flynn (New York: Routledge, 1998), 11.

17 The report of the Second Annual General Meeting of the Fund mentions "the beautiful and highly interesting collections [Petrie] had brought home by the permission of Professor Maspero, who had selected for Boolák a limited series of objects." Egypt Exploration Fund, *Report of the Second Annual General Meeting & Balance Sheet* (London: Egypt Exploration Fund, 1884), 3. Petrie's first full site report likewise mentions that his excavations "yielded us much information on the age of many classes of objects, *besides furnishing the British Museum with several antiquities of types unknown before*" (italics mine). W.M. Flinders Petrie, *Tanis. Part 1, 1883–4* (London: Trübner & Co., 1885), vii.

18 There were exceptions. One particular kind of object, known as a *shabti* (small, usually blue, mummiform objects used in burials), were so common they were given to individual subscribers as well as to public museums.

19 Stevenson, *Scattered Finds*, 38.

20 The EEF/EES kept an official ledger, but the archive is also filled with unbound papers listing institutions and the artefacts that were to be delivered to them. Items are frequently crossed out, checked off, and reallocated to different institutions by multiple hands, including Arthur Hunt's.

21 These dynamics can be encapsulated in Stevenson's notion of "object habits." Alice Stevenson, Emma Libonati, and John Baines, "Introduction – Object Habits: Legacies of Fieldwork and the Museum," *Museum History Journal* 10, no. 2 (2017): 113–26; Stevenson, *Scattered Finds*, 2.

22 See especially MacKenzie, *Museums and Empire*, 44–58, 71.

23 See discussion of the "encyclopaedic museum" in H.H. Frese, *Anthropology and the Public: The Role of Museums* (Leiden: Brill, 1960), 16–19.

24 Thus placing it in contrast to the distinctive dynamics in the US, as described in Johnson, "The Oxyrhynchus Distributions."

25 These events are vibrantly recounted in Currelly, *Ages*, 35–7.

26 Currelly, *Ages*, 38. Misunderstandings of how the subscriptions worked
    were not uncommon. Several copies of letters sent to representatives
    of German libraries responding to inquiries concerning the acquisition
    of papyri contain the identical explanation: "It is a fundamental rule
    of our Society that antiquities (including papyri) can be given only to
    public museums or public libraries, and that the distribution must be in
    proportion to the subscription received" (DIST.32.02a; DIST.32.02b).
27 This quote comes from an undated document typed by Ned Burwash,
    containing recollections of the history of the Victoria College papyrus
    collection, stored in an uncatalogued file associated with the collection at
    the Thomas Fisher Rare Book Library. I am grateful to Timothy Perry for
    providing me with access to the document.
28 See Currelly, *Ages*, 65.
29 See, esp., Henry A. Miers and S.F. Markham, *A Report on the Museums
    of Canada to the Carnegie Corporation of New York* (Edinburgh: T. and A.
    Constable Limited, 1932); cf. Dickson, *The Museum Makers*, 69–71.
30 Stevenson estimates that Victoria College acquired approximately 1,620
    artefacts from EES excavations, placing it in the second tier of public
    institutions that received more than one thousand distributed objects, such
    as Oxford's Pitt Rivers and Ashmolean Museums, the Boston Museum
    of Fine Arts, Edinburgh's Scottish National Museum, and others. The
    British Museum stands alone in the first tier with 14,807 artefacts. See
    Alice Stevenson, "Artefacts of Excavation: The British Collection and
    Distribution of Egyptian Finds to Museums, 1880–1915," *Journal of the
    History of Collections* 26, no. 1 (March 2014): 89–102. This count does not
    include papyri. Evidence of regular contributions to the EES collected by
    Burwash begin to be documented in the Reports of the General Meeting,
    e.g., Egypt Exploration Fund, *Report of the Eighteenth Ordinary General
    Meeting (Twenty-Second Annual General Meeting), Subscription List and
    Balance Sheets: 1903–1904* (London: Kegan Paul, 1904), 70. The Victoria
    College collection was eventually absorbed into the ROM.
31 Grenfell and Currelly were, in fact, friendly, as a set of letters written
    by Grenfell to Currelly attests. Their collegial relationship had helped
    secure artefacts for the Toronto museum in 1906. The letters, however,
    make no reference to the events cited by Currelly in 1926. See Gregory
    Fewster, "Two Letters from B.P. Grenfell to C.T. Currelly in the Royal
    Ontario Museum Archive: New Evidence for the Acquisition of Egyptian
    Antiquities in Canada," *Mouseion* 20, no. 1 (2023): 53–84.
32 Stevenson, *Scattered Finds*, 162.
33 Mary C. Jonas to C.T. Currelly, 13 October 1926 (DIST.23.36).
34 C.T. Currelly to Mary C. Jonas, 26 October 1926 (DIST.23.38). Although
    I have presently found no direct evidence for Currelly's letter to Hunt,

there is indirect evidence for it. Hunt declared to Jonas that "the same post brought an effusion from Mr. Currelly to me" and that he "shall have to acknowledge [Currelly's] letter." Arthur S. Hunt to Mary C. Jonas, 10 November 1926 (DIST.23.39).

35 See, for example, C.T. Currelly to Mary C. Jonas, 9 November 1927 (DIST 49.106); C.T. Currelly to The Committee, 26 November 1927 (DIST 49.107).

36 Hogarth and Hunt each collaborated with Grenfell in a season of excavation at various sites in the Fayyūm region of Egypt, which resulted in the publication *Fayûm Towns and Their Papyri* (London: Egypt Exploration Fund, 1900). Grenfell and Hunt are together best known for their excavations of Oxyrhynchus over the course of several seasons, and the corresponding series of published papyri, beginning with *The Oxyrhynchus Papyri. Part 1* (London: Egypt Exploration Fund, 1898). Both of these efforts were sponsored by the EES.

37 Arthur S. Hunt to Mary C. Jonas, 10 November 1926 (DIST.23.39).

38 D.G. Hogarth to Mary C. Jonas, 26 November 1926, (DIST.23.41).

39 Mary C. to Arthur S. Hunt, 13 October 1926 (DIST.23.35). Jonas went on to note that "in the Report [the donation] is ascribed to Professor Naville's efforts. Of course I do not know exactly where the credit lay, things are not always what they appear, even in the Reports of the Society I expect."

40 Currelly's first season at Deir el-Bahari took place in 1905–6 and the second in 1906–7. See the official excavation reports that mention Currelly's presence in Edouard Naville and H.R. Hall, "Excavations at Deir El-Bahri," in *Archaeological Report, 1905–1906: Comprising the Work of the Egypt Exploration Fund and the Progress of Egyptology During the Years 1905–1906, ed. F.L. Griffith* (London: Egypt Exploration Fund, 1906), 1–7; Edouard Naville, "Excavations at Deir El-Bahri," in *Archaeological Report, 1906–1907: Comprising the Work of the Egypt Exploration Fund and the Progress of Egyptology During the Years 1906–1907*, ed. F.L. Griffith (London: Egypt Exploration Fund, 1907), 1–7; as well as in "A Remarkable Discovery in Egypt," *Nature* 73, no. 468 (15 March 1906): 468; and Currelly's own recollections of that time in his *Ages*, 136–7.

41 For internal discussion about establishing the Laffan Fund, see Egypt Exploration Fund, *Report of the Twentieth Ordinary General Meeting (Twenty-Fourth Annual General Meeting), Subscription List and Balance Sheets: 1905–1906* (London: Kegan Paul, 1906), 10–11. In 1906, the Egypt Exploration Fund is reported to have given as a gift to the Met "a collection of twenty-five antiquities, XI. Dynasty, from the site of temple of King Mentuhotep at Deir el Bahari," though with no special mention of the Laffan Fund. The Metropolitan Museum of Art, *Thirty-Seventh Annual Report of the Trustees for the Year Ending December 31, 1906* (New York: The Metropolitan Museum of Art, 1906), 41. Currelly also reports this event in his memoir,

where he records the total amount promised by Laffan (misspelled as "Laffin") at $5000. Currelly, *Ages*, 133–4, 137–8, 156.

42 See Arthur S. Hunt to Mary C. Jonas, 10 November 1926 (DIST.23.39); cf. Mary C. Jonas to D.G. Hogarth, 25 November 1926 (DIST.23.40). Quotation from Mary C. Jonas to Arthur S. Hunt, 9 November 1926 (DIST.23.36).

43 Mary C. Jonas to D.G. Hogarth, 25 November 1926 (DIST.23.40).

44 The final report of EES papyri distributions appears in Bernard P. Grenfell, Arthur S. Hunt, and H.I. Bell, "Appendix: List of Oxyrhynchus Papyri Distributed," in *The Oxyrhynchus Papyri. Part XVI* (London: Egypt Exploration Society, 1924), 275–9. Papyrus distributions were briefly revived in the middle of the twentieth century, including some that would make it to the University of Toronto's Department of Classics. But not much is currently known about that second wave.

45 Amarna is the site, for example, where the famous bust of Nefertiti was found (held at the Neues Museum in Berlin), which contributed to renewed interest in ancient Egypt among Europeans and North Americans that conformed with the aesthetics of those finds. See discussion in Stevenson, *Scattered Finds*, 145–80. The ROM was a recipient of some materials from Amarna.

46 Jonas wrote concerning a "Mr. Ralph" from Toronto, who had "suggested that a special donation might be raised towards [the EES's] future work on the understanding that a large donation would ensure a fuller participation of any antiquities found." Jonas hoped that Currelly would see that suggestion through. Mary C. Jonas to C.T. Currelly, 7 August 1926 (DIST.48.08).

Chapter Seven

Covenant, Torah, and the Failed Promise of Jewish Museums

YANIV FELLER

The covenant (*brit/bris*) is a central concept in the Hebrew Bible, signifying God's pact with humanity, and his enduring relation with the Israelites. Several promises and pacts are of particular importance. First, with the earth and Noah (Gen. 9:1–17). Second, with Abram (later Abraham) and his offspring (Gen. 15:1–15, 17:1–27). Third, the theophany at Sinai and the giving of the Torah (Exod. 19ff.). Finally, it is customary to discuss the covenant between David and God, which includes the promises of establishing an everlasting Davidic lineage and the eventual construction of the Temple by his son Solomon (2 Sam. 7; Ps. 89:4).

A covenant is a promise made between unequal powers, an idea that can be traced to Near Eastern suzerain-vassal structure. This raises the question of consent. Commenting on Exod. 19:17 – "and they stood at the lowermost part of the mountain" – the Talmudic sage Rabbi Avidimi bar Hama bar Hasa interpreted: "the Holy One, Blessed be He, overturned the mountain, like a tub, and said to them: If you accept the Torah, excellent, and if not, there will be your burial" (Bavli Shabbat 88a). It is quickly added in the text, however, that the Israelites later accepted the Torah willingly, because a coerced promise is never truly a promise. Both the power relation, and the free will of the Israelites, are expressed in this interpretation.[1]

The covenantal promises made by God and humans create essential commitments and expectations that shape religious and social obligations from the Hebrew Bible to contemporary Judaism. Covenants are not abstract ideas; they have physical manifestations and signs in the world. The rainbow is a symbol of God's promise after the Deluge to never destroy the earth. Circumcising one's son in the Jewish tradition is known in Hebrew as *brit milah*, literally bringing him into the covenant through circumcision. The idea's biblical roots are grounded in the promise that Sarah would give birth and that Abraham's descendants would become numerous. The covenant is thereby inscribed on the male body, a tradition that is still very much alive today among Jews and Muslims. At Mount Sinai, we hear of an object, the tablets of the covenant. These tablets were placed in the Ark of the Covenant, later in the Holy of Holies in the Temple.

Since the destruction of the First Temple in 586 BCE, the whereabouts of the Ark have been shrouded in legend.[2] The tablets' iconography is still present in many synagogues and even government institutions in the Netherlands. In Judaism, the Ark of the Covenant has been symbolically replaced by the Holy Ark or Torah shrine (*aron kodesh*). This synagogal niche or closet contains the item that now stands at the centre of worship, the Torah scroll.[3]

This article explores the place Torah, as the document of the covenant and its manifestation, plays in two Jewish museums: the Jewish Museum London (JML), and POLIN: Museum of the History of Polish Jews in Warsaw. I contend that the way a Jewish museum interprets Torah exposes the broader ideology of that museum and its presentation of Judaism. The Torah scroll as an object is central to the following analysis, but the concept of Torah – discussed in the first section – is broader and encompasses other aspects of the covenant such as the text, the Law, and divine sovereignty. The focus on museums means that the theoretical framework derives not only from Jewish thought but also from theories of curation (section two).

The question guiding the analysis of the two museums (section three) is whether a museum can adequately represent the multiple meanings of the covenant between God and the people of Israel. Put differently, what promise do museums make to visitors and can they keep it when it comes to a foundational idea such as Torah? In examining how Jewish museums present the Torah, we see how these institutions navigate the challenge of conveying not only the historical and ritual significance of the Torah but also its role as a testament to God's promises to the Jewish people.

The expectation of a visitor, the implicit promise of the museum, is that the museum would convey knowledge and a certain experience to the visitor. Otherwise, why bother visiting it? Museums convey an aura of authority, through the sheer presence and presentation of the objects in relation to one another, and through the labels and meanings attached to them by the curators.[4] This idea is essential to the emergence of the modern museum as a secular institution of knowledge collection and production in the nineteenth century. Part of museums' self-appointed role has been categorizing, classifying, and creating hierarchies when it came to religion. Many museums, as Ruth Phillips and others noted, have since tried to move away from this approach, for example by including emic voices. The issue of presentation and ascribing meaning remains central to an understanding of museal interpretations of Torah.[5]

The Seventy Faces of the Torah

According to a rabbinic dictum, the Torah has "seventy faces," which is to say the possibilities of textual interpretation are endless. To understand the concept and object of Torah in the context of museums, I identify four especially pertinent meanings: as text, as law, as a material object, and as a subject. Taken together, they create a matrix within which Jewish museums navigate their presentation.[6]

In a narrow sense, Torah stands for the Five Books of Moses, or the Pentateuch. It is the first part of the Hebrew Bible, the Tanakh, followed by the Prophetic books (*Nevi'im*) and the Writings (*Ketuvim*).[7] For the purpose of reading, the canonical text is identical whether one reads it in a book, a scroll, or a smartphone. Treating Torah as text means paying attention to questions of language and translation, especially if one considers the text divine or divinely inspired. Jewish museums in Europe sometimes thematize the translation of the Torah (and the Tanakh as a whole) into vernacular languages as part of the promise and challenges of emancipation and relation of a minority to the majority society. The old permanent exhibition of the Jewish Museum Berlin (2001–17), for example, used Moses Mendelssohn's late eighteenth-century translation of the Torah to German as the starting point of Jewish integration into German society in modern times.[8]

A second understanding of Torah is Law.[9] In this sense, it is the parameters of the covenant, the promise made by the Israelites and later Jews. In the Septuagint, the Alexandrian Greek translation of the Hebrew Bible, the Hebrew word *torah* is translated as *nomos*, Law. The focus on this meaning is taken up by the New Testament, and the apostle Paul in particular came to be identified with a tendency to critique or transcend the Jewish law.[10] The presentation of Torah as Law is therefore a polemical idea in the context of Jewish-Christian relations. In rabbinic Judaism, tradition identifies two Torahs, a Written Torah and the Oral Torah, which are subsequent rabbinic interpretations of the Written Torah. In one understanding, the Oral Torah itself is also divine and was given to Moses on Sinai along with the Written Torah. This is an assertion of authority, for it is the rabbis themselves that describe this idea.[11]

In Jewish museums, Torah as Law is often expanded to incorporate notions of the studying of the Law (Talmud Torah), as well as of the tradition more broadly. A common strategy is placing a volume or whole set of the Talmud, a canonical rabbinical text, next to the Torah scroll, thereby stressing this continuity. Furthermore, Torah as Law can pertain to the treatment of objects. A Jewish museum might reach out – but this is not always the case – to rabbinic authorities in order to consult them about the religious validity of a Torah scroll, because a Torah scroll that is suitable for religious use should ideally be with a community rather than in a museum.[12]

This leads us to the third meaning, central for the present discussion: Torah as a material object. The Torah scroll (*Sefer Torah*) contains the text of the Pentateuch, but it is not identical with it. The text, as mentioned, can theoretically be in any format, language, or material. This is not the case with the Torah scroll. There is inner-biblical evidence to suggest that scrolls and the writing of the text played a role in the Kingdom of Judea. In a scene whose interpretation is debated among scholars, King Josiah receives "a scroll of Torah" found in the Temple. Upon being read its content, Josiah calls for repentance and the restoration of a centralized sacrifice in the Temple in Jerusalem (2 Kings 22:8–23:27). In this scene, it is the text of the scroll, and its confirmation by a prophetess, that matters and not the object itself.[13] Nonetheless, the object serves as a reminder of the covenant and forgotten promises.

It is only at a later period that the Torah scroll as a material object was assigned holiness and became the focal point of ritual in the synagogue. This started no later than the second century CE and came to be fully codified by the Middle Ages. As a ritual object, the scroll is meant to be used and experienced in the synagogue in a certain way. The performative aspect in the spatial and social constellation of the synagogue, in other words, is crucial to the understanding of the Torah as a ritual object.[14]

As sacred objects, Torah scrolls are on a different ontological plane than other religious objects, for example Shabbat candles.[15] Every object that stands in direct relation to the scroll cannot be simply discarded but must be either converted into use for another commandment or be buried away in a genizah, a repository of sacred texts.[16] This group of objects is known as vessels of holiness (*tashmishei kedusah*), e.g., the Torah mantle or case and the wooden rollers upon which the scroll is placed. Vessels of the commandments (*tashmishei mitzvah*), by contrast, are those objects used for ritual purposes that are not ascribed inherent holiness. A candle is just a candle. Shabbat candles are designated as such because they are lit as part of a specific ritual in time and place. As such, they need not be buried.

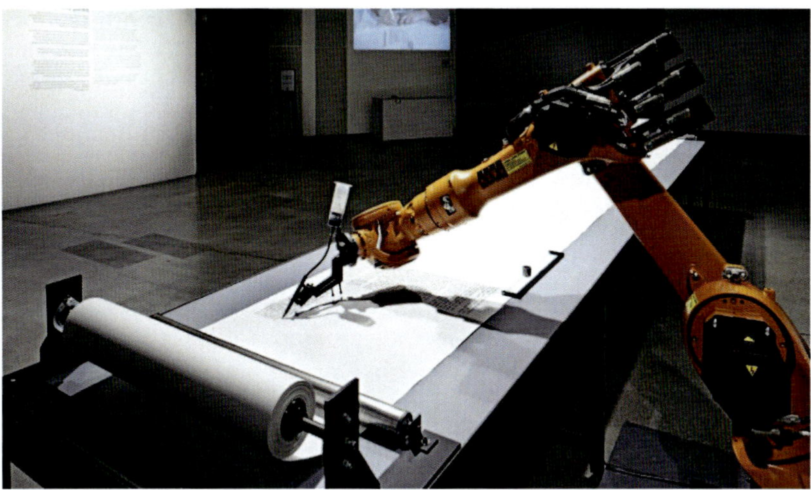

Figure 7.1 Installation "Bios [Torah]" by the artist group robotlab (www.robotlab.de/), Jewish Museum Berlin. Photo by Yves Sucksdorff.

The Torah scroll's production is regulated by a set of halakhic laws: a scribe must write it with great intention on a parchment made from a kosher animal skin, using a quill and special ink. A robot (Figure 7.1) technically capable of writing a flawless scroll – as was presented at the Jewish Museum Berlin's exhibition "The Creation of the World" (2014) – cannot write a valid Torah scroll to be used in the synagogue because it does not have the intentionality required. To continue the above distinction, candles produced in a factory can be used to fulfil the commandment of lighting Shabbat candles, but a mechanically produced Torah scroll is problematic for use in the synagogue. This raises a set of questions related to the preservation and presentation in museums of vessels of holiness in general, and the Torah scroll in particular.

Arjun Appadurai and Igor Kopytoff advocate for an object biography approach that focuses on the development, circulation, and changing meaning of specific objects.[17] Objects emerge from a material that was produced and processed, they come into the world at a certain point in time, are used, misused, repaired, travel from one place to another, are exposed to the weather, get lost, change hands and few find their way into museums. To treat a Torah scroll as a material object means taking its unique history seriously: who produced it and when? Was it used in a synagogue? How did the museum acquire it?[18]

Finally, the Torah is not only a ritual object but a subject. This is a Jewish inflection – attested in ritual practice and textual evidence – that is in line with approaches that treat objects as agents.[19] Lamentations

Rabbah, probably composed between the fifth and seventh century CE, offers a remarkable example: Abraham accuses God of breaking the divine promise by exiling the Israelites and destroying the Temple. God replies that Israel has transgressed the Torah, another breaking of a promise. Abraham then asks for a witness for such a statement. The Torah itself comes to testify and is put to shame by Abraham, who reminds her that Israel accepted her when no one else wanted to.[20] The Torah is clearly an active agent in this story, which expresses anthropomorphism as well as a special relation between the Jews and the Torah.

Similar anthropomorphisms, or rather pointers to the Torah's agency, are found in Jewish ceremonies and holidays. On Yom Kippur (Day of Atonement), the *Kol Nidre* prayer begins the service with a text that releases one from all vows and obligations so that the human can fully repent. It is customarily done while three Torah scrolls are held out of the ark, thereby standing as judges in front of the community. While it can be read symbolically – the Torah as symbolizing divine authority and judgment – another way of understanding it is that the Torah scrolls hold the authority of a court (*beit din*) to release people from their vows. Thought of this way, the Torah scroll is a participant in the process. In Simchat Torah, the holiday celebrating the end of the yearly cycle of reading the Torah, the person invited to read the last portion is called *hatan Torah*, the Torah's groom. In the same celebration, it is customary to dance with the Torah, just as when a new Torah scroll is dedicated, it is often being paraded under a marriage canopy (*chuppah*).

Perhaps the most striking example of the Torah as agent is the seventeenth-century alleged messiah Shabbetai Zevi, who conducted a ceremony in which he married a Torah scroll, thereby proclaiming the unification of the messiah (himself) and the Torah. This was seen by many as a heretical attempt to break the covenant; for Zevi and his followers, however, it was a fulfilment of the messianic promise.[21] In all these instances, the Torah is feminine, serving as the spouse or second half of Israel, the messiah, or God. I have not encountered a museum that would go so far as to thematize the Torah as a subject, with a brief exception of POLIN and its video presentation of the life of another alleged messiah, Jacob Frank.

Thinking of the Torah as a polysemic concept exposes an inherent tension in its representation that curators must confront. Oren Baruch Stier has shown, for example, how the curators in the United States Holocaust Memorial Museum tried to negotiate between the sacrality of desecrated Torah scrolls and the need of the museum as a secular institution to convey knowledge for its visitors.[22] The tension, I argue, is not only between the role of the museum and religion, but also inherent to the idea of Torah. The Torah scroll is the object manifesting the covenant, but it does not capture all its meanings. Neither, however, does treating Torah and covenant as abstract ideas lacking physical substance. The challenge is how to present these meanings and the tensions involved. This is a problem inherent to curatorship, which is always tasked with making decisions as to how to present objects to the visitor. In this sense, it is not unique to the Torah, but the multiple meanings of Torah and its sacredness expose it very poignantly in the context of Jewish museums.

Curating and Silencing

In his introductory essay to this volume, Jeffery Hewitt offers that we turn to the idea of pentimento, a painting over a canvas that was previously painted, in order to highlight not only the colonial violence of erasure and constant breaking of treaties, but also the neglect of historical recognition of that erasure, as well as the potential of recovery of the lost layers. Pentimento exposes previous erasures of meaning, as well as the idea that such erasures are incomplete. It is an apt metaphor, and theoretical model, for dealing with the various, changing meanings objects acquire and lose through inscription, erasure, and placement in the museum.[23] Yet a visual metaphor in the context of the Torah scroll risks an unintended desacralizing thrust. As mentioned in the previous section, the writing of Torah scrolls is highly regulated. A Torah scroll that contains more than a certain number of erasures and mistakes is invalid for ritual use. In other words, a pentimento or palimpsest Torah scroll has lost its function.

Instead of a visual metaphor, I supplement this idea of overwritten promises with an audible component, that of silencing. The theoretical starting point is Paul Valéry's "The Problem of Museums" (1923), an essay in which he complains that works in the museum wish to be treated as rarities, as unique objects. But the fullness of the place, crowded with works and visitors alike, leads to a fight for attention between the works of art.[24] Just as you are not expected to listen to ten orchestras simultaneously, so the visitor to the museum should not be expected to take all the visual cues at once.

The space of the museum, Valéry argues, displaces works from their original context, which in turn leads to the loss of their authentic power as art. Theodor Adorno agrees with Valéry that works die a certain death when coming to the museum.[25] Yet Adorno does not decry the situation or call for a return to a pre-museum state. As a corrective to Valéry's emphasis on the work of art as a thing in and of itself, Adorno turns to Marcel Proust, who epitomized the attitude of the *flâneur*, the observing subject who reads herself into the works in the museum. The *flâneur* is not disturbed by the crowds in the museum or the number of works in a room, because both are merely a catalyst for one's own wandering, ultimately self-centred, thought.

Valéry offers the object-position; Proust the subject-position. Both are right, both are wrong. Adorno argues that objects in museums invite reflection.[26] But this reflection is not a self-reflection that moves away from the objects, as we see in Proust, but rather a reflection on the society that placed these works in the museum. Objects in museums are mediated by their presence in the space of the museum, and it is this mediation that should be reflected upon by the visitors.[27] Museums, according to Adorno, are social agents, embedded in the culture and politics of their time and place. At the same time, objects in museums are not simply passive; they make claims upon the visitor. Adorno therefore suggests that the mediation created by the museum, as the neutralizing space between the object and visitor, is not necessarily to be lamented. On the contrary, it is an occasion for critique of forms of mediation in society. This insight is a reminder that the mediation of objects in museums shapes our understanding of the underlying commitments and the societal values they embody.

Adorno falls short, I believe, in elaborating the question of the *how*, namely the ways in which the museum mediates its objects. The idea of silencing complements this missing piece in Adorno's theory. Silencing can be defined as the negotiation between the curatorial voice and the demands made by the object in the context of the museum. It is part and parcel of the curatorial process, without necessarily implying curatorial intentionality. In fact, silencing might happen against the expressed wishes of the curators.

The mediating power of the museum is not neutral. In the triangle of visitor-object-curator, all parts participate in giving meanings to objects and space. Yet it is the curators who shape the narrative which the visitors confront and in which the objects are placed. The curators are also the ones who decide in the first place what objects to collect and present.[28] At the risk of overstretching Valéry's metaphor, it is not only that objects in museum fight with one another. The curators are the bookies in this fight, the ones who arrange the competition in order to foster a certain agenda. Among the mechanisms they use are positioning in space, the use of labels, multimedia, lighting, and so on.

In *Making and Effacing Art*, Philip Fisher enumerates three ways in which curatorial practices achieve what he calls silencing or "the suppression of images": stripping of context, treating as artwork, and abstraction through art. Of the three, the first two are of importance for this discussion of the Torah scroll. First, in the museum, "images from within the culture [are] stripped from their context."[29] As we have seen, the Torah scroll as an artefact is central to the synagogue. At the risk of oversimplification, one could argue the synagogue is defined by the presence of the Torah scroll and not the other way around.[30] This also could be read, to an extent, the other way around. To paraphrase Fisher, when you take the Torah scroll out of the synagogue, you take the synagogue out of the Torah scroll, thereby silencing a central aspect of it.

The second aspect of silencing objects is by placing them in the museum as artworks. Precious Judaica objects, say Torah accessories, are maintained in their foreignness and treated as art. One representative example is the Victoria and Albert Museum's Europe Gallery, in which a stunning seventeenth-century Torah scroll mantle with its accompanying accessories are presented. As an art and design museum, the Victoria and Albert's main concern is clearly aesthetics, not the religious praxis of the people who used the objects. The accompanying label explaining the object provides an image from Bernhard Picart and Jean Frederic Bernard's *Religious Ceremonies and Customs of All the Peoples of the World*, a 1723 work that might indeed reflect toleration from the period of the objects, but is not giving a voice to their previous unknown Jewish owners or to their meaning for Jews today (Figure 7.2).[31]

Silencing can take many forms, and is a necessary procedure in the process of curation. Listening to the silence, and the process of silencing, is instructive in exposing the ideology of a specific museum. The problem, as mentioned, is not limited to a specific kind of museum. The Victoria and Albert Museum and Jewish museums alike face this type of dilemma when they seek to present the most sacred object in Judaism, and the stand-in for the covenant, as an artefact of craftsmanship rather than religious significance.

The Museums

Before moving to a close reading of the Torah in the exhibitions of the JML and POLIN, the reasons for comparing the two institutions need to be elucidated. To begin with the obvious, both are Jewish museums in respective capitals and thus among the central Jewish cultural institutions in their countries. Second, both permanent exhibitions are twenty-first century creations. The Jewish Museum London opened in 1932, but the present exhibition dates to 2010. The museum closed its doors at the end of 2023, another casualty of the COVID-19 pandemic.[32] POLIN opened in 2013 to much acclaim. The differences between their exhibitions, in other words, cannot be attributed to one being more antiquated than the other.

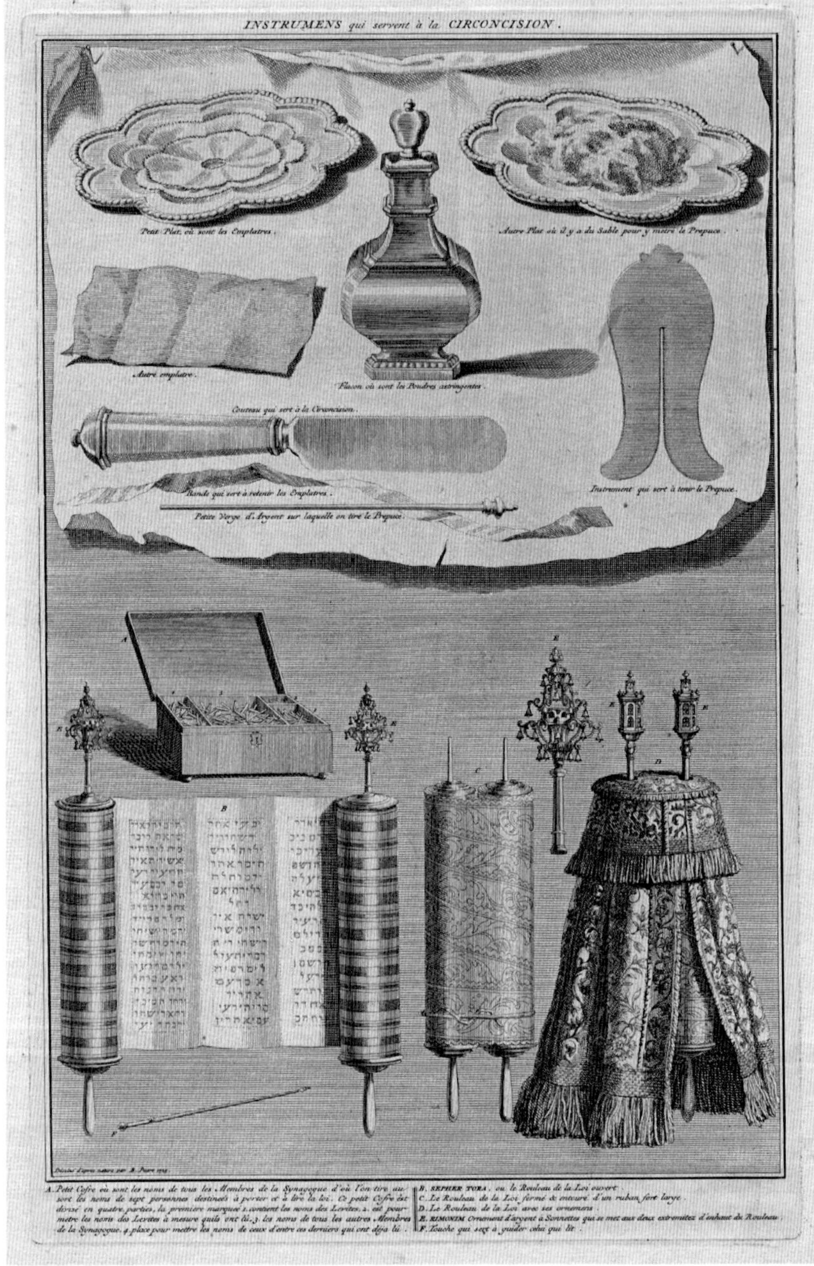

Figure 7.2 Bernard Picart, *Torah Scroll and Its Accessories*, 1725, engraving.
In Bernard Picart, *Cérémonies et coutumes religieuses de tous les peuples du monde.*

The underlying idea informing each museum can be traced to the dual origins of the modern museum, and the two different modes of exhibition that came together around the nineteenth century: on the one hand, collections being opened to the public; on the other hand, public exhibitions such as the World Fairs.[33] The JML is representative of the former, as it started from a private collection. POLIN is an exhibition-oriented museum, drawing on the latter tradition. As its chief curator, Barbara Kirshenblatt-Gimblett, explains, "before there was a museum, before there was a collection, there was a plan for an exhibition."[34]

A comparison of the architecture and locations of the museums tells the background story of the exhibitions from a different perspective. The JML was located in an unremarkable building that formerly served as a piano factory. At the beginning was the collection, not the building. In Warsaw, by contrast, the building is located on the historical site of the Warsaw Ghetto. Even before the visitors enter the museum, they encounter Nathan Rapoport's monumental Ghetto Heroes Monument that was already erected on the site in 1948.[35] As Elżbieta Janicka notes, the construction of the museum coincided with the establishment of ten more memorials in its vicinity, six of which are dedicated to Polish help to Jews, thus reinforcing the dominant Polish national narrative that Poles were victims or helpers, but never perpetrators during the Nazi regime. Unlike the JML, in other words, in POLIN the location is of central importance, even more so than its collection.[36]

A Living Faith

The first exhibition floor of the JML was dedicated to the exhibition "Judaism: A Living Faith," and the second to the historical exhibition about the Jews of England. It is worth pausing on its title of the former. Calling Judaism a "living faith" is revealing. It shows the desire to make clear that Judaism is evolving, as well as that it is something practised in life rather than merely a formal creed.[37] At the same time, the designation as faith is already a distinctly modern, Protestant, understanding that emphasizes belief and delineates religion as a distinct sphere of life. Whereas the covenant is arguably all-encompassing and influences every sphere of life, faith connotes a private matter. This definition, evident for example in Jewish self-designations such as German Citizens of the Mosaic Faith, emerged in the modern period as part of the process of emancipation and reform. It was meant to show that Jews are not a distinct national or racial group but a confession like Catholics and Protestants.[38]

This tendency is evident in the text that greets the visitor to this part of the exhibition, titled "What is Judaism?":

Judaism is the religion and way of life of the Jewish people. [emphasis in the original]

The core teachings of Judaism are set out in the Torah, the first five books of the Bible. It provides a religious and ethical guide and includes the 613 commandments that form the basis of the Jewish way of life. The interpretation of the Torah has been developed over many years by scholars and teachers known as rabbis.

As the Jewish people have spread throughout the world, variations in custom have been developed. However, common practices are shared by observant Jews everywhere. All Jewish communities use Hebrew, the language of the Torah, for prayer and religious observance. They celebrate the weekly day of rest on Sabbath and follow the Jewish calendar to mark the annual cycle of festivals.

Torah is treated in this introduction as text and Law, an approach that frames the visitors' encounter with the exhibition. The claim that "all Jewish communities use Hebrew" is an exaggeration that creates a false sense of a shared unity through language. The treatment of the commandments is also revealing in this regard. Describing Judaism as a "religious and ethical guide" was a common trope in the nineteenth- and twentieth-century descriptions of Judaism meant to counter the Christian prejudice of legalism, namely that Jews focus too much on earthly works in pursuit of salvation, and, by extension, that this leads to absurd hair-splitting legalistic debates.[39]

In the first room of the exhibition, the mode of presentation is what is known as the life cycle approach. The exhibition explains via objects and videos important events in Jewish life from cradle to grave, as well as Jewish holidays and worship. The life cycle presentation, popular since the early days of Jewish museums in the late nineteenth century, has the advantage of serving as a clear presentation of various aspects of Judaism to less informed audiences.[40] The problem with this approach, however, is that "religion" or "Judaism" is artificially separated from the historical narrative, which is one floor above. Although videos describe the meaning of Jewish rituals for contemporary Jews – from kids playing dreidel to a young couple talking about their wedding next to wedding rings – the ritual itself is implicitly deemed timeless.

A Torah scroll is placed at the centre of the room, facing a Torah ark and accessories (Figure 7.3). Whereas the objects in the glass vitrines

Figure 7.3 Entrance to the "Judaism: A Living Faith" gallery at the Jewish Museum London.

might compete for attention among themselves, the Torah scroll dominates the room. The JML imparts here what Joan Branham called "vicarious sacrality."[41] First, quite simply, the Torah scroll is placed in the centre, just as in a traditional synagogue, where it would be read from the *bimah*, or pulpit. Second, the Torah scroll faces directly a historical Torah ark, in the same way it would have been placed in a traditional synagogue during its reading. Finally, the relatively dim lighting and the choice of beautiful objects surrounding the Torah scroll ascribe it unique importance.

The visceral aspects of the Torah are silenced in this presentation. There seems to have been an attempt to present some kind of interactivity in which the visitor touches the screen with a *yad* (Torah pointer) and hears the Ten Commandments, again a nod to universalist tendencies through a choice of an uncontroversial text, unlike detailed sections on sacrificial offerings or the commandment to wipe out the memory of Amalek. During my visits to the museum, unfortunately, one could not listen to the reading as there was a technical problem. But even if it had been possible, the reading, while central, is only one aspect of the visceral experience of the Torah, which includes the sound of the bells on the *rimonim* or watching it being raised for everyone in the synagogue to see. This is a common and unfortunate silencing that is a consequence of placing religious material objects in museums. The glass case fulfils the promise of presenting, and preserving, the object, but at the price of limiting the possibility of experiencing it.[42]

As a material object, the Torah scroll is always situated in time and space, yet one learns nothing about the biography of this specific Torah scroll. Was this Torah used in a synagogue? Where and when? The placement of the scroll at the centre of the room in "Judaism: A Living Faith" is meant to show its relevance for contemporary life, but it does so at the cost of silencing not only the embodied aspects of experiencing the Torah scroll but also at the expense of the biography of this specific scroll.

Silencing, to reiterate, is not always intentional. It is part of a promise the JML cannot keep. In this case, it is likely the result of lack of information. When it is available, the museum gladly provides biographical details of the objects. This is most evident in the case of the Torah ark, placed in the second room of "Judaism: A Living Faith." It was produced in northern Italy in the seventeenth century. Perhaps bought by an English nobleman, it served as a steward's wardrobe in Chillingham Castle before its original purpose was realized in 1932.[43] The illustrious biography of the object, and the fact that it is being told, are examples of the importance the JML, as a collection-based museum, attributes to working with historical objects.

The Torah ark dwarfs a small interactive synagogue model and a wall media installation. It makes these two interactives, meant to express the Oral Torah and its different authority in Jewish denominations, appear more as an afterthought than an integral part of the concept. The video screen on the wall – easy to miss due to the dominance of the Torah ark – presents rabbis from different denominations answering the same questions. It is an effective and common technique to show the plurality of Jewish religious life.[44] The interactive synagogue model is probably meant to achieve the same goal. One can move the characters, so that a woman, for example, could read the Torah from the pulpit. While this sounds liberal and reflective of various denominations of Judaism, it is curious that one cannot move the *bimah*, the pulpit. This is not to be underestimated. Historically, one of the differences between the Reform and Orthodox movements in Judaism is often the location of the pulpit. For the latter it remained in the centre; the former place it near the Torah ark, in line with architecture of many churches.[45] In other words, this activity offers the visitors a variety of synagogue scenarios, but with a certain limit to them.

"Judaism: A Living Faith" conveys the centrality of the Torah through the introductory text, the vicarious sacrality of objects, and multimedia. The focus is on notions of Law and text. The covenant – not named as such as it might be too alienating to visitors – is present through these aspects of the Torah. Yet the life cycle approach is not without its difficulties. The separation of this section from the historical exhibition and calling it "a living faith" point to the attempt to elevate religion as a sphere distinct from history, as does the vicarious sacrality of placing the Torah scroll at the centre. Despite the attempt of the video screens next to the objects, the result is that the covenant remains detached from life, and often from the biography of the objects, such as the Torah scroll and its accessories, that make the covenant's presence felt in peoples' lives.

Warsaw's Theater of History

POLIN takes a very different approach to that of the JML in its permanent exhibition. The promise POLIN makes as a museum is grounded not in the collection but in ideas about storytelling and historical context.[46] In a programmatic essay titled "Theater of History," Barbara Kirshenblatt-Gimblett lays out the principles that guided the curatorial work. The presentation of objects and media was to flow from the narrative and not the other way around. Another organizing principle was the refusal to give normative, ahistorical answers to questions about Judaism. Unlike the JML's exhibition, which began with the question "What is Judaism?," POLIN refuses to provide a clear-cut answer. Instead, writes Kirshenblatt-Gimblett, "There are many ways to be Jewish, and Polish Jews continue to be a work in progress. Answers, provisional at best, are to be found in historically specific moments of the story, in actual situations."[47] It is for these reasons that the curators in POLIN decided against a life cycle presentation, although one was originally planned.[48]

This approach is reflected in the presentation of the different facets of Torah in POLIN. The main discussion of Torah appears within the context of Jewish learning (Talmud Torah) for which Polish Jewry was known. It is part of the section "Paradisus Iudaeorum," which is dedicated to the years 1569–1648 and the revolution in learning brought about by the printing press. Torah as text and tradition, as Oral Torah written down, is explained using media stations that invite the visitor to explore a variety of Jewish canonical works. One example is an interactive presentation that highlights the idea that tradition is in constant movement while still grounded in a fixed origin (Figure 7.4).

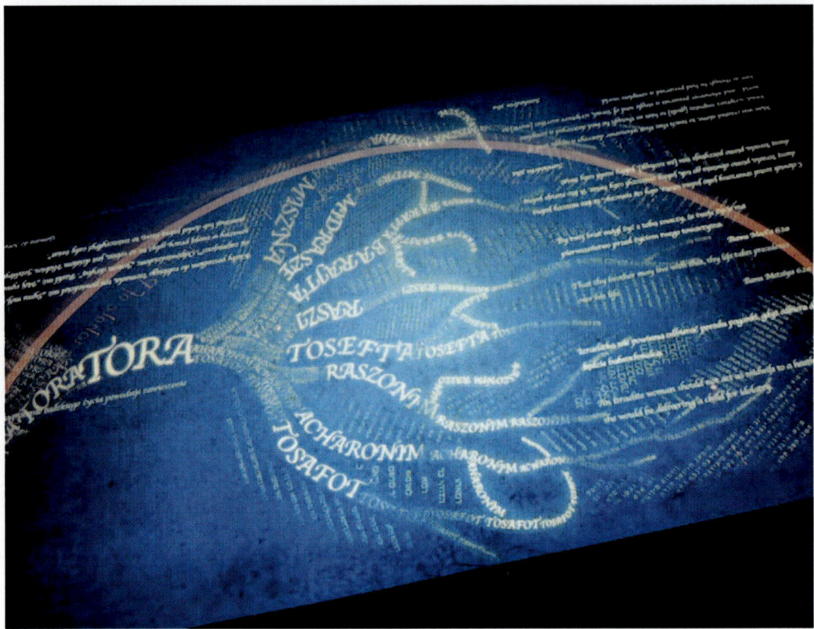

Figure 7.4 Interactive presentation, POLIN, Museum of the History of Polish Jews, Warsaw. Photograph by author.

The visitor learns how Jewish teaching shapes the totality of Jewish life in this period, down to practical questions such as the washing of the hands. This is done through a multimedia station that presents the canonical halakhic work *Shulchan Aruch* by Joseph Karo, and the important commentary on it by the Ashkenazi rabbi Moses Isserles. These works – still highly influential today – are presented in their historical context as part of a gallery dedicated to the era in which they were produced. This presentation reflects both general questions in Judaism, and divergence in custom that is expressed by the difference between Karo and Isserles. It is through engagement with these texts as they relate to specific halakhic questions that the visitor gains knowledge of Judaism.

The most impressive example of the "Theater of History" approach is the Gwoździec synagogue (Figure 7.5). This beautiful wooden synagogue stands for the tradition of wooden synagogues in Poland that did not survive. The Gwoździec's synagogue in POLIN is therefore not the original wooden synagogue, but neither is it a simple reconstruction. It is a new kind of object, especially commissioned for POLIN and

Figure 7.5 The Core Exhibition, *The Jewish Town* gallery at POLIN Museum, photo by M. Starowieyska, D. Golik/POLIN Museum of the History of Polish Jews.

built by a group of volunteers and experts. Yet it is also historical by virtue of having been built according to the old building and painting techniques, which were researched and recovered as part of the project.

The media stations and the audio guide in the synagogue explain the copious illustrations as well as the sacredness of the Torah scroll that is to be read from above the *bimah*.

The Hebrew text above the *bimah* prohibits talking during the reading of the Torah. This is, of course, not a problem. A physical Torah scroll is not to be found near the synagogue, and I was unable to locate any in the exhibition during my visits in 2016. The absence of a Torah scroll shows the tension in the commitment to the story over objects and the inherent silencing involved in curating. Presenting a Torah scroll not from Gwoździec would lead to the silencing of its biography and bring undesired messiness to the narrative by associating it with a synagogue to which it did not belong. The "Theater of History" approach leads, on the one hand, to innovative explorations of what Torah means in the broad sense, as tradition and teaching. On the other hand, the same commitment to the story above all leads de facto to the exclusion of the Torah scroll as a material object. The visitor does not experience the materiality of the Torah as a three-dimensional object belonging in the synagogue.

Conclusion

The Torah as representative of the covenant is a cipher by which to understand the broader agendas of Jewish museums. The different strategies used by the museums show what they see as the relation between Judaism and history, and what they consider to be the main task of the museum. In the JML, Judaism is presented as a "living faith," but one that seems detached from history. In POLIN, the historical narrative takes precedence and Judaism is presented in historical manifestations. Exploring the practice of curatorial silencing is helpful in seeing where each museum succeeds in fulfilling its promise to the visitors, and where it fails. In London, there are historical objects that tell an ahistorical narrative. The Torah scroll as a physical object is present. But this is done without reference to its specific historical circumstances that brought this Torah scroll to the museum, or necessarily for the purpose of celebrating it as a Jewish object. Nor were the visceral aspects associated with the Torah present. The Torah scroll as an object served as a decorative element meant to bring a point across. At once at the centre of the room, and a footnote. In Warsaw, the study of Torah is present, but the scroll is absent. One learns about tradition as historical multifaceted development. The "Theater of History" approach achieves this at the expense of experiencing the Torah scroll qua physical object.

The Jewish museums studied here, like museums more broadly, serve as mediators between objects and visitors through the establishment of a narrative. This narrative, Adorno teaches, merits our reflection as it is a contemporary issue, namely the presentation of Judaism in the twenty-first century. When faced with the idea of covenant and its physical representation, Jewish museums are bound to fail. I do not mean it as a pejorative, but as a matter of museal praxis. There is always a price to be paid for a presentation in a museum.[49]

Torah scrolls are not historical relics; they are tangible embodiments of the enduring promises and commitments that have profoundly shaped Jewish identity and religious practice over centuries. The fulfilment of the promise of the narrative and communication of information entails a silencing of some of the facets of Torah. In London, the result is a material ahistorical Judaism; in Warsaw, a tendency towards a historicized Judaism at the expense of the object. POLIN and JML are just two case studies of the ways covenant and Torah can be used to interpret Jewish museums. As central religious objects and ideas, however, they are revealing about the mediation inherent to curatorial work. Paying attention to the limits and failures of mediation is productive because it exposes the ideology of the museum and the treatment of sacred objects in contemporary society.

NOTES

1 Arnold Eisen, "Covenant," in *20th Century Jewish Religious Thought*, ed. Arthur A. Cohen and Paul Mendes-Flohr (Philadelphia: The Jewish Publication Society, 2009), 107–12; David Novak, *Covenantal Rights: A Study in Jewish Political Theory* (Princeton, NJ: Princeton University Press, 2000).
2 John Day, "Whatever Happened to the Ark of the Covenant?," in *Temple and Worship in Biblical Israel*, ed. John Day (London: T & T Clark, 2005), 250–70.
3 Steven Fine, *This Holy Place: On the Sanctity of the Synagogue during the Greco-Roman Period* (Notre Dame, IN: University of Notre Dame Press, 1997), 72–4; and Lee I. Levine, *The Ancient Synagogue: The First Thousand Years* (New Haven, CT: Yale University Press, 2000), 351–6.
4 Carol Duncan, *Civilizing Rituals: Inside Public Art Museums* (London: Routledge, 1995); Sharon Macdonald, "Exhibitions of Power and Powers of Exhibition: An Introduction to the Politics of Display," in *The Politics of Display: Museums, Science, Culture*, ed. Sharon Macdonald (London: Routledge, 1998), 1–21; Pamela Klassen, "Narrating Religion through Museums," in *Narrating Religion*, ed. Sarah Iles Johnston (New York: MacMillan, 2016), 333–52.
5 Ruth B. Phillips, "Re-Placing Objects: Historical Practices for the Second Museum Age," *The Canadian Historical Review* 86, no. 1 (March 2005): 83–110; Tony Bennett, *The Birth of the Museum: History, Theory, Politics* (New York: Routledge, 1995); Sharon Macdonald, "Enchantment and Its Dilemmas: The Museum as a Ritual Site," in *Science, Magic, and Religion: The Ritual Processes of Museum Magic*, ed. Mary Bouquet and Nuno Porto (Oxford: Berghahn Books, 2022), 209–28.
6 Bamidbar Rabbah 13:16. See Lawrence H. Schiffman, "The Term and Concept of Torah," in *What Is Bible?*, ed. Karin Finsterbusch and Armin Lange (Leuven: Peeters, 2012), 191.
7 This threefold structure is not self-evident. See Marc Zvi Brettler, "The Canonization of the Bible," in *The Jewish Study Bible*, ed. Adele Berlin and Marc Zvi Brettler (New York: Oxford University Press, 2014), 2153–8; Tal Ilan, "The Term and Concept of TaNaKh," in Finsterbusch and Lange, *What Is Bible?*, 173–91.

8   On Bible translations, see Leonard Greenspoon, "Jewish Translations of the
    Bible," in Berlin and Zvi Brettler, *The Jewish Study Bible*, 2005–20; Abigail
    Gillman, *A History of German Jewish Bible Translation* (Chicago: Chicago
    University Press, 2017).

9   Jonathan Klawans, "The Law," in *The Jewish Annotated New Testament: New
    Revised Standard Version Bible Translation*, ed. Amy-Jill Levine and Marc Zvi
    Brettler (Oxford: Oxford University Press, 2011), 515–18.

10 Current scholarship suggests a much more complicated relation to the
    Law in Paul's thought, but regardless of Paul's own position, he often
    came to be understood this way. See David Nirenberg, *Anti-Judaism: The
    Western Tradition* (New York: W.W. Norton, 2013), 64.

11 James Kugel, "Torah," in *Contemporary Jewish Religious Thought: Original
    Essays on Critical Concepts, Movements, and Beliefs*, ed. Arthur A. Cohen
    and Paul Mendes-Flohr (London: Collier Macmillan, 1988), 999–1000.
    For different views on the relation between Written and Oral Torah, see
    Schiffman, "The Term and Concept of Torah."

12 Margalit Schindler, "Religious Values as Conservation Practice: Caring
    for Judaica," in *Prioritizing People in Ethical Decision-Making and Caring
    for Cultural Heritage Collections*, ed. Nina Owczarek (London: Routledge,
    2023), 115–25.

13 What text Josiah's scroll contained is anyone's guess, but the majority
    scholarly opinion suggests that it was some version of the book of
    Deuteronomy. See Michael L. Satlow, *How the Bible Became Holy* (New
    Haven, CT: Yale University Press, 2014), 40–50.

14 David Stern, *The Jewish Bible: A Material History* (Seattle: University of
    Washington Press, 2017), 39–41, 44–8; on locution and performative
    in ritual, see Jonathan Z. Smith, *To Take Place: Toward Theory in Ritual*
    (Chicago: University of Chicago Press, 1987); Catherine M. Bell, *Ritual
    Theory, Ritual Practice* (New York: Oxford University Press, 2009).

15 A similar status is given to other scrolls written under similar guidelines
    and containing portions of the Torah (the scroll of the *mezuzah* and the
    tefillin). Talmud Bavli Megillah 26b; Virginia Greene, "'Accessories of
    Holiness': Defining Jewish Sacred Objects," *Journal of the American Institute
    for Conservation* 31, no. 1 (1992): 31–9.

16 The category of things requiring proper burial (*genizah*) has been expanded
    by some to include among others any objects that contain the divine name.
    For a list of objects, see Amutat Gniza Klalit, accessed 13 March 2025,
    https://gniza.org.il/%D7%9E%D7%99%D7%93%D7%A2-%D7%A9%D7%
    99%D7%9E%D7%95%D7%A9%D7%99/#b.

17 Arjun Appadurai, "Commodities and the Politics of Value," in *The Social
    Life of Things: Commodities in Cultural Perspective*, ed. Arjun Appadurai
    (New York: Cambridge University Press, 1986), 3–63; Igor Kopytoff,

"The Cultural Biography of Things: Commodification as Process," in Appadurai, *The Social Life of Things*, 64–94. For a different approach, that uses the object to tell the human story, see Janet Hoskins, *Biographical Objects: How Things Tell the Stories of Peoples' Lives* (New York: Routledge, 1998); Daniel Miller, *The Comfort of Things* (Cambridge: Polity, 2008).

18 Provenance is a central challenge for Jewish museums in the twenty-first century. See Felicitas Heimann-Jelinek, "Thoughts on the Role of a European Jewish Museum in the 21st Century," in *Visualizing and Exhibiting Jewish Space and History*, ed. Richard Cohen (New York: Oxford University Press, 2012), 243–57.

19 This parallels several Indigenous understandings of the world, while not treating the Torah as kin or ancestor. On the comparison, see Yaniv Feller, "Whose Museum Is It? Jewish Museums and Indigenous Theory," *Comparative Studies in Society and History* 63, no. 4 (2021): 810–16. For Indigenous epistemology, see Craig N. Cipolla, "Taming the Ontological Wolves: Learning from Iroquoian Effigy Objects," *American Anthropologist* 121, no. 3 (2019): 613–27; Cara Ann Krmpotich, *The Force of Family: Repatriation, Kinship, and Memory on Haida Gwaii* (Toronto: University of Toronto Press, 2014); Eduardo Batalha Viveiros de Castro, "The Transformation of Objects into Subjects in Amerindian Ontologies," *Common Knowledge* 10, no. 3 (Fall 2004): 463–84. New materialism theories suggest that such agency is not limited to sacred objects; see Alfred Gell, *Art and Agency: An Anthropological Theory* (Oxford: Clarendon Press, 1998); Jane Bennett, *Vibrant Matter: A Political Ecology of Things* (Durham, NC: Duke University Press, 2010).

20 Lamentations Rabba, ed. Solomon Buber, petichta, 24.

21 Gershom Scholem, *Sabbatai Sevi: The Mystical Messiah, 1626–1676*, trans. Zwi Werblowsky (Princeton, NJ: Princeton University Press, 2016), 159.

22 Oren Baruch Stier, "Torah and Taboo: Containing Jewish Relics and Jewish Identity at the United States Holocaust Memorial Museum," *Numen* 57, no. 3/4 (2010): 505–36.

23 Jeffery Hewitt, "Fragmented Promises, Pentimento, and the Salvage Paradigm," in this volume; Patricia Seed, *American Pentimento: The Invention of Indians and the Pursuit of Riches* (Minneapolis: University of Minnesota Press, 2001). Chip Colwell turns to a similar metaphor: that of the palimpsest, or a text that has been written over. See Chip Colwell, "A Palimpsest Theory of Objects," *Current Anthropology* 63, no. 2 (April 2022): 129–57.

24 Paul Valéry, "Das Problem der Museen," in *Zur Ästhetik und Philosophie der Künste*, ed. Jürgen Schmidt-Radefeldt, trans. Werner Zemp (Frankfurt am Main: Insel, 1995), 6:446–7. Valéry had the Louvre in mind, but his argument can be expanded to other museums as well.

25 Theodor W. Adorno, "Valéry Proust Museum," in *Prisms*, trans. Samuel and Shierry Weber (London: Spearman, 1967), 175.

26 On the object in the museum, see Gottfried Korff, "Zur Eigenart der Museumsdinge (1992)," in *Museumsdinge: Deponieren – Exponieren* (Köln: Böhlau, 2002), 140–5.

27 Adorno, "Valéry Proust Museum," 185.

28 Crispin Paine, *Religious Objects in Museums: Private Lives and Public Duties* (New York: Bloomsbury, 2013); Ruth Phillips, "Why Not Tourist Art? Significant Silences in Native American Museum Representations," in *After Colonialism: Imperial Histories and Postcolonial Displacements*, ed. Gyan Prakash (Princeton, NJ: Princeton University Press, 1995), 98–126.

29 Philip Fisher, *Making and Effacing Art: Modern American Art in a Culture of Museums* (Cambridge, MA: Harvard University Press, 1997), 19.

30 Felicitas Heimann-Jelinek, "Die Synagogen und ihre Metamorphosen: Götteshäuser – Leerstellen – Gedenkstätten," in *Wiederhergestellte Synagogen: Raum – Geschichte – Wandel durch Erinnerung*, ed. Benigna Schönhagen (Berlin: Hentrich & Hentrich, 2016), 23. On the remaining sanctity of the synagogue after the Torah has been taken away, cf. Maimonides, *Mishne Torah*, Laws of Prayer and Priestly Benediction, 11.2.

31 Lynn Hunt, Margaret C. Jacob, and W.W. Mijnhardt, *The Book That Changed Europe: Picart & Bernard's* Religious Ceremonies of the World (Cambridge, MA: Harvard University Press, 2010).

32 Yasmin Rufo, "London's Only Jewish Museum Closes Its Doors," *BBC*, 31 July 2023, www.bbc.com/news/uk-england-london-66357950.

33 For an emphasis on collections, see John E. Simmons, *Museums: A History* (Lanham, MD: Rowman & Littlefield, 2016); for the relation to exhibitions, see Robert Rydell, "World Fairs and Museums," in *A Companion to Museum Studies*, ed. Sharon Macdonald (Oxford: Blackwell, 2006), 135–51; the modern connection between the two is detailed in Anke te Heesen, *Theorien des Museums: Zur Einführung* (Hamburg: Junius, 2012).

34 Barbara Kirshenblatt-Gimblett, "Theater of History," in *Polin: 1000 Year History of Polish Jews*, ed. Barbara Kirshenblatt-Gimblett and Antony Polonsky, trans. Dominika Gajewska (Warsaw: Museum of the History of the Polish Jews, 2014), 9.

35 On Rapaport's monument, before the museum was founded, see James Edward Young, *The Texture of Memory: Holocaust Memorials and Meaning* (New Haven, CT: Yale University Press, 1994); on the site of the Warsaw Ghetto as encapsulating multidirectional memories of suffering and resistance, see Michael Rothberg, "From Gaza to Warsaw: Multidirectional Memory and the Perpetrator," in *The Implicated Subject: Beyond Victims and Perpetrators* (Stanford: Stanford University Press, 2019), 119–45.

36 Elżbieta Janicka, "The Square of Polish Innocence: POLIN Museum of the History of Polish Jews in Warsaw and Its Symbolic Topography," *East European Jewish Affairs* 45, no. 2–3 (2015): 200–14.

37 On lived religion, see Robert A. Orsi, *The Madonna of 115th Street: Faith and Community in Italian Harlem, 1880–1950* (New Haven, CT: Yale University Press, 2002).

38 Leora Batnitzky, *How Judaism Became a Religion: An Introduction to Modern Jewish Thought* (Princeton, NJ: Princeton University Press, 2011); Cynthia M. Baker, *Jew* (New Brunswick, NJ: Rutgers University Press, 2017); Robert Orsi, "Belief," in *Key Terms in Material Religion*, ed. S. Brent Plate (London: Bloomsbury Academic, 2015), 17–23.

39 David Novak, "Avoiding Charges of Legalism and Antinomianism in Jewish-Christian Dialogue," *Modern Theology* 16, no. 3 (2000): 278–80.

40 Cilly Kugelmann, "Museen," in *Enzyklopädie jüdischer Geschichte und Kultur*, ed. Dan Diner (Stuttgart: J.B. Metzler, 2014), 277.

41 Joan Branham, "Sacrality and Aura in the Museum: Mute Objects and Articulate Space," *The Journal of the Walters Art Gallery* 52/53 (1994/1995): 37.

42 Svetlana Alpers, "The Museum as a Way of Seeing," in *Exhibiting Cultures: The Poetics and Politics of Museum Display*, ed. Ivan Karp and Steven Lavine (Washington, DC: Smithsonian Institution Press, 1991), 25–32.

43 "Torah Ark, Piedmont, Northern Italy, 17th Century – Unknown," Google Arts & Culture, accessed 7 April 2021, https://artsandculture.google.com /asset/torah-ark-piedmont-northern-italy-17th-century-unknown /tgEYxWsC5amgig.

44 Such an approach was utilized by the Jewish Museum Berlin in its 2013 temporary exhibition "The Whole Truth … Everything You Always Wanted to Know about Jews." The JMB repeated this idea in a new format in its new permanent exhibition that opened in August 2020. A similar idea is also present in the Frankfurt Jewish Museum's new permanent exhibition, which opened in October 2020.

45 Mirko Przystawik, Andreas Brämer, and Harmen Thies, eds., *Reform Judaism and Architecture* (Petersberg: Michael Imhof, 2017).

46 Pamela Klassen, "Narrating Religion through Museums," 349–50.

47 Kirshenblatt-Gimblett, "Theater of History," 33.

48 The tendency to move away from the life cycle approach is also evident in the new permanent exhibition of The Jewish Museum (New York).

49 The idea to focus on failure is inspired by Arjun Appadurai and Neta Alexander, *Failure* (Cambridge: Polity, 2020).

PART III

The Oath, the Law, and the "Sense of Religion"

BENJAMIN L. BERGER

There is something embarrassing about the contemporary oath. Despite the family resemblance to the promise, it reaches beyond its cousin in its insistent appeal to the metaphysical. The oath is exactly more than a promise, and precisely in this way. This appeal to a transcendent order – or, at least, to something immanent but not quite present – is the source of its distinctively binding character. This order includes the conviction that the consequences of breaking the oath reach beyond the material and interpersonal, affecting the oath-taker at a more fundamental and existential level. This is what Pamela Klassen and Isabel Klassen-Marshall in this volume capture when they describe the oath as "a promise with one foot in the afterlife." All of this underwrites the oath's compelling offer of a peculiar solemnity, force, and even sacrality; the oath evokes, borrowing from Kellen Funk in the section that follows, a "sense of religion." But this is also what makes the oath an awkward device. Inspired by Jeffery Hewitt's introduction to this volume, we might say that Christian theology and the Christian God are never far from view in this "pentimento" of the oath, even as we have painted over it in the various ways that the chapters in this section explore. Why has a device so coloured by this theological pigment persisted in its use and appeal in liberal legal and political orders? How does it survive in the atmosphere of secularism and pluralism? The tenacity of this form of promise appears to be something of a puzzle.

When we acknowledge the liberal rule of law as a system of belief, however, what appears first as a puzzle begins to look more like a key or cipher, helping us to see the way in which modern legal and political life continue to depend on a sacred sensibility. One way in is to step back – adopting a kind of Husserlian epoché that temporarily suspends the accepted concepts that we associate with objects[1] – and see the oath more phenomenologically, as ceremonial form of promise that affirms and draws its strength from a system of beliefs and larger moral order. Whereas a promise binds us to another person, an oath binds us to this order of belief. The oath is, thus, a signpost pointing to the ongoing role of belief in our secular legal and political lives. That "role of belief" encompasses both an ongoing reliance on subjects' religious and otherwise metaphysical commitments and the belief in the liberal rule of law itself. Seen this way, the difficulty of disentangling the religious and secular facets of the oath is simply a faithful measure of the messiness of the interaction of law and religion in modern secular life.

While it is drawing energy, as if by proximity, from its religious roots, the contemporary legal oath affirms a particular belief central to the liberal rule of law: the law's capacity to transcend difference. Managing difference is the foundational liberal political problem to which faith in the rule of law is offered as a solution.[2] The legal oath assists in this task by appealing to something beyond reason and interest that binds our will, and does so despite the various differences that otherwise divide us. To have my oath is to not have to worry about me in the particular: the habits, incentives, beliefs, or circumstances that otherwise direct my actions. The oath purports to cut through all of this with its special form of promise. The oath of allegiance in a diverse society is an emphatic expression of this: the oath is a special commitment to belief in and fidelity to something (not least, the rule of law, often represented by the constitution) despite our many differences. And, as Pamela Klassen and Isabel Klassen-Marshall show in their piece that follows, it is precisely for this reason that the oath of allegiance has become a place to debate the boundaries of community: whose oath, and in what form, can we rely upon, and what oath, asserting what beliefs, can I swear? But it is equally true of the inquisitorial oath that we are most familiar with in the courtroom – the oath to tell the truth. Drawing what assistance it can from whatever theological beliefs might be at hand for the given witness, the oath marks off the courtroom as a sacred space of its own, defined by a common and fundamental belief in the rule of law. This fact is what has made the question of who can properly take this oath – with what beliefs in what moral order – so historically fraught along lines of religious, ethnic, and racial difference, as Catherine Evans shows in her chapter below. In short, we are not done with the oath because we are not yet done with sacred promises that can do this work of managing difference.

The oath does its work by establishing a particular relationship between belief and fact. Confident that the swearer's architecture of belief supports the special moral power of the oath, the oath becomes the warrant to rely on the individual as a source of fact. The oath offers itself as a foundation for factual certainty but is itself fashioned from belief. Evans's chapter shows what happens as state authorities, met with racial and religious difference, lose confidence in the beliefs of the state's legal subjects. She tells the story of a late-nineteenth century Australian murder case, *R v. An Gaa*, involving a Chinese victim and accused, in which the testimonial reliability of the Chinese witnesses is centrally at issue. Uncertainty about the metaphysical commitments and spiritual constitution of the Chinese subject is expressed through worry about the adequacy of the oath and the reliability of the testimony. The case is emblematic of a broader phenomenon, central to this volume: of colonial authorities, desperate to preserve the authority and integrity of the institutions that "sorted, counted, judged, and managed the empire's subjects," met with racial, cultural, and religious difference that exposes and then unsettles the beliefs that allow the legal system to function. In her account of the "candle-based oath," Evans shows these colonial powers struggling to adapt the legal form to comport with what they thought they knew about Chinese spirituality; but these attempts to manage difference always run up against limits. The oath thus becomes a proxy for the digestibility of difference in the colonial legal system. Attention to the oath exposes the legal system as both more dependent on theology and more fragile in the face of difference than is comfortably acknowledged.

The extreme difficulty of extinguishing the sacred/metaphysical components of law, as seen through the life and fate of the oath, is the central teaching of Kellen Funk's chapter in this section. In the mid-nineteenth century, American law saw an ambitious attempt to modernize legal procedure through David Dudley Field's development of what is now known as Field's Code. As Funk reminds us, though, the story of the progressive rationalization of law is as misleading as it is seductive, just as is true of the parallel modernization story about racial equality. Funk's account of Field's treatment of the oath draws these two stories, and their aporias, together. One might reasonably expect that modernization and rationalization of legal procedure would put the oath to bed in favour of fully secularized alternatives. And, indeed, Field had no affection for the theological inheritances of the oath. But he radically expanded the use of the oath, precisely as an attempt to show that its theological foundations were no longer to be taken seriously. It was an effort to disenchant legal procedure by cheapening the metaphysical currency of the oath. Funk shows, however, that "the reform ran headlong against the racial prejudices of the western bar, which insisted that cross-examination required some degree of white Christian piety to work its magic." Just as we continually learn about our current moment, the political and social world was not yet quite ready to be disenchanted, particularly as it met the consequences of colonialism and the fact of racial and gender difference. The oath is an illustration that, in the beliefs that sustain the rule of law, the religious is not succeeded by the secular; they continually mix in new ways.

Through its curious moral force, the oath is not only reflective of these complex and mixing currents of secularism, colonialism, and difference – it is also generative, seeking to create certain kinds of citizens and subjects who believe in certain things. This face of the oath in a plural, multi-jurisdictional world is the focus of Pamela Klassen and Isabel Klassen-Marshall's chapter, as they turn their attention to the oath of allegiance, ultimately wondering what historical and contemporary debates about the oath tell us about what it means to be treaty people. Their three examples variously direct our attention to how the oath can come to serve as a synecdoche for a set of beliefs treasured and courted by the liberal colonial state. For Mennonites in the late nineteenth century, it is precisely the belief-saturated nature of the oath – the idolatry of sovereignty, and willingness for violence – to which they objected and that demanded accommodation if the Canadian state was to succeed in using them in the larger project of Indigenous dispossession. The recent controversy in Canada over the ceremonial form of the oath of citizenship was, similarly, really about anxiety over the substantive beliefs that the oath ostensibly guaranteed and cultivated. When the Minister of Immigration worried that officials would be unable to see a veiled woman's lips moving, he was worrying that Muslim women might not believe in "constitutional values." But as much as oaths are about affirming and establishing certain commitments, Klassen and Klassen-Marshall remind us that they simultaneously expose and make vulnerable "the foundations of authority by speaking them aloud." This important truth is on display in Klassen and Klassen-Marshall's third example: a newly elected Indigenous city councillor's refusal to swear an oath of allegiance to the Queen. Refusing the oath can be an act of affirmative disbelief: here, a denial of the myths of colonialism, the magic of the Crown, and the alchemy of sovereignty. Perhaps, then, the oath has no part in reconciliation; perhaps it is irredeemable.

Attuned to the presence of faith – faith in sovereignty, authority, and legitimacy – at work in this legal form, we have returned, via the oath, to the rule of law as a system of belief. Drawing from Nicholas Aroney's work, Klassen and Klassen-Marshall helpfully describe oaths as "ceremonies designed to cultivate people for whom promises matter." I am tempted to think that, more foundationally, oaths are designed to create people for whom law matters. In multi-jurisdictional, multi-religious, (post)colonial societies, they do so drawing abundantly on their theological and moral origins and energy to sanctify the beliefs at the heart of the rule of law. This is the mechanism by which the oath seeks to do its special work managing difference – by giving the beliefs central to the modern liberal legal order a "sense of religion." This is how we might read Aroney's claim that oaths are "nothing less than the ultimate existential foundation of the rule of law."[3] And yet they are also, therefore, an invaluable point of access to ethical and political deliberation capable of exposing the vulnerability of the law.[4] Once we see that, though powerful and material in its consequences, law is a practice of faith, we are freshly attuned to both the alternatives that it suppresses and the possibility of dissention.

NOTES

1 Husserl called these customarily relied-upon ideas about phenomena, "acceptances." On the use of phenomenological method for critical political and legal reflection, see Sophie Loidolt, "Order, Experience, and Critique: The Phenomenological Method in Political and Legal Theory," *Continental Philosophy Review* 54 (2021): 153–70.
2 This is the very heart of Rawls's political theory. John Rawls, *Political Liberalism*, 2nd ed. (New York: Columbia University Press, 2005).
3 As cited in Klassen and Klassen-Marshall in this volume. Nicholas Aroney, "The Rule of Law, Religious Authority, and Oaths of Office," *Journal of Law, Religion and State* 6 (2018): 212.
4 I am inspired here by Paul Kahn's claim that "[e]very age has its own point of access to ethical and political deliberation. For us, that point is the problem of cultural pluralism." *Putting Liberalism in Its Place* (Princeton, NJ: Princeton University Press, 2005), 1.

Chapter Eight

"However Honestly Meant": Chinese Australians and Truth-Telling in Colonial Victorian Courts

CATHERINE L. EVANS

In an 1871 assault case tried in colonial Melbourne, a Chinese witness declared on the stand that he believed his soul would "transmigrate into a monkey or some other inferior animal" if he lied. He also offered to swear on a Bible; taking a Christian oath could not bind his conscience any further but could do no harm. Colonial officials demurred, instead insisting that the man participate in a ritual invented by British authorities to induce witnesses of "Eastern" confessions to tell the truth in court. The witness, accordingly, blew out a match in "the old style."[1] The colonial practice of asking that Chinese witnesses blow out a candle or match to swear an oath continued sporadically in British courts until as late as the 1940s.[2]

British colonial authorities in the late nineteenth century were preoccupied with lying. As the administrative apparatus of the empire expanded, officials became increasingly invested in preserving the integrity of institutions that sorted, counted, judged, and managed the empire's subjects. However, the fear that colonial agents might be deceived – by a person who lied to a census-taker about their age, who underreported their profits, or concealed evidence of a crime – was perennial. In colonial India, for instance, medical and legal textbooks warned of Indians' supposedly innate mendacity, and offered officials strategies for detecting subterfuge.[3] Lying was considered particularly noxious – and likely – in the legal sphere, where colonial authorities were keen to avoid relying on the testimony of witnesses whom they did not trust.[4] In response, British and British imperial authorities embraced what historians of colonial India have called "truth technologies." New scientific fields such as fingerprinting and serology and bodies of expertise including medical jurisprudence and crime scene investigation emerged.[5]

Courtroom testimony remained, however, integral to the British trial process. Lawyers' techniques like cross-examination flourished, promising to help canny advocates extract truthful statements from unreliable witnesses.[6] Older methods for ensuring the integrity of testimony, such as oath-taking, were renovated and adapted to suit novel contexts and changing understandings of the place of religion and religiosity in nineteenth-century courts.[7] This often involved calibrating oath-taking and swearing practices rooted in Christian tradition to reflect what British officials understood to be the spiritual and cultural beliefs of the empire's diverse subjects. Colonial authorities crafted forms of religious oath-taking and, later, solemn affirmations to coax non-Christian witnesses to tell the truth, or at least to provide lawyers and onlookers with an additional opportunity to assess swearers' credibility.

Cases involving Chinese parties tried in colonial Australia show how British officials struggled to manage spiritual and cultural diversity in court, and in the empire writ large. Oaths in this context operated both as solemn promises that tested the integrity of individual witnesses, and also as set pieces in much broader debates about the interactions of law, religion, and difference in the British empire.[8] The adaptations Britons made to swearing practices to accommodate those of "Eastern" confessions, including candle blowing, often had little basis even in colonial ethnography, let alone Chinese tradition. This was widely acknowledged. A satirical song by goldfield "minstrel" Charles Robert Thatcher, "Chinamen in Court," published in an 1864 Australian collection, claimed that though "each Chinese witness is asked/in every court of law, sir,/If he'll blow out a candle" yet "blowing out a candle/ Appears to some a lark." The implications for Chinese testimony were significant. The rhyme concludes: "It seems to us as if they mean to leave us in the *dark*;/It must be allegorical,/For doubtless of a surety,/ The evidence that's given, is/Enveloped in obscurity."[9]

The notion that elaborate oath-taking processes would guarantee truthful, useful testimony was, to many, increasingly risible. Even Christians' oaths, well-rooted in Anglo-American theological and legal tradition, did not inspire their former awe, when oath-taking had been understood to place the swearer in spiritual peril.[10] As Kellen Funk argues in this volume, perjury charges seemed to many nineteenth-century Americans a better guarantor of truthfulness than threats of eternal damnation. Still, British authorities across the empire clung to their candles. This invented tradition, which lawyers regularly challenged in court, can be located within a broader colonial imaginary that cast Chinese people as fatalistic, mystical, and strange.[11] The candle-blowing ritual was imperfect, to be sure, but its flaws were excused on the basis that Chinese spirituality was fundamentally impenetrable and Western misinterpretations inevitable. Extending to Chinese witnesses the apparent courtesy of an "Eastern" oath also proclaimed the capaciousness and flexibility of British courtroom procedure. The fact that the oath did not guarantee reliable testimony underscored Chinese difference, not colonial incompetence.

Another case tried in Melbourne in the colony of Victoria, *R v. An Gaa* [1875], featured Chinese parties in several roles: victim, accused, police investigator, and witness. This case moves beyond the question of the candle oath to broader colonial beliefs in the metaphysical and ethical differences between European and Chinese Australians. Mendacity, especially among racialized subjects, was of acute concern to colonial legal officials, but untruth could also enter British courts through the testimony of honest witnesses. An oath could not prevent lying if witnesses were telling the truth as they saw it, and inaccurate but honest testimony could withstand even vigorous cross-examination. The possibility that Chinese witnesses might deliberately or inadvertently alter the course of justice, subtly aligning the organs of colonial governance with their own understandings of guilt and innocence, troubled Anglo-Australian officials.

An examination of *R v. An Gaa* shows that doubts about the reliability of Chinese parties in colonial courtrooms extended beyond the spectre of dishonesty, instead casting Chinese Australians as unfathomable and ungovernable. White Australians' anxieties about Chinese migrants' influence echoed those expressed in other jurisdictions populated by Anglo settlers. Beth Lew-Williams argues, for example, that white Americans saw Chinese immigrants both as alien and as threatening to American civic life; they feared not only that Chinese Americans would "contaminate" the nation but also that they "might conquer it."[12] Chinese Australians were seen as similarly corrupt and exotic – untrustworthy even when they told the truth.

In *R v. An Gaa*, both the victim and the accused were Chinese gold diggers with few connections to white settler society. The imagined vulnerability of British colonial justice to Chinese manipulation quickly became an important theme in the case. Cases involving Chinese parties and, especially, the talents of interpreters and policemen of Chinese origin, as this one did, seemed poised to produce Chinese justice in common-law garb, substituting Eastern philosophical principles for British jurisprudence. Jeffery Hewitt, in his introduction to this volume, describes the virtues of parallax. Borrowed from the world of art, parallax describes how objects in a painting can be arranged along different sight lines to create dimension. Hewitt sees beauty in interpretive multiplicity and reminds us that "more than one perspective from a different sight line offers depth, not threats."[13] But for colonial officials in nineteenth-century Australia, differences of perspective were dangerous, creating not depth but distortion. The candle ritual – an artificial creation that even its proponents admitted had at best a hazy relationship to a half-understood cosmology – could not bridge a genuine difference of perception. It was this more intractable problem that most shaped *R v. An Gaa*, and the fortunes of Chinese Australians.

Oaths and Status

By the end of the nineteenth century, non-white witnesses could testify in colonial Australian courts. British justice, at least in principle, was by then equally applicable to all British subjects, to the satisfaction of colonial authorities who trumpeted the fairness and impartiality of imperial governance.[14] And yet, religion, nationality, gender, race, and class inflected how British settlers reckoned the credibility of witnesses, including their ability to swear binding oaths. Those who deviated from the Protestant, propertied, male ideal were imagined to be prone to fabulation or, perhaps worse, alleged to lack a strong sense of the line between reality and fantasy, especially with respect to spiritual and religious matters. In his work on the colonial Caribbean, Miles Ogborn describes oaths as "embodied, localised and particularised verbal performances that enacted power-laden identities and transformed social relationships."[15] Oaths and oral evidence – ideally, sworn testimony – were essential to the functioning and legitimacy of British law in the colonies. Determinations of identity and status were baked into legal rules about who could swear oaths and how, and the weight that their promises carried.[16]

In Victoria, Aboriginal Australians and South and East Asians who did not belong to Abrahamic religions were viewed with particularly acute suspicion. By the late eighteenth century, it had been established that Jews and Muslims could offer sworn testimony in both civil and criminal matters in English courts, their oaths taken upon the holy books of their faiths.[17] Whether a person's oath could be trusted remained a vexed question, even if there were no doubts as to its proper form. Still, uncertainty as to the proper ritual of swearing itself, and the spiritual tradition it supposedly invoked, compounded the problem. Chinese witnesses in British courts, for instance, were sometimes asked to break a saucer instead of extinguishing a match, and there were rumours that

Figure 8.1 "Our Chinamen," *The Australian Sketcher*, 1874, State Library Victoria, Melbourne, Australia.

the correct method might involve slaughtering a live chicken ("A very *fowl* proceeding," joked Thatcher, the satirist).[18]

These anxieties about Chinese testimony were not, however, only a reflection of Britons' ignorance of Asian spiritual – and, for that matter, legal – traditions. Even Chinese Christians were at times asked to swear by saucer-breaking or other putatively "Chinese" methods.[19] Differences of religious affiliation only partly expressed the cultural gap that many Euro-Australians imagined yawned between themselves and their Chinese neighbours. "[T]he testimony of our Celestial brethren, however honestly meant," wrote the author of one 1871 newspaper report, "is desultory and spasmodic, and not altogether comprehensible to the average European mind."[20] Accusations of untruthfulness were deeply significant to Victorian Britons, for whom sincerity was a hallmark of good character. In the colonies, truthfulness became what Wendie Ellen Schneider describes as "a veritable cornerstone of British national identity," especially in India.[21] Chinese Australians' supposed untrustworthiness in court therefore signalled their alleged inability to internalize British values.

Concerns about oath-taking expressed white authorities' sense that Chinese Australians' cosmological and spiritual beliefs (or, rather, colonial caricatures of these beliefs) made them troublesome subjects, unfit for British justice or full civic incorporation.[22] And yet, Chinese migrants and settlers were essential to colonial Victorian social and economic life. They were not, and could not be, excluded from the protections of Australian settler law and legal institutions. The cartoon in Figure 8.1, published in 1874 in a satirical magazine, captures this tension. It shows a Chinese witness blowing out a match on the stand. To his left are an interpreter and, looming behind both Chinese men, a white, bearded bailiff supervising the administration of the oath. The remaining figures depict other Chinese-Australian archetypes: the jovial hawker; the ragpicker in tattered trousers; the portly, vaguely sinister merchant. Titled "Our Chinamen," the image implies at once familiarity and distance. Chinese Australians were essential to the prosperity of the colony, and yet remained apart from white settler society in dress, occupation, language, and custom. The candle-based oath, its dubious authenticity so easily lampooned, symbolized the fragility of Chinese incorporation into the colonial polity.

Chinese Australia

The Australian colony of Victoria underwent a series of demographic and economic shifts over the period from 1850 to 1875. Migrants from across the British world poured into Victoria in search of gold. The population grew from ninety-seven thousand in 1850 to over a million by 1875.[23] From the mid-1850s to the end of the colonial period, between sixty and eighty thousand Chinese migrants arrived in the Australian colonies.[24] Mae Ngai estimates that there were two thousand Chinese people in Victoria in 1854 and forty-two thousand by 1859 – twenty per cent of the adult male population in that year.[25] When the rush was at its peak, there may have been as many as fifty thousand Chinese immigrants in Victoria alone.[26] By 1861, there were still over thirty-eight thousand Chinese immigrants in the Australian colonies, mostly in and around the goldfields of Victoria, New South Wales, and Queensland.[27] However, a diminishing gold supply and an excess of claims meant that few could make a living entirely by digging gold just ten years after its initial discovery.[28] In the 1870s, the Chinese Australian population was in steady decline. One Australian statistician wrote that there were 17,935 Chinese people in Victoria in 1871, almost 30 per cent fewer than had lived in the colony in 1861. He estimated that only thirty-six were women.[29]

With the exhaustion of the alluvial gold deposits, Chinese Australians sought new work in agricultural communities, country towns, and in Melbourne, the bustling colonial capital. One historian describes the "clamour of a hundred thousand ex-miners for farm land" in the 1860s, as they competed with pastoralists who raised sheep for the lucrative wool trade on huge homesteads expropriated from Aboriginal communities.[30] Instead of small farmers, many former miners and new immigrants became urban wage labourers.[31] Others turned to petty trading or cultivating market gardens.[32] Chinese miners, merchants, and labourers had a distinct, but circumscribed, place in Victorian society. They forged social and economic bonds in their communities and enjoyed the protections of colonial justice. Their belonging was incomplete, however, and even respectability and wealth could not assuage white scepticism about their loyalty to British law.

The Crime and the Chinese Detective

An Gaa had come to Victoria from China to hunt for gold.[33] He worked on the goldfields of Vaughan, a settlement in the hills north-west of Melbourne near Castlemaine, a town of about seven thousand residents.[34] He was arrested in June 1875 and charged with murder after authorities discovered the body of Pooey Wah in a bark hut the two shared. A shopkeeper testified that both men were regular opium users, and that he had overheard An Gaa accuse Pooey Wah of cheating him by working their gold claim alone while An Gaa smoked.[35]

An Gaa's trial involved two men, detective Fook Shing and Chinese interpreter Charles P. Hodges who, unlike most anglophone lawyers, jurors, and judges, could speak to An Gaa in his own language. The court relied on Fook Shing and Hodges not only to interpret the defendant's testimony, but also the customs and beliefs of Victoria's Chinese community. But the court's reliance on investigators and professional interpreters as intermediaries made many uneasy.

Fook Shing, who sometimes went by Henry Fooksing, arrived in Victoria in 1854 from Guangzhou. He left his family, struggling farmers, to seek his fortune on the Bendigo goldfields.[36] Fook Shing became a vocal advocate for Chinese political and cultural interests in Bendigo, even leading a secret society (in this context, a fraternal organization that assisted new Chinese immigrants), the Sheathed Sword.[37] He eventually opened a store at Ballarat and began a successful Chinese theatre company. In 1857, he married Ellen Mary Fling.[38] The pair had a daughter, Amelia, in 1859.[39] The relationship quickly soured, and they separated later that year.[40] By 1870, Fook Shing had become a naturalized British subject and had purchased a house near Bendigo.[41]

Fook Shing was the only Chinese detective on the Melbourne force, on which he served from the early 1860s to his retirement in 1886. He might have been hired to replace James Appoo, another China-born expert interpreter and member of the Victorian Detective Police Force who retired in 1863.[42] Like his predecessor, Fook Shing was a valuable asset to the Victorian police, able to extract information from Chinese witnesses who might otherwise have avoided contact with colonial authorities.

Fook Shing was a man in between. In 1871, the Melbourne *Argus* reported that Fook Shing had dismissed a Chinese suspect's claim that he was a Christian with a laugh. The detective, the author wrote, appeared to have become "imbued, by long intercourse with Europeans, with the outer barbarian instinct which leads them to look upon his countrymen with a half-comic feeling of contempt."[43] In 1873, a Chinese prisoner accused Fook Shing of stealing a pipe he had surrendered to police upon his incarceration.[44] These hints of Chinese antipathy towards Fook Shing reprise, in some ways, the rumours that circulated after James Appoo's death. The *Ovens and Murray Advertiser* reported that Chinese residents of a mining encampment refused to enter the house where Appoo died of consumption, "many believing him to have been addicted to trafficking with the devil."[45]

In 1879, Fook Shing married again.[46] His second wife, Ellen Moran, was of mixed Chinese and Irish heritage.[47] Ellen died in 1885 at the age of twenty-four, leaving behind Fook Shing and their two children, Eveline Maud and Henry Burt Fook Shing.[48] The detective retired from the police force the next year. In the wake of the suspected murder of a constable at a Chinese mining camp, one reporter wrote that it was "unfortunate that at this juncture, when a mystery worthy of his calculating brain is to the fore, Fook Shing, the well-known Chinese detective has retired."[49] No one was appointed in his place.[50]

While the press rarely mentioned other Chinese detectives in the Australian colonies, British colonial police forces routinely included non-British members. From the so-called Aboriginal "black trackers" of Queensland to the "native" police forces of India, colonial authorities relied heavily on the knowledge, labour, and linguistic facility of colonized and non-European peoples.[51] These police agents were ethnographers, interpreters, and intermediaries, shaping relations between communities and creating cultural knowledge as they translated it.[52]

Men like Fook Shing were essential to criminal justice in the diverse and rapidly changing landscape of mid-to-late-nineteenth-century

Victoria. While Chinese merchants and policemen were part of the social fabric of Victoria, linguistic and cultural divides remained. In the goldfields, the racial segregation of Chinese and European communities was stark. In some concessions, European and Chinese camps were separated by trenches.[53] Chinese migrants did not choose their isolation freely. White miners, including large populations of Americans and continental Europeans, accused Chinese labourers of spreading disease, wasting water in the arid outback, and of "stealing" gold.

The self-contained camps on the diggings limited Chinese Australians' contact with the English-speaking population. These separate social and linguistic spheres were reflected in the Australian Protectorate system, which operated in the mid-1850s and early 1860s. Modelled on the systems in place in British Hong Kong and the Straits Settlement, the Protectorate regime encouraged the construction of Chinese camps on the peripheries of goldfield towns.[54] A corps of Chinese interpreters and detectives managed the populations of these camps, acting as liaisons between the Chinese population and the colonial state.[55] In 1859, Victorian authorities ended the Protectorates, which had proved expensive and unwieldy to administer. Distrust of Chinese middlemen also motivated colonial officials to place the Chinese population directly under the jurisdiction of the colonial courts.[56] Chinese communities near goldfields remained insular, however. European officials still relied on Chinese-speakers to navigate and police the camps, as well as the growing "Chinese Quarters" of Melbourne and other cities. When crimes occurred in these enclaves, witnesses were often reluctant to tell their stories to colonial authorities who did not speak their language, and who viewed them with suspicion or even hostility.

"Young Sheen"

An Gaa's trial was held at the Castlemaine Assizes on 19 and 20 July 1875 before Redmond Barry, a judge of Irish extraction. A local newspaper, the *Mount Alexander Mail*, carried a detailed account of the case. On the first day, the reporter complained that "the number of Chinese witnesses, and the difficulty of extracting their evidence" would prolong the trial, forcing the jury to be confined to their quarters overnight and delaying Barry's attendance at the Sandhurst Assizes later that week.[57]

The trial, held in a handsome stone courthouse on a grassy hill, resumed the next morning. A policeman who had been patrolling the Vaughan goldfields recalled entering An Gaa and Pooey Wah's hut to find the defendant eating rice by candlelight as his friend's body lay

Figure 8.2 Batchelder & Co., Castlemaine Courthouse, ca. 1865, State Library Victoria, Melbourne, Australia.

nearby, his neck broken and his left hand still clutching an opium pipe. Chinese diggers, hawkers, and shopkeepers, sworn by blowing out matches, related through interpreters that the two friends had quarrelled over their gold claim in the days before Pooey Wah died. An Gaa explained that Pooey Wah and another man had stolen over an ounce of gold while he, An Gaa, had attended a funeral. The claim had been unproductive for some time, and the theft of over a week's worth of gold had dashed his hopes of returning to China.

Fook Shing led the police investigation. He testified that he had interviewed An Gaa in the Castlemaine jail after his arrest. The detective told the court that the prisoner had claimed to have "made up his mind to die, and then said, 'young sheen' meaning 'a feud,' or that if he killed somebody somebody would kill him." Fook Shing added that in a later interview, An Gaa had announced he "had made up his mind life for life – meaning he had killed somebody, and he would give up his life."[58] Under questioning by G.C. Leech, An Gaa's lawyer, Hodges tried to clarify the meaning of "youn sheew" or "young sheen" for the court, which he said meant "resentment and revenge."

What was "young sheen"? While unstable nineteenth-century anglophone transliteration practices cloud the term's Chinese origins, it is possible that it refers to "yao siu" (夭壽), a word often found in nineteenth-century English-Cantonese dictionaries. One dictionary describes the first character, yao (夭), as evocative of "something born incomplete," the shape representing a "crooked neck."[59] With siu (壽; usually given as "shou" or "shoo"), which generally refers to old age or, euphemistically, to death, the whole (夭壽) can mean "premature death" or "an early death."[60] In Hokkien, a widely spoken dialect in Fujian Province in south-eastern China, whence many nineteenth-century Chinese migrated to Australia, "yao siu" is often used as a curse or exclamation, sometimes upon an accident or disaster.[61]

Although Hodges's usual role in Victorian courtrooms was as an interpreter, he had met An Gaa before the crime and took the stand as a witness. In fact, his testimony in the case combined language interpretation, expert commentary on Chinese beliefs, and his direct experience of the circumstances surrounding the crime. He became the case's main authority on "young sheen," which Fook Shing had introduced in his own testimony. Hodges's interpretation went beyond nineteenth-century dictionary definitions of "yao siu" (夭壽), instead advancing an ethnographic account of "young sheen" that emphasized past lives and spiritual realms. He said, for instance, that the Chinese believed that resentment "may be even due to something previous to their being in this world. […] If a man causelessly killed another in this life he did so out of resentment for something that arose in another world." According to this view, "young sheen" explained crimes committed by Chinese accused whose motives were not intelligible to Anglo authorities. While some clearly embraced a concept that dovetailed with stereotypes that cast Chinese Australians as inscrutable, "young sheen" also suggested that Chinese people might commit crimes in response to otherworldly triggers, making their violence difficult to police or predict.

Fatalism and the Chinese Interpreter

Although Hodges had a background in journalism, he had come to Melbourne in the 1850s, like countless others, for the gold. Failing to strike it rich, he still left with a prize: the ability to speak Cantonese.[62] With the collapse of the Protectorate system, government funding for Chinese interpreters fell. Administrators had come to distrust ethnically Chinese interpreters, fearing that they were exploiting white officials' ignorance of Chinese languages to facilitate or commit fraud.[63] Anglo-Australian interpreters like Hodges, who seemed less likely to collude with Chinese criminals, were highly valued.

Hodges saw himself as a protector and patron of the Chinese community in Victoria. On many occasions, he used his position to publicly denounce malicious stereotypes and anti-Chinese legislation.[64] For example, in a letter included in the official report on the Victorian census of 1881, Hodges protested the government's decision to describe the Chinese as "pagans." "In many things," argued Hodges, "the Chinese are misunderstood – therefore misjudged – but in few more than on the subject specially referred to."[65]

Despite his sympathy for Chinese Australians, Hodges's testimony about "young sheen" did little to help An Gaa. The prosecution and even the judge rejected Hodges's efforts to expand the scope of suspicion beyond An Gaa to include anyone potentially bearing a grudge from a past life. Revenge for the theft of his gold supplied An Gaa with a clear, intelligible motive, which did not require consideration of what Barry described as evidence "of a metaphysical kind." After all, Barry reminded the court, "Traditions could not be received as evidence."[66] Here, Barry invoked the legal principle that a defendant's cultural background could not be raised as a distinct defence in British courts.[67] Although cultural evidence was, in fact, routinely considered in cases involving racialized accused, the judge likely hoped the exclusion rule would spare him, and the jury, the need to delve into the intricacies of Chinese metaphysics.

Barry's use of the term "traditions" is also instructive. In the nineteenth-century British Empire, conceptual distinctions among what counted as "tradition," "religion," and "law" were unstable. British Christians tended to espouse a bounded view of religion, with delimited sacred and material spheres, and to consign unfamiliar spiritual practices and beliefs to the realms of culture or "superstition" – or, as here, "traditions."[68] The 1881 Victorian census's classification of Chinese Australians as "pagans," which so irritated Hodges, also reflected Anglo settlers' tendency to view Chinese spirituality as troublingly diffuse, bleeding dangerously into temporal affairs. By attempting to keep traditions out of the courtroom, Barry also sought to restrict consideration of An Gaa's culpability to the material plane over which colonial law claimed exclusive jurisdiction. The candle-blowing oath, a small, cynical concession to diversity conceived to bend Chinese witnesses to the court's needs, was the exception that proved the rule.

Smyth, the prosecutor, disregarded the question of motive entirely, relying instead on the circumstantial evidence tying An Gaa to the crime. While a white defendant's motives might be critical to establishing his or her guilt, Smyth reminded the jury that a Chinese defendant's intentions were often obscure. "[H]owever ignorant they [the jury] were of the motives which influence natives of that country," Smyth argued, the jury could not allow any uncertainty about An Gaa's reasons for killing his friend to affect their verdict.

In reply, the defence insisted that Chinese tradition was essential to the case, and to the jury's understanding of the testimony of the Chinese witnesses who implicated An Gaa.[69] Leech began by telling the jury that "the Chinese were a people who had laws so different from our own as to render it almost impossible to understand them." Differences in law, ethics, and religion made it difficult for Chinese witnesses to adapt to the conventions of British criminal law. The lawyer described Chinese witnesses' "inveterate habit" of lying on the stand to achieve a result they thought was just. Circumstantial evidence, as opposed to confessions or eyewitness testimony, was useful in cases involving white witnesses but not in cases that relied on people of "alien races," who Leech implied were not "manly straight forward witnesses," but feminine dissemblers.[70]

Finally, Leech returned to the crux of his case – "young sheen" and "Eastern" cosmology. He argued that fatalism was a "prominent part of the belief of all Asiatics." Instead of seeing the trial as the moment when the defendant's fate would be decided, Leech argued that Chinese people believed that the course of a defendant's life had been predetermined. To them, the trial was an essentially empty ritual, where they were free to craft narratives that illustrated the defendant's character regardless of their factual accuracy. This rendered Chinese testimony inherently unreliable, in Leech's view.[71]

Inadequate Oaths

The problem of unreliable Chinese testimony, argued Leech for the prosecution, was compounded by the fact that non-Christian Chinese witnesses had a "different form of theology binding on their conscience," and so could not swear binding oaths on pain of divine retribution. Leech also argued that the court's proxy for a Christian oath – blowing out a candle – was "unknown in China" and held no weight in any Chinese belief system.[72]

The law of evidence in Victoria had long been marked by this suspicion of non-Christian oath-taking. In 1854, a Victorian statute stipulated that Aboriginal people could testify in any legal matter without the need for an oath even if they were "uncivilized ... destitute of the knowledge of God and of any fixed belief in Religion or in a future state of rewards and punishments."[73] However, anyone who, in the opinion of the judge, coroner, or justice, seemed to "believe in a God a future state of rewards and punishments [*sic*]" was required to swear an oath.[74] Thus, the personal religious convictions of individual witnesses, often determined with reference to Victorian ethnological understandings of the person's confession, race, or nation, became the province of courtroom inquiry, as legal authorities worked to determine who should be compelled to swear.[75] While belief in an afterlife and the threat of divine punishment for oath-breaking were not required of witnesses, who could instead offer affirmations that they were telling the truth, sworn oaths – and a cosmology that gave them teeth – remained the legal default. The Chinese witnesses in An Gaa's case were duly sworn. British authorities tended to err on the side of caution in moments of theological ambiguity, demanding oaths even when witnesses' precise beliefs about a "future state of rewards and punishments" were unclear. But, as in An Gaa's case, the strength of these oaths was often contested, as "experts" and commentators disagreed about the core precepts of non-Western spiritual traditions and the form of the oaths legal authorities administered.[76]

Leech, An Gaa's lawyer, also discussed "young sheen." The lawyer told the jury that they "knew nothing of the metaphysical belief of the Chinese, but to those people every word and sound had a meaning." Leech did not explain precisely how "young sheen" and the "species of fatalism" it evoked affected An Gaa's guilt. He might have meant to imply that An Gaa's admission to Fook Shing that he "had made up his mind life for life – meaning he had killed somebody, and he would give up his life" was not necessarily a confession to killing Pooey Wah. Perhaps, as a fatalist, An Gaa had accepted that a capital sentence would be his punishment for a murder he committed in a past life, or at least against a different victim. Here, Leech raised the disturbing possibility that his client might have obliquely confessed to a killing committed on another spiritual plane, accepting his arrest and even his death as preordained and just, even if he were innocent of killing Pooey Wah. In such a case, the machinery of colonial criminal justice would send "an innocent man to his doom," a result that the Chinese might consider just, but Anglo-Australians, who prided themselves on the ability of their courts to discover the truth and assign blame fairly, would abhor.[77]

Fook Shing's Instincts and An Gaa's End

Leech bolstered his arguments about fatalism with an attack on Fook Shing's professional ethics. Even though Fook Shing's testimony about his jailhouse conversations with An Gaa supported Leech's contentions about the power of Chinese metaphysical fatalism, Leech hoped to undermine the detective's work in arresting An Gaa in the first place. "The instincts of the detective," Leech told the jury, "were like that of the bloodhound, only thinking of, only searching after, only desiring to fix the guilt on the suspected man ... If there should be a little flaw, the end justified the means."[78] The association of police with bloodhounds was common in the later nineteenth century. Binyamin Blum describes controversies around the use of "bloodhounds" in British and British colonial policing, where dogs, associated with tracking runaway enslaved plantation labourers in the Americas, were considered affronts to liberty.[79] Detectives, especially plainclothes agents, made many nineteenth-century Britons uncomfortable. Their ability to consort undetected with criminals and suspect populations made them a powerful police asset, but also exposed them to the risk of corruption. If detectives could deceive criminals, they could deceive anyone.[80] Even if they were not criminally corrupt, detectives' suspicions could overwhelm their reason, first "marking the quarry" and then manipulating the evidence to ensure a conviction. Fook Shing's status as both a detective and a Chinese immigrant made him doubly suspect. Leech cautioned the jury that Fook Shing was "a Chinese detective, and there was no possibility to check, and therefore there was the more caution to be used."[81] Fook Shing, depicted below in a dapper bowler and cravat, had become a linchpin of the Victorian police and a well-to-do member of Melbourne's middle class. And yet, his familiarity *with* the Chinese criminal underworld made him in some ways *of* it, and so subject to a distrust his respectability could not cure.

Despite the defence's efforts, the jury found An Gaa guilty of murder after an hour of deliberation. Barry announced the death sentence. Of forty-three total executions in Victoria between 1865 and 1879, 9.3 per cent (four) of executed prisoners were born in China. Chinese immigrants comprised roughly 2.5 per cent of the Victorian population, according to the 1871 census.[82] In the aftermath of the trial, Leech made one last plea for his client's life. He wrote to the Executive Council asking for an assessment of An Gaa's sanity. He had come to the conclusion, he wrote, that An Gaa was "so intellectually weak that the weakness amounts to imbecility" and that he ought not, therefore, be hanged.[83] Two doctors interviewed the prisoner, but reported that they found no evidence of insanity.[84]

An Gaa spent his last days imprisoned at Melbourne Gaol. John Buckley Castieau was the prison governor from 1869 to 1884. In August 1875, two Japanese commissioners visited the jail while they were in town to present at the Melbourne Intercolonial Exhibition.[85] Castieau

Figure 8.3 "In the Chinese Quarter," *The Graphic* (London), 13 November 1880, p. 484, State Library Victoria, Melbourne, Australia. Fook Shing is on the bottom left.

and his staff were "anxious to share in the honour & glory of helping to escort the distinguished foreigners." Castieau proudly showed the visitors the labour yard, where male prisoners broke stones, and to workrooms where female prisoners sewed. He then escorted the Japanese delegation to the "place of execution," where "the bolt was drawn for their information & the drop allowed to fall. They looked rather astonished."[86]

Next, Castieau brought the Japanese commissioners, who were by then "interested though perhaps a little frightened," to meet An Gaa, who had been sentenced to death a month before. An Gaa was in shackles in a tiny cell with a thick iron door. Castieau thought that he "looked more like a sulky dog than anything else." Castieau was delighted when his guests, at the conclusion of their macabre tour, asked for An Gaa's name and recorded it, "to be used no doubt when reference is made to their Gaol visit in the Diary which they keep to astonish the Old Folks at Home ... "[87]

An Gaa was executed less than two weeks after he was exhibited to the Japanese travellers. Castieau wrote, "I shall be very glad when the unfortunate China-man is dead & as usual before an execution feel nervous for fear any bungling may occur."[88] At 10:00 a.m. on 30 August 1875, Castieau and the sheriff fetched An Gaa from the condemned cell. A Chinese interpreter, unnamed in the press, spoke at length to the prisoner, who mumbled indistinctly in response. When the rope was placed around his neck An Gaa seemed to swoon, but the bolt was drawn before he could collapse on the trap door. After the execution, a plaster cast of An Gaa's head was taken. Two doctors removed his brain "to make scientific experiments with it."[89]

For Castieau, An Gaa's confinement and execution provided opportunities to play host to visiting dignitaries, and to display the mercy and scientific sophistication of colonial justice. His journal's chatty, workaday tone contrasts sharply with his description of An Gaa, huddled and chained in his dark, stone cell. Prisoners were, and are, often subject to such casual disregard by their keepers. An Gaa's rhetorical transformation from a prisoner into a "sulky dog," however, was likely smoothed by Castieau's assumptions about the inscrutability of his Chinese charge, and the spiritual, even metaphysical, space between them.

British Justice, Chinese Subjects

Legal authorities struggled to apply "British" justice in a rapidly changing, multi-ethnic colony. Castieau's account of the Japanese commissioners' visit to Melbourne Gaol reveals how important it was for Victorian justice to appear modern, competent, and unflinching. To investigate and prosecute crimes, the police and the criminal courts needed the skill and expertise of detectives like Fook Shing. Colonial racism and suspicion, however, injected every interaction with doubt. In the courtroom, that doubt could be wielded by men like Leech to argue that Chinese defendants, witnesses, and officials might appropriate the forms of British justice for their own purposes, adapting them to conform to "alien" moral principles. The only person whose testimony Leech praised was Hodges, a fellow Briton whose race insulated him from the distrust that the barrister heaped on Fook Shing. Hodges's efforts to elucidate the abstruse concept of "young sheen," though, only compounded the confusion about the influence of Chinese fatalism on the case. Ultimately, the jury declined to see the case as "altogether wrapped in helpless mystery." Perhaps they were moved by Barry's summary, in which he argued that "young sheen" was nothing more than "bad feeling in consequence of a supposed injury" – a mundane motive for murder that remained firmly in this life.

Oaths disrupt conceptual boundaries between the sacred and the secular, translating religious conviction into bureaucratic protocol and endowing legal procedure with cosmic heft. In his introduction to this section, Benjamin Berger describes this syncretic quality of the oath, and the resulting complexity of court processes that seek to conscript at least quasi-religious convictions to yield profane truths. The oath, he writes, "offers itself as a foundation for factual certainty but is itself fashioned from belief."[90] An Gaa's case illustrates the risks of relying on belief to produce fact: the possibility raised by his defence lawyers that An Gaa's "Eastern" fatalism inflected his perception of the material world implied that fact could not, in reality, be wrung from belief, or at least from some beliefs.

The oath-taking rites developed by British colonial authorities in Australia and elsewhere were designed to manage difference by disciplining and rationalizing belief – an exercise many admitted was deeply compromised, and perhaps impossible. Why, then, did oaths persist and even proliferate? The answer lies in recognizing even the modern, liberal court as a place of enchantment, where all parties, from witnesses to judges to spectators, are invited to renew their commitments to the prevailing legal order. The candle-blowing oath of the nineteenth century sought to bind the conscience of the oath-taker, but its success did not rest on its efficacy. Rather, such oaths reinforced legal liberalism's own "sense of religion" as a supra-confessional – even imperial – form that could absorb and overwhelm difference.[91] Oaths were at once mechanisms to create "people for whom law matters," as Berger notes, and to sort out whose beliefs were most compatible with the legal ideology of empire.[92] Doubt and suspicion did not mean that oaths had failed or should be abandoned. Instead, officials' and other settlers' qualms expressed their conviction that the work of empire was not yet done, and must continue.

NOTES

1 "City Court," *The Australasian*, 6 May 1871, 23.
2 Julian Frankly, letter to the editor, *Folklore* 68, no. 2 (1957): 371.
3 See, e.g., Norman Chevers, *A Manual of Medical Jurisprudence for Bengal and the North-Western Provinces* (Calcutta: Carbery, 1856).
4 This distrust also extended to local judges, legal experts, and interpreters, whom colonial officers viewed as prone to corruption. See Bernard S.

Cohn, *Colonialism and Its Forms of Knowledge: The British in India* (Princeton, NJ: Princeton University Press, 1996), 29.

5 On "truth technologies" in colonial India, see Elizabeth Kolsky, *Colonial Justice in British India* (Cambridge: Cambridge University Press, 2010); Mitra Sharafi, "The Imperial Serologist and Punitive Self-Harm: Bloodstains and Legal Pluralism in British India," in *Global Forensic Cultures: Making Fact and Justice in the Modern Era*, ed. Ian A. Burney and Christopher Hamlin (Baltimore: Johns Hopkins University Press, 2019), 60–85.

6 On the rise of counsel and cross-examination in England, see John M. Beattie, "Scales of Justice: Defense Counsel and the English Criminal Trial in the Eighteenth and Nineteenth Centuries," *Law and History Review* 9, no. 2 (Autumn 1991): 221–67.

7 On testimonial oaths in the nineteenth-century United States, see Kellen Funk in this volume.

8 On oaths as sites for proxy debates about law and religion, see Klassen and Klassen-Marshall in this volume, and also Benjamin L. Berger, *Law's Religion: Religious Difference and the Claims of Constitutionalism* (Toronto: University of Toronto Press, 2016).

9 Charles Robert Thatcher, *Thatcher's Colonial Minstrel: New Collection of Songs* (Libraries Board of South Australia, 1964), 18. On Thatcher's career and legacy, see Mark Pinner, "Charles Robert Thatcher's Songsters: Politics on the Goldfields of Victoria, Australia," in *Cheap Print and Popular Song in the Nineteenth Century*, ed. Derek B. Scott, Patrick Spedding, and Paul Watt (Cambridge: Cambridge University Press, 2017), 138–58.

10 On the dangers of oath-taking, see James Q. Whitman, *The Origins of Reasonable Doubt: Theological Roots of the Criminal Trial* (New Haven, CT: Yale University Press, 2008).

11 Eric Hobsbawm, "Introduction," in *The Invention of Tradition*, ed. Eric Hobsbawm and Terence Ranger, 2nd ed. (Cambridge: Cambridge University Press, 1992), 1–14.

12 Beth Lew-Williams, *The Chinese Must Go: Violence, Exclusion, and the Making of the Alien in America* (Cambridge, MA: Harvard University Press, 2018), 6.

13 See Hewitt, this volume, 11.

14 On "British justice" and the dream of universalism, see Lyndsay Campbell, "Race, Upper Canadian Constitutionalism and 'British Justice,'" *Law and History Review* 33, no. 1 (2015): 41–92.

15 Miles Ogborn, "The Power of Speech: Orality, Oaths and Evidence in the British Atlantic World, 1650–1800," *Transactions of the Institute of British Geographers* 36, no. 1 (January 2011): 114.

16 Oaths' validity depended on the class, gender, religion, and nationality of the accused, as well as the nature of the alleged offence, in the medieval

period as in the nineteenth century. See Robert Bartlett, *Trial by Fire and Water: The Medieval Judicial Ordeal* (Oxford: Oxford University Press, 1988).

17 Karen A. Macfarlane, "'Does He Know the Danger of an Oath'?: Oaths, Religion, Ethnicity and the Advent of the Adversarial Criminal Trial in the Eighteenth Century," *Immigrants & Minorities* 31, no. 3 (2013): 329.

18 Macfarlane, "Does He Know the Danger of an Oath?," 329.; Thatcher, *Thatcher's Colonial Minstrel*, 18.

19 Macfarlane, "Does He Know the Danger of an Oath?," 329.

20 "The Myrtleford Murder," *The Newcastle Chronicle* (NSW), 7 September 1871, 3.

21 Wendie Ellen Schneider, *Engines of Truth: Producing Veracity in the Victorian Courtroom* (New Haven, CT: Yale University Press, 2016), 5.

22 Lew-Williams describes the similar, and similarly linked, white American notions that Chinese migrants were "heathens" and "inassimilable strangers" who were likely to lie under oath. See Lew-Williams, *The Chinese Must Go*, 33.

23 Asa Briggs, *Victorian Cities* (Berkeley: University of California Press, 1993), 278.

24 Alister Bowen, "The Merchants: Chinese Social Organisation in Colonial Australia," *Australian Historical Studies* 42, no. 1 (2011): 25. On the history of the Chinese in nineteenth-century Australia, see, for example, Kathryn Cronin, *Colonial Casualties: Chinese in Early Victoria* (Melbourne: Melbourne University Press, 1982); Mae M. Ngai, "Chinese Gold Miners and the 'Chinese Question' in Nineteenth-Century California and Victoria," *Journal of American History* 101, no. 4 (March 2015): 1082–105; Iain McCalman, Alexander Cook, and Andrew Reeves, eds., *Gold: Forgotten Histories and Lost Objects of Australia* (Cambridge: Cambridge University Press, 2001); Keir Reeves and Tseen Khoo, "Dragon Tails: Re-interpreting Chinese Australian History," *Australian Historical Studies* 42, no. 1 (2011): 4–9; Keir Reeves and Benjamin Mountford, "Court Records and Cultural Landscapes: Rethinking the Chinese Gold Seekers in Central Victoria," *Provenance: The Journal of Public Record Office Victoria*, no. 6 (January 2007): 30–41.

25 Mae M. Ngai, "Chinese Miners, Headmen, and Protectors on the Victorian Goldfields, 1853–1863," *Australian Historical Studies* 42, no. 1 (2011): 11.

26 Warwick Frost, "Migrants and Technological Transfer: Chinese Farming in Australia, 1850–1920," *Asia-Pacific Economic History Review* 42, no. 2 (July 2002): 117.

27 Ann Curthoys, "'Men of All Nations, except Chinamen': Europeans and Chinese on the Goldfields of New South Wales," in McCalman, Cook, and Reeves, *Gold*, 104.

28 Brian Fitzpatrick, "The Big Man's Frontier and Australian Farming,"
    Agricultural History 21, no. 1 (January 1947): 9.
29 Henry Heylyn Hayter, *Notes on the Colony of Victoria: Historical,*
    Geographical, Meteorological, and Statistical (Melbourne: George Skinner,
    Acting Government Printer, 1876), 58.
30 Fitzpatrick, "The Big Man's Frontier," 11.
31 Fitzpatrick, "The Big Man's Frontier," 12.; On market gardening, see also
    Joanna Boileau, *Chinese Market Gardening in Australia and New Zealand:*
    Gardens of Prosperity (Cham, Switzerland: Springer, 2017).
32 Boileau, *Chinese Market Gardening*, 2.
33 "Castlemaine Court of Assize," *Mount Alexander Mail*, 20 July 1875, 2.
34 Hayter, *Notes on the Colony of Victoria*, 60.
35 "Castlemaine Court of Assize," *Mount Alexander Mail*, 21 July 1875, 2.
36 Benjamin Mountford and Keir Reeves, "Reworking the Tailings: New Gold
    Histories and the Cultural Landscape," in *Creating White Australia*, ed. Jane
    Carey and Claire McLisky (Sydney: Sydney University Press, 2009), 34.
    For more on Fook Shing's biography, see Benjamin Mountford, "In Search
    of Fook Shing: Detective Stories from Colonial Victoria" (undergraduate
    honours thesis, University of Melbourne, 2007).
37 Mountford and Reeves, "Reworking the Tailings," 33; Boileau, *Chinese*
    Market Gardening, 3.
38 Marriage of Fook Shing and Ellen Mary Fling, Victorian Registry of Births,
    Deaths, and Marriages, Event Registration Number 3255, 1857.
39 Birth of Amelia Fook Shing, Victorian Registry of Births, Deaths, and
    Marriages, Event Registration Number 16148, 1859.
40 "Advertising," *Bendigo Advertiser*, 23 August 1859, 1.
41 Mountford and Reeves, "Reworking the Tailings," 34.
42 "James Appoo," *Ovens and Murray Advertiser*, 11 November 1865, 3.
43 "City Court," *The Argus*, 3 May 1871, 4.
44 "Charge Against Detective Fook Shing," *Leader*, 8 March 1873, 23.
45 "Chinese Superstition," *Ovens and Murray Advertiser*, 27 January 1866, 3.
46 Marriage of Fook Shing and Ellen Moran, Victorian Registry of Births,
    Deaths, and Marriages, Event Registration Number 2205, 1879.
47 "Law Report. Supreme Court," *The Argus*, 20 April 1887, 9; Elizabeth
    Malcolm and Dianne Hall, *A New History of the Irish in Australia*
    (Cork: Cork University Press, 2019), 84. Marriages and other romantic
    relationships between Chinese men and Irish women were relatively
    common. The actual frequency of Chinese-Irish marriages is difficult
    to gauge. Scholars have argued that the Australian press's insistence
    that Irish women were overrepresented among the wives of Chinese
    men was designed to soothe white, Protestant concerns about racial

transgression, reinforcing existing stigmas against both the Irish and the
Chinese

48 "Family Notices," *The Age*, 19 March 1885, 1; Death of Ellen Fook Sing
at North Fitzroy, wife of Henry Fook Sing, Victorian Registry of Births,
Deaths, and Marriages, Event Registration Number 1357, 1885; Birth
of Eveline Maud Fook Sing, Victorian Registry of Births, Deaths, and
Marriages, Event Registration Number 16465, 1881; Birth of Henry Burt
Fook Sing, Victorian Registry of Births, Deaths, and Marriages, Event
Registration Number 9287, 1883.

49 "Melbourne," *The Ballarat Star*, 20 March 1886, 2.

50 "Intercolonial Telegrams," *Globe* (Evening), 20 March 1886, 8.

51 On policing in the British empire, see David Arnold, *Police Power and
Colonial Rule, Madras, 1859–1947* (Oxford: Oxford University Press,
1986); David M. Anderson and David Killingray, *Policing the Empire:
Government, Authority, and Control, 1830–1940* (Manchester: Manchester
University Press, 1991); Jonathan Richards, *The Secret War: A True History of
Queensland's Native Police* (St. Lucia: University of Queensland Press, 2008);
Gary Presland, *For God's Sake Send the Trackers: A History of Queensland
Trackers and Victoria Police* (Melbourne: Victoria Press, 1998).

52 On detectives and forensic science, see J.M. Beattie, *The First English
Detectives: The Bow Street Runners and the Policing of London, 1750–1840*
(Oxford: Oxford University Press, 2012); Haia Shpayer-Makov, *The Ascent
of the Detective: Police Sleuths in Victorian and Edwardian England* (Oxford:
Oxford University Press, 2011); Clive Emsley and Haia Shpayer-Makov,
Police Detectives in History, 1750–1950 (Aldershot, UK: Ashgate, 2006);
Philip Paul, *Murder under the Microscope: The Story of Scotland Yard's Forensic
Science Laboratory* (London: Macdonald, 1990); Simon A. Cole, *Suspect
Identities: A History of Fingerprinting and Criminal Identification* (Cambridge,
MA: Harvard University Press, 2009); Ian A. Burney and Christopher
Hamlin, *Global Forensic Cultures: Making Fact and Justice in the Modern Era*
(Baltimore: Johns Hopkins University Press, 2019).

53 Curthoys, "Men of All Nations," 108.

54 Ngai, "Chinese Miners," 12–13.

55 Nadia Rhook, "'The Chief Chinese Interpreter' Charles Hodges: Mapping
the Aurality of Race and Governance in Colonial Melbourne," *Postcolonial
Studies* 18, no. 1 (2015): 4.

56 Rhook, "The Chief Chinese Interpreter," 5.

57 "Items of News," *Mount Alexander Mail*, 20 July 1875, 2.

58 "Castlemaine Court of Assize," *Mount Alexander Mail*, 21 July 1875, 2.

59 Samuel Wells Williams, 漢英韻府: *A Syllabic Dictionary of the Chinese
Language Arranged According to the Wu-Fang Yuen Yin, with the Pronunciation*

of the Characters as Heard in Peking, Canton, Amoy, and Shanghai (Shanghai: American Presbyterian Mission Press, 1874), 1074.

60 Herbert Allen Giles, *A Chinese-English Dictionary* (London: B. Quaritch, 1892), 993, 1273; Ernest John Eitel, *A Chinese Dictionary in the Cantonese Dialect* (London: Trübner and Company, 1877), 199; Williams, 漢英韻府, 1074.

61 I thank Prof. Lynette Chua and Prof. Sida Liu for their generous insights on the possible meaning of "young sheen" and its potential Cantonese origins, including its more colloquial uses in Hokkien.

62 Rhook, "The Chief Chinese Interpreter," 4.

63 Rhook, "The Chief Chinese Interpreter," 5. On the same phenomenon in colonial India, see Cohn, *Colonialism and Its Forms of Knowledge.*

64 Rhook, "The Chief Chinese Interpreter," 13.

65 C.P. Hodges, "Letter Respecting the Belief of the Chinese in God," *Census of Victoria* (1881), 2:183.

66 "Castlemaine Court of Assize," *Mount Alexander Mail*, 21 July 1875, 2.

67 On the "cultural defence" in British colonial courts, see Catherine L. Evans, "Heart of Ice: Indigenous Defendants and Colonial Law in the Canadian North-West," *Law and History Review* 36, no. 2 (2018): 199–234.

68 Elizabeth Elbourne, "Religion in the British Empire," in *The British Empire: Themes and Perspectives*, ed. Sarah E. Stockwell (Malden, MA: John Wiley & Sons, 2008), 132.

69 Later in life, Leech became interested in theological matters, including a mystical sect that espoused "universalism." See "Universalism," *Bendigo Advertiser*, 15 August 1870, 2. See also John Leonard Forde, *The Story of the Bar of Victoria: From Its Foundation to the Amalgamation of the Two Branches of the Legal Profession, 1839–1891: Historical, Personal, Humorous* (Melbourne: Whitcombe & Tombs, 1913), 240. On the supposed trustworthiness of objects over witnesses in early criminalistics, see Ian Burney and Neil Pemberton, "Making Space for Criminalistics: Hans Gross and *fin-de-siècle* CSI," *Studies in History and Philosophy of Science Part C: Studies in History and Philosophy of Biological and Biomedical Sciences* 44, no. 1 (March 2013): 16–25.

70 "Castlemaine Court of Assize," *Mount Alexander Mail*, 21 July 1875, 2.

71 "Castlemaine Court of Assize," *Mount Alexander Mail*, 21 July 1875, 2.

72 "Castlemaine Court of Assize," *Mount Alexander Mail*, 21 July 1875, 2.

73 *An Act to Amend Further the Law of Evidence*, Act XI of 1854, Vic. s. VII.

74 *An Act to Amend Further the Law of Evidence*, s. XII.

75 American jurisdictions adopted a similar approach, at times determining a Chinese witness's fitness to take an oath following an investigation of his or her religious beliefs and understanding of the Christian concept of the

afterlife. See John R. Wunder, "Chinese in Trouble: Criminal Law and Race on the Trans-Mississippi West Frontier," *The Western Historical Quarterly* 17, no. 1 (January 1986): 25–41.

76 On debates about oath-taking and criminal procedure in India, see Kalyani Ramnath, "The Colonial Difference between Law and Fact: Notes on the Criminal Jury in India," *The Indian Economic & Social History Review* 50, no. 3 (July 2013): 341–63, https://doi.org/10.1177/0019464613494624.

77 "Castlemaine Court of Assize," *Mount Alexander Mail*, 21 July 1875, 2.

78 "Castlemaine Court of Assize," *Mount Alexander Mail*, 21 July 1875, 2.

79 Binyamin Blum, "The Hounds of Empire: Forensic Dog Tracking in Britain and Its Colonies, 1888–1953," *Law and History Review* 35, no. 3 (2017): 621–65.

80 Shpayer-Makov, *The Ascent of the Detective*; Clive Emsley and Haia Shpayer-Makov, eds., *Police Detectives in History, 1750–1950* (Aldershot, UK: Ashgate, 2006); Mark Finnane and Dean Wilson, "From Sleuths to Technicians? Changing Images of the Detective in Victoria," in Emsley and Shpayer-Makov, *Police Detectives in History*, 135–56.

81 "Castlemaine Court of Assize," *Mount Alexander Mail*, 21 July 1875, 2.

82 Of all executions, 41.7 per cent (eighteen) were prisoners born in Ireland, even though they made up just over a tenth of the population of the colony. See Malcolm and Hall, *A New History of the Irish in Australia*, 200–1; Arthur Patchett Martin, *Australia and the Empire* (Edinburgh: D. Douglas, 1889), 152.; Official Records of the Registrar-General's Office, *Statistics of the Colony of Victoria, 1871* (Melbourne: Government Printer, 1871), 5.

83 "The Condemned Man, An Gaa," *Bendigo Advertiser*, 3 August 1875, 3.

84 "Melbourne," *Mount Alexander Mail*, 24 August 1875, 3.

85 Peter H. Hoffenberg, "'Nothing Very New or Very Showy to Exhibit'?: Australia at the Great Exhibition and After," in *Britain, the Empire, and the World at the Great Exhibition of 1851*, ed. Jeffrey A. Auerbach and Peter H. Hoffenberg (Aldershot, UK: Ashgate, 2008), 115.

86 Diary of J.B. Castieau, 1875, 19 August 1875, National Library of Australia (NLA), MS Acc. 13.094, Papers of J.B. Castieau.

87 Diary of J.B. Castieau, 1875, 19 August 1875.

88 Diary of J.B. Castieau, 1875, 29 August 1875.

89 Diary of J.B. Castieau, 1875, 30 August 1875.

90 See Berger, this volume, 224.

91 See Funk, this volume.

92 See Berger, this volume.

Chapter Nine

An Oath on the Big Book: Oaths and Examinations in American Codes of Procedure

KELLEN FUNK

On a Sunday in the autumn of 1859, the usually implacable litigator Thomas G. Shearman sat awed by America's most famous preacher. "I never was so *quickly* affected by any sermon I ever heard – it seemed to reach my heart at once," Shearman scribbled in his journal, adding with winking humour that his public display of emotion made his wife "quite cross" with him. Although Shearman was still relatively new to the congregation, his journal marked that Sunday, 9 October, as the day he found a spiritual home under the preaching of Brooklyn's Henry Ward Beecher.[1]

The son of a revivalist Presbyterian and brother to the author of *Uncle Tom's Cabin*, Beecher was renowned for his imaginative metaphors and soothing pulpit oratory. Comparing Beecher to Charles Finney, the firebrand revivalist of an earlier era, Beecher's successor at the Plymouth Church in Brooklyn remarked that "Dr Finney drove men to repentance; Mr Beecher drew them." Indeed, the sermon that Shearman said "melted me right down from the very beginning," was titled "The Gentleness of God."[2]

While most of the sermon might strike more modern ears as so many comfortable bromides, Beecher's conclusion about eternal destiny ended with surprising ambivalence:

> Sometimes, in dark caves, men have gone to the edge of unspeaking precipices, and, wondering what was the depth, have cast down fragments of rock, and listened for the report of their fall, that they might judge how deep that blackness was; and listening – still listening – no sound returns;

Figure 9.1 Printed reproduction of a film portrait of Thomas G. Shearman (1834–1900) when he was twenty-seven years old, around the time David Dudley Field first hired him to perform clerical work on a treatise explaining Field's procedure code. Papers of Thomas G. Shearman, Shearman & Sterling Law Library, 575 Lexington Ave., New York.

no sullen plash, no clinking stroke as of rock against rock – nothing but silence, utter silence! And so I stand upon the precipice of life. I sound the depths of the other world with curious inquiries. But from it comes no echo and no answer to my questions. No analogies can grapple and bring up from the depths of the darkness of the lost world the probable truths.

Beecher left the connection of this passage to the theme of God's gentleness implicit for his audience. The connection was clear to Shearman, though. When he wrote his memoirs in the 1880s, Shearman devoted the first hundred pages to telling not how he became one of New York's wealthiest lawyers, or an unflappable litigator, but rather to how his years-long struggle to remain a devout Christian while rejecting doctrines of perdition finally ended in repose under Beecher's pulpit. In Beecher, Shearman found a kindred spirit, a respectable New Yorker of reputable orthodoxy who nevertheless relaxed Protestant teaching on damnation that had been so crucial to an earlier generation of American revivalists.[3]

In the same era that mainstream American evangelicals might publicly doubt that a gentle God could damn souls to hell, a code drafted by Shearman's law partner David Dudley Field sought to sunder any remaining connection between the practices of US lawyers and Christian ideas of perdition by transforming the civil law's most explicit link to theology: the testimonial oath. While devout jurists and moral theologians in the eighteenth and nineteenth centuries insisted that the obligation of an oath depended on the swearer's belief in supernatural and usually eternal consequences for oath-breaking, Field, Shearman, and their fellow code-writers sought to relocate the obligations of truth-telling fully within a temporal legal system. Under their code, perjury prosecutions and especially the skilful cross-examination of counsel were thought to sufficiently deter and detect falsehood without any further reliance on Christian theology. First promulgated in New York in 1848, Field's Code regulated all aspects of trial practice in the many states that adopted it by century's end. While the Field Code has become a set piece of US legal history, few have examined how the code significantly changed American lawyers' approach to oaths and examinations.[4]

The codifiers' expectations for their work neatly track our received history of the rules of evidence. August accounts by George Fisher, Kenneth Abraham, and G. Edward White tell us that in the nineteenth century Anglo-American law shifted from premodern modes of investigation, marked principally by a reliance on sacral oaths, to a rational system of proofs relying on forensic science and behavioural psychology. In Fisher's memorable imagery, the jury arose as the legal system's principal "lie detector," replacing God as the inscrutable "black box" of deliberation from which the legitimate oracles of judgment flowed.[5]

While this straightforward modernization tale has received some criticism from scholars of eighteenth-century England, it has held a strong sway in American legal history alongside a similar modernization story about race. The Fourteenth Amendment was the linchpin in the transformation of evidence law, Fisher contends, because its admission of racial minorities to the witness stand naturally prompted states to abolish longstanding disqualifications of testimony from parties and interested witnesses, leaving juries to sort through the conflicting testimony that then flooded in.[6] Forensic rationality went hand in hand with a progressing racial egalitarianism – a tale as comforting as any Beecher sermon.

But history did not unfold as neatly as the codifiers expected, nor as smoothly as the accounts report. By ignoring the central place of Field's code of practice in the transformation of American evidence law, we have missed the ways "premodern" and "modern" evidence regimes did not succeed one another but rather swirled together as lawyers rethought their methods of truth-seeking in a civil justice system. Instead of replacing oaths, the codes exponentially multiplied them, dramatically increasing the legal system's reliance on swearing. And although the theological ground underlying the oath shifted over time, many American lawyers remained committed to the notion that some threat of divine displeasure was required to make the oath do its work. Instead of spurring a secular rationalization of evidence law, the codifiers' uptake of racial science convinced them over time of the limits of forensic investigation. Concerned that racialized minorities could not be forced by temporal penalties into testifying truthfully, code lawyers ultimately refused to consign threats of perdition to a premodern legal past.

Oaths in the Civil Legal Tradition

The legal oath had a history more ancient than nearly any other device reformed by New York's 1848 Field Code. Across the High Middle Ages, controversies could be resolved entirely upon the question of which party agreed to swear for the legitimacy of his claim. Ecclesiastical authorities at the time made clear that false swearing was a mortal sin, liable to everlasting punishment in the afterlife.[7] Perhaps for that reason, civil authorities in the sixteenth and seventeenth centuries became extremely guarded in their allowance of oath-taking. Unwilling to become accessories to a witness's damnation, magistrates might permit criminal defendants, children, or "infidels" to speak in court, but they spoke unsworn, disallowed to stake the ultimate wager of their souls on the truthfulness of their testimony. Civil parties, those especially tempted to swear falsely for mere monetary gain, were largely banned from testifying. The only partial exception – discovery procedure at chancery – developed at the time the chancellery was an ecclesiastical office, and the chancellor could administer an oath in his dual capacity as priestly confessor and secular jurist.[8]

Early Modern treatises on evidence tended to focus on guiding practitioners through the technical details of practice rather than explaining the deeper meaning or reason for those practices. Guides on legal evidence elaborated the cases in which oaths were required or excused, but they usually did not undertake to explain what an oath was, what it was for, and how it was supposed to work.[9] An exception was one of the earliest works on evidence, the mid-eighteenth-century treatise by Geoffrey Gilbert, who wrote that the exclusion of certain witnesses from swearing an oath was a matter of "Piety." Gilbert tentatively explained that "the Reason seems to be" that such witnesses "are not admitted to hurt their Consciences by Swearing."[10] Commentators like Gilbert seemed reluctant to admit that jurists relied on religious devotion to make fundamental practices of the legal system workable. For all the advances of eighteenth-century jurisprudence, the law was not an autonomous domain. Barbara Shapiro has shown how frequently assize sermons before court sessions focused on the oath, explaining its theological significance and the necessity of religion to create, as one cleric stated, "the most firm and sacred bond that can be laid upon all that are concerned in the administration of public Justice." But these ubiquitous sentiments in assize sermons do not appear to have been preserved in the judicial instructions or opinions handed down at the assizes themselves.[11]

This same division of genera continued into the nineteenth century: treatises on evidence gave the rules on oath-taking without explaining the act's significance, while moral theologians laboured to make up that deficiency. William Paley's *Principles of Moral and Political Philosophy* explained that "whatever be the form of an oath, the *signification* is the same. It is the calling upon God to witness, *i.e.*, to take notice of what we say, and it is invoking his vengeance, or renouncing his favor if what we say be false."[12] Paley thought that English overuse of the oath might drain it of its solemnity, and he encouraged lawmakers to assess "penalties proportioned to the public mischief of the offence" of false testimony. But so long as the legal system continued to rely on the oath, Paley insisted that oaths "carry with them no *proper* force or obligation, unless we believe that God will punish false swearing with more severity than a simple lie."[13]

Half a century later, moral theologians widely cited and elaborated on Paley's definition of the oath. Field hoped to make plain-spoken legal filings exhibit the same truthfulness as everyday conversation and commercial discourse, but that, explained the mid-nineteenth-century moral theorist William Whewell, was precisely the problem oaths were meant to correct. "If the Witness were to give his Evidence, the Jury their Verdict, the Judge his sentence, with the carelessness and perversion of truth and right, which men often allow themselves in common conversation; the administration of justice would be impossible," Whewell wrote. Legal testimony required more solemnity and care than ordinary conversation, and oaths offered a "natural way of acknowledging and marking this moral solemnity, among religious men, … by acting, and declaring that we will act, as in the presence of God." While jurists avoided linking legal ritual and religious piety, Whewell declared that oath-taking was the fundamental basis of a state's legitimacy, "for a State, not claiming a moral reality for its acts, by means of religious solemnities [i.e., oaths], could not stand against a great body of citizens bound together by religion." Without due regard for the oath, the state itself and its legal apparatus vanished, leaving to any religious oath-taking body the right of revolution.[14]

Whether "religious solemnities" really meant more than "Christian solemnities" was a question whose answer was undergoing significant development across the eighteenth-century British sphere of influence.

In the pivotal case of *Omichund v. Barker* (1745), the English Court of Chancery decided that the sworn testimony of Hindu merchants could be accepted as competent evidence. As Jud Campbell has explained, the differing manuscript reports of *Omichund* left lawyers uncertain whether a proper oath required belief in a deity, belief in an afterlife of potential punishment, or both.[15] In practice, colonial courts in British India satisfied themselves that Jewish, Hindu, and Muslim oaths were sufficiently binding to credit merchant testimony from different faiths. Other essays in this volume show that this settlement was widespread. Pamela Klassen and Isabel Klassen-Marshall's chapter in this volume notes that while "the power behind an oath was usually the Christian God," imperial authorities in Canada adapted to a "wider range" of sacral devices. And as Catherine Evans reports in this volume, by the late nineteenth century, Australian jurists too had become accustomed to "calibrating oath-taking and swearing practices rooted in Christian tradition to reflect what British officials understood to be the spiritual and cultural beliefs of the empire's diverse subjects."[16]

In any event, popular explications of the legal oath in America followed the British moral theologians closely. One of the most widely disseminated tracts in North America – of any kind – was titled "The Swearer's Prayer, or, His Oath Explained." Its lengthy translation of "so help me God" ran in part: "O God! thou hast power to punish me in hell forever: therefore let … every lie that I have told … rise up in judgment against me, and eternally condemn me!" The tract concluded, "Swearer, *this is thy prayer!!!*"[17] And for some laymen, the threat of hell was the foremost, or even the exclusive, safeguard of an honest oath. As late as 1852, a poor Irishman could testify that "I know what perjury is, and that the punishment of perjury is damnation; I never heard that a man could be transported for perjury; I never heard that a man would be punished by the law of the land for perjury."[18]

Accordingly, treatises that were pitched to justices of the peace or magistrates – those who straddled the line between laymen and professionals – were often more explicit about the need for piety to make oaths legally useful. One treatise explained that children could be sworn only if they appeared to have "the sense of religion." New Yorker Oliver Barbour's 1841 "practical treatise," *The Magistrate's Criminal Law* likewise counselled that "a man wholly without religion … shall not be received to give evidence in any case whatever."[19]

Thus, whether the legal treatises made it explicit, the sacral logic of the oath remained largely undisturbed into the early days of the American Republic. When the liberal theorist John Locke famously excluded atheists from his plans for religious toleration, he did so on the basis

Figure 9.2 Frontispiece, *The Publications of the American Tract Society*, vol. 1 (1824).

that atheists denied an afterlife and therefore offered worthless oaths. Likewise, when George Washington urged in his Farewell Address that "religion and morality are indispensable supports" to "political prosperity," his argument relied solely on civil oath-taking: "Let it simply be asked: Where is the security for property, for reputation, for life, if the sense of religious obligation desert the oaths which are the instruments of investigation in the courts of justice?" Accordingly, state after state adopted the common law rule barring non-Christians from oath-taking in the Early Republic.[20]

Verification of Pleadings in Field's Code of Procedure

New York's 1848 procedure code, drafted by Field and explicated in treatises by Shearman, became the basis for modern civil practice in the United States by the end of the century. The code abolished the old ways of making claims in court and instructed lawyers to file simple complaints stating the facts of their cases. "There is no magic in forms," the commentary explained, yet when it came to pleading – the formal statement one party makes when suing another in civil litigation – the code at first appeared to re-enchant legal procedure. "Every pleading," read section 133 in the 1848 Code, "must be subscribed by the party" and "verified by the party, his agent or attorney, to the effect that he believes it to be true." That is, as the note explained, the code proposed to "test" all pleadings by requiring "a verification by the oath of the party."[21] Oaths may have had a long history of crossing the sacred and secular divide in the common law tradition, but for that very reason they had not usually been required of so mundane an activity as civil pleading. The application of the oath to pleadings raised a number of immediate difficulties for the code-writers, but not the one that would have been obvious even a generation earlier: the risk of perdition. Far from reintroducing any "magic" eliminated with the forms of action, Field's expansion of the oath shows just how much American legal practice had become unconcerned with sacral foundations.[22]

The conviction that the threat of hell secured the solemnity, and thus the truthfulness, of an oath rapidly deteriorated in early nineteenth-century America. Jud Campbell and Kathryn Gin Lum argue that the spread of Christian Universalism at the turn of the nineteenth century directly contributed to the demise of state restrictions on oath-takers. Though they never attracted significant numbers, Universalists counted among their members leading statesmen and moral reformers, who seemed to prove by their example that virtue and veracity could be founded on something other than the fear of everlasting perdition. By the 1830s, the exclusion of Universalists and adherents of other varieties of Christian heterodoxy raised significant concerns that the judicial system was subverting constitutional law by preferring certain religious sects and denying religious expression to others.[23] Many states at this time – including New York – amended their constitutions to forbid religious discrimination in oath-taking.[24]

The speed at which the theological foundation of the oath disappeared was dramatic. As late as 1820, a New York appellate court had banned a Universalist from taking a testimonial oath.[25] Yet the sacral logic of future divine retribution was completely absent from every codification report on civil procedure three decades later, both in New York and elsewhere. In his 1847 tract laying out an ideal procedure system, Field expressed incomprehension that "some persons are very tender of the consciences of parties, thinking that the temptation to perjury will prove too strong for human frailty, … if I understand the drift of their argument." Focus on an individual's conscience seemed misplaced to Field, for all that really counted was whether party oaths were more likely in the aggregate to disclose truth or conceal it. Gone was the concern that a court might become complicit in condemning a soul to hell, or that divine retribution secured veracity. Concern for conscience thus struck Field as a "palpable absurdity, that because, in some cases, the motive of interest is stronger than the principle of honesty, therefore those truths which are only known to interested parties shall forever be hidden."[26] A few truthful statements were more valuable than numerous falsehoods and guilty consciences.

Rather than serving as a means to re-sacralize civil proceedings, Field meant oath requirements to be a step towards disenchanting procedure. In a Final Report, Field counselled the legislature to "abolish oaths altogether," so long as pleading and other solemn affirmations still carried temporal penalties for perjury. The rest of the commentary was devoted to other secular concerns. To protect state constitutional rights against self-incrimination, the commissioners decreed that no admissions in civil pleadings could be used as proof in a criminal trial.[27] If parties worried that their knowledge of a dispute was too uncertain to swear to factual veracity, the commissioners provided "a means of amendment of the most liberal character; as liberal, indeed, as we could devise." And earlier drafts of properly amended pleadings would not support a prosecution of perjury.[28]

The secularity of the oath and of Field's Code featured in a curious joke that circulated in the western newspapers in the 1870s. A woman rushed her husband into a clerk's office and demanded her husband take an oath "that he will not strike me again." The clerk protested that he was not empowered to administer oaths, but "'it don't make any difference,' said the woman. 'He's got to take an oath on the big book, before you, that he won't lick me again.'" His protests ignored, the clerk "took down from one of the shelves a copy of the Code of Civil Procedure and laid it before the man, who placed his hand upon it and repeated what his wife told him, and which was as follows: 'I solemnly promise that I will never beat or abuse my wife again, and if I should so far forget myself as to do so, this promise which I now make may be used against me in aggravation of punishment in any criminal proceeding.' The woman then thanked the clerk, and turning to her husband said, 'John, you are a good man after all, and I know you'll keep your promise.'"[29] In the anecdote, the penalty for oath-breaking was described in purely temporal terms – an aggravated criminal punishment. By literally replacing the Bible with the Code of Civil Procedure, the tale drew its humour from the understanding that there could be no magic, no objective spiritual consequence to such an oath. But like its more solemnly administered counterpart, the mock oath could perform its function, so long as those using it believed in it.[30]

From Deterrence to Detection of Oath-breaking

On the face of it, Field's statute requiring all pleadings to be verified by oath seemed like it should have been easy to implement. In practice, oath-taking became one of the more complicated departments of practice under the code. One judge opined in an early ruling that "the nature of the oath which, under the Code, the party is required to make in regard to his pleading [was] necessarily qualified by" the traditional rules of pleading.[31] But it was by no means clear whether a "qualified" oath could give rise to perjury. Remarkably quickly, lawyers in all the early code states abandoned their faith in cross-examination and prosecution as a deterrence to perjury, arguing instead that their skilful cross-examinations, if they could not deter, at least could detect the violation of the oath and thus secure the truth in court. Some argued that they were forced to this position when the code itself seemed to demand perjury from the parties.

From the earliest days of code practice, some lawyers doubted whether perjury could even be committed under code pleading. One New York attorney wrote in to the *Code Reporter*, a magazine founded to share judicial decisions and professional discussion on the new code. The lawyer noted that the code required pleadings to be verified, "but does not state, *in terms*, that it shall be *verified by oath*." The attorney wondered, then, "Can a party who verifies a complaint or answer on oath, knowing it to be wholly false, be convicted of perjury?" The editor bemusedly answered, "We cannot imagine how any doubt can arise on the subject," but in subsequent issues, the *Reporter* admitted the question was more difficult than it first appeared.[32]

The literal provisions of the code seemed to put defendants in an intolerable dilemma. Although a plaintiff generally bore the burden of proof, the defendant could not put the plaintiff to his proof without denying a material allegation under oath, at the risk of perjury. But if a defendant could not deny an allegation he suspected or believed or even knew to be true, the plaintiff would be relieved of the burden of proof the law assigned to him. "Can a party be convicted of the crime of perjury," a Minnesota lawyer exclaimed, "under a law *requiring* him upon *oath* to deny *'all the material facts in the case?'*" If so, the code basically forced defendants into testifying against themselves. If they sought to hold plaintiffs to their proof, as traditional due process demanded, they opened themselves to criminal prosecution for perjury on their pleadings. Thus, the *Code Reporter* ultimately concluded, "the Code does not render it necessary to verify pleading on oath, but if it does, then it is unconstitutional."[33]

Field remained resolute in his Second Report to the New York legislature advising on an amended code. Field's suggested revision waived verification by oath only when an admission would subject a party to prosecution for "an infamous crime" (other than perjury), and expressed "regret, that a more stringent rule in respect to the verification of pleadings is required, but they have reason to believe, that the spirit of the code in this respect has not been always regarded," in that courts had gotten used to regularly excusing the parties from swearing.[34] The New York legislature overruled Field with two new provisions designed to ameliorate the oath requirement. First, the oath was made optional unless the parties themselves insisted on it, which largely reinstituted the rules of pleading at chancery. To force an admission under oath from the defendant, a plaintiff would himself have to swear to his own facts, including the allegation that he could not come by the needed information any other way than the admission of the defendant. Under such a rule, it was no longer clear when an oath was "voluntary" or "required by law," and the distinction was crucial for perjury. Under long-standing rules of equity, derived from biblical injunctions against needless swearing, a voluntary oath was an "unlawful" oath and could not support a charge of perjury. The same year as the New York amendment, the *Code Reporter* favourably cited an Ohio chancery decision recognizing that the voluntary oaths rule was still operative across the common law world, and New York courts applied the rule to code practice in their state a few sessions later.[35]

The second mitigating amendment took Field's commentary on the code and made it a point of law. "It is not required of a party, that he state absolutely, that the matters pleaded are true, inasmuch as his knowledge may not extend to the whole case," Field's Second Report had explained, "but it is intended to put him upon his veracity, and to require him to state nothing, that he does not believe to be true." The legislative amendment accordingly specified that with the oath a party swore not that the facts were true, but that they were *believed* to be true at the time of pleading, a more difficult burden for a prosecutor to prove perjury. Together, the quasi-voluntary nature of the civil oath and knowledge requirement for conviction rendered perjury convictions on civil pleadings largely impractical. Printed reports contain very few instances of a perjury prosecution on civil pleadings – or indeed, on any ordinary civil case.[36] In one peculiar case in the 1870s, the county court in Tompkins, New York, upheld a perjury conviction when a defendant lied in his pleading about paying off a promissory note and sought to escape punishment by arguing that the pleading did not directly claim the note was paid, only that "the defendant says" it was paid, that is, a true allegation of a false statement.[37]

Even in states that adopted Field's more "stringent" rule, the threat of perjury prosecution failed to deter false pleading – or false testimony. In 1853, the Ohio commissioners adopted Field's rules with the comment, "We trust in the general regard of the great mass of the people for truth, in the rigor of the criminal laws of the State to deter the dishonest from perjury, and in the sagacity and skill of judges, counsel, parties, and jurors, to detect and expose falsehood, when perpetuated in a court of justice."[38] But by the end of that same decade, judges in the state had abandoned the deterrence ideal for the promise of detection.

An 1859 Iowa Code Commission solicited surveys from lawyers and law reformers across the Midwest, from New York, and even in London. American jurists expressed indifference as to "whether under this system justice is not purchased at the expense of demoralisation" in the words of an Ohio lawyer recently appointed to the faculty at University of Virginia.[39] Judges on the Ohio Court of Common Pleas agreed that perjury had become rampant under the reformed system, but none found the epidemic particularly troubling. "If perjury is committed, it is very soon disclosed," Judge James L. Bates assured his Iowa correspondents. His colleague, B.F. Hoffman, agreed that "the chief objection is merely, that it produces perjury," but the chance at truth outweighed the objection. Another Ohio judge responded, "Much

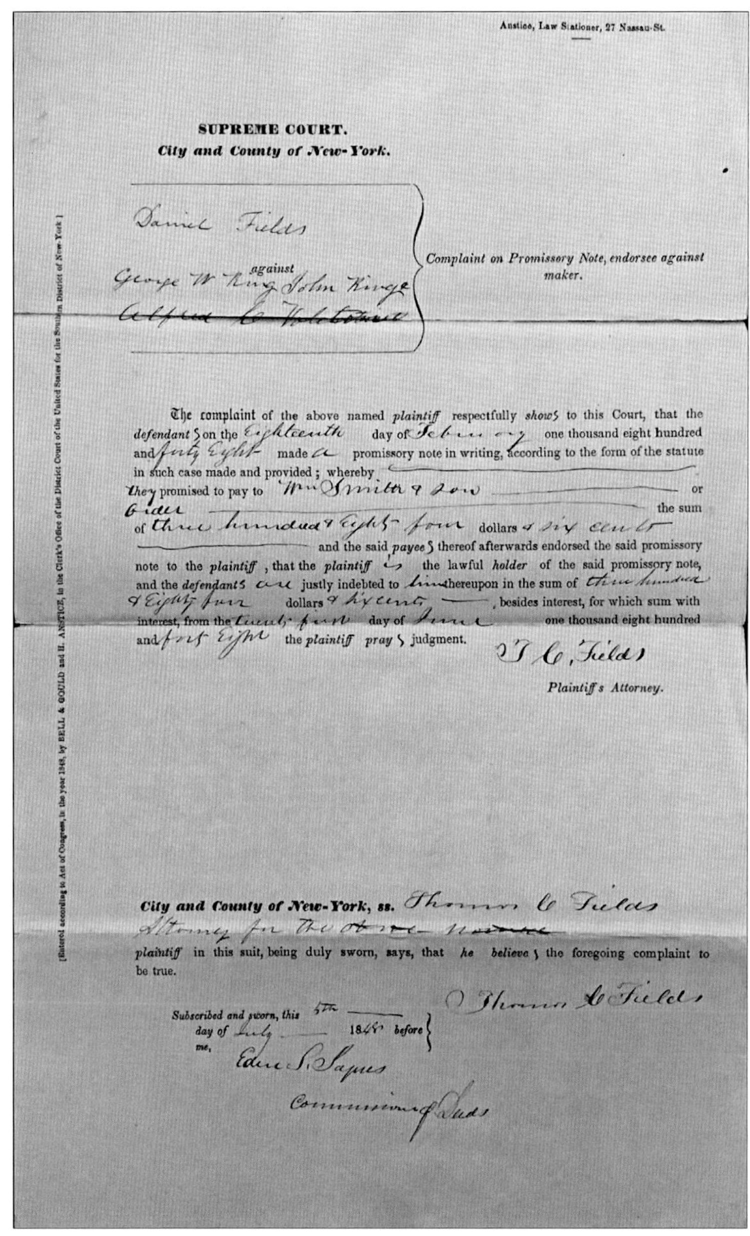

Austice, Law Stationer, 27 Nassau-St.

SUPREME COURT.
City and County of New-York.

Daniel Fields
against
George W. King, John King,
Alfred C. [illegible]
} Complaint on Promissory Note, endorsee against maker.

The complaint of the above named *plaintiff* respectfully *shows* to this Court, that the defendant *s* on the *Eighteenth* day of *February* one thousand eight hundred and *forty Eight* made *a* promissory note in writing, according to the form of the statute in such case made and provided ; whereby *they* promised to pay to *Wm. Smith & Son* or *Order* the sum of *three hundred & Eighty four* dollars *& six cents* and the said *payee s* thereof afterwards endorsed the said promissory note to the *plaintiff* , that the *plaintiff is* the lawful *holder* of the said promissory note, and the *defendant s are* justly indebted to *him* thereupon in the sum of *three hundred & Eighty four* dollars *& six cents* , besides interest, for which sum with interest, from the *twenty first* day of *June* one thousand eight hundred and *forty Eight* the *plaintiff* pray *s* judgment.

T. C. Fields
Plaintiff s Attorney.

City and County of New-York, **ss.** *Thomas C. Fields Attorney for the above named* *plaintiff* in this suit, being duly sworn, says, that *he believe s* the foregoing complaint to be true.

Thomas C. Fields

Subscribed and sworn, this *5th* day of *July* 184*8* before me, *Edwin S. Sayres Commissioner of Deeds*

[Entered according to Act of Congress, in the year 1848, by BELL & GOULD and H. ANSTICE, in the Clerk's Office of the District Court of the United States for the Southern District of New-York.]

Figure 9.3 New York City Municipal Archives, Office of the County Clerk, 31 Chambers St., Manhattan. Pleadings of the Supreme Court of Judicature Collection, PL-1848-F-26, *Fields v. King et al.* The verification on oath became a standard form on preprinted pleadings.

perjury exists in the swearing of parties. It is really alarming, but in many cases does conduce to truth." With truth so easy to detect, codifiers expressed no concerns about presenting conflicting testimony to oath-bound jurors. "The probabilities, the appearance of the witness, the cross-examination, the circumstances, the corroboration of others, etc., almost always makes it easy to see who has the truth on the point in dispute," Judge Hoffman concluded. "The point must be naked and isolated indeed, the contradiction plump and evenly balanced in manner, matter, etc., not to tell where the real truth is."[40]

Rather than following the English example of stepping up perjury prosecutions, American lawyers largely made their peace with perjury.[41] Ignoring criminal sanctions, Judge Hoffman reasoned that perjurers "will soon find their true social and trading position at the lower end of the scale, and out of the good opinion of honest men." A commercial, rather than a spiritual, penalty was apparently the proper punishment of perjury. Some judges would continue to insist into the 1860s that "where, in the course of legal proceedings, the oath of a party is required, the intention is to appeal to his conscience and to his religious sense." Judge Hoffman, however, waved off such concerns, concluding that he "would not be tender of [parties'] internal mental condition, at the expense of others' rights and dues."[42]

The Problem of Racialized Witnesses

"Admission is the rule here," Field explained in defence of the rules that made parties competent witnesses at trial. "Exclusion is the rule of the common law. Let in all the light possible, we ask. Not so the common law; exclude the light, it says, lest perchance it deceive you; unmindful, as it appears to us, that poor light is better than none."[43] The apparent rise of perjured testimony under the code may have meant that the light was much poorer than Field had expected, but at least the compromises of the code allowed truth-seeking that former practices had foreclosed. Even as it became evident that party testimony had opened the floodgates to falsehood, some truth, previously excluded, was streaming in as well, and Field shared the same confidence as the Ohio judges that lawyers could easily detect the truth. "Let us not fear, that judges and juries will be deluded into a belief of an improbable or untrue story, though the parties themselves be the persons who utter it," he urged.[44]

Field's argument was commended outside New York. "I entirely concur with your opinion, that all rules for the exclusion of evidence are rules for the exclusion of light," the Missouri codifier R.W. Wells wrote to Field. In his report, Field reprinted the recommendations of William

Storrs, Chief Justice of the Supreme Court in Connecticut, a state that like New York, had recently allowed parties to testify at trial. "For although, it is obvious that there will be much false swearing by parties in their own behalf," Storrs admitted, "still an intelligent jury can always determine correctly to what weight their evidence is entitled under the circumstances and make the proper allowance for the interest and situation of the witnesses, especially as he is personally before the Court, and is subjected to the searching operation of a cross-examination." The Ohio commission concurred. "The tests of truth are almost innumerable, and tried by them, falsehood is laid bare and recoils upon the head of him who utters it," they wrote in their report.[45]

But just when lawyers in state after state were learning to live with perjury, confident in their ability to detect the truth, many states introduced a new policy of testimonial exclusion in their codes. It began in California, one of the earliest adopters of Field's code outside his home state. As enacted by the legislature, the state's Practice Act tracked the 1849 version of Field's code by requiring pleading on oath and permitting the examination of parties on the stand. The act then provided that "no black, or mulatto person, or Indian, shall be permitted to give evidence in any action to which a white person is a party, in any Court of this State." When Field's brother Stephen J. Field introduced David Dudley's revised draft in the next session, he kept the state's racial exclusion, although he adjusted the blood quantum defining "black" (upward) and "Indian" (downward) from the levels set in 1850.[46] For the latter category, the state assembly briefly considered mitigating the absolute exclusion. Perhaps "Christianized Indians whom two disinterested white persons, citizens of the State, shall, on oath, testify, in open court, that they are known to them, and that they consider their testimony under oath worthy of credit" could testify, "leaving the credibility of such Indians to the jury." With a tied vote, however, the assembly decided to leave the exclusion absolute.[47] Stephen Field and the other codifiers offered no commentary on their change to the New York code. Testimonial exclusions of racialized peoples were not new in American law, and the language of the California rule closely tracked the laws of midwestern states from which many Californians had emigrated.[48]

Commentary would be provided several years later by an infamous case in the state supreme court, *People v. Hall*, which extended the testimonial exclusion of Blacks and Indians to the Chinese as well. *Hall* has become widely noted for its strained attempts to include Chinese people in the statutory construction of "Indian," as well for its reasoning that if "a race of people whom nature has marked as inferior" were admitted to testify, they would next clamour for "all the equal rights of citizenship, and we might soon see them at the polls, in the jury box, upon the bench, and in our legislative halls." What accounts of the case have overlooked, however, is how thoroughly the case subverted the codifiers' faith in cross-examination as an infallible test for truth at trial.[49]

Most of the opinion in *Hall* sought semantic connections between Native American *Indians* and the West *Indies* in order to bring all Asian peoples under the terms of the statute, since the text only excluded Black and Indigenous testimony. In the final pages, the opinion pivoted and argued that "even admitting the Indian of this Continent is not of the Mongolian type," the legislature clearly intended a policy that excluded all non-white testimony in court. "The evident intention of the Act was to throw around the citizen a protection for life and property, which could only be secured by removing him above the corrupting influences of degraded castes," the majority wrote. In elaborating this racial degradation, *Hall* focused on a supposed inability to respect the oath among the Chinese, "whose mendacity is proverbial" and who were "incapable of progress of intellectual development" to respect either oaths of office or of testimony. The most vital clue to legislative intent, the opinion concluded, was the comparison to "domestic Negroes and Indians, who not unfrequently have correct notions of their obligations to society." Surely the legislature did not mean to protect white citizens by excluding the oft true testimony of California's Black and Indigenous populations only to allow foreign races to testify without inhibition.[50]

As a matter of legislative intent, *Hall* seemed to have had the interpretation right. The point of the statute had not been to specifically exclude certain races but to generally exclude all non-white testimony. The specific mention of "black" and "Indian" had been to set the legal levels of blood quantum that would assign race, and a later legislature clarified the law by adding "Mongolians" and "Chinese" to the Indian clause with its requisite one-half blood quantum.[51] However, the admission that the rule excluded the frequently true testimony of these groups for sake of policy entirely undermined the code reforms to witness testimony. If anyone's mendacity had become proverbial by the mid-1850s, it was that of white parties and interested witnesses. Yet, the codifiers had argued, within the totality of the trial, truth was easy to discover and self-interested lying easy to detect. Sensing the contradiction that white lawyers in front of white juries could easily sift truth from white witnesses but not from "inferior" races, Montana's governor Sidney Edgerton vetoed the entire Code of Civil Procedure for its racial exclusions. "Our Juries and Courts are composed exclusively of white men and I consider the Caucasian race competent to weigh evidence coming from any witness of any race wisely, justly and well," he concluded. The Montana legislature overrode the governor's veto without comment.[52]

California's contradictory testimonial rules migrated to other jurisdictions, enjoying an influence almost as widespread as the Field Code itself. Overall, fifteen states and territories – a large majority of pre-Reconstruction Field Code jurisdictions – overwrote Field's competency rules with racist exclusions. Indeed, the only states that admitted party testimony without racial exclusions were in the Reconstruction South under Radical Republican rule.[53] A couple states sought to mitigate the contradiction between the acceptance of white perjury and the abhorrence of non-white mendacity by excluding only "Indians and Negroes who appear incapable of receiving just impressions of the facts respecting which they are examined, or of relating them intelligently and truly."[54] That, too, was a textual borrowing, from Field's exemption of children under ten years old from testifying. On this reasoning, races could be excluded if the chance for truth was minimal because of infantile incapacities. Even racist codifiers like Montana's Governor Edgerton recognized this rule as a fiction. In his reading, the racial exclusions conferred a *benefit* on "the Negro population" because coloured litigants could offer testimony in their cases against each other, while white litigants wishing to rely on Black testimony were deprived of useful evidence – useful, because admittedly true in many cases.[55]

In his monumental study "The Jury's Rise as Lie Detector," Professor George Fisher argues that rules that prohibited witnesses from testifying (disqualification rules, for short) were an "anachronistic survival" of "an age that mistrusted the jury's power to spot the truth and trusted instead the truth-assuring powers of the oath." Focusing mainly on the disqualification of criminal defendants, Fisher admitted that the rules permitting party competency in civil courts (which preceded criminal competency by decades) were mysterious. Although oath-taking and cross-examination were centuries-old practices, lawyers rather suddenly trusted the latter more around the mid-nineteenth century. Fisher noticed that in many states, party disqualification was abolished close to the same time racial exclusionary rules were, and he surmises that states "maintained the old bar against civil parties because their lawmakers saw no good way to reconcile testimony by parties with their racial exclusion laws." Increasing racial egalitarianism thus offers one key to explain how cross-examination came to replace the oath as the security of truth. "In those states that maintained racial exclusion laws, legislators chose to avoid an awkward clash between those laws and rules permitting testimony by civil parties simply by resisting the latter as long as they retained the former," Fisher concludes.[56]

Fisher's study – and subsequent scholarship on oath-taking and cross-examination in America – misses the central importance of the Field Code and its amendments in this history, however. The most popular version of the code in other states did not completely abolish the disqualification of party testimony, but nearly did so. In those codes, parties were not fully competent to testify *exactly* as other witnesses, but they nevertheless offered oath-verified pleadings and could be called to the stand by their adversaries at trial. Further, in most codes, if an adverse examination did not produce anticipated admissions, the examining party could then introduce his own affirmative testimony. The difference between these codes and full party competency was thus only a technical rule of sequence. Moreover, by ignoring several non-state territories that adopted California's version of the Code, Fisher undercounted the number of jurisdictions that basically permitted party testimony but excluded testimony from racial minorities. Fisher's original chart, corrected with the code jurisdictions, follows in Table 9.1. It appears that many lawyers could in fact live with the "awkward clash" of rules allowing party testimony for the sake of truth-seeking while excluding racialized testimony even if it were truthful.

Fisher's comparison of civil and criminal practice is helpful though. Looking mostly at criminal practice, Fisher emphasized the *jury's* rise as lie detector, but within the Field Codes it may be more appropriate to speak of the *lawyer's* rise as lie detector. When Field and his fellow codifiers turned their attention to criminal procedure, it was the truth-seeking powers of the lawyer that they hoped to *keep* from reaching a jury. In an 1849 proposed Code of Criminal Procedure, the Field commission argued that, unlike civil practice, truth-seeking was not the chief goal of criminal practice. If it were, "the French practice" of using cross-examination to "extract from the defendant evidence of his guilt" might be appropriate. But under the New York constitution, truth-seeking in criminal proceedings had to be secondary to protecting civil rights of the accused. The proposed Code of Criminal Procedure thus did not make criminal defendants competent to testify, even though the commission abolished civil party disqualifications the same year. Rather, the criminal code allowed a defendant to offer exculpatory statements without facing the rigors of cross-examination "proceeding on the assumption of his guilt" and driving him "to the alternative of equivocating as to facts, or of denying circumstances plainly true, or of what is occasionally his resort, declining to answer."[57]

Table 9.1 Code-Corrected Version of *Fisher's Comparison of Competency Rules*

Jurisdiction	Date for Racial Exclusion Abolished	Fisher's Date for Party Testimony Allowed	Date for Qualified Party Testimony under the Codes
Kansas	1858	same	
Kentucky	1872	same	**1853**
Louisiana	1867	same	
Oregon	1862	same	**1855**
North Carolina	1866	same	1868
South Carolina	1866	same	1870
Virginia	1866	same	
California	1863	same	**1850**
Florida	1865	same	
Alabama	1865	1867	
Arkansas	1867	1874	1870
Delaware	unknown	1881	
Georgia	1865	1866	
Illinois	1865	1867	
Missouri	1865	1866	**1849**
Ohio	1849	1853	1853
Tennessee	1866	1868	
Texas	1866	1871	
West Virginia	1866	1868	
Indiana	1865	1861	1852
Maryland	1866	1864	
Mississippi	1865	1857	
Iowa	not listed (1860)	not listed	**1851**
Washington	not listed (1877)	not listed	**1855**
Idaho	not listed (1875)	not listed	**1864**
Arizona	not listed (1887)	not listed	**1865**
Montana	not listed (1872)	not listed	**1865**
Wyoming	not listed (1874)	not listed	**1870**
Nebraska	not listed (1925)	not listed	**1855**
Nevada	not listed (1869)	not listed	**1861**

Ultimately, many who adopted Field's Code refused to distinguish between civil and criminal practice. If a policy of protecting civil rights could trump the purposes of fact-finding on the criminal side, it might do so in civil practice as well. And in many western states, codifiers reasoned that the civil rights of white litigants – the protection of their property, their trades, and in some cases their liberty – outweighed the truth value of testimony from what the California supreme court called the "degraded castes."[58]

Moreover, other codifiers disagreed with Field – and with Fisher – about the sanctity of oaths. Fisher argues that religious impulses cannot explain the history of oath-taking or its displacement by cross-examination, but many lawyers – especially in the west – continued to link the two with religious piety into the late nineteenth century. Cross-examination could make a witness sweat, shift his eyes, or stutter his speech, wrote one journalist, only because the witness was under oath and dreaded the cosmic penalties for oath-breaking. In the case of the Chinese, however, "it was difficult to shape an oath solemn enough to bind them."[59] In their perception of Chinese spirituality, western lawyers concluded that merely temporal penalties did not, in fact, make witnesses nervous enough that their prevarication could be detected by cross-examination. Such testimony thus had to be excluded, not because it was frequently untrue, but because it was no longer possible to discern truth from falsehood. Field might have been ready to abandon oath-taking and all pretence of spiritual punishment, but the reform ran headlong against the racial prejudices of the western bar, which insisted that cross-examination required some degree of white Christian piety to work its magic.

The New England Oath

The difference white Christian piety could make would be on full display in a trial conducted twenty-five years after Field introduced his code reforms, a trial involving none other than the Rev. Henry Ward Beecher. Beecher's preaching against hell had drawn Field's partner Thomas Shearman into Beecher's congregation. Shearman's powers to give witnesses hell on the stand had drawn Beecher to retain Shearman as counsel when Beecher was sued for adultery in 1875. The Great Brooklyn Scandal, as the trial has since become known, is a set piece of Reconstruction history. Many works have chronicled the 110-day trial that brought eighty-six witnesses to the stand, including Beecher and his accuser. With only slight exaggeration, one account declares the trial the only thing that "drove Reconstruction off the front pages for two and a half years."[60] The verdict was inconclusive on the question of adultery, but worth considering here is one relatively unremarked episode during the trial when the quality of Beecher's oath became a point of discussion, though not in the ways it did for the Chinese or other racialized witnesses.

When Beecher took the stand at trial, his observance of the formalities caused a small stir, as Beecher refused to place his hand on a Bible but instead held it upright in the air. "The Clerk, supposing he desired to affirm, had begun to administer that form of oath, when" the plaintiff's counsel objected. They demanded that Beecher swear, not simply

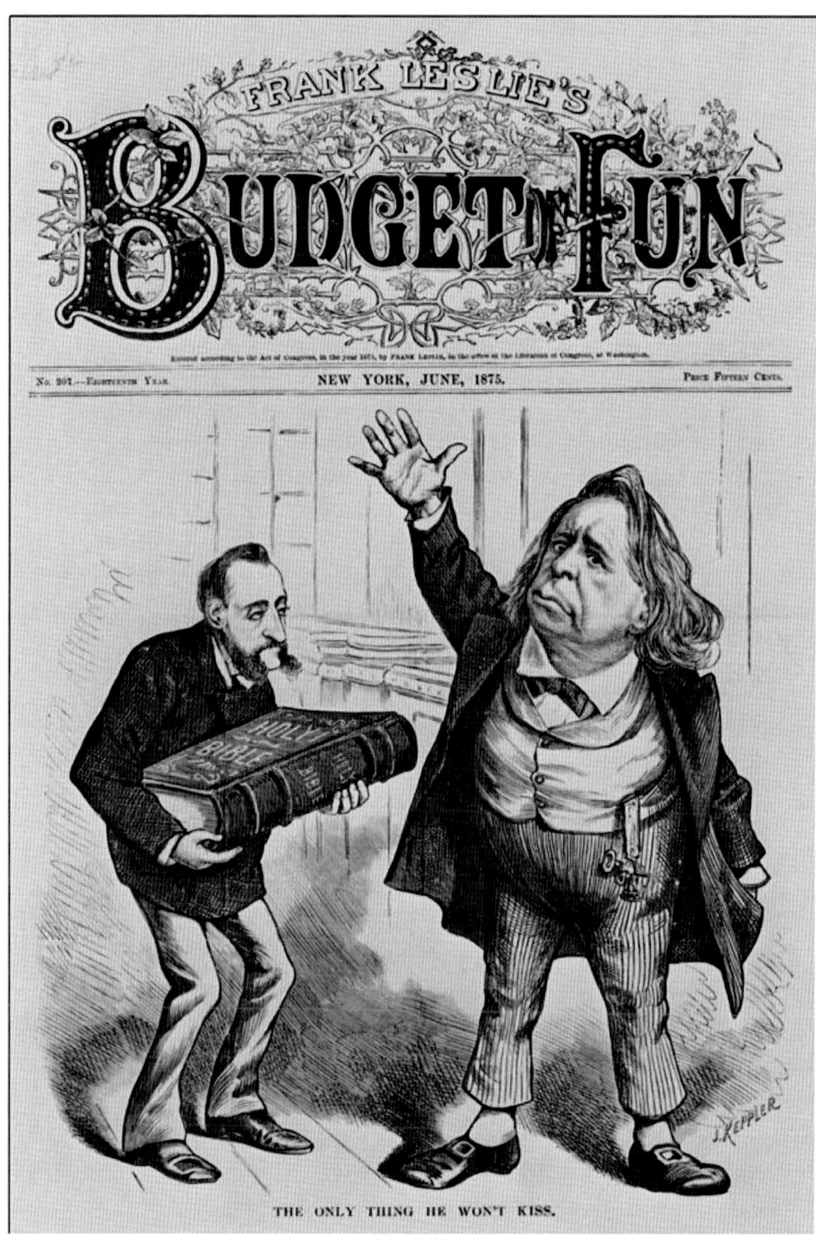

Figure 9.4 The "New England Oath" of the Reverend Henry Ward Beecher.

affirm. Still, Beecher refused the Bible, spurring a local paper to joke it was the "only thing he won't kiss."[61] When questioned about the action later by opposing counsel, Beecher explained he had never really thought about oaths until taking the stand, but having now thought it over, "I should [swear] by nothing else than by God, and not by any lower form or symbol of the Divine presence." Shearman's co-counsel explained that an upraised hand was the usual form of the "New England Oath." No one had any further questions.[62]

This small moment in the Beecher trial illustrates the vast gulf that was then emerging between official doctrines, both legal and religious, and the actual practices US lawyers felt comfortable performing. By this point, Beecher was widely reputed to doubt the existence of hell, while the temporal penalties for lying on the stand were the same regardless of whether Beecher "swore" or "affirmed." Yet the opposing lawyers rejected the bargain Field's Code offered them, refusing to trust solely in the temporal penalties to keep Beecher honest. They insisted on the oath. At the same time, they were content to let the usual formalities slide, dispensing with the Bible (and any other material accommodations lawyers had developed for the heterodox, as documented in other chapters in this volume).[63] Perhaps they were convinced by Beecher's theology of a divine presence that transcended material rites. Or perhaps they understood what was so obvious to their western counterparts: that race, class, and masculinity were key to the oath's magic.[64]

NOTES

1 Diary of Thomas G. Shearman, 9 October 1859, Papers of Thomas G. Shearman, Shearman & Sterling Law Library, 575 Lexington Ave., New York.

2 Henry Ward Beecher, "The Gentleness of God," Sermon Preached at Plymouth Church, Brooklyn, New York, 9 October 1859, in Gaius Glenn Atkins, ed., *Master Sermons of the Nineteenth Century* (Chicago: Willett, Clark, 1940) 84–102; Lyman Abbott, *Henry Ward Beecher: A Sketch of His Career* (Philadelphia: A. Gorton, 1887), 94–5; Shearman Diary, 9 October 1859.

3 Beecher, "The Gentleness of God," 98. See Memoirs of Thomas G. Shearman, vol. 1, esp. 40–92, Shearman Papers. At this time, a confidant observed that "Mr. Beecher believed in retribution … more definitely than he did subsequently." Abbott, *Henry Ward Beecher*, 94.

4 The code of procedure, also known as the code of practice, was adopted in thirty states, including every state west of the Mississippi except civilian Texas (which had its own similar code). Kellen Funk and Lincoln A. Mullen, "The Spine of American Law: Digital Text Analysis and U.S. Legal

Practice," *American Historical Review* 123, no. 1 (February 2018): 132–64. On the code as a "set piece," see Lawrence M. Friedman, *A History of American Law*, 4th ed. (Oxford: Oxford University Press, 2019), 384.

5 George Fisher, "The Jury's Rise as Lie Detector," *Yale Law Journal* 107, no. 3 (December 1997): 575–713; Kenneth S. Abraham and G. Edward White, "The Transformation of the Civil Trial and the Emergence of American Tort Law," *Arizona Law Review* 59, no. 2 (2017): 431–83.

6 Fisher, "The Jury's Rise," 674. Barbara Shapiro has vigorously disputed Fisher's evidence that the legal system did not permit conflicts of testimony before the rise of party qualification, especially in civil cases. Barbara J. Shapiro, "Oaths, Credibility and the Legal Process in Early Modern England: Part 1," *Law & Humanities* 6, no. 2 (2012): 145–78; Shapiro, "Oaths, Credibility and the Legal Process in Early Modern England: Part 2," *Law & Humanities* 7, no.1 (2013): 1–18.

7 John S. Bekerman, "Procedural Innovation and Institutional Change in Medieval English Manorial Courts," *Law and History Review* 10, no. 2 (1992): 203–4; R.H. Helmholz, *The Ius Commune in England: Four Studies* (Oxford: Oxford University Press, 2001), 101–2.

8 William Wake, *A Practical Discourse Concerning Swearing* (London, 1696), 25–35; Jean Domat, *The Civil Law in Its Natural Order*, trans. William Strahan (London, 1772), 462–6; Michael R.T. McNair, *The Law of Proof in Early Modern Equity* (Berlin: Dunckner and Humblot, 1999), 204–19.

9 See, for instance, William Nelson, *The Law of Evidence* (London, 1717); John Morgan, *Essays upon the Law of Evidence* (London, 1789).

10 Geoffrey Gilbert, *The Law of Evidence* (London, 1756), 159.

11 Shapiro, "Oaths, Credibility and the Legal Process in Early Modern England: Part One," 151–2.

12 William Paley, *The Principles of Moral and Political Philosophy* (London, 1785), 162.

13 Paley, *The Principles of Moral and Political Philosophy*, 164–5.

14 William Whewell, *The Elements of Morality: Including Polity* (1845), 2:87–8.

15 Jud Campbell, "Testimonial Exclusions and Religious Freedom in Early America," *Law and History Review* 37, no. 2 (2019): 437–43.

16 See chapters 8 and 10, this volume.

17 [William Rust,] "The Swearer's Prayer, or His Oath Explained," Virginia Religious Tract Society (1813), 1–2. The American Tract Society reported distributing forty-two thousand copies of the tract in Andover alone, marking it among the most widely distributed of its tracts in its annual reports. *The Publications of the New England Tract Society* (Andover, MA: New England Tract Society, 1820), 5:236.

18 Testimony of Jordan, *Report of the Trials at the Petty Sessions of Achill* (1852), 20.

19 Thomas Peake, *A Compendium of the Law of Evidence*, 2nd ed. (1804), 123; Oliver L. Barbour, *The Magistrate's Criminal Law* (Albany: W. and A. Gould, 1841), 380.

20 John Locke, *A Letter Concerning Toleration* (1796), 56; John C. Patrick, ed., *The Writings of George Washington, from the Original Manuscript Sources, 1745–1799*, 39 vols. (Washington, DC: Government Printing Office, 1931–44), 35:229; Sarah Barringer Gordon, "Blasphemy and the Law of Religious Liberty in Nineteenth-Century America," *American Quarterly* 52, no. 4 (December 2000): 686.

21 1848 New York Laws 525; First Report of the Commissioners on Practice and Pleadings: Code of Procedure (Feb. 29, 1848), 145 [hereafter "First Report (New York 1848)"].

22 First Report (New York 1848), 141.

23 Campbell, "Testimonial Exclusions," 451–74; Kathryn Gin Lum, *Damned Nation: Hell in America from the Revolution to Reconstruction* (Oxford: Oxford University Press, 2014), 28–35.

24 See New York Constitution of 1846, art. 1, § 3.

25 Jackson ex dem. Tuttle v. Gridley, 18 Johns. (N.Y.) 98 (1820); Campbell, "Testimonial Exclusions."

26 Field, What Shall Be Done With the Practice of the Courts (1847), 11.

27 1848 New York Laws 525; Final Report of the Commissioners on Practice and Pleadings: The Code of Civil Procedure, in Documents of the Assembly of the State of New York, 73d sess., No. 16 (1850), 2:275, 787 [hereafter "Final Report (New York 1850)"]. On the complicated conflation of party disqualification rules with privileges against self-incrimination, see John Fabian Witt, "Making the Fifth: The Constitutionalization of American Self-Incrimination Doctrine, 1791–1903," *Texas Law Review* 77, no. 4 (March 1999).

28 First Report (New York 1848), 158.

29 "A Husband's Oath – How His Wife Made Him Swear on the Code of Civil Procedure," *Denver Daily Tribune*, 24 January 1877.

30 Catherine Evans's essay in this volume also notes a satirical jab at official courtroom practices (see chapter 8). In both of our instances, the racialized or gendered Other seems to be cast in the role of the wise fool, who sees through the absurdities the officials have to live with to make their system work. See Peter C. Phan, "The Wisdom of Holy Fools in Postmodernity," *Theological Studies* 62, no. 4 (2001); Beatrice K. Otto, *Fools Are Everywhere: The Court Jester around the World* (Chicago: University of Chicago Press, 2007).

31 *Dollner v. Gibson*, 3 Code Reporter 153, 155 (N.Y. Sup. Ct. 1850); 2 Edmonds Select Cases 253, 256.

32 *The Code Reporter* 1 (1848–9): 26–7.

33 Report of Aaron Goodrich, Journal of the House of Representatives of
the State of Minnesota (1860), 220; *The Code Reporter* 1(1848–9): 2. See
also Henry Whittaker, *Practice and Pleading under the Codes* (New York,
1852), 169 (advising plaintiffs always to verify their complaints so as to
effectively shift the burden of proof to defendants).

34 Second Report (New York 1849), 28.

35 On the antiquity of the rule, see R.H. Helmholz, *The Spirit of Classical
Canon Law* (Athens: University of Georgia Press, 1996), 156. Silver v. State,
17 Ohio 365 (Ohio Chancery, 1847); 2 Code Reporter 29; People v. Travis, 4
Parker's Criminal Reports 213 (Buffalo Superior Court, 1854).

36 See, e.g., Frank F. Brightly, *A Digest of the Decisions of All the Courts of the
State of New York from the Earliest Period to the Year 1892* (New York: Banks
and Brothers, 1893), 3:5924–7.

37 People v. Christopher, 4 (11) Hun 805 (1875).

38 Report of the Commissioners (Ohio 1853), 140.

39 The Ohio transplant to Virginia was Professor James P. Holcombe. Report
of the Code Commissioners (Iowa 1859), 232–4.

40 Report of the Code Commissioners (Iowa 1859), 234–6.

41 On English attempts to police party testimony with heightened policing of
perjury, see Wendie Ellen Schneider, *Engines of Truth: Producing Veracity in
the Victorian Courtroom* (New Haven, CT: Yale University Press, 2016).

42 Report of the Code Commissioners (Iowa 1859), 234–5.

43 Final Report (New York 1850), 715.

44 Final Report (New York 1850), 715; First Report (New York), 246.

45 Final Report (New York 1850), 715–17; Report of the Commissioners (Ohio
1853), 129.

46 1850 California Laws 455 § 306; 1851 California Laws 114 § 394. Stephen
Field's code changed the blood quantum to consider a person an Indian
from one-half to one-fourth, and a Negro from one-eighth to one-half.

47 Journal of the House of Assembly of the State of California (1850), 990–1,
1000.

48 See 1807 Ohio Laws 54; Jordan v. Smith, 14 Ohio 499 (1846); 1839 Iowa
Laws 379.

49 People v. Hall, 4 Cal. 399 (1854). Hall was extended to civil cases in Speer
v. See Yup Co., 13 Cal. 73 (1859). On Hall, see also William J. Novak, "The
Legal Transformation of Citizenship in Nineteenth-Century America,"
in *The Democratic Experiment: New Directions in American Political History*,
ed. Meg Jacobs, William J. Novak, and Julian E. Zelizer (Princeton, NJ:
Princeton University Press, 2003), 85–119.

50 4 Cal. 403.

51 1863 California Laws 60.

52 Journal of the House of the Territory of Montana (1865), 201–2, 207–10.

53 In addition to California, the other code states to exclude racialized
    testimony were Arizona, Idaho, Indiana, Iowa, Kansas, Kentucky,
    Missouri, Montana, Nebraska, Nevada, Oregon, Tennessee, Washington,
    and Wyoming. On Southern complaints about the Code and "Negro"
    testimony, see for instance, Diary of David Schenk, 19 January 1864 to 31
    December 1872, MSS vols. 5 and 6, David Schenk Papers, University of
    North Carolina Chapel Hill.

54 1866 Nebraska Revised Statutes 449; 1870 Wyoming Laws 572.

55 Journal of the House of the Territory of Montana (1865), 201–2, 207–10.

56 Fisher, "The Jury's Rise," 661–2, 673–4.

57 Fourth Report of the Commissioners on Pleading and Practice (New York
    1849), xxv-xxix.

58 People v. Hall, 4 Cal. 399, 403 (1854).

59 Fisher, "The Jury's Rise," 598–9; Frank Tuthill, *The History of California* (San
    Francisco: H.H. Bancroft, 1866), 373.

60 Walter A. McDougall, *Throes of Democracy: The American Civil War* (New
    York: HarperCollins, 2009), 551. See also Richard Wightman Fox, *Trials of
    Intimacy: Love and Loss in the Beecher-Tilton Scandal* (Chicago: University
    of Chicago Press, 1999); Barry Werth, *Banquet at Delmonico's: Great Minds,
    the Gilded Age, and the Triumph of Evolution in America* (New York: Random
    House, 2009); Walter K. Earle, *Mr. Shearman and Mr. Sterling and How They
    Grew* (New Haven, CT: Yale University Press, 1963), 97.

61 *Theodore Tilton vs. Henry Ward Beecher, Action for Crim. Con. Tried in the City
    of Brooklyn* (New York: McDivitt, Campbell & Co., 1875), 2:723.

62 *Theodore Tilton vs. Henry Ward Beecher*, 3:5.

63 See chapters 8 and 10, this volume, on rituals of swearing.

64 One historian of religion has recently argued that the Protestant Bible was
    "primarily a medium through which public discourse happened" in the
    nineteenth-century United States, "rather than primarily a substantive
    source for that discourse." That is, "people said what they had to say
    in the language of the Bible." Lincoln A. Mullen, *America's Public Bible:
    A Commentary* (Stanford: Stanford University Press, 2022), https://
    americaspublicbible.supdigital.org/essay/introduction/. We might say
    the same about the Christian theology of oaths, a language to be deployed
    by the end of the nineteenth century rather than a serious source of
    jurisprudence.

Chapter Ten

Ceremonial Promises: Oaths, Treaties, and the Transformation of Christian Privilege in Canada

PAMELA E. KLASSEN AND
ISABEL KLASSEN-MARSHALL

An oath is a promise with one foot in the afterlife. Committing into the future, and sometimes even after death, the oath-taker pledges in front of witnesses, sometimes human, sometimes divine. A treaty, by contrast, is a collective promise in which groups commit to a shared future in specific places, with the land, water, sun, and other living beings as their witnesses. A treaty, when kept, commits future generations to honouring the promises made by their ancestors. Since the earliest commitments made between Indigenous peoples and the British Crown, oath-takers and treaty-makers on Turtle Island have guaranteed their promises through ceremonies. Invoking gods, spirits, and human leaders, including the Creator and a succession of Queens and Kings, treaties and oaths were never mere contracts recorded on paper. These promises were ceremonially enacted, by sharing a pipe together, laying a hand on a Bible, holding an eagle feather, saying the words. They were also materialized – cast into medals and woven into wampum.[1] Despite their spiritual gravity, oaths and treaties are promises made and promises broken; they are fallible commitments that require constant work to renew and repair for those who claim to be guided by them.[2]

In Canada, oaths and treaties are intimately connected, as the Royal Commission on Aboriginal Peoples clarified in 1996: "Treaties were sworn by sacred oaths, announced with great ceremony, and regarded as binding documents of state. The fact that they have been violated time and again does not change their underlying legitimacy."[3] In 2015, the Final Report of the Truth and Reconciliation Commission of Canada echoed this view, noting that treaties were agreements of a "sacred nature," ratified by Indigenous ceremonies. Sharing a pipe ceremony during treaty-making, for example, meant that all participants were "obliged to speak the truth – a stipulation that was not always, or clearly, understood by government negotiators."[4] These very same British and Canadian negotiators, however, also lived within a legal-ceremonial system that cast oaths as sacred promises, made with the Christian God as a witness. So why did they not understand the spiritual and political gravity of their promises?

In this chapter, we reflect on oaths as ceremonial promises at a time when the Canadian government – and the Crown in right of Canada – has committed in new ways to honouring the Treaties it has made with Indigenous nations, exemplified by recent changes to the Oath of Citizenship. In June 2021, in response to Call to Action 94 of the Truth and Reconciliation Commission of Canada, Bill C-8 revised the oath sworn by new Canadian citizens and public servants to include not only a promise of allegiance to the Queen, but also a "faithful" promise to recognize and affirm "Aboriginal and Treaty rights":

> I swear (or affirm) that I will be faithful and bear true allegiance to Her Majesty Queen Elizabeth the Second, Queen of Canada, Her Heirs and Successors, and that I will faithfully observe the laws of Canada, including the Constitution, which recognizes and affirms the Aboriginal and Treaty rights of First Nations, Inuit and Métis peoples, and fulfil my duties as a Canadian citizen.[5]

The only Canadians required to speak this oath (now to King Charles III) are those newly becoming citizens or public servants; Canadians born in Canada or to Canadian parents are generally not required to do so. What difference does it make, then, to add recognition of Treaty rights to the oath of allegiance for Canadians? Should all new Canadians and new public servants be required to make this promise?

From one vantage point, oath-taking might be considered a largely bureaucratized form of ceremonial promise by which secular democratic institutions incorporate citizens into their duties and responsibilities to the nation.[6] Oaths are also a site, however, where the ostensibly secular politics of the Canadian nation state are contested for their Christian, colonial privilege. Reflecting on oaths is one way to foster awareness of the multi-jurisdictional legal orders – Canadian and Indigenous – that have always undergirded treaty promises.[7] The changing history of oaths also helps reveal what the "mythology of assumed Crown sovereignty" rests upon, to borrow Jeffery Hewitt's phrase from the introductory chapter to this volume.

The swearing of oaths in British and British imperial contexts has gradually shifted from being a tool to exclude non-Christians from civic participation to becoming a site of their inclusion.[8] Imperial legal systems privileged Christianity both explicitly and tacitly. Christianity was the de facto religion of the British Empire, with the monarch as both Head of State and Defender of the (Christian) Faith. As in other British colonies, nineteenth-century Canadian lawmakers debated who could give sworn testimony in court. These lawmakers deemed Christians as the most trustworthy due to their belief that their God would punish them if they lied.[9] In nineteenth-century British settler colonies including Canada and New Zealand, colonial courts excluded Indigenous witnesses on the ground that they were "religiously incompetent" and did not swear oaths to the Christian God.[10] Gradually, however, both pragmatic and ethical issues related to religious diversity within the British Empire brought courts to accommodate sworn testimony of non-Anglicans and non-Christians, especially if they too felt bound by a punitive God. An alternate accommodation of making "affirmations" instead of swearing oaths also emerged for Christian groups such as Quakers and Mennonites, as well as atheists, all of whom opposed swearing oaths for both theological and political reasons.[11]

Today, in multi-religious and multi-jurisdictional Canada, an oath is a "sacrament of power" guaranteed by a wide range of "divine witnesses" and symbolic markers.[12] Christians may still place their hands on a Bible when swearing an oath of inquisition to tell the truth or an oath of affirmation when taking on a civil office, but oaths may also be sworn in relation to other sacred texts, such as the Torah or the Qur'an, or while holding an eagle feather in recognition of Indigenous symbols of sacred power. No longer solely oriented to the Christian God, oaths remain an active site of political deliberation and formation.

In considering oaths as a site for the transformation of Christian privilege, we write from our perspectives as white Canadians shaped by Mennonite traditions and kinship. Our ancestors settled on Anishinaabe territory and the Métis homeland just a few years after the making of Treaty 1 in 1871, in what Canada now calls Manitoba. We also write as mother and daughter, both born and raised in Toronto, on Treaty lands of the Mississaugas of the Credit and the traditional territories of the Seneca and the Huron-Wendat peoples.

To develop our concept of "ceremonial promises," we draw from Darcy Lindberg's concept of "ceremonial aesthetics" in his discussion of Nehiyaw/Cree legal pedagogies. [13] Lindberg argues that learning about law is not only something that happens in settings such as law schools or courts, but also takes place through embodied ways of transferring and understanding knowledge and stories. He contrasts the variety of places and modes of Indigenous ceremonial aesthetics (e.g., sweat lodges, pipe ceremonies, dreams) with limited sites of ceremony in Western legal systems. Considering the courtroom in particular, he writes that "protocols surrounding dress, speech and positioning are still important. However, these practices are often viewed as 'formality,' unmoored from any substantive importance they may have had."[14] By centring the oath of allegiance as a ceremonial promise, we seek to show how this "formality" reveals the long history of Christian privilege in Canadian legal systems. At the same time, we argue that reconsidering the oath as a promise provides an opportunity for acknowledging and perhaps redressing the enduring damage of Canadian repression of Indigenous ceremonies and laws.

Indigenous ceremonial repression has a long history in Canada. In the nineteenth century, representatives of the Crown engaged in ceremony when negotiating treaties with Indigenous leaders at the same time that the Canadian government, in alliance with Christian churches and missionaries, created the Indian Act, which outlawed Indigenous legal and spiritual ceremonies.[15] First enacted in 1876, frequently amended, and still extant, the Indian Act has been the legislative means by which the Canadian government classified and regulated the lives of Indigenous peoples in minute detail, making them "wards of the state" in an attempt to assimilate Indigenous peoples and deny their sovereignty.[16] In the same decades that representatives of the Queen engaged in Indigenous rituals for truthtelling during treaty negotiations, such as pipe ceremonies, Canadian courts declared Indigenous people to be "religiously incompetent" to swear oaths. Canadians recognized and participated in Indigenous ceremony when it enabled them to seize Indigenous land, while refusing to acknowledge it in their courts of law.[17] When courts denied legal efficacy to Indigenous ceremonial promises they also privileged Christian rituals as properly legal and political, relegating Indigenous ceremony to superstition.

We open our reflections on oaths as a window onto changing expectations of what it means to be treaty people by comparing three debates in which questions of religion, sovereignty, and ceremonial aesthetics were central: 1) the Canadian government's accommodation of Mennonites as a group whose religious principles kept them from swearing oaths of allegiance as they sought land as "New Canadians" in the 1870s; 2) the debate during the 2010s over whether Muslim women wearing niqabs could take the oath of citizenship with their faces covered; and 3) the refusal in 2019 of a newly elected Indigenous city councillor to swear an oath of allegiance to the Queen, due to his respect for Indigenous sovereignty and treaty principles. We then place these debates within the longer history of oaths in British colonial jurisdictions, highlighting the significance of "ceremonial law" in imperial contexts in which courts privileged Christianity as the guarantor of the truthful subject. Returning to the ceremonial aesthetics of the citizenship oath, we consider the Anishinaabemowin concept of Mino-bimaadiziwin, or practices of living in good way, as a potential pathway to redressing Christian privilege and centring treaty relations. Here, we draw especially from the work of John Borrows on Anishinaabe ethics embodied in the Seven Grandmother Teachings, and their importance for Canadian public life.[18]

Oaths as Multi-jurisdictional Promises

There have been three main kinds of oaths in British and British imperial contexts: oaths of inquisition, oaths of allegiance, and oaths of office.[19] In different ways, all are promises often understood as "religious acts" in which a person is "bound by one's words and affirmations."[20] Oaths of allegiance, in particular, pledge the swearer's loyalty to the monarch and/or state in a way that explicitly names their responsibilities. In Canada, oaths play a pedagogical and performative role in the making of moral subjects, as a description on a Canadian House of Commons web page demonstrates:

> The taking of an oath or indeed an affirmation is essentially a question of morality. It is generally believed that people do not take the oath or affirmation lightly, and will consider themselves bound by it. If the person taking the oath lies, on one level that is a matter between that person and his or her conscience or God. At the same time, just as witnesses lie in court, despite having been sworn to tell the truth, people do on occasion break their oaths. Moreover, in the present, less religious era, it is likely that many people are not as intimidated by oaths as was previously the case.[21]

Even in a "less religious" – or multi-religious – era, oaths remain ceremonies that both "ritualise and emotionalise" citizenship, binding a person to a morally responsible way of living in community.[22] Promises made in acknowledgment of the power of another, whether a Queen, the nation state, or the Creator, oaths can both constrain hubris and admit multiple sovereignties: "they are both instruments of power and instruments of resistance."[23]

Controversies about oaths are often "proxy debates," in the sense that Benjamin Berger uses the term to discuss debates about religion that seem on a surface level to be about one topic, but that obscure or distract from the deeper significance of religion in legal orders. Proxy debates, he writes, "become a normative shell game, surreptitiously shifting around the more perplexing and fundamental questions raised by the interaction of law and religion."[24] The example of the debate about whether a woman's oath can be efficacious when her face is covered is a prominent instance of such a proxy debate: was the argument really about the effectiveness of the oath or a different, and more insidious, concern about whether devout Muslim women could truly become Canadians?[25]

As symbolic acts open to varied interpretations, oaths risk becoming superficial. In his discussion of ceremonial aesthetics, Darcy Lindberg warns of the danger of "celebratory" inclusion of Indigenous legal traditions as "ceremonial 'window-dressing' for the continuation of pedagogies that are largely informed by Canadian common and civil laws."[26] The revision of the citizenship oath in response to Call to Action 94 does risk becoming window-dressing, if promising to recognize and affirm Treaty rights assimilates Indigenous sovereignty into "Canada," instead of teaching Canadians about what it means to live out nation-to-nation relations with Indigenous peoples.[27]

For Canadian citizens to recognize and affirm Treaty rights requires learning new ways of "belonging to law" – to adapt Benjamin Berger's phrase – that include both Indigenous and Canadian legal orders.[28] Such multi-jurisdictional belonging requires awareness of Indigenous jurisdiction and ceremony, ongoing learning and engagement with Indigenous knowledge and knowledge holders, and concerted remembering, repairing, and enacting of ceremonial promises. We begin, then, with this image (Figure 10.1) to guide our way.

What does it mean to make a promise with a Queen? Anishinaabe artist Christian Chapman's 2013 painting of Queen Elizabeth II and the Duchess of Cambridge (now the Princess of Wales after the death of the Queen) asks this question in a visual medium. Chapman transposes the ubiquity of the Queen as a Canadian symbol into a generative image of a woman and grandmother surrounded by powerful Anishinaabe symbols of growth. During her reign, the Queen's image was displayed on money, her name appeared on every court case prosecuted by the state, and her authority was represented via an ornamental mace in every legislature across the country. Chapman wraps symbols of the Queen's spiritual power, especially her crown and her lineage, represented by her granddaughter-in-law, in the recognizable style of Anishinaabe Woodland art.[29] His painting also suggests the fragility of

Figure 10.1 Christian Chapman, *The Past, Present, and Future of the Anishinaabe People*, 2013, mixed media, three panels, private collection.

the Royal Family as a symbol of colonial sovereignty. For example, during a March 2022 visit of the (then) Duke and Duchess of Cambridge to the Caribbean, William and Kate were repeatedly called to account for the British role in slavery and colonialism.[30] The Queen and her kin embody the spiritual and moral vulnerability of British claims to authority in former colonies: a vulnerability also brought to light in saying the oath of allegiance.

Oaths of Allegiance as Ceremonial Promises: Three Examples

Perched at the unstable crossing of religious and secular authority, and of inner conscience and outer testimony, oaths are ritualized pledges of loyalty meant to display current allegiances and compel future moral conduct. Spoken by the oath-maker and fixed in the memories of the witnesses, oaths are an embodied form of public speech shaped by ceremonial aesthetics; an oath of allegiance is a performative act said in a specific way in a particular place. It is not enough just to sign a document in the privacy of one's own home or to make a whispered commitment in your mind. Before the COVID-19 pandemic, when Canadian citizenship ceremonies temporarily shifted online, everyone fourteen or older becoming a Canadian citizen had to utter the oath at an in-person citizenship ceremony, with exceptions for those with "mental disabilities" who may not understand the oath.[31] A large roomful of soon-to-be citizens would gather in rows to speak the pre-2021 version of the citizenship oath out loud: *"I swear (or affirm) that I will be faithful and bear true allegiance to Her Majesty Queen Elizabeth the Second, Queen of Canada, Her Heirs and Successors, and that I will faithfully observe the laws of Canada, and fulfil my duties as a Canadian citizen.*" Citizens-to-be had the option of "swearing" or "affirming" their allegiance to the Queen. If they chose to swear, they could "bring a holy book of their choice on which to swear the Oath."[32] Government officials walked the aisles during the recitation, watching new citizens moving their lips.

In Canada, state accommodation of religious difference has often worked particularly well for Christians, including where oaths are concerned. Mennonites, for example, an Anabaptist group that emerged from the Radical Reformation of the sixteenth century with a stripped-down ceremonial aesthetic, have been able to flourish in Canada as a Christian community that understood itself to be set apart from the world. Mennonites have long been suspicious of too close a connection between the church and the state, due in part to their theological commitments to pacifism and their consequent refusal of military service. Mennonite convictions about oaths also led to tensions with state-based legal orders. Not only did they consider swearing allegiance to a monarch to be idolatrous, placing a worldly ruler above God, they also worried that to swear such allegiance might put one at the risk of being forced into military service. In addition, they thought the act of swearing on a Bible to guarantee one's honesty denigrated the Christian obligation to be truthful in all of one's worldly dealings.[33] Mennonites based their suspicions on a New Testament biblical source, James 5:12: "But above all, my brothers, do not swear, either by heaven or by earth or by any other oath, but let your 'yes' be yes and your 'no' be no, so that you may not fall under condemnation." Mennonites preferred to "affirm" their trustworthiness by their words alone.

The Mennonite separation of church and state, however, was not as distinct when it came to their acceptance of state recognition and support when settling on the Treaty lands of the Anishinaabeg and the homeland of the Métis Nation. Enabled by their reputations as good farmers, Mennonites were attractive immigrants for many settler states, leading them to play a pivotal role in expanding the frontiers of settler colonies in the Americas. Their migratory history of joining state projects of colonization depended on their successful negotiations of jurisdictional and ceremonial privileges, quite literally. Mennonites who emigrated in the 1870s from southern Russia (now Ukraine) to Manitoba negotiated what they came to call "the Privilegium of 1873," an agreement signed between male representatives of prospective Mennonite emigrants and the Secretary of the Department of Agriculture.[34] The Canadian state extended the Mennonites "the fullest privilege of exercising their religious principles," including exemption from military service and exemption from swearing affidavits and oaths. (See Figures 10.2 and 10.3). It also gave them the privilege to teach their children in their own German-language schools and granted them large reserves of land, sections of which they could hold as private property, and which they could exchange if they were not suitable for farming. This Christian privilege, along with their agricultural labour, was key to Mennonites' ability to dispossess Indigenous nations.

As Aimee Craft and others have shown, the land that Mennonites settled in southern Manitoba was already the subject of promises made between the Anishinaabeg, the Red River Métis, the Crown, and the Dominion Government, through Treaty 1 and the Manitoba Act.[35] Contrary to these earlier promises and laws, the Canadian government created two "reserves" for Mennonite settlement, while simultaneously denying the Métis the collective land base they had been promised. What is particularly noteworthy about this wave of Mennonite immigration to Canada is that the many exceptions that Mennonites were afforded by the Canadian government were not only religious in nature, but also affected land distribution and patenting, furthering Indigenous land dispossession.

In one example, the connection between oaths and land grants in the nineteenth century was made explicit. To receive the patent to their lands after the necessary requirements were met, settlers were expected to become citizens of Canada. The process of naturalization required them to swear an oath of allegiance. Mennonites raised concerns with Canadian officials, as they worried that to swear an oath of allegiance would entail being expected to perform military service.[36] In response to these concerns, then-Canadian Minister of the Interior, Richard Scott, wrote a memorandum in 1877 coming up with a solution so that Mennonites could receive their land patents. He recognized that "Mennonites hesitate to take the Oath of Allegiance from the fear that doing so will render them liable to Military Service, to which they are opposed, the same being contrary to the doctrine of their religion."[37] Noting that the Dominion Government had promised them exemption from military service prior to their emigration from Russia, Scott reiterated to Mennonites that swearing the oath, though necessary to receive a land patent, would not infringe on the immunity from military service previously promised to them.[38] As Adolf Ens has shown, most Mennonite immigrants were satisfied by this official guarantee and exception, and agreed to be "naturalized" via the oath in order to receive their land patents.[39] The Dominion government recognized Mennonite religious difference, enabling many, but not all, Mennonites to agree to take the oath in order to acquire their land.

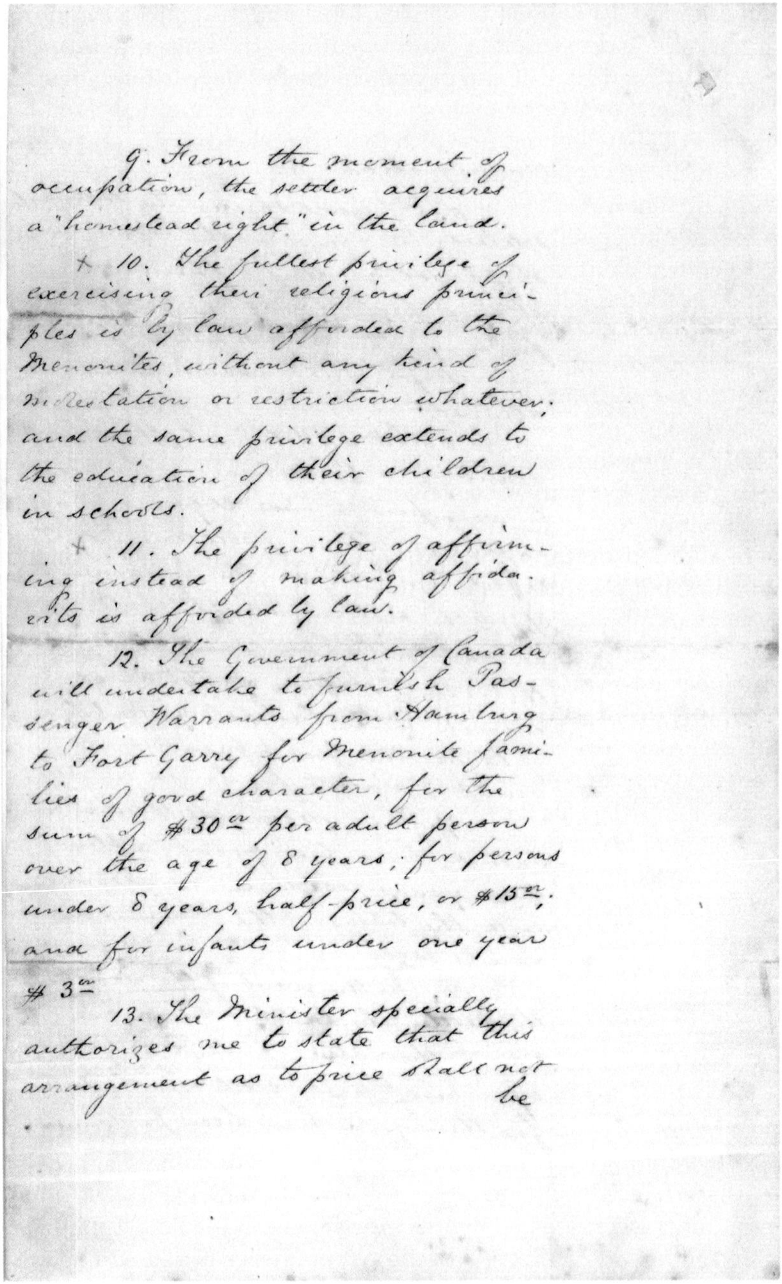

9. From the moment of occupation, the settler acquires a "homestead right" in the land.

✝ 10. The fullest privilege of exercising their religious principles is by law afforded to the Menonites, without any kind of molestation or restriction whatever; and the same privilege extends to the education of their children in schools.

✝ 11. The privilege of affirming instead of making affidavits is afforded by law.

12. The Government of Canada will undertake to furnish Passenger Warrants from Hamburg to Fort Garry for Menonite families of good character, for the sum of $30.00 per adult person over the age of 8 years; for persons under 8 years, half-price, or $15.00; and for infants under one year $3.00

13. The Minister specially authorizes me to state that this arrangement as to price shall not be

Figure 10.2 Letter of Invitation, English, 1873, p. 4, Mennonite Heritage Archives, Winnipeg.

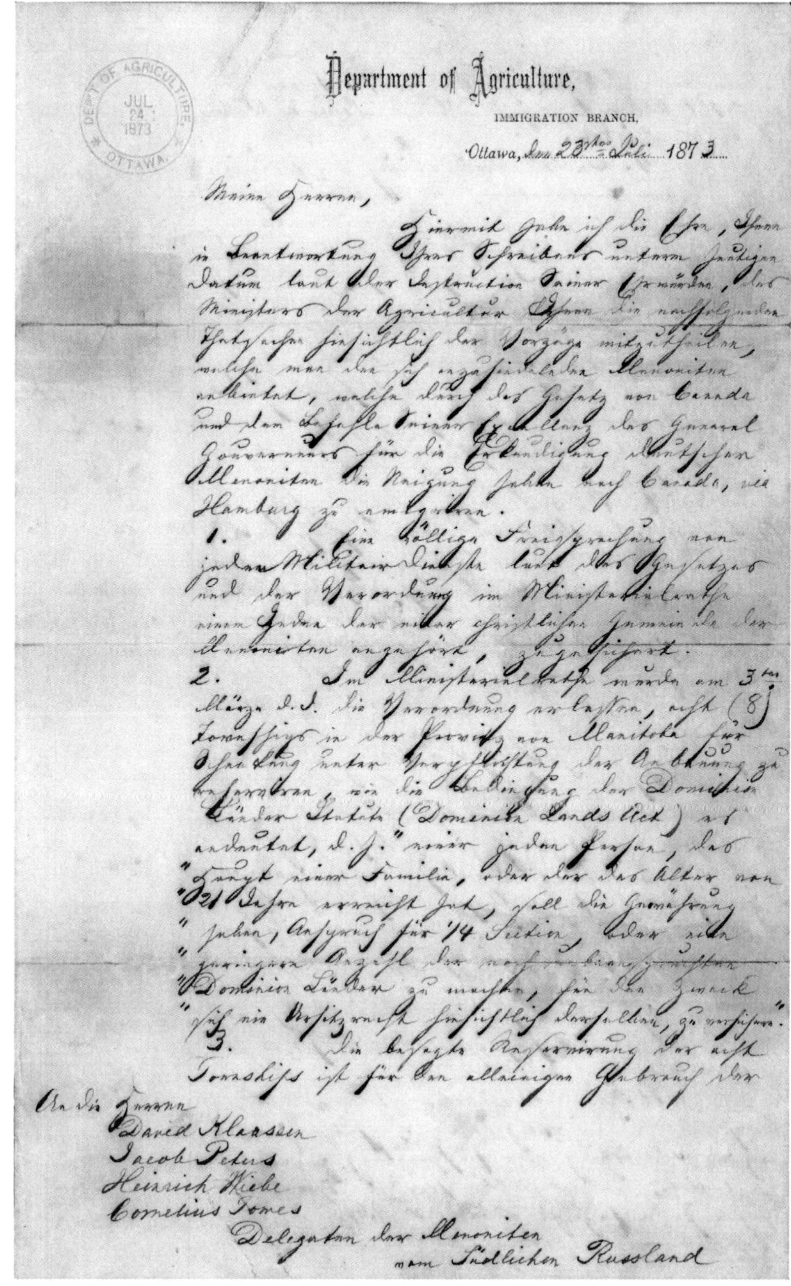

Figure 10.3 Letter of Invitation, German, p. 1, Mennonite Heritage Archives, Winnipeg.

The Mennonite controversy over oaths could be seen as a proxy debate, or distraction, in which questions of allegiance to the Queen were secondary to the Dominion's overarching goal of settling Mennonite families on Indigenous land and to the Mennonites' goal of property ownership. The Dominion Government found ways to recognize and accommodate Mennonites in their desire to preserve their ability to live collectively, protect their spiritual traditions, and transfer their language and values to future generations in their own schools. At the same time and place, the government denied Indigenous parents these same goals, instead further developing the residential school system that took children from their families and forced them to speak English and attend Christian ceremonies. Throughout the twentieth century to this day, Mennonites have continued to seek official exemptions, often still known as a "Privilegium," frequently at the expense of Indigenous peoples across Central and South America.[40]

More recent debates over the citizenship oath continue to reveal how Christian privilege undergirds the ceremonial aesthetics of the secular state. By the twenty-first century, however, politicians tried to exclude non-Christians from courts and citizenship ceremonies because they were overly religious. In 2011, then-federal Minister of Immigration Jason Kenney unilaterally banned face veils for those taking the Citizenship Oath, arguing that such face-covering practices "clash with Canadian 'constitutional values.'"[41] If citizenship officials could not see a woman's lips moving, could they be sure she was taking the oath? In response, a Muslim woman named Zunera Ishaq took the Crown to court for the right to take her oath of Canadian citizenship while her face was covered.

Ishaq's case was part of a wider resistance by Muslim women to a growing trend of legislation that denied them the right to cover their faces in legal settings, such as in citizenship ceremonies and when testifying in court.[42] As legal scholar Natasha Bakht has written, "Women who wear the niqab or the full-face veil have borne the brunt of oppressive government tactics internationally to limit their choice of clothing. These tactics to ban certain public displays of religiosity are 'justified' by numerous explanations that reveal more about niqab objectors' illogical, bias-laden, and viscerally negative reactions than any legitimate concerns that the niqab may actually raise."[43] Opposing the niqab to constitutional values, Kenney used controversies over the Oath of Citizenship as a proxy debate to cloak underlying hostility to Muslim difference.

After Ishaq's success at the Federal Appeals Court in 2015, people who wear face coverings due to a "sincerely held religious belief" can now recite their oath in private before the ceremony, in front of a female

Figure 10.4 Portrait of the Queen at the front of the hall before a citizenship ceremony, February 2020. Photo by Pamela Klassen.

official if appropriate. Ishaq took her oath in 2015 with her face covered from the nose down by a colourful scarf, holding a Canadian flag.[44] In part a proxy debate adjudicating just how far anti-Muslim rhetoric and legislation could go, Zunera Ishaq's case also became the provocation for new rituals of citizenship. Reflecting on the niqab debate, Benjamin Berger contends that the citizenship ceremony is "the most literal moment of citizen formation through law."[45] The secular state requires citizens to "belong to law" through rituals such as the citizenship ceremony, as "an explicit act of submission to sovereignty."[46] But what happens when multiple sovereignties and ways of belonging to law are invoked in the ceremonies of the secular state?

Ceremonies of political office, which also require of oaths of allegiance to the monarch, provide one answer. In fall 2018, Gaetan Baillargeon, a newly elected councillor in the northern Ontario town of Hearst and a member of Constance Lake First Nation, refused to pledge allegiance to Queen Elizabeth II during the swearing-in ceremony for his elected office. Initially told by the town clerk that he could not take his seat without speaking these words of allegiance, Baillargeon declined, backing up his refusal with reference to the long and devastating history of the Canadian government breaking its Treaties with Indigenous nations.[47] To swear allegiance to the Queen, Baillargeon argued, was to dishonour the Treaties.[48]

Baillargeon was eventually provided with an alternate form in which he could tick a box stating that as Indigenous person, declaring allegiance to the Queen "would be inconsistent with my views regarding the relationship between the Crown and Indigenous peoples." His "solemn promise" when taking office was considered to have the same effect "as if made under oath."[49] Shortly after the Ontario government accommodated Baillargeon, James McCrae, a former Attorney General of Manitoba, published an op-ed entitled "No Special Canadians" in the *Winnipeg Sun*, excoriating Baillargeon:

> Mr. Baillargeon is a member of Constance Lake First Nation, located near Hearst. The band is a signatory to Treaty No. 9 (1905), which includes the following promise: " … and the undersigned Ojibeway, Cree and other chiefs and headmen, on their own behalf and on behalf of all the Indians whom they represent, do hereby solemnly promise … *to conduct and behave themselves as good and loyal subjects of His Majesty the King*." By his disloyal conduct, Mr. Baillargeon is violating his Band's Treaty obligation to the Crown. He talks about "broken Treaties" justifying his conduct. He should look in the mirror.[50]

McCrae's argument is interesting, and mistaken, for two reasons. First, when it comes to accommodations for swearing oaths of allegiance, there have indeed been "special Canadians," as the Mennonite example of the Privilegium attests. Second, as a former Attorney General, McCrae would likely know that many Indigenous people do not consider themselves to be Canadian and that treaties were not one-way obligations in which Indigenous people became "loyal subjects" who had "extinguished" their sovereignty.[51]

Once again, oaths prompted a proxy debate over a fundamental issue: Canada insisting on Crown supremacy at the expense of Indigenous sovereignty. Gaetan Baillargeon's refusal was rooted in an understanding of treaties as nation-to-nation land-sharing agreements, in which representatives of Indigenous nations made solemn promises with representatives of the Crown. As a member of the Constance Lake First Nation, he could not make a new promise to the Queen as an individual outside of that historic and ongoing collective Treaty promise.

It would be wrong, however, to think that just because oaths are used in proxy debates, they are not important kinds of promises on their own. Practices of "intentional moral formation," as Nicholas Aroney argues, oaths are ceremonies designed to cultivate people for whom promises matter. Oaths have staying power in secular jurisdictions in part because "they are nothing less than the ultimate existential foundation of the rule of law."[52] Herein lies the power and vulnerability of oaths: they both establish and expose the foundations of authority by speaking them aloud.

A Short Survey of Oaths and Christian Privilege

In Britain and its imperial jurisdictions, debates over oaths were often arguments about Christian and white privilege. Since at least the seventeenth century, British legal systems debated whether "infidels" (non-Christians) or non-white people were capable of taking oaths as "credible" witnesses in court.[53] If an oath-taker did not believe that God would punish them if they lied, then how could laying their hand on the Bible properly guarantee their promise?

Beginning in the eighteenth century, British law increasingly allowed for Jews, and later Muslims and other non-Christians, to swear their oaths on their own holy texts. Karen Macfarlane has shown, however, that both in London and in courts around the empire, English Christian oaths remained the most powerful form of legal promise. Even once British law granted non-Christians the right to swear their oaths by other deities, lawyers used this difference against them: "questioning of the oaths of non-whites and non-Christians in criminal trials was a way of establishing that a witness did not share the common English values or identity."[54] Writing about the history of Māori oaths under the laws of the colony of New Zealand, Shaunnagh Dorsett points out how British law refused to recognize any ceremonial promises beyond those rooted in Christianity. In the British view: "problematically, most indigenous peoples, particularly in the Australian colonies, did not adhere to any recognisable religion. They were entirely 'destitute of the knowledge of God' and therefore unable to swear any oath, even under the common law 'infidel' exception."[55] Catherine Evan's chapter in this volume, on nineteenth-century Australian debates about admitting evidence from Chinese people in courts of law, also demonstrates how the swearing of oaths revealed ways that British imperial law fundamentally privileged Christianity as its basis.

Nineteenth-century Canadian colonial courts were shaped by these trans-imperial legal debates; so too were US courts, as discussed in Kellen Funk's chapter in this volume. As Reginald Good has shown, non-Christian Indigenous people were regularly barred from giving testimony at trial because they were deemed "heathens" who did not have the "religious competency" to do so. In this view, they had neither "natural religion" nor a belief in a punitive God.[56] And even when a court did deem Indigenous people religiously competent, their testimony was often disallowed because the state did not recognize any Indigenous ceremony as akin to swearing an oath.[57] As Sidney Harring notes, some Canadian courts found ways of admitting Indigenous testimony without directly addressing the question of Christian orthodoxy, especially when Crown prosecutors depended on Indigenous witnesses for the success of their cases.[58] Indigenous witnesses, for their part, sometimes avoided testifying in Canadian trials that were adjudicating the guilt of their kin via Canadian laws.[59]

Canadian legal assessments of Indigenous religious competency were concurrent with the rise of the Indian Act and its dehumanizing categorizations of Indigenous people and repression of Indigenous ceremony. As John Borrows has written, the Indian Act's "formal operation has devastating effects. Its underlying philosophy damages most everyone it touches."[60] Countless government reports by Indian Agents labelled Indigenous people who were not Christians as "pagans," a categorization used to justify sending children to the church-state system of residential schools. Canadian attempts to repress Indigenous ceremony, however, did not destroy the foundations of Indigenous law.

In addition to truth-telling practices such as pipe ceremonies, Indigenous nations have also used oaths for their own governance processes. Discussing the role of oaths in the constitutions written by Tribal Nations in the United States in the twentieth century, David Wilkins and Sheryl Lightfoot situate Indigenous-written oaths within a longer history. They note the shift from the oath as a "self-curse" to a promise with God as the witness, arguing that Tribal Nations have adopted the oath in their own ceremonies of governance because of the voluntary self-constraint at its core: "In all cases where oaths have been employed, their central purpose has been to restrain the exercise of power by appeal to morality and a sense of responsibility, especially pertaining to the duties of public office."[61] Almost all the Tribal oaths of office detailed by Wilkins and Lightfoot, which were largely written between the mid-nineteenth and mid-twentieth centuries, include the phrase "swear (or affirm)," perhaps to accommodate a wide diversity of Christian and Indigenous ceremonial traditions.[62] As Wilkins and Lightfoot argue and Baillargeon's example shows, much more research is needed to explore the political and governance effects of oaths of office on Indigenous leaders – especially in the cases in which the oaths place loyalty to a monarch or the US Constitution before loyalty to the Indigenous nation.[63]

Forty years ago, Vine Deloria Jr., Dakota scholar of religion and legal theorist, explained how denigration of Indigenous ceremony was the grounding of colonial sovereignty, rooted in the Christian concept of the Doctrine of Discovery and the subsequent writings of theorists such as Locke and Montesquieu:

> The white Europeans were to have the Indian lands because the Indians were infidels rather than Christians, hunters rather than farmers, monsters rather than men, or by reason of the generous gifts of European civilization or technology, or by reason of conquest, or by reason of the fact that the king owned everything. We are now aware of the logical or factual errors of these writers, and of their resort of pure fabrication in concepts such as conquest.[64]

In an 1895 revision to the Indian Act, itself a pure fabrication, the Canadian government made it illegal for anyone to encourage or participate in an "Indian festival, dance or other ceremony of which the giving away or paying or giving back of money, goods or articles of any sort forms a part."[65] Missionaries and government officials knew that the Potlatch, Sun Dance, and other ceremonies were powerful forms of Indigenous law, governance, sovereignty, and generational redistribution of land and wealth, so they criminalized them.[66]

Ceremonial Law and the Politics of Recognition

Throughout the British Empire, dichotomizing "secular" law and "spiritual" religion rendered non-Christian ceremony not as law but as superstition.[67] Writing about India under British colonial rule, Robert Yelle (drawing from Gil Anidjar) argues: "By defining the terms of the discourse in such a way as to make the question of the origins and limits of the secular unthinkable, Christian colonialism rendered its own, ostensibly secular, form immune to the objectifying and transformative power it directed against other traditions and, by the same token, made itself invisible, and therefore potentially invulnerable."[68] Anglo-American and European biblical scholars, anthropologists, and moral philosophers assisted in obscuring the Christian privilege within secular law; they studied the intersection of ceremony, morality, and law with the Bible as an interpretive lens, even when thinking about non-Western societies.

These nineteenth-century scholars built on older traditions of thinking about "ceremonial law." In different ways, European Jewish and Christian interpreters turned to Mosaic law, including the Ten Commandments, to develop an understanding of law that was universal, rooted in the natural world designed by the Creator, and attained through reason. Christians – most famously Thomas Aquinas – came to think of law by way of a supersessionist story in which Christian moral law overcame Jewish "ceremonial law."[69] In this Christian view, the coming of Jesus Christ as the Messiah abrogated Jewish rituals, making them invalid and unnecessary.

The distinction between "moral" and "ceremonial" law stemmed from anti-Jewish readings on the part of Christians, who saw Jewish law as mere ritual, overcome by the sacrifice of Christ.[70] After the Reformation, this theological view was deeply shaped by what historian Peter Burke has called the Protestant "repudiation" of ritual, in which Protestant theologians, in various ways, framed both Jewish and Catholic rituals as irrelevant, or worse, superstitious and dangerous.[71] It was only one small step for Protestants to include in this ritual repudiation the rituals of the non-Christian peoples they labelled as "primitive" and "heathen," and in need of Christian civilization.[72]

Beginning in the late nineteenth century, scholars working within a "science of religion" paradigm turned to evolutionary and racist hierarchies to structure their thinking about the link between ceremony and morality. They separated non-Christian ceremony – often dubbed magic or superstition – from the properly moral and the properly political.[73] British colonial officials were often inspired by this racist scholarship when writing the laws that justified their monarch's sovereignty across what they considered to be their empire. As Robert Yelle has argued about the Indian concept of dharma in the context of British India,

> [it] was at once a legal code, a metaphysics, a cosmology, a system of morals, and a set of ritual techniques. The British viewed this mixture, and especially its ritual elements, as evidence of a "primitive" stage of development in which law and religion had not yet assumed their proper and distinct identities. These evolutionary theories, although ostensibly secular and objective, emerged from and retained the traces of Christian theology.[74]

These theories lumped together Hindu dharma with Jewish ceremonial law, classing both as antithetical to what Christians and secularists understood to be moral law rooted in universal reason. In India, colonial recognition of religious difference became a tool for controlling groups of people by way of religious categories such as Muslim or Hindu.[75]

In Canada, the Indian Act attacked Indigenous sovereignty by trying to destroy Indigenous ceremonies, in part by denying that Indigenous peoples had "religion."[76] Canada's systematic attempts at what Katherine Pettipas called "ceremonial repression" struck at the heart of Indigenous families, sovereignty, and generational knowledge sharing.[77] In addition to privileging Christian testimony on the witness stand and when taking oaths, the Indian Act also privileged Christianity as the only recognizable, and legal, source of religious ritual and pedagogy in the case of weddings, marriage, and most devastatingly, in the educational system.[78] Residential schools became a systematic attempt at cultural genocide, in which Christian conversion and the English language would erase Indigenous languages and spiritual traditions throughout generations.[79]

Considering the continued legacies of this colonial history, some Indigenous scholars advocate another approach to state recognition: they reject it. Glenn Coulthard argues that recognition in multicultural states, as elaborated in the work of Charles Taylor and others, has assumed the legitimacy of the state's sovereignty. In a settler-colonial context, this very sovereignty was achieved through colonizers taking Indigenous land by the fabricated authority of colonial law. In Coulthard's view, for Indigenous groups to then seek recognition from the Canadian state, exemplified in the revisions to the Oath of Citizenship, would be to perpetuate "colonial relations of power."[80] Indigenous people who refuse recognition under the terms of the colonial state – both in the US and in Canada – often refuse the concept of religion as itself a colonizing tool, preferring words such as spirituality or the sacred (with their own histories).[81] Increasingly, Indigenous scholars are turning away from English terms altogether to articulate the relationship between law and spirituality in Indigenous languages, thereby reclaiming terrain both ceremonial and political.[82]

Mino-bimaadiziwin: Living Together in a Good Way

John Borrows, an Anishinaabe legal scholar who has written extensively on the history of treaties and ceremony in a multi-jurisdictional Indigenous and Canadian frame, orients his book, *Law's Indigenous*

Figure 10.5 Holy Cross Catholic Church in Wiikwemkoong Unceded Territory. Photo by Pamela Klassen, 2019.

Ethics, with the Anishinaabemowin concept of Mino-bimaadiziwin, or practices of living in good way, the "good life," or the "good path."[83] Written at the intersection of Anishinaabe law and Canadian constitutional law, Borrows's book is structured by the Seven Grandmother (or Grandfather) Teachings: Zaagi'idiwin, Love; Debwewin, Truth; Zoongide'iwin, Bravery; Dabaadendizowin, Humility; Nibwaakaawin, Wisdom; Gwayakwaadiziwin, Honesty; and Manaaji'idiwin, Respect.[84] As Borrows demonstrates, thinking with Mino-bimaadiziwin and the Seven Grandmother Teachings as orienting concepts helps to disrupt the linguistic familiarity of the English words for morality and justice, while also pointing to the importance of land, place, and stories for ceremonial promises.

Canadians living on Anishinaabe territory can find Mino-bimaadiziwin orienting them at many places, including in exhibits at the Art Gallery of Ontario in downtown Toronto and at the Ojibwe Cultural Foundation on Manitoulin Island, a spiritual and political centre for the Anishinaabeg.[85] They can also find the Seven Grandmother/ Grandfather Teachings carved into wood at ceremonial settings, both religious and political. For example, when we participated in the Manitoulin Island Summer Historical Institute in 2019, led by Professors Alan Corbiere and Carolyn Podruchny, we read these teachings etched into the wood of the Holy Cross Catholic Church in Wiikwemkoong Unceded Territory on Manitoulin Island.[86]

John Borrows notes that there is debate among Anishinaabeg over the cultural legitimacy of the "codification" of Anishinaabe law into the Seven Grandmother Teachings, with some claiming it is a recent innovation and others rooting it in ancient traditions.[87] Either way, Borrows contends, the Seven Grandmother Teachings offer guidance for Mino-bimaadiziwin, and how to live a good life in a world suffering from human-caused climate crisis. As Nookomis, the grandmother, says in Borrows's text: "healing requires more than the gathering of plants, though this is necessary too. You need good principles and practices; you need standards, criteria, guides, measures, authorities, and traditions to help out. As the old one taught, you need law: chi-inaakonigewin."[88] She continues: "The world won't survive if we live only for ourselves."[89]

Borrows has argued throughout his work that Indigenous stories, ethics, and law have played an important, but often misrecognized or ignored, role in Canadian law and constitutionalism. This misrecognition, he argues, comes from false distinctions imposed between law, morality, and ceremony: "The transformation of moral, spiritual, economic, social, and philosophical questions into legal issues can deceive us. We can be lulled into believing that metaphysics is not at play when courts and legislatures consider questions concerning choice, life, death, security, and liberty of the person."[90] Borrows has also connected Canadian misrecognition of the relationship between law and spirituality to wilful ignorance among Canadians about the historical and ongoing significance of ceremony for treaty relationships. Treaties made between Indigenous nations and the Crown were not surrenders of land written on pieces of paper. Neither treaties nor the Indian Act "extinguished Aboriginal governance powers."[91] Instead, treaties were solemn promises to share the land that referenced a Creator on both sides, marked by ceremonies of pipe-smoking, drumming, and storytelling.[92]

Since 2021, the Seven Grandfather Teachings can now be found in the Chamber of the Ontario Legislature in Toronto, where a carving by Anishinaabe artist Garrett Nahdee of Walpole Island First Nation is located over the entrance, directly facing the Speaker's Chair (Figure 10.6).

A pamphlet accompanying a display in the lobby of the Legislature explains that the "Seven Grandfather Teachings are [a] set of Anishinaabe guiding principles that give people the tools for how to live a good life. They have been passed down from generation to generation for thousands of years through stories and ceremonies."[93] The Seven Grandfather Teachings display is placed directly below two large portraits of early colonial officials in Upper Canada: John Graves Simcoe,

Figure 10.6 Garrett Nahdee, *Seven Grandfather Teachings*, wood carving, Ontario Legislative Chamber. Photo by Pamela Klassen, 2022.

a key actor in Indigenous dispossession throughout Anishinaabe and Haudenosaunee territories, and Isaac Brock, a British general known as a hero in the War of 1812, who allied with the Shawnee leader and warrior, Tecumseh, to capture Fort Detroit.[94]

The significance of this juxtaposition might not be evident to a passerby who did not know the men in the paintings, or their roles as leaders in the colonial expansion of Upper Canada. Whether or not the Seven Grandfather Teachings display in the Ontario Legislature is an example of ceremonial aesthetics as call to action or mere window-dressing depends on who is looking and who is animating the teachings.

As Anishinaabe writers and artists who invoke Mino-bimaadiziiwin show, the power of colonial governance is neither invisible nor invulnerable. Some of this vulnerability lies in the fact that Canadian assertions of sovereignty were rooted in Christian "ceremonies of possession" that, as Vine Deloria Jr. argued, repudiated Indigenous ceremony as irrational, amoral, and even immoral.[95] Taking seriously the Seven Grandmother/Grandfather Teachings as relevant to the deliberations in the Chamber of the Ontario Legislative Assembly requires

Figure 10.7 Seven Grandfather Teachings Exhibit, with portrait of John Graves Simcoe above, Ontario Legislative Assembly. Photo by Pamela Klassen, 2022.

recognizing the ways that provincial and federal political legitimacy have been rooted in Christian privilege. But even more importantly, these teachings require understanding that any legitimacy of the Ontario and Canadian Parliaments depends on centuries of treaties with the Anishinaabeg, Haudenosaunee, and other Indigenous nations that must be honoured and activated now and into the future.[96]

It took the Government of Canada many years to bring forward the Bill that would incorporate Aboriginal and Treaty rights into the Oath of Citizenship. That it eventually passed in 2021 was in large part because of the ongoing insistence of Indigenous nations that ceremony and politics are always connected. As examples of Mennonites and Muslims show in different ways, the Canadian state can change the ways it understands and enacts oaths according to varying ceremonial aesthetics. Though the citizenship ceremony may seem like mere ritual to some, imagine the scene of immigration officials walking up and down the aisles to make sure that every new Canadian audibly says the words of the oath to signal their commitment to recognize and affirm the Aboriginal and Treaty rights of Indigenous nations. What might such promises portend?

The Commissioners of the Truth and Reconciliation Commission defined ten principles of reconciliation, including the following: "Reconciliation requires sustained public education and dialogue, including youth engagement, about the history and legacy of residential schools, Treaties, and Aboriginal rights, as well as the historical and contemporary contributions of Aboriginal peoples to Canadian society."[97] Reconciliation requires actively remembering and engaging with treaties in a way that acknowledges and enables the resurgence of Indigenous law and ceremony. Promising to uphold and honour treaties in an oath of citizenship does necessarily make it so. Mino-bimaadiziwin, however, offers a path of living together well rooted in teachings that make visible Anishinaabe ceremonial aesthetics that center treaties as promises in place and across generations. Amid ongoing Treaty violations across Canada at both provincial and federal levels, it is time for all Canadians to learn about, articulate, affirm, and enact the Treaty promises to which we are called.

What difference could it make for all Canadians, and not only new citizens or certain public servants, to make an oath that faithfully recognizes and affirms Treaty rights? The ceremonial is a space in which the ongoing power of Christianity in the secular state of Canada is rendered visible, but it can also be a place where it is challenged and resisted. In the nineteenth century, Canadian lawmakers, shaped by a Christian view in which they thought loyalty to the Queen gave them supremacy over all others, invented ceremonies to legitimize the new Canadian nation state while they criminalized Indigenous ceremony and sovereignty. In the twenty-first century, however, after centuries of Indigenous insistence that Canada and Canadians honour their Treaty promises, new ceremonial promises are a step in making visible and audible the reality of Indigenous jurisdiction.

NOTES

1 Alan Ojiig Corbiere, Bne Doodeman, and Mchigiing Njibaa, "Parchment, Wampum, Letters and Symbols: Expanding the Parameters of the Royal Proclamation Commemoration," *ActiveHistory.ca* (blog), 2 October 2013, http://activehistory.ca/2013/10/parchment-wampum-letters -and-symbols-expanding-the-parameters-of-the-royal-proclamation -commemoration/.
2 John Borrows, "Origin Stories and the Law: Treaty Metaphysics in Canada and New Zealand," in *Indigenous Peoples and the State: International Perspectives on the Treaty of Waitangi*, ed. Mark Hickford and Carwyn Jones (London: Routledge, 2019), 30–56, https://doi.org/10.4324 /9781351240376-3; Jacinta Ruru, "The Failing Modern Jurisprudence of the Treaty of Waitangi," in Hickford and Jones, *Indigenous Peoples and the State*, 111–26, https://doi.org/10.4324/9781351240376-7.
3 Royal Commission on Aboriginal Peoples, "Highlights from the Report of the Royal Commission on Aboriginal Peoples," 3 November 2008, www.rcaanc-cirnac.gc.ca/eng/1100100014597/1572547985018; See also Royal Commission on Aboriginal Peoples, René Dussault, and Georges Erasmus, *People to People, Nation to Nation: Highlights from the Report of the Royal Commission on Aboriginal Peoples* (Ottawa: Minister of Supply and Services Canada, 1996).
4 Truth and Reconciliation Commission of Canada, *Canada's Residential Schools: The History, Part 1, Origins to 1939: The Final Report of the Truth and Reconciliation Commission of Canada* (Montreal: McGill-Queen's University Press, 2016), 1:118.
5 "Legislative Summary of Bill C-8: An Act to Amend the Citizenship Act (Truth and Reconciliation Commission of Canada's Call to Action Number 94)," Research Publications, Library of Parliament, 22 October 2020, https://lop.parl.ca/sites/PublicWebsite/default/en_CA /ResearchPublications/LegislativeSummaries/432C8E.
6 Ben Chen, "Diminution and Secularisation of Oaths in Australian Courts," *Australian Bar Review* 37, no. 3 (2013): 291–306. For an imaginative reflection on changes to the citizenship oath, see Jeremy Webber's concluding chapter to this volume.

7 Not all Indigenous nations entered into historical Treaty-making with Canada, especially in British Columbia, where there are now several "modern" Treaties. As with Indigenous nations with Treaties, Indigenous nations without Treaties also retain inherent rights.

8 Enid Campbell, "Oaths and Affirmations of Public Office under English Law: An Historical Retrospect," *The Journal of Legal History* 21, no. 3 (2000): 1–32, https://doi.org/10.1080/01440362108539614; Jonathan Gray, *Oaths and the English Reformation* (Cambridge: Cambridge University Press, 2013), 45.

9 Reginald Good, "Admissibility of Testimony from Non-Christian Indians in the Colonial Municipal Courts of Upper Canada/Canada West," *Windsor Yearbook of Access to Justice* 23, no. 1 (2005): 62.

10 Good, "Admissibility of Testimony"; Shaunnagh Dorsett, "Sworn on the Dirt of Graves: Sovereignty, Jurisdiction and the Judicial Abrogation of 'Barbarous' Customs in New Zealand in the 1840s," *The Journal of Legal History* 30, no. 2 (2009): 175–97, https://doi.org/10.1080/0144036090 3069775.

11 Campbell, "Oaths and Affirmations." On the changing status of Christianity in relation to oaths in US courts, see Kellen Funk's chapter in this volume.

12 Nicholas Aroney, "The Rule of Law, Religious Authority, and Oaths of Office," *Journal of Law, Religion and State* 6, no. 2–3 (2018): 196, https://doi .org/10.1163/22124810-00602003.

13 Darcy Lindberg, "Miyo Nêhiyâwiwin (Beautiful Creeness): Ceremonial Aesthetics and Nêhiyaw Legal Pedagogy," *Indigenous Law Journal* 16/17, no. 1 (2018): 51–65.

14 Lindberg, "Miyo Nêhiyâwiwin," 53n10.

15 Sa'ke'j Henderson, *Indigenous Diplomacy and the Rights of Peoples: Achieving UN Recognition* (Vancouver: University of British Columbia Press, 2008); Anishinaabe Grand Council of Treaty #3, "'The Creator Placed Us Here': Timeline of Significant Events of the Anishinaabeg of Treaty #3" (Kenora, ON: Anishinaabe Grand Council of Treaty #3, 2013); Douglas Cole and Ira Chaikin, *An Iron Hand upon the People : The Law against the Potlatch on the Northwest Coast* (Vancouver: Douglas & McIntyre, 1990); Katherine Pettipas, *Severing the Ties That Bind: Government Repression of Indigenous Religious Ceremonies on the Prairies* (Winnipeg: University of Manitoba Press, 1994).

16 Mary-Ellen Kelm and Keith D. Smith, *Talking Back to the Indian Act: Critical Readings in Settler Colonial Histories* (Toronto: University of Toronto Press, 2018).

17 Borrows, "Origin Stories and the Law"; Dale Antony Turner, *This Is Not a Peace Pipe: Towards a Critical Indigenous Philosophy* (Toronto: University of Toronto Press, 2006).

18 John Borrows, *Law's Indigenous Ethics* (Toronto: University of Toronto Press, 2019).

19 Aroney, "The Rule of Law"; Gray, *Oaths and the English Reformation.*

20 Aroney, "The Rule of Law," 212.

21 "Oaths of Allegiance and the Canadian House of Commons (BP-241E)," Government of Canada Publications, October 1990, http://publications. gc.ca/Collection-R/LoPBdP/BP/bp241-e.htm.

22 Tine Damsholt, "'I Didn't Think I Would Be Emotional until I Started Saying the Oath' – Emotionalising and Ritualising Citizenship," *Journal of Ethnic and Migration Studies* 44, no. 16 (2018): 2701–16, https://doi.org/10 .1080/1369183X.2017.1389038.

23 Aroney, "The Rule of Law," 208.

24 Benjamin L. Berger, *Law's Religion: Religious Difference and the Claims of Constitutionalism* (Toronto: University of Toronto Press, 2015), 168.

25 Natasha Bakht, "In Your Face: Piercing the Veil of Ignorance About Niqab-Wearing Women," *Social & Legal Studies* 24, no. 3 (2015): 419–41, https:// doi.org/10.1177/0964663914552214.

26 Lindberg, "Miyo Nêhiyâwiwin," 64.

27 Borrows, "Origin Stories and the Law." For a strong critique of the oath of allegiance as a barrier to Indigenous sovereignty, see Thomas McMahon, "Reconcile This: Canada's Oath to the Queen, the Doctrine of Discovery, Indigenous Peoples, New Canadians and Freedom of Expression," SSRN (March 2017), https://doi.org/10.2139/ssrn.2886896.

28 Benjamin L. Berger, "Belonging to Law: Religious Difference, Secularism, and the Conditions of Civic Inclusion," *Social & Legal Studies* 24, no. 1 (2015): 47–64, https://doi.org/10.1177/0964663914549408.

29 David W. Penney, Gerald McMaster, and Kevin Gover, *Before and after the Horizon: Anishinaabe Artists of the Great Lakes* (Washington, DC: Smithsonian National Museum of the American Indian, 2013).

30 Rachel Hall and Amelia Gentleman, "'Perfect Storm': Royals Misjudged Caribbean Tour, Say Critics," *The Guardian*, 25 March 2022, www.theguardian.com/uk-news/2022/mar/25/ william-and-kate-caribbean-tour-slavery-reparations-royals.

31 "The Oath of Citizenship: Backgrounder," Immigration, Refugees and Citizenship Canada, 28 May 2019, www.canada.ca/en/immigration -refugees-citizenship/news/2019/05/the-oath-of-citizenship.html.

32 "Oath of Citizenship," Government of Canada, 8 July 2021, www.canada .ca/en/immigration-refugees-citizenship/corporate/publications -manuals/operational-bulletins-manuals/canadian-citizenship/ceremony /oath.html.

33 John Perry, "Not Pledging as Liturgy: Lessons from Karl Barth and American Mennonites on Refusing National Oaths," *The Mennonite*

Quarterly Review 76, no. 4 (2002): 431–59; Virgil Wiebe, "Oath Martyrs," *British Journal of American Legal Studies* 2, no. 1 (2013): 205.

34 Adolf Ens, *Subjects or Citizens?: The Mennonite Experience in Canada, 1870–1925* (Ottawa: University of Ottawa Press, 1994): 17.

35 Aimée Craft, *Breathing Life into the Stone Fort Treaty: An Anishnabe Understanding of Treaty One* (Saskatoon: UBC Press, 2013); Gerhard J. Ens, *Homeland to Hinterland: The Changing Worlds of the Red River Metis in the Nineteenth Century* (Toronto: University of Toronto Press, 1996).

36 Ens, *Subjects or Citizens?*, 38.

37 Order-in-Council. Minister of Interior, 8 August 1877. Library and Archives Canada, RG2, Series A-1-a. Volume 359, Reel C-3320, Access Code 90.

38 Order-in-Council. Minister of Interior, 8 August 1877.

39 Ens, *Subjects or Citizens?*, 38.

40 Yann le Polain de Waroux, Janice Neumann, Anna O'Driscoll, and Kerstin Schreiber, "Pious Pioneers: The Expansion of Mennonite Colonies in Latin America," *Journal of Land Use Science* 16, no. 1 (2021): 1–17, https://doi.org/10.1080/1747423X.2020.1855266; Paola Canova, "Intimate Sovereignty: Mennonite Self-Government in 'Green Hell' and the Politics of Belonging in Paraguay's Chaco," *The Journal of Latin American and Caribbean Anthropology* 26, no. 1 (March 2021): 65–83, https://doi.org/10.1111/jlca.12530.

41 Craft, *Breathing Life*.

42 Bakht, "In Your Face"; Amélie Barras, Jennifer A. Selby, and Melanie Adrian, eds., *Producing Islam(s) in Canada: On Knowledge, Positionality, and Politics* (Toronto: University of Toronto Press, 2022); Berger, "Belonging to Law."

43 Bakht, "In Your Face," 420.

44 "Zunera Ishaq, Who Challenged Ban on Niqab, Takes Citizenship Oath Wearing It," CBC News," 5 October 2015, www.cbc.ca/news/politics/zunera-ishaq-niqab-ban-citizenship-oath-1.3257762.

45 Berger, "Belonging to Law," 54, 60.

46 Berger, "Belonging to Law," 55.

47 "Hearst Councillor Gaetan Baillargeon Says Province Changing Rules on Pledging Allegiance to the Crown," *CBC News*, 11 December 2018, www.cbc.ca/news/canada/sudbury/gaetan-baillargeon-hearst-council-seat-1.4939808.

48 Also see the case of Patricia Monture: Cynthia Gray, "A Question of Sovereignty: Patricia Monture v. the Queen," *Canadian Woman Studies* 10, no. 2–3 (1988): 146–7; Patricia A. Monture, *Thunder in My Soul: A Mohawk Woman Speaks* (Halifax: Fernwood Publishing, 1995).

49 Government of Ontario, "Declaration of Office: Alternate Option for
    Indigenous Persons; Section 232 of the Municipal Act, 2001," Revised 2018,
    www.mah.gov.on.ca/Page219.aspx; See also Government of Ontario,
    "O. Reg. 373/07: Oaths and Affirmations, Public Service of Ontario Act,
    2006, S.O. 2006, c. 35, Sched. A," Ontario.ca, July 24, 2014, www.ontario.ca
    /laws/view.
50 James C. McCrae, "No Special Canadians," *Winnipeg Sun*, 22 December
    2018, https://winnipegsun.com/news/national/guest-column
    -no-special-canadians.
51 John S. Long, *Treaty No. 9: Making the Agreement to Share the Land in Far
    Northern Ontario in 1905* (Montreal: McGill-Queen's Press University Press,
    2010).
52 Aroney, "The Rule of Law," 212.
53 Shaunnagh Dorsett and Ian Hunter, *Law and Politics in British Colonial
    Thought: Transpositions of Empire* (New York: Palgrave Macmillan, 2010).
54 Karen A. Macfarlane, "'Does He Know the Danger of an Oath'?: Oaths,
    Religion, Ethnicity and the Advent of the Adversarial Criminal Trial in the
    Eighteenth Century," *Immigrants & Minorities* 31, no. 3 (2013): 338.
55 Jonathan Michael Gray, "Conscience and the Word of God: Religious
    Arguments against the *Ex Officio* Oath," *The Journal of Ecclesiastical History*
    64, no. 3 (July 2013): 494–512, https://doi.org/10.1017
    /S0022046913000535.
56 Good, "Admissibility of Testimony," 62.
57 Good, "Admissibility of Testimony," 92.
58 Sidney L. Harring, *White Man's Law: Native People in Nineteenth-Century
    Canadian Jurisprudence* (Toronto: University of Toronto Press, 1998), 102.
59 Good, "Admissibility of Testimony."
60 John Borrows, "Unextinguished: Rights and the Indian Act," *University of
    New Brunswick Law Journal* 67 (2016): 5.
61 David E. Wilkins and Sheryl Lightfoot, "Oaths of Office in Tribal
    Constitutions: Swearing Allegiance, but to Whom?," *American Indian
    Quarterly* 32, no. 4 (Fall 2008): 393.
62 Wilkins and Lightfoot, "Oaths of Office," 396.
63 Wilkins and Lightfoot, "Oaths of Office," 407.
64 Vine Deloria, *Behind the Trail of Broken Treaties: An Indian Declaration of
    Independence* (Austin: University of Texas Press, 1985), 89.
65 Keith D. Smith, *Strange Visitors: Documents in Indigenous-Settler Relations in
    Canada from 1876* (Toronto: University of Toronto Press, 2014), 96.
66 Henderson, *Indigenous Diplomacy*; Anishinaabe Grand Council of Treaty #3,
    "The Creator Placed Us Here"; Cole and Chaikin, *An Iron Hand upon the
    People*; Pettipas, *Severing the Ties That Bind*.

67 Robert A. Yelle, "The Hindu Moses: Christian Polemics against Jewish Ritual and the Secularization of Hindu Law under Colonialism," *History of Religions* 49, no. 2 (November 2009): 145, https://doi.org/10.1086/649524.

68 Yelle, "The Hindu Moses," 142.

69 "Ceremonial law" is a designation still used by many Christian theologians and by some scholars of Judaism. Meirav Jones, "Philo Judaeus and Hugo Grotius's Modern Natural Law," *Journal of the History of Ideas* 74, no. 3 (July 2013): 339–59; Yelle, "The Hindu Moses."

70 Yelle, "The Hindu Moses"; Mark Elliott, "Calvin and the Ceremonial Law of Moses," *Reformation and Renaissance Review* 11, no. 3 (2009): 275.

71 Peter Burke, *The Historical Anthropology of Early Modern Italy: Essays on Perception and Communication* (Cambridge: Cambridge University Press, 1987). See also Pamela E. Klassen and John W. Marshall, "Saint as Cipher: Paul, Badiou, and the Politics of Ritual Repudiation," *History of Religions* 51, no. 4 (May 2012): 344–63, https://doi.org/10.1086/664722.

72 See also Jonathan Boyarin's argument about Catholic concepts of Christendom and Europe as concepts that "naturalise rhetorical links between a doctrine known as Christianity and the exercise of legitimate power." Jonathan Boyarin, *The Unconverted Self: Jews, Indians, and the Identity of Christian Europe* (Chicago: University of Chicago Press, 2009), 117.

73 See Terence Keel, *Divine Variations: How Christian Thought Became Racial Science* (Stanford: Stanford University Press, 2018); David Chidester, *Empire of Religion: Imperialism and Comparative Religion* (Chicago: University Of Chicago Press, 2014).

74 Yelle, "The Hindu Moses," 144.

75 Lauren A. Benton, *Law and Colonial Cultures : Legal Regimes in World History, 1400–1900* (New York: Cambridge University Press, 2002); Anver M. Emon, "Pluralizing Religion: Islamic Law and the Anxiety of Reasoned Deliberation," in *After Pluralism: Reimagining Religious Engagement*, ed. Courtney Bender and Pamela E. Klassen (New York: Columbia University Press, 2010), 59–81; Anver M. Emon, "Conceiving Islamic Law in a Pluralist Society: History, Politics and Multicultural Jurisprudence," *Singapore Journal of Legal Studies* (December 2006): 331–5.

76 Christopher L. Tomlins, *Freedom Bound: Law, Labor, and Civic Identity in Colonizing English America, 1580–1865* (Cambridge: Cambridge University Press, 2010); Philip Girard, "Imperial Legacies: Chartered Enterprises in Northern British America," in *Legal Histories of the British Empire: Laws, Engagements and Legacies*, ed. Shaunnagh Dorsett and John Mclaren (London: Routledge, 2014): 127–40. See also Tisa Wenger, *We Have a Religion: The 1920s Pueblo Dance Controversy and American Religious Freedom* (Chapel Hill: University of North Carolina Press, 2009).

77 Pettipas, *Severing the Ties That Bind*, xii. See also Lindberg, "Miyo Nêhiyâwiwin"; Nicholas Shrubsole, *What Has No Place, Remains: The*

Challenges for Indigenous Religious Freedom in Canada Today (Toronto: University of Toronto Press, 2019), https://doi.org/10.3138/9781487530730.

78 Sarah Carter, *The Importance of Being Monogamous: Marriage and Nation Building in Western Canada to 1915* (Edmonton: University of Alberta Press, 2008).

79 Truth and Reconciliation Commission of Canada, *Canada's Residential Schools: Reconciliation: The Final Report of the Truth and Reconciliation Commission of Canada*, vol. 6 (Montreal: McGill-Queen's University Press, 2016); Paulette Regan, *Unsettling the Settler Within: Indian Residential Schools, Truth Telling, and Reconciliation in Canada* (Vancouver: UBC Press, 2010).

80 Glen Sean Coulthard, *Red Skin, White Masks: Rejecting the Colonial Politics of Recognition* (Minneapolis: University of Minnesota Press, 2014).

81 Michael David McNally, *Defend the Sacred: Native American Religious Freedom beyond the First Amendment* (Princeton, NJ: Princeton University Press, 2020); Shrubsole, *What Has No Place, Remains.*

82 Borrows, *Law's Indigenous Ethics*; E. Richard Atleo/Umeek, *Principles of Tsawalk: An Indigenous Approach to Global Crisis* (Vancouver: UBC Press, 2011).

83 Nookomis in Borrows, *Law's Indigenous Ethics*, 12.

84 Borrows, *Law's Indigenous Ethics.*

85 "Artist Isaac Murdoch and the Stories of the Seven Grandfather Drums," Art Gallery of Ontario, accessed 7 July 2022, https://ago.ca/events/artist-isaac-murdoch-and-stories-seven-grandfather-drums; "About Us," Ojibwe Cultural Foundation, accessed 7 July 2022, https://ojibwe-cultural-foundation.myshopify.com/pages/frontpage.

86 "Aanii/Welcome," Wiikwemkoong Unceded Territory, 2025, https://wiikwemkoong.ca/.

87 Borrows, *Law's Indigenous Ethics*, 13.

88 Nookomis in Borrows, *Law's Indigenous Ethics*, 13.

89 Nookomis in Borrows, *Law's Indigenous Ethics*, 12.

90 Borrows, "Origin Stories and the Law," 34.

91 Borrows, "Unextinguished," 32.

92 John Borrows, "Wampum at Niagara: The Royal Proclamation, Canadian Legal History, and Self-Government," in *Aboriginal and Treaty Rights in Canada: Essays on Law, Equality, and Respect for Difference*, ed. Michael Asch (Vancouver: University of British Columbia Press, 1997), 155–72. Our discussion here also draws from Pamela E. Klassen, "Spiritual Jurisdictions: Treaty People and the Queen of Canada," in *Ekklesia: Three Inquiries in Church and State*, by Paul Christopher Johnson, Pamela E. Klassen, and Winnifred Fallers Sullivan (Chicago: University of Chicago Press, 2018): 107–74.

93 "The Seven Grandfather Teachings," Legislative Assembly of Ontario, accessed 7 July 2022, www.ola.org/en/seven-grandfather-teachings.

94 Victoria Freeman, "'Toronto Has No History!' Indigeneity, Settler Colonialism, and Historical Memory in Canada's Largest City," *Urban History Review* 38, no. 2 (2010): 21–35; James Laxer, *Tecumseh & Brock: The War of 1812* (Toronto: House of Anansi, 2012).

95 Patricia Seed, *Ceremonies of Possession in Europe's Conquest of the New World, 1492–1640* (Cambridge: Cambridge University Press, 1995); Vine Deloria, *God Is Red: A Native View of Religion* (Golden, CO: Fulcrum Publishing, 2003).

96 Two Toronto-specific books that activate Treaties are Denise Bolduc, Mnawaate Gordon-Corbiere, Rebeka Tabobondung, and Brian Wright-McLeod, eds., *Indigenous Toronto: Stories That Carry This Place* (Toronto: Coach House Books, 2021); Talking Treaties Collective, *A Treaty Guide for Torontonians*, 1st ed. (Toronto: Jumblies Press, 2022).

97 Truth and Reconciliation Commission of Canada, *Truth and Reconciliation Commission of Canada: Calls to Action* (Winnipeg: Truth and Reconciliation Commission of Canada, 2015).

CONCLUSION

Promises That Make Us Who We Are

JEREMY WEBBER

Oaths. Covenants. Vows. Treaties.

These are members of a class of promises that are neglected, perhaps even mischaracterized, in contemporary legal scholarship. Nevertheless, they continue to play an important role in today's constitutional orders. I will call them "covenantal promises" (in French, *promesses solonelles* or *promesses constitutionnelles*). Such promises are central to the papers in this volume. They include oaths (of office, of citizenship, to tell the truth, and so on) and the promises made in treaties with Indigenous peoples. In this contribution, I examine how they relate to other types of promises in today's legal orders (especially contractual promises), suggest how we should conceive of covenantal promises in today's societies (an enterprise of reconsideration necessary not least because, in their traditional form, covenantal promises have tended to have a marked religious dimension), and seek to engage a conversation about their contemporary relevance in a specific class of oath (citizenship oaths). In so doing, I address a subject that I, like many contemporary constitutional lawyers, have generally found uncomfortable, namely the responsibilities of citizens in a constitutional order or, to put the same observation another way, the role of a commitment to the good, not merely to the just, in the governance of today's societies. On the rare occasions when responsibilities are invoked, that invocation tends to turn towards conservative ends, emphasizing conformity rather than citizens' critical engagement and contribution. My proposals will be of the latter tendency, not the former, but they share with conservative variants the fact that they are unapologetic in their attention to questions of strong moral evaluation, of the good, in the governance of contemporary societies. I accept the view of Charles Taylor and others that strong evaluations lie behind our conceptions of justice and that striving for a better society is integral to our work as citizens.[1]

I begin with an exploration of what have been paradigmatic, classically liberal, theories of contractual promises. I do so because I suspect that those understandings continue to shape lawyers' impressions of all promising, including the covenantal promises discussed here. They do so despite the fact that there has long been a large body of scholarship that challenges the classical conception even in what had been its conceptual heartland: contracting in commercial transactions.[2] My reason for using the classical theory as a point of contrast, then, is not that it presents an accurate picture of all contractual promising. It doesn't. But rather that it remains a common, even dominant way of conceiving of promises in both the Civil Law and Common Law. Examining those classical theories enables one to establish, by contrast, the particular nature of covenantal promises. It allows us to recover an alternative and venerable form of promising, one that remains important in today's constitutional orders. It brings us back – as so many of the essays in this collection do – to a plural world of promising.

The Classical Model of Promising

At least since the adoption of the Code Napoléon in 1804 – and in the Common-Law world since the triumph of liberalism in the courts of the nineteenth century – promises of all kinds have been subjected to a predominant model: promises are understood to be the product of individual choice and decision. Their content is determined by the willed stipulations of the parties. Their binding character is the result of individuals' binding themselves. The paradigmatic example of a legally enforceable promise is a contract, which, in the Civil Law, creates "the law between the parties."[3] Even one's relationship to one's political community is conceived as the product of a "social contract." Indeed, all of legal history is, in Maine's famous terms, an evolution from status to contract.[4]

This model – what I will call the "classical model" – has lost much of its hegemony even in the law of contract, but it nevertheless retains an influence that surpasses that of any competing theory. It does so directly in provisions on the law of contractual obligations in civil codes, in treatises on contract law, and in the decisions of courts. Indeed, many departures from the classical model have been patched onto that model, not challenging it directly. They are conceived as either a) an attempt to correct inequalities of bargaining power between the parties in order to ensure that the result conforms more closely to what the decision-maker presumes would be the parties' will; or b) the state's imposition of policies which override the will of the parties but where, in areas not touched by the policies, the parties' relationship is still seen as one of mutually willed agreement. Important trends in contemporary contracts scholarship have sought to displace the classical model, especially given contemporary contracting practices that depart markedly from it, such as the extensive use of standard-form contracts that are (and indeed often are designed to be) unread, or the relational contracts emphasized by Stewart Macaulay and Ian Macneil.[5] Although that scholarship has cast significant doubt on the descriptive accuracy of the classical theory, it has yet to displace the ideological force of the model, perhaps because it has tended to point to the range of uses of contract rather than advance a comprehensive theory of its own.[6]

Thus, while challenged, the classical model still has a prominent place in the conceptual field. A cluster of ideas converge towards that model, ideas most elaborated in the Civil Law tradition. The germ of the approach can be perceived in the writings of Hugo Grotius, whose influential work, *De iure belli ac pacis* (1625), dealt with the law that should govern relations among states. Because Grotius was seeking to identify legal principles that might exist beyond the level of any human sovereign, he developed those principles within natural law: law that was derived from God's will or, in its increasingly secular variants, legal actors' intrinsic faculties of reason and volition. An individual could, he argued, make binding promises by using their will to bind their will, a capacity that Grotius patterned upon God's ability to bind himself in his covenants with humanity.[7] Grotius's theory was not fully secular. His argument not only drew upon biblical accounts but also required better conduct from parties than could be derived from their wills alone. He expected, for example, that parties had to meet a high standard of disclosure in contractual negotiations and, although he conceded that states had good reason to require formalities for the conclusion of certain contracts, he suggested that agreements that failed to comply with those requirements could still be binding in conscience.[8] His discussion of contracts also led directly into his discussion of oaths (it is difficult to conceive of any modern-day contracts textbook including a chapter on oaths).[9] Nevertheless, Grotius's emphasis upon an individual's ability to make binding promises through the deliberate exercise of their will alone could be readily secularized. This secularization ultimately gave rise to the centrality of the "autonomy of the will" in accounts of contracting in the French tradition of the Civil Law. Indeed, in its most ambitious formulations, any acceptable normativity – any legitimate body of law – ultimately could be traced back to the rationality and volition of a legal actor, conceived as an autonomous, self-sufficient, sovereign individual.[10]

One commentator summarizes this notion as follows: "will theory holds that a contract is an instrument of self-government in which the parties' stipulations, their subjective law, reign supreme: a contract is law unto the parties ... "[11] To be sure, not every jurist adopted the farthest-reaching expressions of the autonomy of the will, in which individual volition was understood to be the fount of all legal obligation, but the classical jurists of the Civil Law did consider the concurrence of parties' wills to be the essence of contracts. Robert-Joseph Pothier, whose *Treatise on Obligations* (1761) anticipated the codification of French Civil Law and which remained a canonical source for its interpretation thereafter, placed the operation of the parties' wills at the foundation of contract: "Le contrat renferme le concours des volontés de deux personnes, dont l'une promet quelque chose à l'autre, et l'autre accepte la promesse qui lui est faite" (Contracts embody the conjunction of the wills of two persons, in which one promises something to the other and the other accepts the promise that is made to them).[12]

The notion of the autonomy of the will came to dominate interpretation of the Code Napoléon's provisions on contractual obligations, especially from the second half of the nineteenth century.[13] It was often said to underlie other codal provisions, notably, in Quebec, freedom of testamentary disposition.[14] For contracts, three implications were derived from the principle: first, freedom of contract – the parties' freedom to conclude a contract or not, to choose with whom to contract, and to determine the terms of a contract, together with the principle that contracts are formed by the parties' consent alone (the law did impose additional formalities on some contracts, but these were understood to be exceptions); second, the determining role of the parties' original accord, so that contracts could not be modified by a judge or by either party acting alone; third, the limiting of the contract's legal effect to the parties themselves.[15] Many jurists still affirm that the exercise of the parties' wills is foundational to contractual obligation. When, in the 1990s, the Civil Code of Lower Canada was replaced by the Civil Code of Québec, Article 1378 of the new code reaffirmed the initiatory role of the parties' wills: "[a] contract is an agreement of wills" (*un accord de volonté*). Ghestin, Loiseau, and Serinet in the most recent edition of their treatise on contracts in French Civil Law similarly adopt "un accord de volontés" as an indispensable element in their "functional definition," although they reject the far-reaching claims for the autonomy of the will. For them, the binding force of a contract depends upon the contract's validity within a pre-existing legal order: the parties' wills alone are insufficient to create a legal obligation, and it is crucial that the exercise of the parties' wills be weighed against considerations of social utility and arguments of justice.[16] The recent decision of the Supreme Court of Canada in *6362222 Canada inc v. Prelco inc* (15 October 2021) – unanimous, although it overturned contrary decisions by both the Superior Court and the Court of Appeal – is expressly and emphatically based on the principle of the autonomy of the will.[17]

Of course, historically, the power of the parties' wills was never the only theory employed to justify the enforcement of contracts. It was often combined with the utilitarian argument that individually directed economic activity would create prosperity, maximizing the welfare of society as a whole. Ghestin therefore speaks of freedom of contract having "a double origin" in individualistic theories of natural rights and in liberal economic theory.[18] The influence of utilitarian arguments is especially evident in the range of promises that the law will enforce: above all, bilateral transfers of economic value.[19] Utilitarian arguments also shape the remedies courts will order. This is true of the marked preference for damages over specific performance as the standard remedy for breach of contract (in the Common Law but not to the same extent in the Civil Law): in most cases an injured party cannot insist that their counterpart perform the precise obligations undertaken but must instead be satisfied with an objectively determined monetary value for their loss.[20] Indeed, one problem with a theory based strictly on the wills of the individuals is that, while it purports to capture reasons why the parties themselves should treat their promises as binding, it is much less persuasive as to why the rest of society should enforce them. One suspects that, to justify enforcement, utilitarian arguments play a substantial role, with the result that both the Civil Law and the Common Law have generally enforced only a subset of promises.[21]

Common Lawyers have been less ambitious than Civil Lawyers in their philosophical expositions.[22] This has meant that the Common Law has tolerated more ambiguity in its premises and incorporated more readily a plurality of normative concerns. Utilitarian purposes in particular have played a greater role, a role reflected, for example, in the greater emphasis of Common Law judges upon a bilateral exchange of value – a bargain – as the paradigmatic example of a contract. Nevertheless, the making of promises remained an essential element. Frederick Pollock began the 1889 edition of his influential treatise on contracts as follows, capturing both the Common Law's empiricism and the continued role of promises:

> The law of Contract may be described as the endeavour of the State, a
> more or less imperfect one by the nature of the case, to establish a posi-
> tive sanction for the expectation of good faith which has grown up in

the mutual dealings of men of average right-mindedness. Accordingly, the most popular description of a contract ... is also the most exact one, namely that it is a promise or set of promises which the law will enforce. The specific mark of contract is the creation of a right, not to a thing, but to another man's conduct in the future. He who has given the promise is bound to him who accepts it, not merely because he had or expressed a certain intention, but because he so expressed himself as to entitle the other party to rely on his acting in a certain way.

...

The first and most essential element of an agreement is the consent of the parties. There must be a meeting of two minds in one and the same intention.[23]

The centrality of promises to Common Law contracts has sometimes been doubted. The requirement, in the Common Law's doctrine of consideration, that there be a substantive exchange of value has led some theorists to argue that the Common Law enforces bargains rather than promises.[24] Others have argued that a party's *reliance* on the other party, rather than the full expectation created by a promise, is contract law's principal concern.[25] These are the most prominent examples in a rich and extended set of debates which I need not recount. The debates are not about promising versus no promising but about whether the parties' assent to the terms of the contract is truly voluntary, the importance to be ascribed to the parties' assent, the extent to which the manifestation of assent should be considered sufficient to determine the terms of contracts and control the consequences of breach, and the manner in which those undertakings ought to be weighed against other considerations. Most of those who argue that contract law is not about the value of keeping one's promises acknowledge that the assent of the parties, even if marred by differences in power, brings a contract into being. And even the most passionate advocate of promising, Charles Fried (who adopts the Civil Lawyers' notion of the autonomy of the will), acknowledges that a bundle of normative considerations, not just the parties' wills, shapes contract law. Indeed, he says that promising is neither necessary nor sufficient to create a contract.[26]

Such arguments of relative importance need not preoccupy us. Our concern is the way in which promising has been understood in all these accounts – even those in which promising plays a minor role or is said to be vitiated. These common features constitute what I have called the classical model. They are as follows:

1. Promises are the product of an act of commitment by one party to
    another. The relationship established by such a promise begins,
    then, as a private relation between two parties. That relation may or
    may not be enforced by the state. The state may impose conditions
    on the set of promises made by the parties. But, if and when it
    does so, the state is understood to be attaching consequences to
    a relationship that is generated by the parties' autonomous acts
    of will. The state is outside the contractual nexus, sometimes
    imposing conditions, sometimes attaching consequences to it, but
    not itself participating in the promises.
2. This means that, in the paradigmatic case, the terms of the promises
    are determined by the parties. Even during the heyday of the liberal
    model of contracting, the principal obligations of the nominate
    contracts were specified in civil codes but this specification could
    be reconciled with the classical model on the basis that it was
    essentially a shorthand method of contracting, in which the code
    merely summarized obligations associated with common types of
    contracts. This explanation may well have understated the extent to
    which the obligations were imposed – the imposition of obligations
    has certainly grown with the expansion of the regulatory state – but
    here as elsewhere, scholars' adherence to ideologically inflected
    theories has tended to resist factual refutation.
3. In the paradigmatic case, the moment of the parties' assent, the
    moment when the obligation is born, also crystallizes the obligatory
    content of the relationship. A court will scrutinize the terms
    expressed or implied at that moment to determine the parties'
    undertakings for the duration of the contractual relation.
4. The fact that the parties' obligations arise from a relationship that
    is particular to them means that, in principle, only the parties have
    rights and obligations in relation to the promises. The promises
    belong to the parties and the parties alone. They can agree to put
    an end to the promises or to modify them. In the standard case
    of a contract in which one party's promise is given in exchange
    for another's promise, if one party fails to perform the other can
    decline to perform their part.

All these features are central to accounts of promising based primarily upon the parties' wills but note that they are also integral to
common utilitarian justifications for the enforcement of contracts. The
utilitarian accounts emphasize the value of the parties' autonomy in
making, enforcing, and modifying contractual promises, arguing that
overall welfare will be maximized if property is privately owned and

economic activity driven by owners' self-directed decision-making. Rather than emphasizing the parties' responsibilities within a broader moral or political order, the most common utilitarian justifications tend to reduce those responsibilities by de-emphasizing moral arguments for fulfilling one's promises and thereby maximizing the space for privately directed action. That reduction of promissory obligation is epitomized in the doctrine of the efficient breach of contract in the law and economics literature, under which parties should be free to breach their contracts – perhaps even be encouraged to do so – if the benefit they would gain would be greater than the damages they would have to pay.[27] The promises are written down to their economic value in exchange.

The emphasis on the parties' exercise of will, set out in the four features above, is certainly idealized. Legal regimes have always recognized that rules of public order might justifiably restrict contractual freedom.[28] Moreover, the most prominent theme in contract-law scholarship over the last hundred years has been how the law might protect against or compensate for differences in bargaining power. Nevertheless, the classical model continues to exercise a significant influence. It furnishes the general rule in relation to which restrictions operate as exceptions. It serves as the ideal that many correctives seek to restore.[29] The classical model has not been the sole normative principle shaping that law. That model has had to compete, even within civil codes, with substantially different visions of human relationships – a competition that, in French and Quebec law, has mirrored the conflict between liberal republican and conservative Catholic conceptions of society. This was true especially in the treatment of the family – a zone frequently fenced off from the notions of individual autonomy, social equality, and free disposition of property affirmed in the classical model.[30] Indeed, the classical model itself has often incorporated presuppositions that conflict with its purported individualism and equality so that its supposed deference to the parties' wills plays a more ideological than determinative role. Its purported emphasis upon rationality and volition has been invoked historically to justify the *limitation* of the autonomy of those discriminatorily presumed to have diminished capacity for such reasoning, such as women and racialized minorities.[31] It certainly leaves out beings who do not exercise humanly understandable rationality and volition (such as humans of substantially diminished capacity, animals, and other entities within the natural world).[32] It has been used to normalize inequality by treating unequal relations as contracted when the "consent" is simply imputed, vitiated by the prior situation of the parties, or undermined by the reduction of aspects of personhood to property.[33] Who truly believes that the obligations implied in the contract of employment (e.g., the duty of fidelity) are a matter of the unfettered volition of the parties, as opposed to the imposition of status-based presumptions long attached (by masters) to the relation of master and servant?[34]

The classical model is not, then, a description of empirical reality but a striking image, an influential portrayal – at best an aspiration, at worst an ideology – about the nature and value of promising. But there are forms of promising that have never been adequately described within that model. Those forms become clear when one turns to oaths, covenants, vows, and treaties.

Oaths, Covenants, Vows, Treaties

There is overlap and indeed ambiguity in the manner in which these terms are used. They share many of the features that contrast with the classical model. It will be most efficient, then, to deal with them together, setting out the features that distinguish covenantal promising from the classical model. As will become clear, the forms have, in their original signification, a markedly religious dimension. That poses the question of how they might be adapted to a secular or religiously plural society. We will return to that question at a number of points, especially in the fourth section of this chapter.

To begin, let me give a thumbnail sketch of what I take to be the core meaning of each of the terms.

For **oaths**, I adopt Grotius's definition (borrowed in turn from Cicero), namely: "An Oath is a religious Affirmation, and whatever is promised after such a Manner, calling GOD, as it were, for a Witness to your Words, ought punctually to be performed." It was, then, originally a promise before God, not specifically to God, but one in which God's vengeance was invoked to give added sanction to the promise should it be broken.[35]

The term **covenant** has been applied to a greater range of circumstances. These uses have generally focused on promises made in a particularly solemn or formal manner, such as (in the Common Law) promises contained in a deed under seal. Here, I will focus upon the ultimate in solemn promises: agreements among members of a community either before or with their God. These may contain oaths, but they are characterized by the fact that they typically constitute agreements – compacts – in which each party undertakes obligations to the other, and they are also typically collective, undertaken by an entire community before or with God.

Vows are less common in law because they are rarely enforceable, but they are a familiar part of our normative experience and have substantial affinities to the other terms canvassed here. These, too, are solemn promises, but the promises are typically made to oneself or, in a less secular age, to one's deity. This will be the least discussed of the four terms.

When I speak of **treaties**, I will be referring to treaties between Indigenous peoples in North American Indigenous legal traditions and the extension of that legal form to historic treaties between Indigenous peoples and the governments of settler societies.[36] As we will see, these treaties have significant affinities to covenants.[37] Modern-day treaties lie beyond this chapter's scope. As a result of governments' focus on achieving "certainty," modern treaties have tended to take a markedly contractual form. That said, I suspect that more attention to their constitutional and covenantal character, described below, would produce greater success.[38]

Here are the ways in which these types of promises differ from those in the classical model.

1. The parties to the promise are not limited to the individuals doing the promising

In each of these promises God – or, if one wants to take a first step towards secularization, the moral order – is integrally involved in the promissory relationship. That is patent in the religious forms of oaths, covenants, and vows. As Grotius says of oaths: "it is not so much the Persons to whom we swear, as GOD, whom we invoke as a Witness to what we swear, that creates this Obligation."[39] God is directly and purposefully brought into the promissory nexus. The same is true of treaties although, depending on the Indigenous tradition, the moral order may not be personified and is generally not separated from the natural order. Thus, at the conference from which this volume emerged, Eileen Antone of the Oneida of the Thames First Nation–Turtle Clan began our meetings with a series of invocations, in which (among other things) she thanked the Creator for the earth and for the stars and for all creation. Similar invocations are universal in the proceedings that created the historic treaties.[40] The order of life, the moral and cosmological order, was called upon to inform, sustain, and guarantee the work to be done.

Frequently, especially in covenants and treaties, the promissory nexus is expanded in another way as well. The parties to the promises are not merely those present at the time of the promises but all members of their communities, including descendants. There is an intergenerational dimension to the promises.

2. What is promised – the content of the obligation – is not determined by the expression of the parties' wills

The content of covenantal promises is typically dictated by the moral order itself, not fashioned by the parties. The role of the promises is to bring the promisors into conformity with the moral order, not achieve their personally directed aims. The promisor still engages in a recognizable act of will. They affirmatively embrace and agree to conform to the moral order. But this is an act of accession to something beyond themselves, not the making of commitments that are defined by their personal wills.

This is patent in the case of covenants in the Abrahamic religions, the essence of which is the affirmation of – often a return to – what is required by right relationship with God.[41] It is also true of such oaths as the promise to tell the truth in criminal proceedings, discussed by Catherine Evans and Kellen Funk, the citizenship oaths in Pamela Klassen and Isabel Klassen-Marshall's chapter, or oaths of office. The content of such promises is dictated by the state in the interest of the state's normative order. To be sure, the modalities of that order may be contested and contestable. Contestation is central to the chapters of Evans and Sujith Xavier. But the arguments described by Evans and Xavier are themselves driven by an aspiration to a truly moral order – in this case, a perfected, not a discriminatory, order.

A comparable analysis could be made of most vows. Mohandas Gandhi was a great fan of vows. He urged the taking of vows upon others. He spoke of vows as a means of strengthening one's will. But even though the terms of his vows could seem arbitrary (especially in their extreme precision) and his engagement in them at times more of a moral exercise than, in their content, a conformity to moral perfection, it is also clear that the strengthening of one's will was, for him, ultimately in aid of a purpose to which one was called, not a purpose one had chosen.[42]

In contrast, the terms of treaties may appear to be squarely about negotiation, their content determined through protracted treaty councils. Treaties do involve the deliberate adjustment of the parties' potentially conflicting aims, but the invocations of the Creator and the natural order, the language of kinship between the parties, the ceremonies of sacredness, and the parties' conscious aspiration to conclude a permanent relationship all make clear that, at least for the Indigenous parties, there was a definite sense that the process ought to be guided by responsibility to a broader vision of good sociability, one that stands beyond the particular preferences of the parties.[43] That vision might not yet be delineated, it might be one that the participants are searching to identify, it might be unattainable, it might be a work in progress, but, even if its specific terms are only clarified as the councils proceed, an ethic of responsibility to such an aspiration is built into the ceremonies. Indeed, I suspect that the non-Indigenous negotiators also felt the force of these obligations if nothing else because they participated in the language and practices of the ceremonies. Those negotiators may have toyed with their obligations, invoked them for instrumental rather than deontological reasons, or otherwise acted in bad faith. Certainly, all too frequently, the obligations went unrecognized or were poorly recognized by actors outside the councils. But that is our tragedy and our responsibility. It is part of the pentimento to which Jeffery Hewitt refers in his chapter – a persisting presence ingrained within our foundational relationships.

3. These promises frequently have a constitutional dimension, underpinning a normative, indeed often a political, community

Often, these forms of promising don't simply reflect a normative order. They realize that order, bringing it into effect.

The constitutional character of such promises is patent in the Abrahamic covenants, which bound together Abraham's descendants, defined the people of Israel, and specified the people's foundational commitments. These covenants later served as a model for church organization in non-conformist Protestant denominations, which in turn contributed important strands to constitutional theories during the English Civil War and the founding of the United States.[44] Now, covenants with God can have a sting in their tail. They can place a premium on fidelity to a one true way so that disagreements, even within the religion broadly defined, can be tantamount to apostasy. They can divide or limit at the same time that they unite. Nevertheless, one can understand why covenants frequently have constitutional effect. They create a bond between a people and a normative order. Moreover, they can do so through time, intergenerationally.

Indigenous treaties differ from the religious covenants in that they forge a relationship between two or more normative orders. Tolerance for diversity and continued normative autonomy is therefore built into their foundations.[45] Yet, as the literature on treaties eloquently affirms, they, too, typically have a constitutional character. They provide a framework of principles for the parties' future interactions, creating a composite normative order that derives its legitimacy from both component orders. They create a federated normative community in which the components are not subsumed.[46]

4. These promises frequently define what it means to be a member
of the political community

The constitutional function of these promises also operates at the individual level. Most obviously, oaths are a common mechanism by which individuals are admitted to membership. Oaths speak of the responsibilities of membership both generally, as in the case of citizenship oaths, or in relation to specific roles, as in the case of the promise to tell the truth in judicial proceedings or oaths of office.[47]

Oaths thereby evoke the reciprocity inherent in membership. Members' rights do not exist in gross but only in relation to one or more normative communities. Those communities can only be sustained through human action. Thus, membership is dependent upon at least some members shouldering responsibilities to sustain the community. That does not mean that one's responsibilities must be all-consuming and one's requirement to conform absolute. The responsibilities exist to sustain a community regulated by some aspiration to justice, and that objective may require criticism as well as support. I am tempted to say that the reciprocity of membership and responsibility is not so much a matter of free-standing obligation as a truth about the conditions of justice, conditions that the true friends of justice will work to sustain. This reciprocity of membership and community need not be limited to a single national community. It is compatible with adherence to more than one collectivity. Indeed, such an assortment of memberships is the norm, not the exception, as members act as citizens of countries, citizens of provinces and states, members of their local community, members of the community of all humanity, family members (and of course the list goes on), each of these relationships requiring some shouldering of responsibility if they are to be sustained. One's vision of normative community therefore can be, ought to be, federal.

The demands of reciprocity can also run in the other direction, so that the community itself is subject to moral demands. In particular, a community's desire to draw upon individuals' contributions can trouble the boundaries of membership and non-membership. Isn't that what is happening in Catherine Evans's chapter, in the grudging extension of rights to testify in court proceedings? The desire to have non-members' testimony, while still excluding them, sets up tensions that are familiar, in much starker terms, from the history of slavery, where the desire to dominate absolutely is continually challenged by enslaved people's lived humanity. The domination can be sustained but at large cost, not least to the dominators' conception of themselves as just (although one should not underestimate the dominators' ability to resist the appeals of conscience, meeting enslaved persons' humanity with indifference, anger, or violence).[48] If a society is at all responsive to its moral experience, it can find itself incrementally reconstructing its boundaries. Non-citizens' contributions, even if reluctantly sought and ungenerously received, can end up transforming the community's understanding of itself and its membership.

Indeed, the practices of promising involved in oaths aspire to be constitutional in a still deeper sense. They seek to shape the very identities of their participants, establishing a sense of belonging, instilling discipline, cultivating practices of truth-telling, and affirming a commitment to a society that aspires to justice and truth. Making and keeping promises can provide mettle for one's intentions and build trusting relations among citizens. It was precisely to train oneself in such capacities that Gandhi continually experimented with vows and encouraged his followers to do likewise. Oaths, covenants, vows, and treaties can therefore be particularly significant promises. They can make us who we are, individually and collectively.

If that conclusion seems overblown, consider the following story. In the late 1970s, I studied political science at the University of British Columbia. On one occasion we engaged in a negotiations exercise designed to introduce us to game theory. It was understood – I think even expected – that parties might defect from their promises. I did defect – agreeing to an alliance with Murray and then concluding a secret alliance with another student, leaving Murray's position in tatters. I will never forget his disgust at what I had done. It wasn't the game, which meant nothing to him or me; it was the fact that I would be so cavalier with my promises. It was a lesson that I have never forgotten. Did I want to live my life according to the presuppositions of a game, or did I want to be trustworthy?

5. The obligational content of these promises evolves over time

Under the classical model the parties' obligations are crystallized at the moment of the parties' meeting of minds. The situation is different under covenant and treaty. There, the effective content of the obligations is expected to evolve with time.

This is true in part because those commitments operate in the very long term. The parties therefore do not know, at the time of the covenants' and treaties' conclusion, the circumstances they will have to address, although they do know that the foundational obligations will have to adapt. But this goes further than merely an expectation of adaptation; the obligations themselves are conceived in different terms. When the promises are made, one is not committing to a highly specific course of conduct: one is embarking on a course of discovery and development, the nature of which one does not yet know. One is committing oneself to that endeavour.

Think of religious covenants. Their primary obligations are typically very few and either very abstract (e.g., to be faithful to one's God) or very specific but where the sole purpose is to call to mind the primary, largely unstated, obligations (e.g., one is to circumcise one's male offspring on the eighth day). Then, once begun, one's task is to discover what it means to be faithful as one lives one's life. The initial commitment matters – it is, in one sense, everything – but its meaning, its requirements, are to be worked out continually as one proceeds.

The same is true of treaties. Much has now been written about the parties' differential understanding of the nature of treaties. Some of that literature has focused, importantly, on the treaties' terms: were they about the surrender of land or about the sharing of land?[49] But the literature has also drawn our attention to the different character ascribed to the agreements (a difference closely related to the question of terms). Were they contracts, so that their content was crystallized at the time of their conclusion with the result that anything that was not specifically provided is implicitly excluded? Or were they covenants: the start of a relationship, the demands of which would only become clear in the fullness of time – indeed, would never become fully clear because the relationship would develop indefinitely?[50] This chapter has lent its voice to the second alternative. The consequences for treaty interpretation are substantial. The standard approach is borrowed from contract law: one searches for the "common intention of the parties" determined at the time of the treaty's adoption.[51] But there is often, empirically, no such common intention – or rather the only truly common intention exists at a very high level of generality: that the parties are concluding a treaty or, to give that phrase a little more content, that they seek to live together in peace and justice, in a manner that takes full account of the needs of each party.[52] The treaties' interpretation requires that one reflect, continually, upon that relationship and consider what it should mean for us today.

This brings us back to the realization that treaties are like constitutions. They are about the forging of a relationship, initiating a normative community. Their content is the work of the parties through time. They are not contracts, the obligational content of which is crystallized at the instant of their conclusion. The relationship is the treaty.[53] The methods of interpretation appropriate to treaties are those appropriate to constitutions.

6. The "parties" do not own the promises

When they first encounter treaties, many students note the long history of settler governments failing to perform treaty obligations and conclude that, in response, First Nations should renounce their obligations. The students are surprised to learn that the attitude of First Nations tends to be quite different. Treaty Nations typically take the position that they promised for (in the common phrase) as long as the sun shines, the grass grows, and the river flows, and that their obligations endure, even if the non-Indigenous governments do not live up to theirs.[54] The students are left wondering, how can that be?[55]

Again, the difference comes down to the different nature of promises. The classical model treats the promising parties as, in principle, the only actors that control the operation of a contract. In contract law, that has consequences throughout the agreement's administration. For example, once a contract is concluded, only the parties can vary the terms of the agreement (they must do so by a further agreement). In addition, when they do so, they need not seek approval from or consider the interests of any other party. Moreover, their obligations are typically conditioned on each other's performance. If the obligations are to be sequentially performed, and the party that is first to perform neglects to do so, the other can withhold its performance until the first acts.[56] The Common Law allows a party, faced with a sufficiently important breach by its co-contractor, to treat the contract at an end.[57] In contrast, Indigenous parties do not consider that they and the government are the only parties to the obligational nexus of the historic treaties. They commonly see their promises as binding before the Creator, binding upon their honour. They are not freed from their obligation to behave honourably if their co-contracting party turns out to be dishonourable.[58] Once again, we see the consequence of promises that extend beyond the will of the parties alone.

The Contemporary Relevance of Covenantal Promises

There are, then, promises that do not conform to the classical model: promises that include oaths, covenants, vows, and treaties in North American Indigenous legal traditions. The distinctive feature of these promises – the feature that drives all the other consequences – is that one's deity (or often, in treaties, the cosmic order) is integral to the promissory nexus. In promising, one does not pursue one's own will. Instead, one brings one's will into conformity with the moral order. Nor are covenantal promises archaic holdovers. They are part of our contemporary experience: they are the mechanism by which newcomers are admitted to citizenship; they form a central element in court proceedings; they confirm us in important public roles; they are crucial to understanding the historic treaties.

This form of promising offers the best explanation for the idea that society's normative order should be based upon a "social contract." Accounts of the social contract are generally founded on the classical model of promising. They are deeply unpersuasive.[59] Their purported reliance upon individuals' free choice is illusory. There is no real opportunity, at the individual level, to negotiate the terms of one's political and legal order and although there is, in some cases, a better argument that the terms have been negotiated by groups, that raises the question of how those groups obtained authority to act. Immigration offers the closest case to the free agreement of individuals and, even there, immigrants manifestly do not negotiate the terms of the order. At best the social contract is a thought experiment. Even then, the artificiality of its premise (that individuals approach the contract from a position outside established relationships and norms), combined with the fact that there is disagreement among citizens upon matters at the heart of the "contract," renders the contractual model highly suspect. The model of a covenant is much better.[60] One is typically born into a social order, one develops one's commitment to an order that is ongoing, the content of that order is the continual work of time, and a conception of mutual obligation, reciprocal responsibility, is foundational to the relationship. Covenants therefore capture two important intuitions that give some credence to the idea of a social contract, namely a) the hope that government can secure the voluntary adherence of the governed, combined with b) the idea that there ought to be some reciprocity between governors and governed.

In fact, if we turn our minds seriously to the class of promises in this volume, I suspect we will find them in many other situations as well. They regulate some of our most important relationships, marriage among them. We have not always done a good job of realizing that fact. In the Supreme Court of Canada's decision in *Quebec (Attorney General) v. A*, 2013 SCC 5, the Court addressed whether the default matrimonial regime applicable to married spouses in Quebec must, as a result of the guarantee of equality in section 15 of the Canadian Charter of Rights and Freedoms, also apply to unmarried spouses. The court split four ways, but all four tended to treat the ultimate regime as a matter of choice in a manner equivalent to one's exercise of will in contractual negotiations. Their disagreement was over whether and how, in order to have true choice, it was necessary to compensate for gendered differences in power between prospective spouses. Now, this focus on contractual choice and its vagaries was justified: even in the case of married spouses, the parties can choose their regime; the central question is what should be the default regime. Moreover, the law with respect to matrimonial regimes has indeed been reshaped (thank goodness) by the need to respond to gendered economic inequality. Nevertheless, one can't help suspecting that more was in play here, namely a belief among some that, in principle, the most appropriate regime for spouses is a pooling of family property so that, although the parties might be free to vary this regime, they should be required to do so expressly. There should be a presumption in favour of common property in any conjugal relationship, not just as a corrective to differences in contractual power but in support of a marital relationship based on equality of contribution and decision-making.[61]

We have tended in judicial proceedings to avoid interpretations that are so rich in visions about how one ought to lead one's life. They seem presumptuous, paternalistic, insufficiently respectful of individuals' moral autonomy, preferring a vision of the good life to individuals' rights, perhaps even reflecting an illiberal drift back from contract to status. It is much easier to speak in the language of contractual equality. Canadian courts have often had a hard time articulating the nature of and justification for complex status regimes and their closely associated rites of passage, such as citizenship, distinctions based on age similar to the now disaggregated age of majority (e.g., the driving, drinking, or voting age), and marriage and family relations. Often, courts appear to sidestep what is most at issue.[62] To be clear, I am not suggesting that we abandon a commitment to individual autonomy and equality, nor that we stop using those concepts to reform status-based regimes, but I am suggesting that our relationship to law may not be sufficiently understood through freedom of choice alone. Although we should hold legal regimes to account, those regimes can also hold us to account, summoning us to better lives. Law is one way of learning – indirectly, by both example and counterexample – from those who came before.

Indeed, commitment to some conception of the good life is unavoidable, implicit even in equality and autonomy. The force of this argument may be clearer once one realizes that equality, too, is a status, achieved through a normative order.[63] This is true historically. The ending of slavery needed to be fought for and then protected through law. It still needs to be fought for. One could say the same about married women's equality and women's equal participation in political or economic life. There are now serious arguments about whether non-human animals or natural phenomena should be granted some form of legal status.[64] Equality needs to be established within a functioning and effective normative order in order to be operative in fact, and the instantiation of that equality always involves definition and elaboration – ideally continued reflection upon and revision of our definitions – all of which require that one draw upon conceptions of what it takes to have a good life.

One might well make a similar argument with respect to individual autonomy. Charles Taylor argues convincingly that the commitment to autonomy is itself premised on a vision of what makes for the good life, specifically the capacity to realize one's own self-chosen ends, and that accepting this aim requires that one value the institutions and associations that help one to develop this capacity.[65] Feminist theories of relational autonomy, such as the important work of Jennifer Nedelsky, similarly affirm autonomy as a value and emphasize that, in a world in which we are born into relationship, exist in relationship with others, and depend upon those relationships to cultivate and sustain our freedom of action, autonomy must be defined in terms of the nature and qualities of relationships.[66] It is not about being left utterly alone.

Indeed, in contractual scholarship itself, there is increasing realization that the democratic state's endorsement of contracting ought to impel a richer affirmation of normative principle than the classical doctrine of the autonomy of the will provides, and that contract law ought to be reconceived in ways that seek to guarantee and extend parties' autonomy and freedom, not merely presume autonomy even when it manifestly does not exist. See, for example, the important work of Pascale Dufour.[67]

This is not to say that we lack grounds for criticizing and revising (or replacing) the normative orders affirmed by our societies. Our various experiences – such as our encounters with people to whom we once thought ourselves superior, with those of another culture or class, or with animals – can furnish us with reasons to contest a society's apportionment of status (as we see in the context of both slavery and the ability of racialized individuals to serve as witnesses in legal proceedings).[68] But victory in those struggles itself takes the form of changes in the recognition and activation of status. Such regimes are sufficiently complex that changes are unlikely to be once and for all. They will be subject to continued reassessment and revision, as has been true of matrimonial regimes.

This brings us to the question of the secularization of oaths, covenants, vows, and treaties. We saw that, in their original form, these promises were bound up with religious commitments. The visions of the good to which they appealed, the moral orders they invoked, were conceived in specifically religious terms. Can they be adapted to secular or religiously plural societies? Even if those conceptions are secularized, will they still embody too great a commitment to a particular, contentious, moral order, so that they are open to the same objections as religious commitments?

In Canada, the making of oaths has already been pluralized by the authorization of witnesses to solemnly affirm,[69] but one might ask whether, without more than a name change, solemn affirmations are equivalent to oaths. What is the nature of the solemnity in solemn affirmations? Is there any calling of one to a sense of responsibility as there is in oaths? Solemn affirmations do expose the affirmer to prosecution for perjury, but is that sufficient? If the only encouragement to tell the truth is the penalty, might an affirmer, weighing whether to tell the truth or not, properly apply the kind of reasoning that supports an efficient breach of contract? Should we embrace a theory of the efficient breach of one's oath?

One might take the position that, having rejected any kind of enforced religious commitment, the only thing a secular society can do is impose a penalty for lying under oath or affirmation. Any further consequence must be left to the promisor's personal character, to the promisor's sense of honesty, and potentially the private sanction of loss of reputation. There is a religious variation on this argument, some nonconformist denominations taking the position (on the basis of Matthew 5:34–7) that oaths are superfluous: that *all* one's affirmations ought to be true.[70] Grotius and Pothier, in their increasingly secularized contexts, tended to treat oaths as superfluous, or nearly so, in contractual relations.[71] But note that, at least for the nonconformists, this position did not reduce the expectation of moral conduct but rather increased it, so that the same high standards were applied in all situations – a levelling up of promises rather than a levelling down.

I suggest that something more than the imposition of a penalty is possible – something that approaches the effect of an oath but is consistent with a religiously diverse society. Oaths, covenants, vows, and treaties all emphasize the promisor's responsibility to the normative order by drawing that order into the promissory nexus. In the classical form of these promises, the order is conceived in distinctively religious terms. The promises are dependent, for their full effect, on the promisor sharing those religious commitments. But living in a religiously diverse society requires that the society not presume specifically religious commitments. The society must tolerate a wide range of beliefs, not because those beliefs are intrinsically worthwhile (some members may think they are, but others may believe they are profoundly mistaken), but rather because one is reconciled to living peaceably in society with those who do hold such beliefs. One accepts the presence of the beliefs by ricochet, not because one respects the beliefs, but because one respects the members who hold them. Conviviality – the recognition that one is fated to live together, and one had better do so in peace – rather than some rich sense of substantive agreement, is what holds such diverse societies together.[72]

This doesn't mean that one is prevented from committing oneself to the pursuit of a just normative order. On the contrary, the very desire to live together in peace requires that the society sustain some order, but the content of that order will always be at one remove from the content of any particular religious or other set of commitments. It will be a cobbled-together and compromised order, one that represents a rough amalgam of the commitments of the various members. For that reason, it may well be less systematic than the beliefs of society's members. (Although one should not presume that members' beliefs are as systematic as religious or philosophical doctrines. On the contrary, individual opinions are generally more approximate, heterodox, and open to adjustment. Most humans are natural convivialists.)[73] The compromise order will also be, like all human creations, shaped by power and open to criticism and counter-mobilization for reform on those grounds. But the great virtue of such an order – one that should not be cast aside lightly – is that it enables an approximation of justice to be achieved in a community in which people disagree.[74]

John Rawls suggests a similar objective in his notion of an "overlapping consensus,"[75] but there are crucial differences in what I am advocating. Rawls describes such a consensus as endorsing a conception of justice with which members reason, on public issues, in a manner independently of their "comprehensive doctrines." He excludes from this public reasoning arguments founded in religious commitments because such arguments are, he claims, incapable of being shared by others. Both these limitations are wrongheaded. The compromised order can never be so firmly settled, never so consistent and complete, and never so exhaustive in its implications that it can regulate society without continual reference to the deeper commitments of its members, and individuals are whole people, drawing upon the full range of their commitments. Even among non-religious members, many of these commitments will be disputed. To exclude such arguments would disenfranchise those members or require them to be disingenuous in their arguments. Of course, there may be prudential reasons for members to frame their arguments in terms that others can accept but, to do so, they will almost certainly have to provide reasons that engage with members' particular concerns, not apply a separate set of ostensibly neutral reasons. They will expand the scope of reasons they offer, not limit them. This will require *more* consideration of believers' positions, not less.[76] Fortunately, as Jeffrey Stout has argued, there is more potential for deliberation across religious differences than many theorists presume.[77]

There will of course be limits. There will be positions that are so intolerable to members that those members cannot imagine continuing in community with people who hold them.[78] Indeed, I suspect that Rawls postulates the existence of a "public reason," hedged off from the hazards of democratic debate, precisely in order to guarantee such limits. But it is disingenuous to suggest that limits will be the subject of latent agreement.[79] Limits need to be argued for among the citizenry and sustained through the society's structures. Rawls's own theories are contributions to those arguments; they are not beyond disagreement. And that realization serves as an important reminder of the responsibilities of citizenship. It brings home the seriousness of limitations imposed on others – that they are impositions on people who disagree, not matters of natural agreement. Such judgments are necessary if one is to have any normative community – they may well attract very extensive popular support – but they are still impositions on those outside the consensus. That realization reminds us that affirming, reinforcing, and enforcing standards of justice is central to the responsibility of citizenship. Maintaining a normative order – the work of a community governing itself – is serious and ongoing business.

It is to this fundamental work of sustaining normative community that members are called when they take an oath, enter a covenant, or conclude a treaty. They bind themselves to building a community that aspires to justice and goodness. Their commitment is not to a highly specific, thoroughly elaborated, theoretically determined vision of that society. Rather, they make their promises as co-creators, co-definers, of a vision continually to be developed.[80] This involves respect for other members, their colleagues in those tasks, including some respect for decisions from which they dissent. Their oaths, covenants, and treaties can even invoke (though not impose) religious commitments, which, for a believer, emphasizes the solemnity of the obligations they are undertaking. But, in a diverse society – even in an ostensibly uniform society in which members understand their beliefs in their own way – the beliefs cannot be the essence of their obligations. Their commitment is to the continual work of community.

This is an emphatically democratic vision of oaths, covenants, vows, and treaties. It embodies the reciprocity between members and government that our best theories of law, individual autonomy, and sovereignty affirm.[81] In recent years, there have been sporadic attempts in countries of immigration to stipulate the obligations immigrants should fulfil. Typically, those obligations have been focused upon compliance, instructing newcomers on what they must obey. They neglect the most characteristic feature of democratic citizenship: that newcomers are to join with their citizen-colleagues in making and remaking their society. Our most important promises are founded upon that responsibility.

Conclusion

Covenantal promises are, then, promises that make us who we are, individually and collectively. They engage our wills, emphasizing our responsibility for advancing a good and just society. They are a fundamental part of our lives in society, one that can help us make better sense of our most important institutions. They can help us to build upon those institutions.

The elaboration of such consequences will have to be left to future efforts. However, as one last example, consider the most comprehensive promises that citizens make to their legal and political communities: citizenship oaths. In preparation for this paper, I looked back to the two oaths that apply to me. Here they are:

Canada:

> I swear (or affirm) that I will be faithful and bear true allegiance to His Majesty King Charles the Third, King of Canada, His Heirs and Successors, and that I will faithfully observe the laws of Canada, including the Constitution, which recognizes and affirms the Aboriginal and treaty rights of First Nations, Inuit and Métis peoples, and fulfil my duties as a Canadian citizen.[82]

Australia:

> From this time forward, under God, I pledge my loyalty to Australia and its people, whose democratic beliefs I share, whose rights and liberties I respect, and whose laws I will uphold and obey.[83] [The phrase "under God" may be omitted by the person making the pledge.]

Having been born in Canada, I have in fact never sworn the Canadian oath, nor would I have seen it had I not attended my spouse's citizenship ceremony. Countries are much more willing to insist upon the responsibilities of immigrants than those of the native-born. But I know which oath I prefer. Note the differences. The promisor's allegiance in the first oath is to the King (in his role as representative of the Canadian political order as a whole). In the second, one pledges one's loyalty to one's country and one's fellow citizens. The first emphasizes obedience and compliance, the second one's participation in a democratic and rights-respecting society. The Australian version contains a promise to obey the law (as it should), but that obligation comes last in the list and is combined with the more active commitment to "uphold" the law. The Australian is a democratic oath, one designed for citizens who govern themselves, the Canadian for a people who are subjected to law and government.

Here is one attempt to revise the Canadian oath to emphasize the active responsibilities of citizenship expressed in this chapter, stated in general terms so that they do not foreclose the debates that any democratic society must have. It begins by shamelessly plagiarizing the Australian version.[84]

> I pledge my loyalty to Canada and to my fellow citizens, and my respect to its peoples, whose democratic beliefs I share, whose rights and liberties I cherish, and whose laws I will uphold and obey. I promise to work to make Canada a better and more just society, so that, as citizens and as a country, we fulfil our responsibilities to all who live within it, to Indigenous peoples, to French and English as the principal languages of public life, to Canadians of all origins, and to the world at large, including the environments upon which this world depends. And, in doing so, I will draw upon my best understanding [under God] of what it means to be a citizen of a good and just society.

This draft retains the form of an oath, but if citizenship involves a reciprocal relationship between citizen and country, should we recast these promises as a covenant? If so, then we might draft a response from the people of Canada that acknowledges the new citizen's promises, makes promises in return, and expresses the Canadian people's anticipation of what the new citizen will bring to the country.

That is my attempt at an oath appropriate to the promises we make to a country's legal and political order. What would be yours?

NOTES

1 Charles Taylor, "Atomism" and "What's Wrong with Negative Liberty," in *Philosophy and the Human Sciences: Philosophical Papers 2* (Cambridge: Cambridge University Press, 1985), 187–229.

2 See, for example, the literature on relational contracting, especially the works of Stewart Macaulay, beginning with "Non-Contractual Relations in Business: A Preliminary Study," *American Sociological Review* 28, no. 1 (February 1963): 55–67; Ian R. Macneil, beginning with "The Many Futures of Contracts," *Southern California Law Review* 47 (May 1974): 691–816; and Jean-Guy Belley, beginning with "La théorie générale des contrats. Pour sortir du dogmatisme," *Cahiers de Droit* 26, no. 4 (1985): 1045–58.

3 This is the language of the Code Napoléon, art. 1134: "Les conventions légalement formées tiennent lieu de loi à ceux qui les ont faites."

4 Henry Sumner Maine, *Ancient Law*, 1st ed. (London: John Murray, 1861), 170. For a recent discussion, see Coel Kirkby, "Law Evolves: The Uses of Primitive Law in Anglo-American Concepts of Modern Law, 1861–1961," *American Journal of Legal History* 58, no. 4 (December 2018): 538–42.

5 See Macaulay, "Non-Contractual Relations"; Macneil, "The Many Futures of Contracts"; Belley, "La théorie générale"; and André Bélanger, Pascale Dufour, and Éric Fokou, *Le contrat de droit civil comme artefact social: constats, prospections et utopies* (Quebec: Presses de l'Université Laval, 2023).

6 See Bélanger, Dufour, and Fokou, *Le contrat de droit civil*, vi. See also David Sandomierski's emphasis on the prominent role of legal realism and its heirs in the teaching of contracts in Canadian (and American) law schools. Sandomierski, *Aspiration and Reality in Legal Education* (Toronto: University of Toronto Press, 2020), especially at 46–53. Legal realism is, of course, characterized precisely by its scepticism towards claims for the internal rationality of law.

7 Hugo Grotius, *The Rights of War and Peace*, ed. Richard Tuck (Indianapolis: Liberty Fund, 2005), 704–5.

8 Grotius, *Rights of War and Peace*, 736–8, 708.

9 Grotius, *Rights of War and Peace*, bk. 2, ch. 13. Pothier, too, includes a section on oaths, but it is clear that, by his time, he considers them an anachronism that ought to make no difference to contractual promises'

binding force. Robert-Joseph Pothier, *Oeuvres de Pothier: traité des obligations* (Paris: M. Siffrein, 1821), 1:149–56.

10 André-Jean Arnaud, *Les origines doctrinales du Code civil français* (Paris: Librairie Générale de droit et de jurisprudence, 1969), 197–8; Jean-Louis Baudouin, Pierre-Gabriel Jobin, and Nathalie Vézina, *Les obligations*, 7th ed. (Cowansville, QC: Éditions Y. Blais, 2013), 132–5; Jacques Ghestin, *Le contrat dans le nouveau droit québécois et en droit français: principes directeurs, consentement, cause et objet* (Montreal: Institut de droit comparé, Université McGill, 1982), 3.

11 Rosalie Jukier, in *Quebec Civil Law: An Introduction to Quebec Private Law*, ed. John E.C. Brierley and Roderick A Macdonald (Toronto: E. Montgomery, 1993), 390.

12 Pothier, *Oeuvres de Pothier*, 1:81. See also Arnaud, *Les origines doctrinales*, 206–9.

13 Arnaud, *Les origines doctrinales*, 197ff; Jean-Philippe Lévy and André Castaldo, *Histoire du droit civil*, 2nd ed. (Paris: Dalloz, 2010), 825–9; Ghestin, *Le contrat*, 3 and 6; Christophe Jamin, "Une brève histoire politique des interprétations de l'article 1134 du code civil," *Recueil Dalloz* 11 (2002): 901–7; Baudouin, Jobin, and Vézina, *Les obligations*, 132–5; Jukier, *Quebec Civil Law*.

14 Brierley and Macdonald, *Quebec Civil Law*, 160, 178.

15 This list follows that in Ghestin, *Le contrat*, 3–5. See also Arnaud, *Les origines doctrinales*, 198; Brierley and Macdonald, *Quebec Civil Law*, 178–9; Jacques Ghestin, Grégoire Loiseau, and Yves-Marie Serinet, *Traité de droit civil: La formation du contrat. Tome 1: Le contrat, Le consentement*, 4th ed. (Paris: LGDJ, 2013), 156–8; Baudouin, Jobin, and Vézina, *Les obligations*, 141–7; Jukier, *Quebec Civil Law*, 390.

16 Ghestin, Loiseau, and Serinet, *Traité de droit civil*, 47–9, 177–9.

17 *6362222 Canada inc v. Prelco inc* 2021 SCC 39 (which dealt with a clause in a commercial contract that purported to limit a contractor's liability for breach). The fact that the Supreme Court's decision overturned both trial and appellate judgments is, however, indicative of the fact that the theory of the autonomy of the will has long been contested in Quebec, a contestation reflected in, for example, an expansive duty of good faith in the law of obligations (art. 1375 CCQ). (My thanks to Mireille Fournier.)

18 Ghestin, *Le contrat*, 3. See also Brierley and Macdonald, *Quebec Civil Law*, 160n31; Ghestin, Loiseau, and Serinet, *Traité de droit civil*, 147–56; Jukier, *Quebec Civil Law*, 390. In his 1982 work (at 6–7), Ghestin suggests that these two arguments became dominant only in the late nineteenth and early twentieth centuries and that the Napoleonic codifiers placed much more emphasis on limitations on contractual rights. It is true that the codifiers did emphasize that rights were subject to restrictions

in the public interest, but it goes much too far to say, as Ghestin does, that there were, in the *travaux préparatoires*, "pas du tout des références au libéralisme économique ou à la philosophie individualiste." Such references may have been sparse in relation to contracts but the two were clearly – indeed stridently – paired in the presentation of property rights in the code, in which private ownership was said to be justified on the dual bases of natural rights acquired by occupation and labour and of the great increase in productivity resulting from private industry (see "Présentation au Corps Législatif, et exposé des motifs, par M. Portalis," in *Recueil complet des travaux préparatoires du Code civil*, ed. P.-A. Fenet [Paris: Videcoq, 1836], 11:112–34). One suspects that the reason for the difference is that, at the beginning of the nineteenth century, the protection of newly acquired property and the employment of the newly allodial rights of ownership, rather than freedom of contract, were the principal focus of liberal concern: Levy and Castaldo, *Histoire du droit civil*, 481–5. Ghestin, Loiseau, and Serinet are on stronger ground in their 2013 work (*Traité de droit civil*, 147–64) when they soften Ghestin's claims about the period of codification and attribute the dominance of the "autonomy of the will" to the later nineteenth century, as a classically liberal reaction to what those liberals considered to be the threat of social legislation. This interpretation complements Martin's emphasis upon a disenchanted individualism as the dominant spirit of the Code Napoléon, still seeing individuals' pursuit of their own purposes as the source of society's dynamism but concerned that egoism needed to be contained by sources of stability and authority. Xavier Martin, *Mythologie du Code Napoléon: aux soubassements de la France moderne* (Bouère: D.M. Morin, 2003). Martin, however, confines his use of the term "natural law" to rights that are understood to be capable of existing within the state of nature, neglecting those branches of natural law theory that ground rights' justification in nature but maintain that their realization can only occur within society.

19 This is a simplification. The notion of "cause" in the Civil Law is, of course, more encompassing than the Common Law's concept of "consideration" but enforceable promises are nevertheless analysed in bilateral terms: the promise must be intended to convey, generally implicitly, a right to demand performance to the promisee, and a promise must be accepted by the promisee to be enforceable.

20 Quebec judges originally followed the Common Law's approach, but Quebec's Civil Law has now moved towards a general right to specific performance, subject to exceptions. Baudouin, Jobin, and Vézina, *Les obligations*, 857–9.

21 See Ghestin, Loiseau, and Serinet, *Traité de droit civil*, 139–40.

22 Although see the empiricism evident in the approach to the definition of contracts in Ghestin, Loiseau, and Serinet, *Traité de droit civil*, 35–56.
23 Frederick Pollock, *Principles of Contract*, 5th ed. (London: Stevens and Sons, 1889), 1 and 3.
24 For useful discussions, see Angela Swan, Jakub Adamski, and Annie Y. Na, *Canadian Contract Law*, 4th ed. (Toronto: LexisNexis, 2018), 3–5, 31; S.M. Waddams, *The Law of Contracts*, 7th ed. (Toronto: Thomson Reuters, 2017), 17–19.
25 For two classic discussions, see L.L. Fuller and William R. Perdue Jr., "The Reliance Interest in Contract Damages," *Yale Law Journal* 46, no. 1 (November 1936): 52–96 and no. 3 (January 1937): 373–420; P.S. Atiyah, *The Rise and Fall of Freedom of Contract* (Oxford: Oxford University Press, 1979).
26 Charles Fried, *Contract as Promise: A Theory of Contractual Obligation*, 2nd ed. (Oxford: Oxford University Press, 2015), 3, 25, 35.
27 For a useful summary of different forms of the theory of efficient breach, see Seana Valentine Shiffrin, "The Divergence of Contract and Promise," *Harvard Law Review* 120, no. 3 (2007): 730–3.
28 See art. 6, Code Napoléon and art. 13, Civil Code of Lower Canada, and the many articles in the Civil Code of Québec in which the protection of public order is invoked. Similarly, property rights, although ultimately founded on natural law, were subject to regulation "par les lois et par les règlements": art. 544, Code Napoléon; Fenet, *Recueil complet*; Arnaud, *Les origines doctrinales*, 193–4. See also the concessions of the strongest advocate of contract as promise in the contemporary Common Law, Fried, *Contract as Promise*, 3.
29 Ghestin, Loiseau, and Serinet, *Traité de droit civil*, 180–1; Baudouin, Jobin, and Vézina, *Les obligations*, 147–9 (although they treat four principles as concurrent values, with autonomy of the will being "le grand principe général" and "le principe dominant"); Maurice A. Tancelin, *Des obligations en droit mixte du Québec*, 7th ed. (Montreal: Wilson and Lafleur, 2009), 64–79.
30 Jean Carbonnier, "Le Code civil" in *Les lieux du mémoire: La Nation*, ed. Pierre Nora (Paris: Gallimard, 1986), 2:297–8, 301. In his iconoclastic work, *Mythologie du Code Napoléon*, Martin, e.g., at 205–8, argues persuasively that the codifiers consciously relied upon Catholic principles as a source of social stability following the upheaval of the revolutionary period, and that the Napoleonic Code and Concordat should therefore be seen as complementary (although, one could add, the conflict between the church's and the Bonapartist regime's aims became evident in the history of both Code and Concordat). An example of a jurist emphasizing these conservative elements is *Les aspects généraux du droit privé dans la province du Québec* (Paris: Librairie Dalloz, 1967) by Louis Baudouin (not to be

confused with his son, Jean-Louis Baudouin, the distinguished jurist of the law of obligations in Quebec). Baudouin père devotes several pages to the autonomy of the will in Quebec Civil Law (especially 125–32), but those pages contain a brief invocation of the principle and extensive emphasis upon its limitations. Quebec's code was, at its adoption, more embracing of individual autonomy than the French code in one striking respect: it enshrined freedom of testamentary disposition at a time when French law, in the interest of surviving family members, substantially restricted disposition by will: John E.C. Brierley in Brierley and Macdonald, *Quebec Civil Law*, 333–4. Martin, *Mythologie du Code Napoléon*, 201–2 and 251–70, notes that the drafters of the Code Napoléon themselves sought to weaken the restrictions on testamentary disposition of the revolutionary period and re-establish a sphere of testamentary freedom (although one much more constrained than that in Quebec). They did so specifically in order to buttress paternal authority. That example reminds us that the autonomy of the will is not a freestanding principle. Its effect depends upon the attribution of property rights; how those rights and the capacity to exercise them are attributed, within the family and in other domains, can substantially alter the principle's sphere of operation.

31 See e.g., Carole Pateman, "'The Disorder of Women': Women, Love, and the Sense of Justice" in Carole Pateman, *The Disorder of Women: Democracy, Feminism and Political Theory* (Stanford: Stanford University Press, 1989), 17–32; Martin, *Mythologie du Code Napoléon*, 22–3, 270–82, and 442–5 (noting the reintroduction of African slavery when the legislators were developing the Code Napoléon and the treatment of the family within the Code).

32 See e.g., Maneesha Deckha, *Animals as Legal Beings: Contesting Anthropocentric Legal Orders* (Toronto: University of Toronto Press, 2021).

33 See, e.g., Carole Pateman, *The Sexual Contract* (Stanford: Stanford University Press, 1988).

34 In the Common Law, see Stacey Reginald Ball, *Canadian Employment Law*, loose-leaf (Toronto: Carswell, 1996), 5:30 n36 (when discussing implied terms): "Status has always had an important role to play in determining the rights and obligations associated with the employment relationship, and it still does." For the transmutation of these obligations in form, but not in substance, during the transition from status to contract, see John V. Orth, *Combination and Conspiracy: A Legal History of Trade Unionism, 1721–1906* (Oxford: Clarendon Press, 1991), 107–17. In the Civil Law, see Philippe Remy, "Droit des contrats: questions, positions, propositions," in *Le droit contemporain des contrats: bilan et perspectives*, ed. Löic Cadiet (Paris: Economica, 1987), 271–82; Ghestin, Loiseau, and Serinet, *Traité de droit civil*, 2. Finally, see Fried, *Contract as Promise*: " … even among legally

binding arrangements that are initiated by agreement, certain ones are singled out and made subject to a set of rules that often have little to do with that agreement. Marriage is the most obvious example, but contracts of employment, insurance, or carriage exhibit these features as well. Thus the conception of the will binding itself – the conception at the heart of the promise principle – is neither necessary nor sufficient to contractual obligation" (3).

35 Grotius, *Rights of War and Peace*, 769–70 (capitalization in original). Pothier, *Oeuvres de Pothier*, 149, adopts a similar definition.

36 In Canada, a distinction is often made between the "historic" and "modern" treaties with Indigenous peoples. "Historic treaties" were concluded from the start of treaty-making in northern North America up until the signing of Treaty 11 in 1921. There was then a long gap, as Canadian governments refused to recognize Aboriginal title, no longer negotiated treaties, pared back existing entitlements, and imposed a coercive administrative regime on Indigenous peoples. However, following the recognition of Aboriginal title in *Calder v. Attorney-General of British Columbia* [1973] S.C.R. 313 (SCC), Canadian governments began once again to negotiate treaties. These are the "modern" treaties, the first of which was the James Bay and Northern Quebec Agreement (1975). As note 38 below indicates, modern treaties are significantly different in form from historic treaties in a manner germane to this chapter's argument.

37 See, however, Sébastien Grammond, *Les traités entre l'État canadien et les peuples autochtones* (Cowansville, QC: Éditions Y. Blais, 1995), who accepts the premise that treaties are essentially contracts and explores how contract law ought to apply to treaties in a manner that supplements the public-law principles applicable to treaties (the law of contract therefore applying as *droit supplétif*). In Grammond's analysis, the unique features of treaties tend to be attributed to public-law rules that depart from and supersede the general law of contract, not as features of a distinct species of promising. He treats them as exceptions to general principles of contract so that, in effect, the public law serves as the *droit supplétif*. Nevertheless, his careful and insightful analysis can be read as an exploration of the possibilities and limitations of applying the law of contract to treaties.

38 J.R. Miller notes the change in form from the historic treaties, remarking on the "marked legalism" of the modern treaties: J.R. Miller, *Compact, Contract, Covenant: Aboriginal Treaty-Making in Canada* (Toronto: University of Toronto Press, 2009), 298–9. This legalism is in tension with the relational nature and constitutional role of these treaties. Modern treaties contain extensive self-government provisions, powers for determining the membership of the peoples party to the agreement, joint institutions for the management of resources across broad swathes of country, and,

in one instance, a commitment to create the territory of Nunavut. They initiate continuing relationships rather than once-and-for-all settlements, the most obvious example being the 1975 James Bay and Northern Quebec Agreement which has now been supplemented by more than twenty complementary or related agreements. One wishes that the modern treaties' covenantal and constitutional character were better recognized in their negotiation and implementation.

39 Grotius, *Rights of War and Peace*, 788.

40 Royal Commission on Aboriginal Peoples, *Report of the Royal Commission on Aboriginal Peoples, Vol. 1: Looking Forward, Looking Back* (Ottawa: Indian and Northern Affairs Canada, 1996), 129–30; Robert A. Williams, *Linking Arms Together: American Indian Treaty Visions of Law and Peace, 1600–1800* (New York: Oxford University Press, 1997), 40–61; Harold Cardinal and Walter Hildebrandt, *Treaty Elders of Saskatchewan: Our Dream is That Our Peoples Will One Day Be Clearly Recognized as Nations* (Calgary: University of Calgary Press, 2000), 7–8, 70; Aimée Craft, *Breathing Life into the Stone Fort Treaty: An Anishnabe Understanding of Treaty One* (Saskatoon: Purich, 2013), 79–82; Heidi Kiiwetinepinesiik Stark, "Changing the Treaty Question: Remedying the Right(s) Relationship," in *The Right Relationship: Reimagining the Implementation of Historical Treaties*, ed. John Borrows and Michael Coyle (Toronto: University of Toronto Press, 2017), 248–76; John Borrows, "Sun – As Long as the Sun Shines – Revitalize Others" in John Borrows, *Along Life's Thin Edge* (unpublished manuscript, 2021).

41 The literature in English on religious covenants in the Jewish and Christian traditions is of course immense. For covenants in Islam, see Wadad Kadi Al-Qadi, "The Primordial Covenant and Human History in the Qur'ān," *Proceedings of the American Philosophical Society* 147, no. 4 (December 2003) 332–8; Joseph E.B. Lumbard, "Covenant and Covenants in the Qur'an," *Journal of Qur'anic Studies* 17, no. 2 (2015): 1–23.

42 See, e.g., *The Collected Works of Mahatma Gandhi* (New Delhi, Publications Division Government of India, 1958–94), 12:238, 13:225–35, 15: 76–7, 29:87–90, 31:240–1, 39:167–71, 41:272–4, and 44:264–5, https://www.gandhiheritageportal.org/the-collected-works-of-mahatma-gandhi.

43 See especially Stark, "Changing the Treaty Question"; Williams, *Linking Arms Together*, 50–1, 61; Cardinal and Hildebrandt, *Treaty Elders of Saskatchewan*, 6–7, 14–20, 31–47, 53–5, 70–1; John Borrows, *Law's Indigenous Ethics* (Toronto: University of Toronto Press, 2019), 37–41; Leanne Simpson, "Looking after Gdoo-naaganinaa: Precolonial Nishnaabeg Diplomatic and Treaty Relationships," *Wicazo Sa Review* 23, no. 2 (Fall 2008): 29–42; Craft, *Breathing Life*, especially 64.

44 See especially Andrew C. McLaughlin, *The Foundations of American Constitutionalism* (Gloucester, MA: Peter Smith, [1932] 1972).

45 See especially James (Sakej) Youngblood Henderson, Marjorie L. Benson, and Isobel M. Findlay, *Aboriginal Tenure in the Constitution of Canada* (Scarborough, ON: Carswell, 2000), 98; Michael Asch, *On Being Here to Stay: Treaties and Aboriginal Rights in Canada* (Toronto: University of Toronto Press, 2014).

46 Grammond, *Les traités*, 85 and 112–14, also emphasizes this constitutional character, especially treaties' role in establishing a relationship between two political communities. He sees this as the essence of the "solemnity" commonly attributed to treaties. On the constitutional character of treaties see generally, Royal Commission on Aboriginal Peoples, *Report of the Royal Commission on Aboriginal Peoples, Vol. 2: Restructuring the Relationship* (Ottawa: Minister of Supply and Services Canada, 1996), 20–1; Williams, *Linking Arms Together*, 98–123; Aaron Mills/Waabishki Ma'iingan, "What is a Treaty? On Contract and Mutual Aid," in Borrows and Coyle, *The Right Relationship*, 208–47; Stark, "Changing the Treaty Question"; Janna Promislow, "Treaties in History and Law" *UBC Law Review* 47, no. 3 (2014): 1091–1106, 1141–53. On federated normative communities, see the literature on treaty federalism, e.g., Russel Lawrence Barsh and James Youngblood Henderson, *The Road: Indian Tribes and Political Liberty* (Berkeley: University of California Press, 1980), 270–82; Andrew Bear Robe, *Treaty Federalism: A Concept for the Entry of First Nations into the Canadian Federation, And Commentary on the Canadian Unity Proposals* (Gleichen, AB: Siksika Nation Tribal Administration, 1992); James [Sákéj] Youngblood Henderson, "Empowering Treaty Federalism," *Saskatchewan Law Review* 58, no. 2 (1994): 241–329; Kiera L. Ladner, "Treaty Federalism: An Indigenous Vision of Canadian Federalism," in *New Trends in Canadian Federalism*, ed François Rocher and Miriam Catherine Smith, 2nd ed. (Peterborough, ON: Broadview Press, 2003), 167.

47 In this section we will be focusing primarily on non-Indigenous examples, but a similar argument could be made with respect to individuals' obligations under relations of kinship, including the fictive kinship established by treaties. See Williams, *Linking Arms Together*, 64ff, 124ff.

48 See Eugene D. Genovese, *Roll, Jordan, Roll: The World the Slaves Made* (New York: Vintage, 1974), 88–91. For important examinations of the operation of sympathy and slave owners' resistance to it, and the ways in which the logic of property and domination counteracted considerations of humanity, see Thavolia Glymph, *Out of the House of Bondage: The Transformation of the Plantation Household* (Cambridge: Cambridge University Press, 2008), chs. 1–3 (especially her discussion of "ambivalence" at 24ff); Stephanie E. Jones-Rogers, *They Were Her Property: White Women as Slave Owners in the American South* (New Haven, NJ: Yale University Press, 2019).

49 See e.g., Craft, *Breathing Life*, 60–5; Cardinal and Hildebrandt, *Treaty Elders*, 57–8, 62–7; Neil Vallance, "The Earliest First Nations Accounts of the Formation of the Vancouver Island (or Douglas) Treaties of 1850–54," in *To Share, Not Surrender: Indigenous and Settler Visions of Treaty Making in the Colonies of Vancouver Island and British Columbia*, ed. Peter Cook, Neil Vallance, John S. Lutz, Graham Brazier, and Hamar Foster (Vancouver: UBC Press, 2021), 123–54.

50 See especially Royal Commission on Aboriginal Peoples, *Report of the Royal Commission on Aboriginal Peoples, Vol. 1* (which draws upon a contrast between "business contracts" and "the forms of marriage, adoption and kinship"); Royal Commission on Aboriginal Peoples, *Report of the Royal Commission on Aboriginal Peoples, Vol. 2*, 18–20; Mills, "What is a Treaty?"

51 *R v. Marshall*, [1999] 3 S.C.R. 456 at para 14 (*per* Binnie, J.).

52 Compare Craft, *Breathing Life*, 11–12; Promislow, "Treaties in History and Law," 1130–2, 1165–71; "Introduction" in Cook, Vallance, Lutz, Brazier, and Foster, *To Share*, 8–9; Royal Commission on Aboriginal Peoples, *Report of the Royal Commission on Aboriginal Peoples, Vol. 1*, 175–6; Royal Commission on Aboriginal Peoples, *Report of the Royal Commission on Aboriginal Peoples, Vol. 2*, 41–2.

53 Mills, "What is a Treaty?"; Stark, "Changing the Treaty Question," especially 274–6; Cardinal and Hildebrandt, *Treaty Elders*, 25; Craft, *Breathing Life*, 92–3, 113; Henderson, Benson, Findlay, *Aboriginal Tenure*, 95–99; Simpson, "Looking after Gdoo-naaganinaa," 35; Arthur J. Ray, J.R. Miller, and Frank Tough, *Bounty and Benevolence: A History of Saskatchewan Treaties* (Montreal: McGill-Queen's University Press, 2000), 202–3. See generally Williams, *Linking Arms Together*, 62–82, 124–33; Promislow, "Treaties in History and Law," 1099–1100; Michael Coyle and John Borrows, "Introduction," in Borrows and Coyle, *The Right Relationship*, 3, and the rest of the papers collected in that volume. Miller, *Compact, Contract, Covenant*, emphasizes the role of kinship as a model for the treaty relationship (e.g., 284ff) and, in charting governments' move towards contract as the model, strikingly contrasts the contestation that occurred around surveying (e.g., 292 and 303).

54 Royal Commission on Aboriginal Peoples, *Report of the Royal Commission on Aboriginal Peoples, Vol. 2*, 41.

55 Grammond shares their puzzlement: *Les traités*, 136–9.

56 This, in the Civil Law, is the *exceptio non adimpleti contractus*: Baudouin, Jobin, and Vézina, *Les obligations*, 1016–21.

57 Waddams, *Law of Contracts*, 410ff; Swan, Adamski, and Na, *Canadian Contract Law*, 643ff.

58 Cardinal and Hildebrandt, *Treaty Elders*, 25–8; Harold Johnson, *Two Families: Treaties and Government* (Saskatoon: Purich, 2007), 29; John

Borrows, "Covenants and Treaties" in Borrows, *Along Life's Thin Edge*. Compare, however, Grotius, *Rights of War and Peace*, 790, who strikes an intermediate position: he allows that oaths may be implicitly conditioned upon performance by the other party, thereby allowing the promisor not to perform if the other party does not perform; but he nevertheless holds that in oaths, unlike regular contractual promises, an inequality in contractual obligations does not free a party from their promises.

59 The argument in this paragraph is much briefer than the complexity of the social contract tradition requires. For a fuller canvassing, see Jeremy Webber, "The Meanings of Consent," in *Between Consenting Peoples: Political Community and the Meaning of Consent*, ed. Jeremy Webber and Colin M. Macleod (Vancouver: UBC Press, 2010) 3–41. Compare Williams, *Linking Arms Together*, 30; Mills, "What is a Treaty?"

60 See McLaughlin, *The Foundations of American Constitutionalism*, especially at 70–1 (although he does not expressly distinguish between covenant and contract).

61 Such a presumption does of course exist by statute in jurisdictions across Canada, including Quebec with respect to married spouses. The question in *Quebec (Attorney General) v. A* was whether it need be applied to spouses in Quebec who were not formally married.

62 See Jeremy Webber, *The Constitution of Canada: A Contextual Analysis*, 2nd ed. (Oxford: Hart, 2021), 176.

63 This is the essential insight in Hannah Arendt, *The Origins of Totalitarianism* (New York: Harcourt, 1968) at 290–302, where she argues that the existence of rights is dependent upon membership in an effective political and legal order. She made her argument specifically in relation to states, but it is important to realize that non-state orders can also achieve sufficient effectivity to guarantee rights.

64 See, e.g., Deckha, *Animals as Legal Beings*.

65 Charles Taylor, "Atomism."

66 Jennifer Nedelsky, *Law's Relations: A Relational Theory of Self, Autonomy, and Law* (New York: Oxford University Press, 2011).

67 Pascale Dufour, *La théorie générale du contrat au prisme des travaux d'Axel Honneth* (Brussels: Larcier, 2023).

68 For a moving exploration of how experience can prompt moral reflection, see Brian Slattery, "Rights, Communities and Tradition," *University of Toronto Law Journal* 41, no. 3 (Summer 1991): 447–67.

69 See, e.g., Canada Evidence Act, R.S.C. 1985, c C-5, section 15.

70 This position is by no means limited to nonconformists but it has come to be identified especially with Anabaptists, Mennonites, and Quakers. See the useful historical summary of its reception (and the various grounds for evading what appears to be a clear prohibition) in Ulrich Luz, *Matthew*

1–7: A Continental Commentary, trans. Wilhelm C. Linss (Minneapolis: Fortress Press, 1989), 318–21.

71 See, e.g., Grotius, *Rights of War and Peace*, 797–801; Pothier, *Oeuvres de Pothier*, 150–6.

72 Jeremy Webber, "A Two-Level Justification for Religious Toleration," *Journal of Indian Law and Society* 4 (Winter 2012): 34–7. See also Jeremy Webber, "Governing Ourselves: Reflections on Reinvigorating Democracy Stimulated by Gitxsan Governance," in *Democratic Multiplicity: Perceiving, Enacting, and Integrating Democratic Diversity*, ed. James Tully et al. (Cambridge: Cambridge University Press, 2022), 295–8.

73 Hence the wisdom of Jeffrey Stout's argument that there is more scope for deliberation across religious difference than is often suggested: Jeffrey Stout, *The Flight from Authority: Religion, Morality, and the Quest for Autonomy* (Notre Dame, IN: University of Notre Dame Press, 1981), 266; Jeffrey Stout, *Ethics After Babel: The Languages of Morals and Their Discontents* (Boston: Beacon Press, 1988), 64ff. See also Webber, "Two-Level," 37–43.

74 Jeremy Webber, *Las gramáticas de la ley: derecho, pluralismo y justicia*, trans. Francisco Beltrán Adell and Álvaro Córdova Flores (Barcelona: Anthropos, 2017), 32–5.

75 John Rawls, *Political Liberalism* (New York: Columbia University Press, 1993), 133–72.

76 Webber, "Two-Level," 48–50. This, then, is a special case of the "enlarged mentality," which Hannah Arendt took to be the standard of impartiality in judgment. See Hannah Arendt, *Lectures on Kant's Political Philosophy*, ed. Ronald Beiner (Chicago: University of Chicago Press, 1992), 42–4, 71–5; Jennifer Nedelsky, "Communities of Judgment and Human Rights," *Theoretical Inquiries in Law* 1, no. 2 (2001): 249ff; Jeremy Webber, "A Judicial Ethic for a Pluralistic Age," in *Multiculturalism and Law: A Critical Debate*, ed. Omid A. Payrow Shabani (Cardiff: University of Wales Press, 2007), 67–100.

77 Stout, *The Flight from Authority*; Stout, *Ethics After Babel*; Webber, "Two-Level."

78 Jeremy Webber, "Multiculturalism and the Limits to Toleration" in *Language, Culture and Values in Canada at the Dawn of the 21st Century*, ed. André Lapierre, Patricia Smart, and Pierre Savard (Ottawa: Carleton University Press, 1996), 269–79; Webber, "Two-Level," 51–3.

79 Jeremy Waldron, *Law and Disagreement* (New York: Oxford University Press, 1999).

80 I have dropped vows from the list of promises because their contemporary use tends to be associated with individual rather than collective endeavours, but they are very similar. Gandhi called his autobiography

The Story of My Experiments with Truth, the notion of experiments capturing well his use of vows.

81 For law, see Kristen Rundle, *Forms Liberate: Reclaiming the Jurisprudence of Lon L. Fuller* (Oxford: Hart, 2013). For autonomy, see Taylor, "Atomism." For sovereignty, see Martin Loughlin, *The Idea of Public Law* (Oxford: Oxford University Press, 2003), although Loughlin sees the location of sovereignty as necessarily single within any political order, a restriction that I reject: Jeremy Webber, "We Are Still in the Age of Encounter: Section 35 and a Canada beyond Sovereignty" in *From Recognition to Reconciliation: Essays on the Constitutional Entrenchment of Aboriginal and Treaty Rights*, ed. Patrick Macklem and Douglas Sanderson (Toronto: University of Toronto Press, 2016), 90–4.

82 *Citizenship Act*, R.S.C. 1985, c C-29, Schedule (last amended 2021).

83 *Australian Citizenship Act 2007* (Cth), Schedule 1 (last amended 1993).

84 As in the Australian version, the King does not appear in this draft. That is not the result of republican zeal, at least not on my part and I suspect not on the part of all the Australian drafters as well. At their best, the monarch and their representatives in Canada serve as representatives of the Canadian people who stand above partisan affiliation (in contrast, for example, to the US president) and as a personification of the Canadian state's responsibility for the fulfilment of its responsibilities in, for example, treaties with Indigenous peoples. See Jeremy Webber, "Constitutional Poetry: The Tension between Symbolic and Functional Aims in Constitutional Reform," *Sydney Law Review* 21 (1999): 275–6. These representative roles are in addition to the significant functions of the King's representatives in the formation of governments in parliamentary systems. I could not, however, find a way to express those ideas without the oath sounding like a civics lesson.

Contributor Biographies

Benjamin L. Berger is Professor at Osgoode Hall Law School, York University, in Toronto, Canada. His areas of research interest and expertise include law and religion; legal and social theory; criminal and constitutional law; and law, mental health, and psychoanalysis. He has written broadly in these areas and is the author or editor of multiple books, including *Law's Religion: Religious Difference and the Claims of Constitutionalism* (University of Toronto Press, 2015). He is a Member of the College of the Royal Society of Canada and held the York Research Chair in Pluralism and Public Law. Professor Berger convenes the Osgoode Colloquium on Law, Religion & Social Thought.

Elizabeth Elbourne is Associate Professor in the Department of History and Classical Studies, McGill University. Among her publications are *Empire, Kinship and Violence: Family Histories, Indigenous Rights and the Making of Settler Colonialism, 1770–1842* (Cambridge University Press, 2022) and *Blood Ground: Colonialism, Missions, and the Contest for Christianity in the Cape Colony and Britain, 1799–1853* (McGill-Queens University Press, 2002). She is currently co-editor, with Shino Konishi (University of Western Australia), of volume three (1750–1914) in the forthcoming five-volume *Cambridge History of Colonialism and Decolonization*, and is a former co-editor of the *Journal of British Studies*. In 2024–5 she holds a Smuts Visiting Research Fellowship at the University of Cambridge.

Catherine L. Evans is Associate Professor at the Centre for Criminology and Sociolegal Studies at the University of Toronto. She is a legal historian of the British Empire with interests in the histories of criminal law, forensic science, psychiatry, and incendiarism in the nineteenth century. She is the author of *Unsound Empire: Civilization and Madness in Late-Victorian Law* (Yale University Press, 2021).

Yaniv Feller teaches at the Religion Department and the Bud Shorstein Center for Jewish Studies at the University of Florida. A scholar of Jewish thought and museum studies, his publications include *The Jewish Imperial Imagination: Leo Baeck and German-Jewish Thought* (Cambridge University Press, 2023), the co-edited volume *Covenantal Thinking: Essays on the Philosophy and Theology of David Novak* (University of Toronto Press, 2024), and articles in various journals and edited collections. Yaniv's current book project is titled "Jew in a Box: The Past and Future of Jewish Museums."

Gregory Fewster is Wendy and Leslie Rebanks Postdoctoral Fellow at the Royal Ontario Museum. He writes on the textual and material culture of Mediterranean antiquity and its modern reception in the West. Recent publications include *The Authentic Paul: Critical Scholarship and the Making of a Christian Book* (McGill-Queen's University Press, 2025).

Kellen Funk is the Michael E. Patterson Professor of Law at Columbia Law School, where he teaches courses on American civil litigation and legal history. His book, *Law's Machinery: Reforming the Craft of Lawyering in America's Industrial Age* (Oxford University Press, 2025), relates the history of codification to law reform in the mid-nineteenth-century United States, intertwining stories of economic, religious, and political developments across the highly inventive era of American litigation reform.

Jeffery Hewitt joined Osgoode Hall Law School in 2019 and is mixed-descent Cree. After graduating from Osgoode in 1996, being called to the Bar in Ontario in 1998, Professor Hewitt returned to complete his LLM in 2016. He is currently working on a PhD in art history. Professor Hewitt's research interests include Indigenous legal orders and governance, constitutional law, human rights, legal education, art + law, and visual legal studies. Professor Hewitt mainly teaches constitutional law and Indigenous-related courses, and is a co-director of Osgoode's Intensive Program in Indigenous Lands, Resources, and Governments.

Pamela Klassen is Professor in the Department for the Study of Religion at the University of Toronto. Her books include *The Story of Radio Mind: A Missionary's Journey on Indigenous Land* (2018) and the co-authored *Ekklesia: Three Inquiries in Church and State* (2018), both published by University of Chicago Press. Her digital storytelling project "Kiinawin Kawindomowin Story Nations" (storynations.utoronto.ca) is in collaboration with Kay-Nah-Chi-Wah-Nung Historical Centre of Rainy River First Nations, in Treaty #3 Territory. She was awarded the Anneliese Maier Research Award from the Humboldt Foundation, which she held at University of Tübingen from 2015–20. She is a Fellow of the Royal Society of Canada.

Isabel Klassen-Marshall holds a Joint Honours BA from McGill University in History and Political Science and a Juris Doctor from the University of Toronto Law School. In 2025–6, she is clerking at the Superior Court of Justice in Toronto. She is grateful to have worked for Indigenous communities through her experiences at JFK Law LLP in Toronto, the Algoma Community Legal Clinic in Sault Ste. Marie, and the Maya Leaders Alliance in Belize.

Monique Scheer is Professor of Historical and Cultural Anthropology at the University of Tübingen, where she currently also serves as Vice-Rector for International Affairs and Diversity. Among her research interests are religion, secularity, and cultural diversity in modern Germany, the history of emotions, and cultural theory. Recent publications include *Enthusiasm: Emotional Practices of Conviction in Modern Germany* (Oxford University Press, 2020), *Secular Bodies, Affects, and Emotions: European Configurations* (edited with N. Fadil and B.S. Johansen, Bloomsbury, 2019) and *The Public Work of Christmas: Difference and Belonging in Multicultural Societies* (edited with P. Klassen, McGill-Queen's University Press, 2019).

Jennifer A. Selby is Professor and Graduate Coordinator in Religion and Culture, jointly appointed to Political Science, affiliate member of Gender Studies, and director of the Nexus Centre for Humanities and Social Sciences Research at Memorial University of Newfoundland, Canada. Her ethnographic-based research examines secularism in contemporary France and Canada. She is currently principal investigator of two SSHRC-funded research projects, one on secularism in the francophone world and the second on Muslim life in Newfoundland and Labrador. Selby is the author most recently of *Secular Sensibilities: Romance, Marriage, and Contemporary Algerian Immigration to France and Québec* (University of North Carolina Press, 2025).

Kate Stoehr is an elementary teacher with the Toronto District School Board. Prior to her teaching career, she earned an MA from the Department for the Study of Religion at the University of Toronto. Her research and study focused on the influence of Christian worldviews on the Canadian colonial state's policies of assimilation related to agriculture in the nineteenth century.

Pooyan Tamimi Arab is Assistant Professor of Religious Studies at Utrecht University's Department of Philosophy and Religious Studies. He is the author of *Amplifying Islam in the European Soundscape* (Bloomsbury, 2017), a book about Dutch secularism and the broadcasting of the Islamic call to prayer with loudspeakers, and *Why Do Religious Forms Matter?* (Palgrave, 2022), about materiality and aesthetics in the political writings of Spinoza, Locke, and Rawls. He co-edited the volume *Spinoza's Theological-Political Treatise (1670–2020): Commemorating A Long-Forgotten Masterpiece* (MDPI, 2021) and co-edited *The Routledge Handbook of Material Religion* (Routledge, 2024).

Jeremy Webber is Professor Emeritus of Law at the University of Victoria (Canada), Honorary Professorial Fellow at the University of Melbourne, and Doctor et Professor iuris constitutionalis honoris causa at Eötvös Loránd University in Budapest. He has written widely in legal theory, constitutional theory, Indigenous rights, federalism, cultural diversity, and constitutional law in Canada and in relation to other countries (especially Australia).

Sujith Xavier is Associate Professor in the Faculty of Law, University of Windsor. His research spans Third World Approaches to International Law and domestic public law and racialization. He has experience working with local grassroots NGOs in Sri Lanka. He has also served as legal intern with Al-Haq (Palestine) and law clerk at the International Criminal Tribunal for the Former Yugoslavia/International Criminal Tribunal for Rwanda Appeals Chamber. Sujith has appeared before several courts including the Supreme Court of Canada.

Index

Note: The letter *f* following a page number denotes a figure and the letter *t* a table